Advanced Computational Intelligence Techniques for Engineers

This book presents a thorough examination of computational intelligence and its significant influence on solving intricate engineering challenges. It covers fundamental theories as well as advanced applications, illustrating how techniques in computational intelligence are transforming engineering practices. The book is organized into distinct sections, each concentrating on specific engineering domains in which computational intelligence assumes a critical role. The book

- presents a methodical coverage of computational intelligence principles and techniques, illustrated by examples from various engineering domains,
- emphasizes a problem-solving approach, demonstrating how computational intelligence can be used to tackle complex problems,
- offers use cases and real-world examples to facilitate targeted learning and understanding, and
- includes discussion on ethical considerations, advocating for the responsible use of technology and consideration of societal impacts.

This reference book is for engineers, researchers, and scholars interested in computational intelligence techniques in engineering.

Advanced Computational Intelligence Techniques for Engineers

Edited by

T. Joshva Devadas, Naveenkumar Jayakumar,
N. Narayanan Prasanth, P. Anandhakumar and
Shrikant Jadhav

CRC Press
Taylor & Francis Group
Boca Raton London New York

CRC Press is an imprint of the
Taylor & Francis Group, an **informa** business
A CHAPMAN & HALL BOOK

Designed cover image: ShutterStock

First edition published 2026
by CRC Press
2385 NW Executive Center Drive, Suite 320, Boca Raton FL 33431

and by CRC Press
4 Park Square, Milton Park, Abingdon, Oxon, OX14 4RN

CRC Press is an imprint of Taylor & Francis Group, LLC

ISBN: 978-1-032-87342-8 (hbk)
ISBN: 978-1-032-87344-2 (pbk)
ISBN: 978-1-003-53215-6 (ebk)

DOI: 10.1201/9781003532156

Typeset in Times
by Deanta Global Publishing Services, Chennai, India

Contents

Preface

In a world increasingly shaped by technological innovation, computational intelligence has become a vital tool for addressing complex challenges across industries. The book *Advanced Computational Intelligence Techniques for Engineers* emerges as a response to the growing need for solutions that are not only technically robust but also ethically grounded and socially impactful. This edited volume paves the way for leading experts to explore how AI, machine learning, and hybrid algorithms can transform engineering, healthcare, and sustainability efforts by bridging the gap between cutting-edge research and real-world implementation.

The book uncovers the most pressing issues starting with equitable healthcare access to climate-resilient agriculture and the need for interdisciplinary collaboration. Each chapter reflects this ethos, blending rigorous computational methods with practical case studies. Readers will discover how AI accelerates early disease diagnosis in low-resource settings, how swarm intelligence optimizes smart manufacturing, and how multiomics data drives personalized cancer therapies. Contributions also highlight tools like federated learning for data privacy and nonlinear unmixing for advanced imaging, illustrating the diversity of modern computational intelligence.

Chapters confront ethical dilemmas head-on, whether addressing algorithmic bias in healthcare AI, ensuring transparency in deep-fake detection, or prioritizing sustainability in agricultural systems. By integrating global perspectives from Ethiopian soil fertility projects to smart factories, the book underscores the importance of context-aware solutions. It is designed for engineers, researchers, and practitioners in AI, biomedical fields, and industrial automation. It equips readers to tackle challenges with predictive maintenance, emotion recognition, and drug discovery through methods like genetic algorithms, CNN-GA hybrid, and ensemble models.

The editors extend their sincere gratitude to the contributors and reviewers whose expertise and dedication shaped this work. Ultimately, this book encourages readers to innovate while prioritizing humanity and the planet, thus offering a roadmap for progress that is both transformative and inclusive.

—The Editors

About the Editors

T. Joshva Devadas is a computer technocrat with Doctor of Philosophy in Computer Science, with distinctions in Master of Technology and Master of Science degrees in Computer Science. He has more than two decades of experience in teaching and guiding young computer scientists. He has contributed to projects using current, cutting-edge technologies and programming languages and also guided young students in choosing and experimenting with current computing trends for the past two and a half decades of academic work. He works towards creating state-of-the-art computing facilities for visually and physically challenged individuals to navigate and use computers independently.

Naveenkumar Jayakumar, PhD, is Associate Professor at VIT, Vellore, India, specializing in Computational storage systems and Information Management, cybersecurity, and intelligent computing. He has more than 15 years of academic and industrial experience. His research is centered on secure cyber-physical systems, edge computing, and applied machine learning, evidenced by multiple Scopus-indexed publications, patents, and funded projects. With over a decade in academia, he has guided postgraduate research in areas such as natural language processing (NLP), deep learning, and software engineering, driving innovations from automation to advanced cloud platforms.

N. Narayanan Prasanth, PhD, is Professor at the School of Computer Science and Engineering, Vellore Institute of Technology, Vellore, India, having more than 16 years of experience in academics and research. His research interests include network switch scheduling algorithms, switching architectures, parallel and distributed computing, high-performance computing, and IoT. He has published more than 30 papers in reputed conferences and journals. He is a life member of ISTE and a member of Internet Society. He has also served as a technical committee member and session chair for several conferences and journals.

P. Anandhakumar, PhD, is Professor in the Department of Information Technology at Anna University, Chennai, India. He completed his doctorate in the year 2006 from Anna University. He has produced 20 PhDs in the field of image processing, cloud computing, multimedia technology, and machine learning. His ongoing research lies in the field of digital twin technology, machine learning, and artificial intelligence. He has published more than 150 papers indexed in SCI, SCOPUS, WOS, etc. He has more than 27 years of teaching experience in the field of computer science and information technology.

Shrikant Jadhav joined SJSU as Assistant Professor of Electrical Engineering in Fall 2021. Before joining SJSU, he worked as Assistant Professor for a year at Fort Lewis College, Durango, CO. He moved to the United States in 2013 to pursue a PhD. He received his PhD in Electrical Engineering from the North Carolina A & T State University, Greensboro, NC, in 2018. His research includes developing methodologies for accelerating computationally intensive applications like image processing, bioinformatics, machine learning, etc. He was hired as a postdoc from 2018 to 2020 to work on the "A Mobile High-Performance Computing System for Deployment in the Field" project, supported by the DoD grant. During his PhD and postdoc period, he mentored several high school, undergraduate, and graduate students. He has also served as a technical committee member and session chair for several conferences and journals.

List of Contributors

A. Kannan
College of Engineering Guindy
Chennai, India

Madhura Abnave
Pimpri Chinchwad College of Engineering
Pune, India

Solomon Adane
Woldia University
Ethopia

Palak Agrawal
KPMG
GTA, Canada

Anusha B.
Marian Engineering College
Trivandrum, India

Balabhadra Nikhitha
Kalasalingam Academy of Research and Education
India

Bandikattu Snehalatha
Kalasalingam Academy of Research and Education
India

Bedamsetty Visali
Kalasalingam Academy of Research and Education
India

Bokkisam Akshitha
Kalasalingam Academy of Research and Education
India

Atharv Chougule
Pimpri Chinchwad College of Engineering
Pune, India

D. Roja Ramani
New Horizon College of Engineering
India

Pratiksha Darekar
Pimpri Chinchwad College of Engineering
Pune, India

Vishakha Despande
Pimpri Chinchwad College of Engineering
Pune, India

Prateek Goyal
CISCO
ATX, USA

Savita Gupta
Panjab University
India

Thomas Abraham J. V.
Vellore Institute of Technology
India

Naveenkumar Jayakumar
Vellore Institute of Technology
India

Karthik K.
Vellore Institute of Technology
India

Priya K.
Kannur University
India

Rajkumar K. K.
Kannur University
India

K. Shivani
Vellore Institute of Technology
India

Suresh P. K.
Vellore Institute of Technology
India

Varsha K.
Kannur University
India

Gholamreza Kakamanshadi
Islamic Azad University
Iran

Manish Kumar
Pondicherry University
India

Rohit Kumar
Universitat de Barcelona
Spain

Anandha Meenachi M.
Vellore Institute of Technology
India

M. Kaliappan
Ramco Institute of Technology
India

R. M. Rajeshwari
Ramco Institute of Technology
India

Sushmithaasri K. N.
Vellore Institute of Technology
India

Narayanan Prasanth
Vellore Institute of Technology
India

R. Raja Subramanian
Kalasalingam Academy of Research and Education
India

R. Raja Sudharsan
Velammal College of Engineering and Technology
India

R. Subramanian
Pondicherry University
India

Ankit Raj
Pondicherry University
India

Ashwin T. S.
Vanderbilt University
USA

Salini S.
Vellore Institute of Technology
India

S. Sridevi
Thiagarajar College of Engineering
India

Swati V. Shinde
Pimpri Chinchwad College of Engineering
Pune, India

Sukhwinder Singh
Panjab University
India

Prince Thomas
Woldia University
Ethopia

T. Joshva Devadas
Vellore Institute of Technology
India

V. Pandiyaraju
Vellore Institute of Technology
India

Section A

Computational Intelligence

Healthcare and Biomedical Applications

1 Artificial Intelligence in Healthcare

Rohit Kumar

1.1 INTRODUCTION

Artificial intelligence (AI) is reshaping the landscape of healthcare around the world. Once seen as a futuristic tool, AI is now playing an active role in patient diagnosis, treatment planning, health monitoring, and even hospital management. Its ability to process vast amounts of data, recognize patterns, and support decision-making has made it a valuable partner for healthcare professionals.

AI refers to a set of technologies that allow machines to perform tasks that typically require human intelligence, such as reasoning, learning, problem-solving, and understanding language (Russell & Norvig, 2020). In healthcare, these technologies are being used to automate administrative processes, interpret complex medical images, and support clinical judgments with data-driven insights.

The journey of AI in healthcare began decades ago with early rule-based expert systems like MYCIN in the 1970s, which was designed to assist with infectious disease diagnosis. Although limited by computing power and data availability, such systems laid the groundwork for today's more sophisticated approaches (Topol, 2019). The recent surge in AI's effectiveness is largely due to improvements in machine learning algorithms, access to large datasets, and advances in computing infrastructure.

Modern healthcare generates a massive amount of data—from electronic health records (EHRs) and genomic sequences to medical imaging and wearable device outputs. Analyzing this data manually is time-consuming and prone to error. AI, particularly machine learning, can analyze these datasets quickly and with a high degree of accuracy, uncovering patterns that may not be evident to human observers (Jiang et al., 2017).

The value of AI became particularly evident during the COVID-19 pandemic. AI tools were used to forecast infection trends, analyze CT scans for signs of the virus, and support drug repurposing efforts. In one case, the AI platform BlueDot issued alerts about an unusual respiratory illness in Wuhan days before global awareness grew (Bogoch et al., 2020).

Despite its promise, AI adoption in healthcare also presents major challenges. Issues such as data privacy, algorithmic bias, lack of interpretability, and regulatory uncertainty must be addressed thoughtfully. It is essential to ensure that these technologies serve all patients equitably and ethically.

DOI: 10.1201/9781003532156-2

This chapter provides a comprehensive overview of how AI technologies are transforming healthcare. We begin with an exploration of the application of AI in clinical and operational applications of healthcare. This is followed by an analysis of the challenges involved and a forward-looking discussion on future directions and current research.

1.2 CLINICAL APPLICATIONS OF AI

The clinical applications of artificial intelligence (AI) are perhaps the most visible and impactful demonstrations of its transformative potential in healthcare. From improving diagnostic accuracy to supporting treatment decisions and monitoring patients remotely, AI is increasingly integrated into the core processes of patient care. These applications are not futuristic concepts—they are being piloted and deployed in hospitals, clinics, and laboratories around the world.

1.2.1 AI in Diagnosis and Prognosis

AI's most prominent clinical role is in disease diagnosis and risk stratification. Diagnostic tasks often involve pattern recognition, a strength of machine learning algorithms—particularly those based on deep learning. In radiology, for example, AI has shown remarkable success in interpreting imaging studies such as X-rays, CT scans, and MRIs.

A landmark study by Esteva et al. (2017) demonstrated that a deep convolutional neural network could classify skin lesions at a level comparable to dermatologists. Similar models have been trained to detect diabetic retinopathy, pneumonia, lung nodules, and even early-stage cancer from various types of medical imaging (Gulshan et al., 2016; Ardila et al., 2019).

AI is also applied in pathology, where digital slides are scanned and analyzed to detect malignancies, grade tumors, and count mitotic figures. In cardiology, machine learning algorithms can interpret ECGs, identify arrhythmias, and predict adverse cardiac events.

Beyond diagnosis, AI models are being used to predict disease progression and outcomes. For instance, predictive analytics can forecast the likelihood of complications in ICU patients or identify those at high risk for hospital readmission. These prognostic tools allow clinicians to intervene earlier and allocate resources more efficiently.

1.2.2 Drug Discovery and Development

The process of bringing a new drug to market is costly, time-consuming, and fraught with failure. AI is revolutionizing this process by accelerating drug discovery, improving candidate selection, and optimizing clinical trial design.

Machine learning models analyze vast chemical libraries, genetic data, and biological networks to identify molecules with therapeutic potential. Companies such as Atomwise and Insilico Medicine use deep learning to model drug-target interactions, while others apply AI to predict pharmacokinetics and toxicity.

During the COVID-19 pandemic, AI was used to repurpose existing drugs. Notably, BenevolentAI identified baricitinib, an anti-inflammatory drug, as a potential treatment by analyzing biomedical literature and molecular pathways (Richardson et al., 2020).

In clinical trials, AI helps recruit eligible participants, optimize trial protocols, and monitor patient responses in real time. These innovations not only reduce costs but also improve the likelihood of success.

1.2.3 Personalized and Precision Medicine

One of AI's most exciting contributions is in personalized medicine—the tailoring of medical treatment to the individual characteristics of each patient. By integrating data from genomics, electronic health records, lifestyle patterns, and wearable devices, AI systems can support precision diagnoses and targeted therapies.

In oncology, AI platforms analyze tumor genomics to match patients with specific therapies, predict treatment responses, and assess the risk of recurrence. IBM's Watson for Genomics, for example, provides clinicians with insights into the most effective targeted treatments based on a patient's DNA profile.

In chronic disease management, predictive models identify patients at risk for conditions such as diabetes, hypertension, or heart failure, allowing preventive strategies to be implemented early. Personalized medicine holds the promise of reducing unnecessary treatments, improving outcomes, and optimizing healthcare resource utilization.

1.2.4 AI in Surgery and Robotics

Surgical practice is undergoing a transformation with the integration of AI-enhanced robotic systems. While surgical robots like the da Vinci system have been in use for over two decades, recent advances have introduced greater autonomy and decision support into these platforms.

AI assists surgeons by enhancing visualization, guiding incisions, and alerting users to potential errors or deviations from the planned procedure. In minimally invasive procedures, machine vision helps track instruments, analyze tissue characteristics, and optimize movement.

Autonomous robotic procedures, while still in experimental stages, are being explored for suturing, biopsy collection, and orthopedic drilling (Shademan et al., 2016). These systems aim to increase precision, reduce human error, and improve surgical outcomes, particularly in repetitive or delicate tasks.

1.2.5 Virtual Health Assistants and Chatbots

AI-powered virtual assistants and chatbots are increasingly used for triage, health education, appointment scheduling, and chronic disease management. These systems use natural language processing (NLP) to interact with users in conversational formats and provide tailored responses based on symptoms and health history.

Tools such as Ada, Babylon, and Florence guide users through symptom checkers and suggest whether to seek medical care. Others, like Woebot, offer mental health support using evidence-based cognitive behavioral therapy techniques (Fitzpatrick et al., 2017).

While not intended to replace clinical encounters, these tools expand access to care, especially for individuals in rural or underserved areas. They also reduce the administrative burden on healthcare providers.

1.2.6 Wearables and Remote Patient Monitoring

Wearable devices such as smartwatches, fitness trackers, and biosensors have become common tools for health monitoring. These devices continuously collect data on heart rate, physical activity, sleep patterns, and even electrocardiogram (ECG) signals.

AI algorithms process this data to detect anomalies, predict health risks, and send alerts to patients or providers. For instance, Apple's ECG-enabled watch has received FDA clearance to detect atrial fibrillation. In diabetes care, continuous glucose monitors (CGMs) paired with AI models guide insulin dosing and dietary recommendations.

Remote monitoring reduces the need for frequent clinic visits and supports early detection of deterioration in patients with chronic conditions. This is especially valuable in post-operative care, geriatrics, and during pandemics when minimizing in-person contact is necessary.

1.3 AI IN HEALTHCARE OPERATIONS

While AI's clinical applications receive significant attention, its impact on healthcare operations is equally important. Hospitals and health systems face challenges related to cost, efficiency, staffing, and logistics. AI technologies help optimize workflows, reduce administrative burdens, and support strategic decision-making.

1.3.1 Hospital Operations and Patient Flow

Managing hospital resources effectively is a complex task involving bed allocation, surgery scheduling, discharge planning, and staffing. AI can assist administrators by forecasting patient admissions, identifying bottlenecks, and suggesting interventions.

For example, predictive models can estimate emergency department demand based on historical data, weather, and public events (Helm et al., 2020). AI-powered scheduling systems allocate operating rooms and staff based on urgency and expected duration of procedures, helping reduce delays and cancellations.

Hospitals have also implemented AI to improve discharge planning by predicting which patients are likely to need extended care, thus ensuring smoother transitions and reducing readmissions.

1.3.2 Supply Chain and Inventory Management

Efficient supply chain management is vital for uninterrupted patient care. AI systems analyze usage patterns, expiration dates, and vendor performance to optimize ordering and inventory.

Machine learning algorithms forecast demand for medications, surgical supplies, and personal protective equipment (PPE), reducing stockouts and overstocking. During the COVID-19 pandemic, AI models were used to monitor supply levels and predict future shortages, aiding public health preparedness (Ghosh et al., 2020).

AI-enabled logistics systems also streamline delivery routes within large hospital networks, minimizing transit times for laboratory samples or critical medications.

1.3.3 Electronic Health Records (EHRs) and Clinical Documentation

EHRs are essential for modern healthcare but are often cited as a source of clinician burnout due to their time-consuming nature. AI addresses this by automating routine documentation tasks, extracting insights from clinical notes, and enabling more efficient data entry.

Natural language processing (NLP) tools like ambient scribes listen to physician-patient interactions and automatically generate encounter summaries. Companies such as Nuance and Suki offer AI-driven dictation tools that convert speech to structured notes, saving time and reducing clerical errors.

AI also assists in identifying missing information in records, flagging drug interactions, and suggesting diagnostic tests. When integrated into clinical workflows, these systems enhance data quality and decision-making.

1.3.4 Fraud Detection and Revenue Cycle Management

Healthcare fraud and billing errors cost billions of dollars annually. AI systems are now used by insurers and healthcare organizations to identify suspicious patterns in billing, coding, and claims.

For example, AI algorithms analyze large datasets to detect anomalies such as overbilling, upcoding, or duplicate claims. These tools can flag claims for review before payment, reducing financial loss and improving compliance (Obermeyer et al., 2019).

In revenue cycle management, predictive models forecast payment delays and recommend actions to accelerate reimbursements. They also help identify underpaid or denied claims that merit appeal.

1.3.5 Human Resource Management and Workflow Automation

Staffing is a critical component of healthcare delivery. AI-based tools help forecast workforce needs, identify skill gaps, and match staff availability to patient demand. By analyzing shift patterns, absenteeism, and patient acuity levels, AI supports dynamic scheduling that balances workload and reduces staff fatigue.

Workflow automation tools handle administrative tasks such as appointment reminders, preauthorization requests, and patient registration. These systems free up staff to focus on clinical care and enhance the patient experience through faster, more responsive service.

1.4 CHALLENGES AND LIMITATIONS

Despite its promise, the use of AI in healthcare presents significant challenges that must be carefully addressed.

1.4.1 Data Privacy and Security

AI systems rely on vast amounts of patient data, raising concerns about privacy and consent. Health data is highly sensitive, and breaches can have serious consequences.

To address this, regulations such as the General Data Protection Regulation (GDPR) and Health Insurance Portability and Accountability Act (HIPAA) mandate strict data protection standards. Techniques like federated learning allow model training without centralizing data, enhancing privacy (Rieke et al., 2020).

1.4.2 Algorithmic Bias and Fairness

AI models are only as good as the data they are trained on. If training datasets are skewed or unrepresentative, models may perform poorly or unfairly—especially for underrepresented populations.

For example, an algorithm used to allocate healthcare resources in the United States was found to underestimate the needs of Black patients due to biased training data (Obermeyer et al., 2019). Ensuring fairness requires diverse datasets, bias audits, and transparent evaluation.

1.4.3 Explainability and Trust

Many AI models, especially deep learning systems, function as "black boxes" whose internal decision-making is opaque. This lack of explainability hinders adoption by clinicians who must trust and understand these systems.

Explainable AI (XAI) methods, such as SHAP values or attention maps, help make model decisions interpretable. Regulatory bodies increasingly require explainability for clinical AI tools (Arrieta et al., 2020).

1.4.4 Integration with Clinical Workflows

AI tools that are not well-integrated into daily clinical routines can create more problems than they solve. Poorly designed systems may disrupt workflows, increase documentation time, or lead to alert fatigue.

Successful integration requires user-centered design, clinician involvement, and interoperability with existing IT systems (Sendak et al., 2020).

1.4.5 Regulatory and Ethical Concerns

AI in healthcare is regulated by agencies such as the U.S. Food and Drug Administration (FDA), the European Medicines Agency (EMA), and national health authorities. These bodies are still evolving guidelines for AI-based systems, especially those that learn continuously.

Ethical issues also arise, such as accountability for errors, patient autonomy, and the potential replacement of human labor. Developing trustworthy AI requires collaboration among ethicists, regulators, engineers, and clinicians (Char et al., 2018).

1.5 CASE STUDIES AND REAL-WORLD IMPLEMENTATIONS

1.5.1 DeepMind and the NHS: AI in Eye Disease Diagnosis

One of the most widely cited examples of successful clinical AI deployment is the collaboration between Google's DeepMind and Moorfields Eye Hospital in the United Kingdom. This partnership led to the development of an AI system capable of analyzing optical coherence tomography (OCT) scans to detect more than 50 eye diseases, including diabetic retinopathy and age-related macular degeneration.

The system, trained on thousands of labeled OCT scans, demonstrated diagnostic performance comparable to expert ophthalmologists (De Fauw et al., 2018). What made the project especially noteworthy was its use of a dual-network architecture: one neural network produced the diagnosis, and a second provided an explanation and confidence level for the result. This move toward "explainable AI" helped foster clinician trust in the tool.

However, the project also faced criticism early on for its handling of patient data. In 2016, DeepMind was found to have received access to 1.6 million NHS patient records without proper patient consent. This incident prompted public backlash and regulatory scrutiny, leading to stricter governance and transparency requirements in subsequent AI projects (Powles & Hodson, 2017).

This case illustrates both the promise of AI for clinical diagnostics and the importance of ethical data stewardship and public trust.

1.5.2 IBM Watson for Oncology: Hype, Limitations, and Lessons Learned

IBM's Watson for Oncology was launched with great anticipation as a cognitive computing platform designed to assist oncologists in selecting personalized cancer treatments. Trained on a combination of medical literature, clinical guidelines, and expert-curated datasets, Watson was expected to deliver treatment recommendations based on individual patient profiles.

While the system showed potential in early pilot studies, particularly in structured environments, its broader deployment revealed several challenges. Reports surfaced that Watson often recommended unsafe or irrelevant treatments, largely due to poor data quality and a lack of contextual understanding (Strickland, 2019). Additionally,

Watson struggled to adapt to local practices, differing treatment protocols, and varying patient populations.

The case of Watson highlights a crucial lesson in AI deployment: high-performing algorithms alone do not guarantee clinical utility. The effectiveness of AI systems depends heavily on the quality of data they are trained on, the context in which they are used, and their integration into clinical workflows. Overreliance on marketing rather than empirical validation also risks damaging public confidence in healthcare AI.

1.5.3 AI and the COVID-19 Pandemic: A Global Test of Capability

The COVID-19 pandemic created an unprecedented testbed for AI tools across the healthcare continuum. From early outbreak detection to vaccine development and hospital management, AI played multiple roles in responding to the crisis.

One of the earliest signals about the outbreak came from BlueDot, a Canadian health surveillance company that used natural language processing and machine learning to scan news reports and airline data. BlueDot flagged the potential epidemic in Wuhan days before official announcements by public health bodies (Bogoch et al., 2020).

AI was also deployed to aid in diagnosis. In China, AI systems were developed to analyze chest CT scans to detect COVID-19 pneumonia, especially in situations where testing kits were scarce. Hospitals used predictive algorithms to identify patients at high risk of deterioration, helping clinicians allocate scarce ICU resources.

Moreover, AI played a pivotal role in drug discovery and vaccine development. Machine learning was used to identify candidate molecules, simulate protein structures, and predict immune responses—contributing to the acceleration of vaccine research.

Despite these successes, the pandemic also exposed some limitations. Many AI tools failed to generalize across settings due to overfitting or biased training data. Others were deployed too quickly, without sufficient clinical validation. The COVID-19 experience serves as a reminder of the need for rigorous evaluation, transparency, and the alignment of AI tools with public health goals.

1.5.4 Indian Startups and Innovations: AI in Low-Resource Settings

India has emerged as a hub for AI-driven healthcare innovation, particularly focused on low-cost, scalable solutions tailored to the needs of resource-constrained environments. Several startups have gained international recognition for their use of AI in diagnostics and health screening.

Qure.ai, based in Mumbai, has developed deep learning models to interpret chest X-rays and head CT scans. Their AI system, qXR, is used to screen for tuberculosis, pneumonia, and lung nodules, particularly in rural clinics and public health programs. It has been validated in multiple countries and integrated into mobile screening vans and tele-radiology platforms (Qure.ai, 2023).

Niramai, another Indian startup, uses AI and thermal imaging to detect breast cancer. Unlike traditional mammography, which requires expensive equipment and trained radiologists, Niramai's solution is portable, is non-invasive, and does not involve radiation exposure. It is especially useful for screening women in rural or semi-urban areas where access to cancer diagnostics is limited.

These examples demonstrate that AI can be both technologically advanced and socially inclusive. By designing for affordability, portability, and simplicity, these startups have shown how AI can be adapted to meet the needs of diverse populations.

1.5.5 AI for Global Health and Public Sector Applications

Beyond individual startups and health systems, AI is increasingly being used in public health programs, particularly in disease surveillance and resource planning. International organizations such as the World Health Organization (WHO) and national health agencies have begun incorporating AI into their public health strategies.

In sub-Saharan Africa, AI tools have been piloted to predict malaria outbreaks based on climate data, mobility patterns, and historical case reports. Similar approaches are being used to track dengue fever, Ebola, and other vector-borne diseases.

AI is also being used to optimize vaccination campaigns. For instance, predictive models help identify geographic areas with low immunization coverage and suggest targeted interventions. This kind of data-driven planning can significantly improve outcomes in large-scale public health initiatives.

However, deploying AI in global health contexts comes with unique challenges. Data quality, internet connectivity, local regulatory frameworks, and community acceptance all influence the success of such projects. Additionally, there is an ongoing need to avoid "tech colonialism"—the imposition of external solutions without sufficient local participation and capacity building.

1.6 FUTURE DIRECTIONS AND RESEARCH OPPORTUNITIES

1.6.1 Explainable Artificial Intelligence (XAI)

One of the most pressing areas of development is explainable AI or XAI. The majority of high-performing AI models, particularly those using deep learning, function as "black boxes"—they produce accurate outputs but offer little insight into how they arrived at a decision. In medicine, this lack of transparency is a significant barrier. Clinicians must be able to understand, validate, and trust AI-generated recommendations, especially in high-stakes decisions such as cancer diagnosis or surgical planning.

Research in XAI focuses on making AI models more interpretable without sacrificing performance. Techniques like SHAP (Shapley Additive Explanations), LIME (Local Interpretable Model-agnostic Explanations), and attention mechanisms are being used to highlight which features influenced a model's decision (Arrieta et al., 2020). For example, an AI system predicting sepsis may indicate that a sudden rise in heart rate and white blood cell count was the primary trigger for its alert.

Going forward, the development of inherently interpretable models—those designed from the ground up for transparency—could be crucial for clinical adoption. There is also a growing recognition that interpretability is not merely a technical issue but a sociotechnical one: explanations must be meaningful to the people using the system, which includes clinicians, patients, and administrators.

1.6.2 Federated Learning and Privacy-Preserving AI

Another transformative area of research is federated learning. In traditional machine learning, data from multiple sources must be centralized for model training. This approach raises serious concerns about privacy, especially with sensitive health data. Federated learning flips this model: instead of moving data to a central server, the model is sent to where the data resides at hospitals or clinics, trained locally, and then aggregated into a global model.

This approach allows collaboration across institutions without ever sharing raw patient data. Not only does this preserve privacy, but it also helps improve the generalizability of AI models by incorporating diverse data sources (Rieke et al., 2020). For example, a federated model trained on radiology data from hospitals across continents could potentially perform better across demographic and geographic groups.

Privacy-preserving AI also includes research into differential privacy, homomorphic encryption, and secure multi-party computation. These techniques allow data to be analyzed without exposing sensitive information, thus maintaining compliance with data protection regulations such as GDPR and HIPAA. The future of scalable, trustworthy AI in healthcare likely depends on the successful implementation of these tools.

1.6.3 AI for Global Health and Equity

As AI technologies develop, a critical question emerges: Who benefits? The current distribution of AI development and deployment is heavily skewed toward high-income countries. Yet, some of the most compelling use cases for AI lie in low- and middle-income settings, where healthcare access is limited, and infrastructure is strained.

AI has the potential to support global health by enabling more equitable access to diagnostics, decision support, and health education. For example, smartphone-based AI tools can assist in screening for eye diseases or skin conditions in rural areas without specialist access. Chatbots can deliver maternal health information to expectant mothers in multiple languages. AI can also help in planning vaccine distribution or predicting outbreaks in resource-constrained settings (Ienca & Vayena, 2020).

However, equity is not just about extending existing tools to new regions. It also involves building context-specific AI that reflects local health priorities, languages, disease profiles, and cultural norms. This requires involving local stakeholders (clinicians, patients, and policymakers) in the design and validation process. It also demands open access to AI tools and datasets to empower innovation in the Global South.

1.6.4 AI in Preventive and Proactive Healthcare

Most current healthcare systems are reactive. They focus on diagnosing and treating diseases after symptoms appear. AI offers an opportunity to shift this paradigm toward prevention and early intervention. Predictive models can identify individuals at high risk for chronic diseases like diabetes or cardiovascular disease based on routine health checks, wearable data, and lifestyle information.

For example, AI models can analyze longitudinal data from wearable devices to detect subtle changes in behavior or physiology that precede the onset of illness. An elevated resting heart rate, reduced sleep quality, and changes in physical activity patterns may signal the early stages of a depressive episode or respiratory infection. AI can trigger alerts or nudges to encourage patients to seek care earlier, potentially avoiding hospitalizations or complications.

In the public health sphere, AI can help monitor population-level risks, such as tracking air pollution exposure, analyzing dietary patterns, or forecasting the spread of vector-borne diseases. This kind of proactive surveillance and intervention can make healthcare more sustainable and cost-effective in the long term.

1.6.5 Multimodal AI and Foundation Models

The human body is a complex system, and understanding it requires synthesizing information from many sources—genomic data, clinical notes, medical images, lab results, and patient behavior. Multimodal AI aims to integrate these different data streams to provide a more holistic and accurate view of health.

Recent advancements in foundation models—large-scale models pre-trained on vast datasets—are pushing the boundaries of what AI can achieve. Models like Med-PaLM, BioGPT, and Clinical BERT are being adapted to understand and reason across multiple data types (Singhal et al., 2023). These models can answer clinical questions, summarize research papers, generate discharge notes, and even simulate diagnostic reasoning.

The vision for multimodal AI is a "digital twin" of the patient—a comprehensive, evolving model that reflects the individual's health status and predicts how it might change under different interventions. While still in early stages, this approach could revolutionize personalized medicine and clinical decision-making.

However, there are challenges. Multimodal models are computationally intensive, require massive and well-curated datasets, and are prone to compounding biases from multiple data sources. Furthermore, their complexity makes them even harder to explain and validate. These issues must be addressed to ensure safety, effectiveness, and acceptance in clinical settings.

REFERENCES

Ardila, D., Kiraly, A. P., Bharadwaj, S., Choi, B., Reicher, J. J., Peng, L., ... Tse, D. (2019). End-to-end lung cancer screening with three-dimensional deep learning on low-dose chest computed tomography. *Nature Medicine*, 25(6), 954–961.

Arrieta, A. B., Díaz-Rodríguez, N., Del Ser, J., Bennetot, A., Tabik, S., Barbado, A., ... Herrera, F. (2020). Explainable Artificial Intelligence (XAI): Concepts, taxonomies, opportunities and challenges toward responsible AI. *Information Fusion*, 58, 82–115.

Bogoch, I. I., Watts, A., Thomas-Bachli, A., Huber, C., Kraemer, M. U., & Khan, K. (2020). Pneumonia of unknown aetiology in Wuhan, China: Potential for international spread via commercial air travel. *Journal of Travel Medicine*, 27(2). DOI: 10.1093/jtm/taaa008

Char, D. S., Shah, N. H., & Magnus, D. (2018). Implementing machine learning in health care—addressing ethical challenges. *New England Journal of Medicine*, 378(11), 981–983.

De Fauw, J., Ledsam, J. R., Romera-Paredes, B., Nikolov, S., Tomasev, N., Blackwell, S., ... Suleyman, M. (2018). Clinically applicable deep learning for diagnosis and referral in retinal disease. *Nature Medicine*, 24(9), 1342–1350.

Esteva, A., Kuprel, B., Novoa, R. A., Ko, J., Swetter, S. M., Blau, H. M., & Thrun, S. (2017). Dermatologist-level classification of skin cancer with deep neural networks. *Nature*, 542(7639), 115–118.

Ghosh, D., Pushan K. D., & Mostafa A. (2024). Harnessing the power of hybrid models for supply chain management and optimization. *Hybrid Information Systems: Non-Linear Optimization Strategies with Artificial Intelligence*, 407–426.

Fitzpatrick, K. K., Darcy, A., & Vierhile, M. (2017). Delivering cognitive behavior therapy to young adults with symptoms of depression and anxiety using a fully automated conversational agent (Woebot): A randomized controlled trial. *JMIR Mental Health*, 4(2), e19.

Gulshan, V., Peng, L., Coram, M., Stumpe, M. C., Wu, D., Narayanaswamy, A., … Webster, D. R. (2016). Development and Validation of a Deep Learning Algorithm for Detection of Diabetic Retinopathy in Retinal Fundus Photographs. *JAMA*, 316(22), 2402–2410.

Ienca, M., & Vayena, E. (2020). On the responsible use of digital data to tackle the COVID-19 pandemic. *Nature Medicine*, 26(4), 463–464.

Helm, J. E., AhmadBeygi, S., & Van Oyen, M. P. (2020). Design and analysis of hospital admission control for operational effectiveness. *Production and Operations Management*, 29(1), 201–222.

Jiang, F., Jiang, Y., Zhi, H., Dong, Y., Li, H., Ma, S., ... Wang, Y. (2017). Artificial intelligence in healthcare: past, present and future. *Stroke and Vascular Neurology*, 2(4), 230–243.

Obermeyer, Z., Powers, B., Vogeli, C., & Mullainathan, S. (2019). Dissecting racial bias in an algorithm used to manage the health of populations. *Science*, 366(6464), 447–453.

Qure.ai. qXR: AI-Powered Chest X-Ray Interpretation Tool. Qure.ai, 2023, https://www.qure.ai/product/qxr.

Powles, J., & Hodson, H. (2017). Google DeepMind and healthcare in an age of algorithms. *Health and Technology*, 7(4), 351–367.

Richardson, P., Griffin, I., Tucker, C., Smith, D., Oechsle, O., Phelan, A., … Stebbing, J. (2020). Baricitinib as potential treatment for 2019-nCoV acute respiratory disease. *The Lancet*, 395(10223), e30–e31.

Rieke, N., Hancox, J., Li, W., Milletari, F., Roth, H. R., Albarqouni, S., ... Cardoso, M. J. (2020). The future of digital health with federated learning. *NPJ Digital Medicine*, 3(1), 1–7.

Russell, S., & Norvig, P. (2020). *Artificial Intelligence: A Modern Approach* (4th ed.). Pearson Education.

Sendak, M. P., D'Arcy, J., Kashyap, S., Gao, M., Nichols, M., Corey, K., ... Ratliff, W. (2020). A path for translation of machine learning products into healthcare delivery. *NPJ Digital Medicine*, 3(1), 1–10.

Shademan, A., Decker, R. S., Opfermann, J. D., Leonard, S., Krieger, A., & Kim, P. C. W. (2016). Supervised autonomous robotic soft tissue surgery. *Science Translational Medicine*, 8(337), 337ra64.

Singhal, K., Azizi, S., Tu, T., Mahdavi, S. S., Wei, J., Chung, H. W., ... Touvron, H. (2023). Large language models encode clinical knowledge. *Nature*, 620(7972), 172–180.

Strickland, E. (2019). IBM Watson, heal thyself: How IBM overpromised and underdelivered on AI health care. *IEEE Spectrum*, 56(4), 24–31.

Topol, E. (2019). *Deep Medicine: How Artificial Intelligence Can Make Healthcare Human Again*. Basic Books.

2 An Extensive Survey of Gene-Centric Approach to Parkinson's Disease Identification

Anusha B., V. Pandiyaraju,
Thomas Abraham J. V. and A. Kannan

2.1 INTRODUCTION

Environmental factors (toxins, chemicals, and head trauma) and genetic factors [1] are the major reasons for the occurrence of PD [2]. It is a brain disease. This progressive disorder affects the nerve cells that exist in deep parts of the brain called the basal ganglia and the substantia nigra. Nerve cells in the substantia nigra produce the neurotransmitter dopamine, which is responsible for relaying messages that plan and control body movements [3]. It affects both facial expressions and behavioral features [4].

The various symptoms associated with PD are dementia (memory loss) and tremor (muscle movement), which starts from one side of the body, one hand, arms, legs (walking difficulty), feet, and face [5]. The various features used to detect PD are medical images [6], face [7], gait [8, 9], gene [10–12], handwriting [13], motion [14], and voice [15].

Only 15% of individuals with Parkinson's disease have a family history of the condition. For the rest, the cause of PD is usually unknown. Research suggests that a combination of genetic and environmental factors may cause Parkinson's disease. It's rare for Parkinson's disease to be passed down from parent to child. Most cases of Parkinson's aren't hereditary. However, people who get early-onset Parkinson's disease are more likely to have inherited it. Having a family history of Parkinson's disease may increase the risk of developing the condition. Having a first-degree family member with Parkinson's disease raises the risk to 3%. This means that having a parent or sibling with Parkinson's disease slightly increases the risk [16]. In PD, this genetic-based inheritance occurs in two ways: autosomal dominant and autosomal recessive. In autosomal dominant, one copy of the abnormal gene is inherited from a parent. In autosomal recessive, two copies of abnormal genes are present [17]. These genes are located on chromosomes. Genes contain DNA, which is the fundamental unit of heredity [18].

DOI: 10.1201/9781003532156-3

Based on age, PD is classified into three categories as juvenile-onset (<20), young-onset (20–40), and late-onset PD (>40) [19]. In order to identify PD in all age groups, there are various genes that exist in the DNA responsible for the cause of PD. In a PD person's gene, the substitution of one amino acid for another in the protein sequence is called a missense mutation [20].

The main objectives of this survey are as follows:

- To understand the background of genes.
- To identify the genes responsible for the cause of PD.
- To highlight the genes only responsible for the cause of PD.
- To briefly describe available datasets that can be useful for further research.
- To analyze the different available gene processing methods.
- To analyze the different gene processing methods that have already been used for PD detection.
- To identify the genetic variant features associated with genes responsible for the cause of PD.
- To propose a generic framework for coded sequence extraction and mutation detection.
- To study techniques for coded region detection and sequence matching.

2.2 EXTRACTION OF GENE DATASET

Deoxyribonucleic acid (DNA) is a molecule that forms a double helix structure and carries genetic instructions for the development, functioning, growth, and reproduction of all known organisms, including *Homo sapiens*. DNA consists of a set of genes. Genetic and environmental factors cause modifications which in turn are the reason for the occurrence of gene-based diseases. Genes are made up of nucleotides – adenine (A), guanine (G), cytosine (C), and thymine (T) [21]. These nucleotides within the gene have coding and noncoding regions. Only the coding regions (exons) code the proteins with the help of amino acids. The noncoding regions (introns) do not code the proteins. Therefore, there is a need to identify the exons [22].

In order to identify PD, after exon identification, it is necessary to check whether any single mutation exists in the sequence. This single mutation occurs due to both dominant and recessive patterns of inheritance. In PD, the single mutation belongs to missense mutations in genes [23]. If a missense mutation exists in the corresponding gene, the amino acid and its position must be identified in order to rectify the problem correctly.

Early detection of mutations helps to prevent further variations of getting PD by having proper treatment and is helpful to avoid the various factors that can lead to further variations developing in the gene.

2.2.1 Genes Responsible for the Cause of PD

There are 20,000 to 25,000 genes present in *Homo sapiens* [24]. However, not all genes are responsible for the cause of PD. Some gene variations cause PD. At the

TABLE 2.1
List of PD Genes Associated with Other Diseases

Genes	No. of Patients Tested	Mutation Rate	Family History	Detected Age (Years)	Disease Name
GBA gene [25]	119	5.4%	Yes (4.9%)	>60 (65–85)	Type 1 Gaucher disease [69]
GLA gene [27]	90 families	2 PD	Yes	–	Fabry disease
ATP13A2 gene [17]	–	–	–	–	Kufor-Rakeb syndrome
PLA2G6 [17]	–	–	–	–	Early-onset dystonia parkinsonism, Kufor-Rakeb syndrome
FBXO7 [17]	–	–	–	–	Early-onset Parkinsonism pyramidal syndrome, Kufor-Rakeb syndrome
CYP2D6 (in white people) [30, 31]	528 (Chinese)	–	–	–	Dementia with Lewy bodies and low frequency of genetic polymorphism in Chinese

same time, a few genes are the reasons for the cause of PD as well as some other diseases. Such genes may have a greater number of variations in their exons. In order to identify PD genes, we have been conducting a survey over the past few years. Based on that survey, the resulting genes responsible for the cause of PD are listed in Table 2.1.

From this, genes such as GBA [26], GLA [27], ATP13A2 [28], PLA2G6, FBXO7 [29], and CYP2D6 [30] are associated with PD as well as other syndromes. Such genes may or may not have other types of mutations. Therefore, we need to identify the unique genes solely responsible for the cause of PD. Based on a survey [17], missense mutations exist in genes that are solely responsible for the cause of PD. The unique genes only responsible for the cause of PD are listed in Table 2.2.

The CYP2D6 gene has a low frequency of occurrence in PD. In SNCA, copy number variation (CNV) issues are observed. However, it remains a high-prevalence gene associated with PD. Two-thirds of studies state that there exist single nucleotide polymorphisms (SNPs) in PD genes. Based on Table 2.2, SNCA, LARK2, PRKN, PINK1, and DJ-1 [40] are the prominent genes related to PD in *Homo sapiens*. The generic information, age-based PD groups, and inheritance information are presented in Table 2.3. Juvenile-onset Parkinson's disease (JOPD) and young-onset Parkinson's disease (YOPD) are categorized under early-onset Parkinson's disease (EOPD).

TABLE 2.2
Genes Solely Responsible for the Cause of PD

Genes	No. of Patients Tested	Mutation
PARKIN (PARK 2) [32]	259	8.5%
	138	7.24%
	102	25%
	69	8.7%
	16	68%
LARK2 [32]	800	No
	140	G2019S
	150	No
	300	No
PINK 1 [32]	250	6%
DJ-1 [32]	150	No
DJ-1 [32]	308	3.9%
MAPT [32]	301	No
VPS35 [32]	320	No
E1F4G1 [32]	320	No
SNCA	181 – PD	CNV occur
PARK2	67 – control	CNV occur
PARK7		No CNV
ATP13A2		No CNV
PINK1		No CNV
LARK2		No CNV
[33]		
SNCA	–	Yes (high prevalence)
LARK2		Yes
[34]		
ATF4	–	Switching
PINK1		Yes
PARKIN		Yes
[35]		
ATP13A2	–	Yes
LARK2		Yes
PARK7		Yes
PINK1		Yes
PRKN		Yes
SNCA		Yes
VPS35		Yes
GBA		Mutation does not occur PD (may/may not cause PD)
UCHL1		
[19]		

TABLE 2.3
Prominent PD Gene Information

Gene	Inheritance	Chromosome Position	Nucleotide Length	Amino Acid Length	Disease [46]
α-Synuclein (SNCA)	AD [36, 37]	4q22.1 [41, 112]	420	140	F, YOPD, LOPD
Leucine-rich repeat kinase 2 (LRRK2)	AD [36, 37]	12q12 [42, 113]	7563	2521	F, YOPD, LOPD
PRKN gene make a protein called parkin (PARK2)	AR [36, 38]	6q26 [43, 114]	1395	465	F, (≤80–90%), JOPD, YOPD, LOPD
PTEN-induced putative kinase 1 (PINK1)	AR [36, 38]	1p36.12 [44, 115]	1743	581	F, JOPD, YOPD, LOPD
DJ-1 (PARK7)	AR [38, 39]	1p36.23 [45, 117]	567	189	F, JOPD, YOPD, LOPD

AD, autosomal dominant; AR, autosomal recessive; F, familial; JOPD, juvenile-onset Parkinson's disease; YOPD, young-onset Parkinson's disease; LOPD, late-onset Parkinson's disease.

2.2.2 PD Gene Datasets

In order to apply informative techniques that combine computer science with biological information, it is necessary to identify the gene databases. There are numerous gene datasets available, each based on different representations of genes. The following are various gene datasets used in the analysis for the detection of PD using informative techniques:

1. BioGPS – Transcription profiling by array of human substantia nigra from patients with Parkinson's disease [47, 118].
2. ParkDB – Annotated microarray dataset [48].
3. NCBI-GEO (Gene Expression Omnibus) – Microarray data [49–51].
4. NCBI – Gene Sequences [52].
5. Ensemble – Gene Sequences [53].
6. PD mutation – Gene Sequences [54].
7. UniProtKB – Gene Sequences [55].

Among the above-mentioned datasets, BioGPS, NCBI-GEO, and ParkDB have annotated microarray data. Microarray data are useful for identifying the crucial genes associated with PD [56]. They are also used to identify Parkinson's disease-associated pathways [57] and the differential expression profile of the genetic network for Parkinson's disease [58]. Genetic variants that occur in genes cause PD. In

TABLE 2.4
Gene Sequence Dataset Information

Gene Name	Sequence Dataset
SNCA	NCBI, PD mutation
LARK2	NCBI, PD mutation, Ensemble
PRKN	NCBI, PD mutation, UniportKB
PINK1	PD mutation, Ensemble, UniportKB
PARK7	NCBI, PD mutation, UniportKB

order to identify the genetic variants, gene sequences are needed. The availability of gene sequences in various datasets is presented in Table 2.4.

The different datasets use different gene sequence formats for sequence representation. Plain sequence format, FASTQ format, FASTA format, EMBL format, GCG format, GCG-RSF (Rich Sequence Format), GenBank format, 1G format, and Genomatix annotation syntax are the widely used genomic sequence representation formats [59]. Each and every representation uses different indexing and spacing formats. If there is a need to use sequences from the different datasets, there is a need to ensure the sequence representation formats. There is a difference in sequence format representation; there is a need to align the sequences before processing. For aligning the sequences, a lot of sequence alignment algorithms are available. We will discuss such a sequence alignment algorithm in Section 2.4.

There are numerous genome sequencing techniques available. Once the sequencing of the genome is done, the data becomes available for computer-based interpretations. In particular, variations within the genome are detected using data points that exist in the sequence, which will be analyzed and interpreted to provide results. The genetic variants associated with PD genes are discussed in Section 2.3. Interpreted mutation results can help identify the reason (cause) and ultimately cure various diseases. For making such interpretations, manual calculations are infeasible. Nowadays, computational biological techniques are available to detect mutations. Pattern-matching algorithms and mathematical models are widely used to identify the mutations. It is anticipated that these computational models may be helpful in discovering new treatments for a number of diseases.

2.2.3 Genetic Variants Associated with PD

Possessing a particular gene variant does not necessarily mean one will develop the disease, while lacking a particular gene variant does not necessarily mean the disease will not occur. Therefore, we need to identify the various genetic variants associated with PD. The genetic variants associated with each gene are presented in Table 2.5.

For the purpose of identifying genetic variants that exist in a sequence, various sequence matching algorithms are available. These methods are discussed in Section

TABLE 2.5
Gene Variants Responsible for the Cause of PD

Gene	Variants
SNCA	A30P, E46K, A53T [60]
LARK2	R1441C, R1441G, R1628P, Y1699C, G2019S, I2020T, G2385R [61]
PRKN	G144A, C211T, G226C, G237C, G336T [62]
PINK1	P209A [63], S419P [64], W437X [65], Q456X [66]
DJ-1	A39S [67], G150S [68]

2.4. Before identifying variants from exons, it is necessary to extract exons from the genomic sequence. Exon extraction methods are discussed in Section 2.3. In this survey, we examine how the biological information of an organism is processed using computational techniques with the knowledge of computer science. For this purpose, we introduced an automated approach of biological signal-based exon identification and sequence matching-based process, which can be useful in the medical diagnosis of PD up to some extent.

2.3 CODED REGION DETECTION IN GENOMIC SEQUENCES

In eukaryotic organisms, coding regions in genomic sequences are used to regulate gene expression. They form mature mRNA. They are the coding portions of the sequence of the genes, which code for protein. In PD, a number of mutations exist in the protein sequences. So, there is a need to identify the protein-coding region beneficial for the identification of known variants. Therefore, systems easily identify the targeted mutations in the gene sequence. This is the major cause of a single incorrect nucleotide coding a different amino acid.

Genomic DNA sequences are given as the input to the system, and the location of genes and transcripts is collected from different sources. Intrinsic signals such as start and stop codons, statistical properties, transcript sequences (either full-length cDNAs or partial ESTs), and protein sequences are the required information. A plethora of programs and strategies associate these sources of information in order to obtain consistent gene predictions. Sequence signal-based 'intrinsic' evidence and statistical bias can be combined using hidden Markov models to yield the exact gene predictions. These programs are known as ab initio or de novo gene finders [89]. A lot of gene prediction or coding region (CDs) identification online tools are available [90]. The Marple Algorithm and Wavelet Packets Transform are integrated for identifying exons. In this, DNA was converted into a numerical sequence using the code13 method before applying the integrated algorithm, which increased the accuracy of detecting CDs [91]. Time-frequency filtering is an efficient approach used for CD detection in DNA sequences. It uses a multi-resolution method to analyze CDs of varied sizes. It effectively handles promoter regions and splice site detection

[92]. The Data Normalized Data Clipped LMS (DNDCLMS) algorithm takes input as the binary representation of DNA. A feedback signal is generated for updating filter coefficients. Whenever the feedback signal was minimum, the accurate location of CDs was predicted [93]. SVD algorithms are used to identify the exons at the nucleotide level based on spectral peaks at 1/3 frequency component position [94].

Coding measure schemes (indicator sequences), window functions, digital filters, Fourier transforms, wavelet transforms, continuous wavelet transforms, discrete wavelet transforms, and spectrum estimation are the different coding region identification methods [95]. Exons within a gene exhibit three-base periodicity (TBP). When signal processing methods are applied, TBP can be easily determined. It is the basis for all exon identification techniques. In this maximum normalization, the technique is used to reduce the complexity. In addition, the MDNLMS algorithm is integrated with sign-based algorithms [96]. Walsh codes of order four numerical encoding generate the 1D binary discrete sequence. Then, the modified Gabor wavelet transform (MGWT) was applied to the DNA discrete sequence for spectrum analysis, which effectively identifies the CDs of unknown gene sequences [97].

Various algorithms and tools used for detecting CDs are presented in Table 2.6. Based on biological principles, splicing signals are used for encoding CDs. In over 60%, splicing signals themselves are sufficient to extract the CDs that have splice donor, splice acceptor, and branch-site information [98]. This information is sufficient to develop a novel algorithm for extracting CDs.

2.4 GENE SEQUENCE ALIGNMENT METHODS AND SEQUENCE MATCHING TECHNIQUES

Gene sequence alignment methods are used to arrange DNA, RNA, and protein sequences in order to identify the similarity between sequences. This process will be helpful to identify evolutionary and structural relationships between two or more sequences. For aligning the sequence, a wide variety of sequence alignment tools and techniques are available.

NCBI developed BLAST, which utilizes multi-core processors in its algorithm. It compares a query sequence and returns the best matches found in the data. This program compares and calculates the statistical significance between nucleotide or protein sequences and the sequence databases [70]. In BLAST, Graphical Processing Units (GPU) are introduced because of their exceptionally high performance-to-cost ratio. The GPU increases the speed of processing as compared with NCBI-BLAST. This is widely used for protein sequence alignment [71]. Sequence alignment models incorporate substitutions, insertions, and deletions. During sequence alignment, Cactus graphs use complementary algorithms, which have the ability to find intragene duplication and properly align the sequences [72]. The SILVA Incremental Aligner (SINA) utilizes *k*-mer searching and partial order alignment algorithms. It dynamically selects a set of sequences and constructs the alignment. It is particularly effective for aligning RNA genes, achieving high accuracy as well as throughput [73, 74]. Dynamic reconstruction of sequences is done using Merge Align, which improves the performance of sequence alignments. In this, Merge Align produces

TABLE 2.6
Coded Region Detection Algorithms/Tools

References	Algorithms/Tools used	Dataset	Inference
[89]	• Ab initio or de novo gene finders • GENCODE	Mammalian transcriptomes: • Ensemble genome browser • National Center for Biotechnology Information (NCBI) • University of California Santa Cruz (UCSC)	In mammalian transcriptomes, whole genome analysis has different overlapping transcripts. In this low fraction of transcriptional complexity was discovered. GENCODE translates the larger transcripts to minimal protein per locus. It effectively removes noncoding transcripts.
[90]	AUGUSTUS – Handles alternative transcripts using ab initio. CSTminer – A web tool used to identify the coding and noncoding sequence tags. FeatureExtract x97 – For GenBank format files, it extracts sequences such as exon structure, intron structure, etc. GeneAlign – Identify CDs.	–	Various tools are available for the prediction of coding sequences and genes.
[91]	Marple Algorithm Wavelet Packet Transform	Eukaryotic DNA Sequence Datasets: • GENSCAN65 • HMR195 • BG570	Algorithms use the Code13 numerical mapping approach for increasing the accuracy in identification. The marble algorithm is time-consuming.
[92]	S-Transform-Based Time-Frequency Filtering Approach	• HMR195 – 195 sequences of the human, rat. • GenBank No. AF099922: DNA sequence of gene F56F11.4a	S-transform provides low-frequency resolution at higher frequencies and low time resolution at lower frequencies due to the scaling nature of the Gaussian window. It affects the time-frequency filtering operation and accuracy.

(*Continued*)

TABLE 2.6 CONTINUED
Coded Region Detection Algorithms/Tools

References	Algorithms/Tools used	Dataset	Inference
[93]	• Data Clipped LMS (DCLMS), Error Clipped LMS (ECLMS), Data Error Clipped LMS (DECLMS) • Data Normalized LMS (DNLMS) • Data Normalized Data Clipped LMS (DNDCLMS) • Data Normalized Error Clipped LMS (DNECLMS) • Data Normalized Data Error Clipped LMS (DNDECLMS)	National Center for Biotechnology Information (NCBI) database: Human Genomic Sequences • OCIF gene • tat gene • TCL6 gene • FAA gene • CCR-5 gene • FGF gene • RP58 gene • TTN gene • Beta globin sequence on chromosome 11 • Gene for prolactin inducible protein (GPIPI)	DNDCLMS based Adaptive Exon Predictor (AEP) is better in exon prediction applications. Based on feedback signal algorithms updates the filter coefficients. Minimum feedback signal results the location of coding region sequence.
[94]	Pseudoeiip-Singular Value Decomposition (SVD) algorithm	• Gene of *C. elegans* (F56F 11.4) and accession no. AF099922 • *Mus musculus* (PSMB5) • *Homo sapiens* stubulin gene for accession number BC111374	It is a faster algorithm. It produces the precision results as 83%.
[95]	Techniques used for coding region extraction: • Coding measure schemes • Window functions • Digital filters • Fourier transform-based methods • Wavelet transform-based methods • Spectrum estimation	–	This paper review various possible algorithms for coding region identifications. Each technique includes various algorithms/methods helpful for identifying the coding regions.

(Continued)

TABLE 2.6 CONTINUED
Coded Region Detection Algorithms/Tools

References	Algorithms/Tools used	Dataset	Inference
[96]	Adaptive signal processing techniques: • MDNLMS • MDNSRLMS • MDNSLMS • MDNSSLMS	National Center for Biotechnology Information (NCBI) genomic sequence database	Based on computational complexity, MDNSRLMS is more accurate for identifying exons.
[97]	Modified Gabor wavelet transform	HRM195 database	Walsh numerical encoding method and modified Gabor wavelet transform (MGWT) are used to discretize the DNA sequence for spectrum analysis. Computational complexity is lower compared to the GENSCAN tool.
[98]	–	–	Biological signals are useful for predicting CDs.

a consensus alignment of two sequences on the basis of independent MSAs. The numerical representation is used for representing MSA. A graph alignment is used to identify nodes. Based on edge weight, alignment could be done. Traceback is used to construct the aligned sequence [75].

Dynamic programming (DP)-based sequence alignment uses global (Needleman-Wunsch algorithm) and local (Smith-Waterman algorithm) alignment algorithms. These algorithms use a substitution matrix to assign scores to input sequences (i.e., either nucleotide sequence or amino acid sequence). Once the alignment matrix is filled, a traceback operation is performed to align the sequences. It requires more memory for larger sequences [76]. DIALIGN combines local and global features and has the ability to identify local homologies among sequences without requiring detectable global homology, which helps to analyze the relevant protein families or genomic sequences [77].

Pairwise sequence alignment is used to identify the similarity region between two biological sequences. GapMis is a tool used for pairwise sequence alignment [78]. The dynamic algorithm can only process short-length sequences because of processing speed and low memory. However, with the help of GPU, pairwise sequence alignment was done for longer sequences using the Smith-Waterman algorithm [79]. A maximum entropy probability model was used to infer the pairwise interactions between the sequences [80]. Major issues associated with dynamic programming are space and time complexity, and for overcoming such issues, hybridization of soft computing algorithms such as Particle Swarm Optimization with Gravitation Search Algorithm (PSOGSA) have been proposed. It effectively reduces complexity issues and provides optimal results for alignment problems [81]. Minimap2 is an online tool used for aligning nucleotide sequences. It uses DP to extend from the ends of chains and to close regions between adjacent anchors in chains [82]. The two gene sequences are input into the pairwise alignment algorithm for very long nucleic acid sequences (PAAVLS) algorithm. It successfully generates alignment results with the help of the Smith-Waterman [83] and Needleman-Wunsch [84] algorithms. It calculates the scoring matrix and performs a traceback operation for effective alignment results [85].

Nowadays, evolutionary algorithms are used for aligning the sequences. The genetic algorithm selects the population that is divided into three zones based on the objective function's score. Then it performs crossover depending on cut-points and the location of gaps. It guarantees to provide fitness in each succeeding generation. In the end, the offspring of populations provide better fitness value. As a result, GA has the ability to find the finest alignment score [86]. For increasing the pairwise algorithm's alignment performance, it uses deep reinforcement learning. It handles very large sequences effectively. It makes decisions for any input without using manual methods of state spaces [87].

Each and every method has its own pros and cons. DP-based global alignment identifies site homology between sequences. It simplifies ancestral-descendant relationships as an inference over molecular phylogenetics. DP-based local alignment identifies sequence similarities that occur due to inheritance or convergence [88].

Sequence matching techniques are used to identify the missense mutation associated with PD. Missense mutation functionality can be detected by using sequence alignment algorithms. Sequence alignment algorithms also provide the incorrectly coded amino acid. SIFT, Polyphen-2, Uniprot, and a manually curated alignment tuned for Align-GVGD. Sequence alignments vary with respect to sequence composition and their evolutionary depth [99]. A genetic algorithm-based sequence matching technique matches pairwise sequences as well as a sequence with a database that contains a set of sequences [100]. Constructing a sorting machine using apriori, K-means, SVM, decision tree, and neural network is used to classify whether the gene is normal or a mutation has occurred. It classifies Alzheimer's disease dementia and Lewy body disease. This machine can help doctors predict or diagnose the exact disease the patient has. The result of the sorting machine provides the most commonly occurring amino acid. There exists a lot of similarity between high error rates due to the large similarity between Alzheimer's disease and Parkinson's disease. Neural network considering the sum of squared error (SSE) of k-means provides the best result [101].

Mutations present in DNA could be identified using distance-based pattern matching algorithms. In this chapter, Hamming method-based distance matching was done for identifying the mutations [102]. In the same manner, the phylogenetic distance between two DNA sequences was measured using the Jukes-Cantor distance algorithm. It calculates the number of *k*-mer matches between two DNA sequences. It is an alignment-free method [103]. The dissimilarity between DNA sequences was measured using Mahalanobis and Euclidean distance. Mahalanobis compares the frequency of words as the value of n-adjacent letters and Euclidian distance corrects the variance of n-words. This type of combined approach reduces the error rate [104]. To avoid the alignment delay, dissimilarity measurements are carried out by probabilistic model-based pairwise distance measure [105]. The probabilistic model measures the evolutionary distance between sequences using Jensen-Shannon divergence and Euclidean distance [106]. The grammar-based distance method was used to measure pairwise dissimilarity between sequences in a larger dataset [107]. Protein stability predictors are widely used to detect pathogenic missense mutations [108].

For achieving proper alignment and matching scores, a single objective function is insufficient. There is a need to consider multiple objectives such as sequence length, minimum gap length, maximizing the number of conserved columns, and achieving the maximum scoring. Multi-objective functions combined with genetic algorithms provide a better solution for handling sequence matching problems [109]. However, with the help of alignment-free methods, there is a possibility of reducing computation time because they don't depend on dynamic programming [110]. The sequence alignment and matching algorithms are summarized in Table 2.7.

23andMe is a direct-to-consumer genetic testing toolkit. At-home DNA tests are useful for detecting disease risk. They provide meaningful health information directly to individuals. Even if a variant is not found, the reports provide a lot of information, helping people understand how genetics as well as other factors affect their health [111]. In order to obtain results, we propose a generic framework for the detection of missense mutations from genomic sequences, as illustrated in Figure 2.1.

TABLE 2.7
Sequence Alignment and Matching Algorithms

References	Sequence Alignment/Sequence Matching Algorithms or Tools	Dataset	Inference
[70]	BLAST: Basic Local Sequence Alignment Tool	NCBI and other nucleotide or protein sequences	BLAST algorithm identifies the region of similarity in the input sequence. Input may be in the form NCBI GI numbers, database accession numbers, sequences, etc.
[71]	GPU-BLAST: Graphics processing unit – Basic Local Sequence Alignment Tool	NCBI protein database UniProt database	For long and short sequences comparison was carried out in a parallel execution manner with the help of GPU. GPU speeds up the processing of NCBI-BLAST.
[72]	Cactus: Multiple sequence alignment algorithm	Mammals: Blanchette dataset	Cactus graphs are used for proper sequence alignment representation and also identify the intra-gene duplications.
[73]	SILVA Incremental Aligner (SINA)	SILVA ribosomal RNA project gene database (BRAliBase III)	SINA uses *k*-mer searching in fusion with partial order alignment (POA) for accurate alignment.
[75]	MergeAlign	Archaeal sequence dataset	Merge align dynamically construct consensus MSA from independent MSAs and assign precision score for that alignment.
[76]	Dynamic Programming Algorithm: • Needleman-Wunsch algorithm • Smith Waterman algorithm	isCj1293 and HP0840 enzymes	It provides optimal alignment results for distantly related protein sequences.
[77]	DIALIGN	PFAM database	It exactly detected low similarity sequences based on local homologies present in the sequences.
[78]	GapMis	–	It pairwise aligns the sequence with single gap with the help of dynamic programming matrix.

(Continued)

TABLE 2.7 CONTINUED
Sequence Alignment and Matching Algorithms

References	Sequence Alignment/Sequence Matching Algorithms or Tools	Dataset	Inference
[79]	GPU with Smith- Waterman algorithm	–	Helpful for performing pair wise alignment of long sequences.
[80]	Pairwise Maximum-Entropy Probability Models	Biological sequence database	Similarity in model parameters reflects interactive coupling results. It is used to predict the global properties such as 3-D structure prediction, association of gene–gene networks, gene alteration patterns, etc., present in biological systems.
[81]	Hybrid Gravitational Search Algorithm – Particle Swarm Optimization (GSAPSO) algorithm	UniProt Database	GSAPSO overcomes the complexity problem occurs during alignment.
[82]	Minimap2 uses the seed-chain-align procedure	Multi-species databases such as nt from NCBI	Minimap2 acts as a versatile mapper in addition to pairwise aligner intended for nucleotide sequences. It makes use of fast base-level alignment algorithm along with precise chaining algorithm.
[83]	Pairwise Alignment Algorithm for Very Long Sequences (PAAVLS) algorithm	RNA sequences: lncRNAs contain 91,667 nucleotides in ENST00000597346.1 located on human chromosome 11. lncRNAs contain 84,332 nucleotides in ENST00000623130.1 located on human chromosome 22	PAAVLS reduces the demand of memory need while using the Smith-Waterman algorithm. It performs well with longer sequences.

(Continued)

TABLE 2.7 CONTINUED
Sequence Alignment and Matching Algorithms

References	Sequence Alignment/Sequence Matching Algorithms or Tools	Dataset	Inference
[84]	Longest common substring within a sliding window was identified with the help of dot matrix. Needleman-Wunsch's algorithm was used to align the prefix strings. Linear comparison can be carried out if more than one sequences have more similarity.	NCBI – 102 SARS sequences	It performs well for similar sequences.
[85, 88]	Dynamic Programming Algorithm: • Needleman-Wunsch algorithm • Smith-Waterman algorithm	–	It effectively performs global and local pairwise alignments.
[86, 100]	Genetic algorithm (GA)	–	During selection, the GA splits the population into three zones on the basis of the objective function. The crossover approach depends on the cut-points and location of the gaps. The fitness value improves the coverage and generates offspring in each generation. These off spring have better fitness values (i.e., alignment scores).
[99]	Alignment algorithm for missense mutation prediction • SIFT • Polyphen-2 • Uniprot • Align-GVGD	Cancer-associated genes from online Breast Cancer Information Core (BIC) mutation database, • BRCA1 • MSH2 • MLH1 • TP53	Missense mutation was predicted with the help of four alignment algorithms. Align-GVGD predicted all variants when provided with alignments containing a large number of sequences.

(Continued)

TABLE 2.7 CONTINUED
Sequence Alignment and Matching Algorithms

References	Sequence Alignment/Sequence Matching Algorithms or Tools	Dataset	Inference
[101]	Constructing a sorting machine using, • Apriori • Decision tree • Support vector machine • K-means • Neural network (NN)	–	The sorting machine identifies whether the PD-responsible gene belongs to normal or mutated. In this, NNs make use of the sum of squared error (SSE) of k-means as a good classification machine. But if there is a need to distinguish two similar diseases, higher similarity led to the generation of a higher error rate.
[102]	Distance-based methods,Hamming • Hamming-Normalization	DNA Hepatitis data –World Gen Bank	Linear normalization added to the Hamming method balances the dissimilarity of the score pattern.
[103]	Slope-SpaM	–	It is an alignment-free sequence matching software. It extracts phylogenetic distances (distance matrix method) for distances up to 0.5 replacements for each position. The disadvantage addressed here is that it uses only spaced words instead of continuous sequences.
[104]	Mahalanobis distance and Euclidean distance	HSLIPAS (Human mRNA for lipoprotein lipase) dataset	The dimensionality of *n*-words was reduced by using relative count vectors. After that, the dissimilarity between the sequences was identified.

(Continued)

TABLE 2.7 CONTINUED
Sequence Alignment and Matching Algorithms

References	Sequence Alignment/Sequence Matching Algorithms or Tools	Dataset	Inference
[105]	Nearest-neighbor interaction using various parameters, • Gotoh • Vologodskii • Breslauer • Blake • Benight • SantaLucia • Sugimoto • Unified	GenBank sequence database	Without alignment it identifies the similarity between two biological sequences. Nearest-neighbor parameters such as Blake's and Sugimoto's have high sensitivity values. This method does not require complex calculations during comparison.
[106]	Online space word matching software: http://spaced.gobics.de/	Allows all datasets in FASTA sequence file	Maximum sequence capacity is 500 sequences. The evolutionary distance between two DNA sequences is calculated based on the number of (spaced) word matches without alignment.
[107]	Grammar-based distance metric (GramAlign) Online: http://bioinfo.unl.edu/GramAlign.html	BAliBASE 3.0 database	It is helpful to align larger dataset.
[108]	Protein stability predictors Online: https://www.nature.com/articles/s41598-020-72404-w/tables/1	Protein Data Bank – ClinVar database	It is helpful to identify the missense mutation present in the sequences. 13 protein stability predictors are available. Out of 13, FoldX is the best variant predictor.
[109]	Multi-objective genetic algorithm	BAliBASE 2.0. database	It is a multi-sequence alignment algorithm. The stochastic method, i.e., GA, solves complex optimization problem.

(Continued)

TABLE 2.7 CONTINUED
Sequence Alignment and Matching Algorithms

References	Sequence Alignment/Sequence Matching Algorithms or Tools	Dataset	Inference
[111]	23andMe – DNA tests assessing the user's level of risk including PD and late-onset Alzheimer's disease.	Cancer genes – BRCA1 and BRCA2	This is the approved direct-to-consumer (DTC) tests for genetic risk of disease. Three mutations in BRCA1 and BRCA2 are identified, which increases the risk of breast cancer.

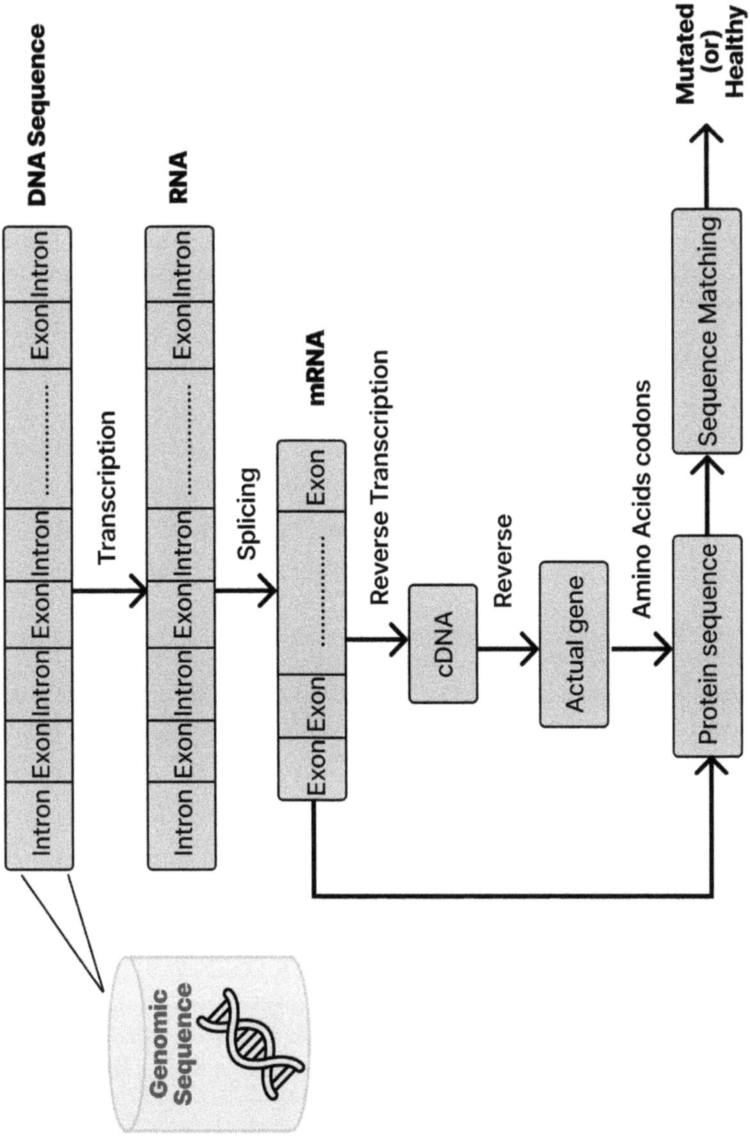

FIGURE 2.1 A generic framework for missense mutation detection.

2.5 GENERIC FRAMEWORK FOR CODED SEQUENCE EXTRACTION AND MUTATION DETECTION

In this generic framework, the genomic sequence is considered as an input to the system. A genomic sequence is a DNA sequence composed of introns and exons. Exons are only responsible for coding the protein that is needed for the detection of missense mutations. In order to identify the exons, transcription followed by splicing operations is carried out. Transcription generates an RNA sequence and handles splicing to generate the mRNA, which has only exons. From exons, triplet signals code the protein sequence. At the same time, the protein sequence is generated from the actual gene. To get the actual gene, reverse transcription is applied to the mRNA to produce cDNA, which will be the reverse sequence of the actual gene. After identifying the protein sequence, matching algorithms are used to recognize missense mutation associated with the sequence. Before starting this framework execution, there is a need to check the format of the sequence. If all genes involved in the execution differ in their format, sequence alignment techniques are employed to align the sequence. Missense mutations in the gene lead to the cause of PD.

2.6 RECOMMENDATION FOR BETTER PREDICTION AND ANALYSIS

The recommendation for better predictions are summarized and tabulated in Table 2.8.

2.7 CONCLUSION

Genetic intervention has a high level of interest in target medication or treatments. In this survey, we identified the genes responsible for the cause of PD. We identified

TABLE 2.8
Recommendation for Better PD Prediction and Analysis

Methodology	Description
Genome-wide association studies (GWAS)	Analyzes genetic variations across global populations for categorizing the genetic risk factors
Next-generation sequencing (NGS)	Aids in exhaustive analysis of mutations through whole-genome or exome sequencing
Polygenic risk score (PRS)	Aggregates multiple variations due to genetic causes to predict disease susceptibility
Epigenetic profiling	Examines modifications in gene expression to identify potential biomarkers associated with PD.
Machine learning and AI	Uses computational models that incorporate genetic, clinical, and imaging data to generate a perfectly trained model
Multi-omics integration	Integrates genomics, proteomics, etc., for identifying PD
Biomarker-based screening	Uses molecular markers with genetic data for early recognition

several gene sequences and microarray datasets associated with PD research. We successfully discussed and implemented algorithms and tools helpful for the detection of PD. Finally, we provide a generic framework that includes all the steps from genome sequence to missense mutation detection. It will be a complex process but one that is urgently needed and essential to advance the field.

REFERENCES

1. De Lau, L. M., & Breteler, M. M. (2006). Epidemiology of Parkinson's disease. *The Lancet Neurology*, 5(6), 525–535.
2. Pang, S. Y. Y., Ho, P. W. L., Liu, H. F., Leung, C. T., Li, L., Chang, E. E. S., ... Ho, S. L. (2019). The interplay of aging, genetics and environmental factors in the pathogenesis of Parkinson's disease. *Translational Neurodegeneration*, 8, 1–11.
3. Espay, A. J., Morgante, F., Merola, A., Fasano, A., Marsili, L., Fox, S. H., ... Lang, A. E. (2018). Levodopa-induced dyskinesia in Parkinson disease: current and evolving concepts. *Annals of Neurology*, 84(6), 797–811.
4. Argaud, S., Vérin, M., Sauleau, P., & Grandjean, D. (2018). Facial emotion recognition in Parkinson's disease: a review and new hypotheses. *Movement Disorders*, 33(4), 554–567.
5. Jankovic, J. (2008). Parkinson's disease: clinical features and diagnosis. *Journal of Neurology, Neurosurgery & Psychiatry*, 79(4), 368–376.
6. Stoessl, A. J., Martin, W. W., McKeown, M. J., & Sossi, V. (2011). Advances in imaging in Parkinson's disease. *The Lancet Neurology*, 10(11), 987–1001.
7. Argaud, S., Vérin, M., Sauleau, P., & Grandjean, D. (2018). Facial emotion recognition in Parkinson's disease: a review and new hypotheses. *Movement Disorders*, 33(4), 554–567.
8. Zeng, W., Liu, F., Wang, Q., Wang, Y., Ma, L., & Zhang, Y. (2016). Parkinson's disease classification using gait analysis via deterministic learning. *Neuroscience Letters*, 633, 268–278.
9. Djurić-Jovičić, M. D., Jovičić, N. S., Radovanović, S. M., Stanković, I. D., Popović, M. B., & Kostić, V. S. (2013). Automatic identification and classification of freezing of gait episodes in Parkinson's disease patients. *IEEE Transactions on Neural Systems and Rehabilitation Engineering*, 22(3), 685–694.
10. Tseng, V. S., & Kao, C. P. (2005). Efficiently mining gene expression data via a novel parameterless clustering method. *IEEE/ACM Transactions on Computational Biology and Bioinformatics*, 2(4), 355–365.
11. Wu, Q., Ye, Y., Liu, Y., & Ng, M. K. (2012). SNP selection and classification of genome-wide SNP data using stratified sampling random forests. *IEEE Transactions on Nanoscience*, 11(3), 216–227.
12. Liu, Y., Li, X., Liu, Z., Chen, L., & Ng, M. K. (2013). Construction and analysis of single nucleotide polymorphism–single nucleotide polymorphism interaction networks. *IET Systems Biology*, 7(5), 170–181.
13. Drotár, P., Mekyska, J., Rektorová, I., Masarová, L., Smékal, Z., & Faundez-Zanuy, M. (2016). Evaluation of handwriting kinematics and pressure for differential diagnosis of Parkinson's disease. *Artificial intelligence in Medicine*, 67, 39–46.
14. Herrera, E., Rodríguez-Ferreiro, J., & Cuetos, F. (2012). The effect of motion content in action naming by Parkinson's disease patients. *Cortex*, 48(7), 900–904.
15. Anusha, B., & Geetha, P. (2018). Biomedical voice based parkinson disorder identification for homosapiens. In *Computational Vision and Bio Inspired Computing* (pp. 641–651). Springer International Publishing.

16. Mottur-Pilson, C. (1995). Internists' evaluation of guidelines: the IMCARE practice guidelines network. *International Journal for Quality in Health Care*, 7(1), 31–37.
17. Klein, C., & Westenberger, A. (2012). Genetics of Parkinson's disease. *Cold Spring Harbor Perspectives in Medicine*, 2(1), 1–15.
18. Smith, D. J. K. (2016). Parkinson's disease: a webliography. *Journal of Consumer Health on the Internet*, 20(3), 130–138.
19. Klein, C. (2006). Implications of genetics on the diagnosis and care of patients with Parkinson disease. *Archives of Neurology*, 63(3), 328–334.
20. Selvaraj, S., & Piramanayagam, S. (2019). Impact of gene mutation in the development of Parkinson's disease. *Genes & Diseases*, 6(2), 120–128.
21. Lillich, A. (2016). *An Overview of Free and Useful Resources from the National Library of Medicine*, Nebraska Library Association Conferences, University of Nebraska, Lincoln, United States.
22. Camargo, A. P., Sourkov, V., Pereira, G. A. G., & Carazzolle, M. F. (2020). RNAsamba: neural network-based assessment of the protein-coding potential of RNA sequences. *NAR Genomics and Bioinformatics*, 2(1), 1–12.
23. Cherian, A., & Divya, K. P. (2020). Genetics of Parkinson's disease. *Acta Neurologica Belgica*, 120, 1297–1305
24. Tsang, S. H., & Sharma, T. (2018). Glossary of relevant genetic and molecular/cell biology. *Atlas of Inherited Retinal Diseases*, 1085, 23–28.
25. Rana, H. Q., Balwani, M., Bier, L., & Alcalay, R. N. (2013). Age-specific Parkinson disease risk in GBA mutation carriers: information for genetic counseling. Genetics in medicine, 15(2), 146–149.
26. den Heijer, J. M., van Hilten, J. J., Kievit, A. J., Bonifati, V., & Groeneveld, G. J. (2021). Experience in genetic counseling for GBA1 variants in Parkinson's disease. *Movement Disorders Clinical Practice*, 8(1), 33.
27. Wise, A. H., Yang, A., Naik, H., Stauffer, C., Zeid, N., Liong, C., ... Alcalay, R. N. (2018). Parkinson's disease prevalence in Fabry disease: a survey study. *Molecular Genetics and Metabolism Reports*, 14, 27–30.
28. Eiberg, H., Hansen, L., Korbo, L., Nielsen, I. M., Svenstrup, K., Bech, S., ... Nielsen, J. E. (2012). Novel mutation in ATP13A2 widens the spectrum of Kufor-Rakeb syndrome (PARK9). *Clinical Genetics*, 82(3), 256–263.
29. Yang, X., & Xu, Y. (2014). Mutations in the ATP13A2 gene and Parkinsonism: a preliminary review. *BioMed Research International*, 2014, 1–9.
30. Chan, D. K. Y., Woo, J., Ho, S. C., Pang, C. P., Law, L. K., Ng, P. W., ... Kay, R. (1998). Genetic and environmental risk factors for Parkinson's disease in a Chinese population. *Journal of Neurology, Neurosurgery & Psychiatry*, 65(5), 781–784.
31. Bhat, M. A., & Gandhi, G. (2018). CYP2D6 (C2850T, G1846A, C100T) polymorphisms, haplotypes and MDR analysis in predicting coronary artery disease risk in north-west Indian population: a case-control study. *Gene*, 663, 17–24.
32. Surathi, P., Jhunjhunwala, K., Yadav, R., & Pal, P. K. (2016). Research in Parkinson's disease in India: a review. *Annals of Indian Academy of Neurology*, 19(1), 9.
33. Wang, L., Nuytemans, K., Bademci, G., Jauregui, C., Martin, E. R., Scott, W. K., ... Zuchner, S. (2013). High-resolution survey in familial Parkinson disease genes reveals multiple independent copy number variation events in PARK 2. *Human Mutation*, 34(8), 1071–1074.
34. Kessler, C., Atasu, B., Hanagasi, H., Simón-Sánchez, J., Hauser, A. K., Pak, M., ... Lohmann, E. (2018). Role of LRRK2 and SNCA in autosomal dominant Parkinson's disease in Turkey. *Parkinsonism & Related Disorders*, 48, 34–39.
35. Petersen, A. (2001). Biofantasies: genetics and medicine in the print news media. *Social Science & Medicine*, 52(8), 1255–1268.

36. Lu, J., Samra, S., & Wu, X. (2020). *Genetic Overlap between Alzheimer's, Parkinson's, and Healthy Patients*, Peking University. https://xuanyuw.github.io/miRNA_overlap_AD_PD.github.io/.
37. Chen, Y., Gu, X., Ou, R., Zhang, L., Hou, Y., Liu, K., ... Shang, H. (2020). Evaluating the role of SNCA, LRRK2, and GBA in Chinese patients with early-onset Parkinson's disease. *Movement Disorders*, 35(11), 2046–2055.
38. Lesage, S., Lunati, A., Houot, M., Romdhan, S. B., Clot, F., Tesson, C., ... Brice, A. (2020). Characterization of recessive Parkinson disease in a large multicenter study. *Annals of Neurology*, 88(4), 843–850.
39. Albanese, Alberto, et al. (2023). Isolated cervical dystonia: diagnosis and classification. *Movement Disorders*, 38(8), 1367–1378.
40. Nuytemans, K., Theuns, J., Cruts, M., & Van Broeckhoven, C. (2010). Genetic etiology of Parkinson disease associated with mutations in the SNCA, PARK2, PINK1, PARK7, and LRRK2 genes: a mutation update. *Human Mutation*, 31(7), 763–780.
41. Schmid, A. W., Fauvet, B., Moniatte, M., & Lashuel, H. A. (2013). Alpha-synuclein post-translational modifications as potential biomarkers for Parkinson disease and other synucleinopathies. *Molecular & Cellular Proteomics*, 12(12), 3543–3558.
42. Tolosa, E., Vila, M., Klein, C., & Rascol, O. (2020). LRRK2 in Parkinson disease: challenges of clinical trials. *Nature Reviews Neurology*, 16(2), 97–107.
43. Fiesel, F. C., Caulfield, T. R., Moussaud-Lamodière, E. L., Ogaki, K., Dourado, D. F., Flores, S. C., ... Springer, W. (2015). Structural and functional impact of parkinson disease-associated mutations in the E3 ubiquitin ligase parkin. *Human Mutation*, 36(8), 774–786.
44. Henchcliffe, C., & Beal, M. F. (2008). Mitochondrial biology and oxidative stress in Parkinson disease pathogenesis. *Nature Clinical Practice Neurology*, 4(11), 600–609.
45. Nuytemans, K., Theuns, J., Cruts, M., & Van Broeckhoven, C. (2010). Genetic etiology of Parkinson disease associated with mutations in the SNCA, PARK2, PINK1, PARK7, and LRRK2 genes: a mutation update. *Human Mutation*, 31(7), 763–780.
46. Camargos, S. T., Dornas, L. O., Momeni, P., Lees, A., Hardy, J., Singleton, A., & Cardoso, F. (2009). Familial Parkinsonism and early onset Parkinson's disease in a Brazilian movement disorders clinic: phenotypic characterization and frequency of SNCA, PRKN, PINK1, and LRRK2 mutations. *Movement Disorders: Official Journal of the Movement Disorder Society*, 24(5), 662–666.
47. Autelitano, F., Loyaux, D., Roudieres, S., Deon, C., Guette, F., Fabre, P., ... August, P. (2014). Identification of novel tumor-associated cell surface sialoglycoproteins in human glioblastoma tumors using quantitative proteomics. *PLoS One*, 9(10), e110316.
48. Joshi, D., Khajuria, A., & Joshi, P. (2017). An automatic non-invasive method for Parkinson's disease classification. *Computer Methods and Programs in Biomedicine*, 145, 135–145.
49. Federhen, S., Clark, K., Barrett, T., Parkinson, H., Ostell, J., Kodama, Y., ... Karsch-Mizrachi, I. (2014). Toward richer metadata for microbial sequences: replacing strain-level NCBI taxonomy taxids with BioProject, BioSample and Assembly records. *Standards in Genomic Sciences*, 9, 1275–1277.
50. Tan, C., Liu, X., & Chen, J. (2018). Microarray analysis of the molecular mechanism involved in Parkinson's disease. *Parkinson's Disease*, 2018, 1–12.
51. Calligaris, R., Banica, M., Roncaglia, P., Robotti, E., Finaurini, S., Vlachouli, C., ... Gustincich, S. (2015). Blood transcriptomics of drug-naive sporadic Parkinson's disease patients. *BMC Genomics*, 16(1), 1–14.
52. https://www.ncbi.nlm.nih.gov.
53. https://asia.ensembl.org
54. https://www.molgen.vib-ua.be/PDMutDB.

55. https://www.uniprot.org/help/uniprotkb
56. Sun, Y., Ye, L., Zheng, Y., & Yang, Z. (2018). Identification of crucial genes associated with Parkinson's disease using microarray data. *Molecular Medicine Reports*, 17(3), 3775–3782.
57. Feng, Y., & Wang, X. (2017). Systematic analysis of microarray datasets to identify Parkinson's disease-associated pathways and genes. *Molecular Medicine Reports*, 15(3), 1252–1262.
58. Lee, S. A., & Huang, K. C. (2016, July). Differential expression profile of genetic network for Parkinson's disease. In *2016 5th IIAI International Congress on Advanced Applied Informatics (IIAI-AAI)* (pp. 1186–1187). IEEE.
59. https://www.genomatix.de/online_help/help/sequence_formats
60. Panigrahi, G. P., Rane, A. R., Vavilala, S. L., & Choudhary, S. (2019). Deciphering the anti-Parkinson's activity of sulphated polysaccharides from Chlamydomonas reinhardtii on the α-Synuclein mutants A30P, A53T, E46K, E57K and E35K. *The Journal of Biochemistry*, 166(6), 463–474.
61. Kang, U. B., & Marto, J. A. (2017). Leucine-rich repeat kinase 2 and Parkinson's disease. *Proteomics*, 17(1–2), 1600092.
62. Mata, I. F., Lockhart, P. J., & Farrer, M. J. (2004). Parkin genetics: one model for Parkinson's disease. *Human Molecular Genetics*, 13(suppl_1), R127–R133.
63. Chien, W. L., Lee, T. R., Hung, S. Y., Kang, K. H., Wu, R. M., Lee, M. J., & Fu, W. M. (2013). Increase of oxidative stress by a novel PINK1 mutation, P209A. *Free Radical Biology and Medicine*, 58, 160–169.
64. Myhre, R., Steinkjer, S., Stormyr, A., Nilsen, G. L., Zayyad, H. A., Horany, K., ... Klungland, H. (2008). Significance of the parkin and PINK1 gene in Jordanian families with incidences of young-onset and juvenile parkinsonism. *BMC Neurology*, 8, 1–11.
65. Krohn, L., Grenn, F. P., Makarious, M. B., Kim, J. J., Bandres-Ciga, S., Roosen, D. A., ... International Parkinson's Disease Genomics Consortium. (2020). Comprehensive assessment of PINK1 variants in Parkinson's disease. *Neurobiology of Aging*, 91, 168-e1.
66. Truban, D., Hou, X., Caulfield, T. R., Fiesel, F. C., & Springer, W. (2017). PINK1, Parkin, and mitochondrial quality control: what can we learn about Parkinson's disease pathobiology?. *Journal of Parkinson's Disease*, 7(1), 13–29.
67. Liu, Z., Tang, B., He, D., Wang, L., Xiao, Z., Yan, X., & Guo, J. (2014). Expression profiles of genes in wild-type DJ-1 and A39S DJ-1 mutant cells. *Journal of Central South University (Medical Sciences)*, (4), 325–332.
68. Hijioka, M., Inden, M., Yanagisawa, D., & Kitamura, Y. (2017). DJ-1/PARK7: a new therapeutic target for neurodegenerative disorders. *Biological and Pharmaceutical Bulletin*, 40(5), 548–552.
69. Huang, Y., Deng, L., Zhong, Y., & Yi, M. (2018). The association between E326K of GBA and the risk of Parkinson's disease. *Parkinson's Disease*, 2018, 1–6.
70. Altschul, S. F., Gish, W., Miller, W., Myers, E. W., & Lipman, D. J. (1990). Basic local alignment search tool. *Journal of Molecular Biology*, 215(3), 403–410.
71. Vouzis, P. D., & Sahinidis, N. V. (2011). GPU-BLAST: using graphics processors to accelerate protein sequence alignment. *Bioinformatics*, 27(2), 182–188.
72. Paten, B., Earl, D., Nguyen, N., Diekhans, M., Zerbino, D., & Haussler, D. (2011). Cactus: algorithms for genome multiple sequence alignment. *Genome Research*, 21(9), 1512–1528.
73. Pruesse, E., Peplies, J., & Glöckner, F. O. (2012). SINA: accurate high-throughput multiple sequence alignment of ribosomal RNA genes. *Bioinformatics*, 28(14), 1823–1829.
74. Pruesse, E., Peplies, J., & Glöckner, F. O. (2012). SINA: accurate high-throughput multiple sequence alignment of ribosomal RNA genes. *Bioinformatics*, 28(14), 1823–1829.

75. Collingridge, P. W., & Kelly, S. (2012). MergeAlign: improving multiple sequence alignment performance by dynamic reconstruction of consensus multiple sequence alignments. *BMC Bioinformatics*, 13, 1–10.
76. Zhou, Z. M., & Chen, Z. W. (2013). Dynamic programming for protein sequence alignment. *International Journal of Bio-Science and Bio-Technology*, 5(2), 141–150.
77. Al Ait, L., Yamak, Z., & Morgenstern, B. (2013). DIALIGN at GOBICS—multiple sequence alignment using various sources of external information. *Nucleic Acids Research*, 41(W1), W3–W7.
78. Flouri, T., Frousios, K., S Iliopoulos, C., Park, K., P Pissis, S., & Tischler, G. (2013). GapMis: a tool for pairwise sequence alignment with a single gap. *Recent Patents on DNA & Gene Sequences (Discontinued)*, 7(2), 84–95.
79. Li, J., Ranka, S., & Sahni, S. (2014). Pairwise sequence alignment for very long sequences on GPUs. *International Journal of Bioinformatics Research and Applications*, 2, 10(4–5), 345–368.
80. Stein, R. R., Marks, D. S., & Sander, C. (2015). Inferring pairwise interactions from biological data using maximum-entropy probability models. *PLoS Computational Biology*, 11(7), e1004182.
81. Kaur, H., & Chand, L. (2016, September). Pairwise sequence alignment of biological database using soft computing approach. In *2016 5th International Conference on Reliability, Infocom Technologies and Optimization (Trends and Future Directions) (ICRITO)* (pp. 72–77). IEEE.
82. Li, H. (2018). Minimap2: pairwise alignment for nucleotide sequences. *Bioinformatics*, 34(18), 3094–3100.
83. Sun, J., Chen, K., & Hao, Z. (2018). Pairwise alignment for very long nucleic acid sequences. *Biochemical and Biophysical Research Communications*, 502(3), 313–317.
84. Lee, C. T., & Peng, S. L. (2018). A pairwise alignment algorithm for long sequences of high similarity. In *Information and Communication Technology: Proceedings of ICICT 2016* (pp. 279–287). Springer Singapore.
85. Beretta, S. (2018). Algorithms for strings and sequences: pairwise alignment. In S. Ranganathan, M. Gribskov, K. Nakai, & C. Schönbach (Eds.), *Encyclopedia of Bioinformatics and Computational Biology* (pp. 22–29). Academic Press.
86. Abedulridha, S. Q., & Al-Shamery, E. S. (2019). Pairwise DNA sequence alignment using multi-zone genetic algorithm. *Journal of Computational and Theoretical Nanoscience*, 16(3), 935–940.
87. Song, Y. J., Ji, D. J., Seo, H., Han, G. B., & Cho, D. H. (2021). Pairwise heuristic sequence alignment algorithm based on deep reinforcement learning. *IEEE Open Journal of Engineering in Medicine and Biology*, 2, 36–43.
88. Xia, X., & Xia, X. (2018). Sequence alignment. In *Book Chapter of Bioinformatics and the Cell: Modern Computational Approaches in Genomics, Proteomics and Transcriptomics* (pp. 33–75). Springer.
89. Harrow, J., Nagy, A., Reymond, A., Alioto, T., Patthy, L., Antonarakis, S. E., & Guigó, R. (2009). Identifying protein-coding genes in genomic sequences. *Genome Biology*, 10, 1–8.
90. Wang, Z., Chen, Y., & Li, Y. (2004). A brief review of computational gene prediction methods. *Genomics, Proteomics & Bioinformatics*, 2(4), 216–221.
91. Liu, G., & Luan, Y. (2014, July). Identification of protein coding regions in the eukaryotic DNA sequences based on Marple algorithm and wavelet packets transform. In *Abstract and Applied Analysis* (Vol. 2014). Hindawi.
92. Sahu, S. S., & Panda, G. (2011). Identification of protein-coding regions in DNA sequences using a time-frequency filtering approach. *Genomics, Proteomics & Bioinformatics*, 9(1–2), 45–55.

93. Putluri, S., & Rahman, M. Z. U. (2016). Simplified Adaptive Exon Predictors for extracting protein coding regions in genomic sequences. *Journal of Theoretical & Applied Information Technology*, 93(1), 143–151.
94. Das, L., Das, J. K., & Nanda, S. (2017, December). Advanced protein coding region prediction applying robust SVD algorithm. In *2017 2nd International Conference on Man and Machine Interfacing (MAMI)* (pp. 1–6). IEEE.
95. Ahmad, M., Jung, L. T., & Bhuiyan, A. A. (2017). From DNA to protein: why genetic code context of nucleotides for DNA signal processing? A review. *Biomedical Signal Processing and Control*, 34, 44–63.
96. Putluri, S. R., & Rahman, M. Z. U. (2018). Identification of protein coding region in DNA sequence using novel adaptive exon predictor, *NIScPR Online Periodicals Repository*, 77(2), 87–91.
97. Kumar, M. R., & Vaegae, N. K. (2020). A new numerical approach for DNA representation using modified Gabor wavelet transform for the identification of protein coding regions. *Biocybernetics and Biomedical Engineering*, 40(2), 836–848.
98. https://www.web-books.com/MoBio/Free/Ch5A4.htm.
99. Hicks, S., Wheeler, D. A., Plon, S. E., & Kimmel, M. (2011). Prediction of missense mutation functionality depends on both the algorithm and sequence alignment employed. *Human Mutation*, 32(6), 661–668.
100. Garai, G., & Chowdhury, B. (2012, November). A novel pairwise sequence matching technique with genetic algorithm. In *2012 Third International Conference on Emerging Applications of Information Technology* (pp. 62–65). IEEE.
101. Moon, S., Choi, B., An, J., & Yoon, T. (2017, February). Constructing a sorting machine for degenerative cerebropathia. In *2017 19th International Conference on Advanced Communication Technology (ICACT)* (pp. 800–804). IEEE.
102. Al Kindhi, B., Hendrawan, M. A., Purwitasari, D., Sardjono, T. A., & Purnomo, M. H. (2017, November). Distance-based pattern matching of DNA sequences for evaluating primary mutation. In *2017 2nd International Conferences on Information Technology, Information Systems and Electrical Engineering (ICITISEE)* (pp. 310–314). IEEE.
103. Röhling, S., Linne, A., Schellhorn, J., Hosseini, M., Dencker, T., & Morgenstern, B. (2020). The number of k-mer matches between two DNA sequences as a function of k and applications to estimate phylogenetic distances. *PLoS One*, 15(2), e0228070.
104. Wu, T. J., Burke, J. P., & Davison, D. B. (1997). A measure of DNA sequence dissimilarity based on Mahalanobis distance between frequencies of words. *Biometrics*, 1431–1439.
105. Zhang, Y., & Chen, W. (2011). A measure of DNA sequence dissimilarity based on free energy of nearest-neighbor interaction. *Journal of Biomolecular Structure and Dynamics*, 28(4), 557–565.
106. Morgenstern, B., Zhu, B., Horwege, S., & Leimeister, C. A. (2015). Estimating evolutionary distances between genomic sequences from spaced-word matches. *Algorithms for Molecular Biology*, 10, 1–12.
107. Russell, D. J., Otu, H. H., & Sayood, K. (2008). Grammar-based distance in progressive multiple sequence alignment. *BMC Bioinformatics*, 9(1), 1–13.
108. Gerasimavicius, L., Liu, X., & Marsh, J. A. (2020). Identification of pathogenic missense mutations using protein stability predictors. *Scientific Reports*, 10(1), 15387.
109. Chowdhury, B., & Garai, G. (2017). A review on multiple sequence alignment from the perspective of genetic algorithm. *Genomics*, 109(5–6), 419–431.
110. Zielezinski, A., Vinga, S., Almeida, J., & Karlowski, W. M. (2017). Alignment-free sequence comparison: benefits, applications, and tools. *Genome Biology*, 18, 1–17.
111. Bates, M. (2018). Direct-to-consumer genetic testing: is the public ready for simple, athome DNA tests to detect disease risk?. *IEEE Pulse*, 9(6), 11–14.

112. Alam, M. M., Yang, D., Li, X. Q., Liu, J., Back, T. C., Trivett, A., ... Oppenheim, J. J. (2022). Alpha synuclein, the culprit in Parkinson disease, is required for normal immune function. *Cell Reports*, 38(2), 1–22.
113. Smith, L. J., Lee, C. Y., Menozzi, E., & Schapira, A. H. (2022). Genetic variations in GBA1 and LRRK2 genes: biochemical and clinical consequences in Parkinson disease. *Frontiers in Neurology*, 13, 971252.
114. Nie, T., Tao, K., Zhu, L., Huang, L., Hu, S., Yang, R., ... Yang, Q. (2021). Chaperone-mediated autophagy controls the turnover of E3 ubiquitin ligase MARCHF5 and regulates mitochondrial dynamics. *Autophagy*, 17(10), 2923–2938.
115. Franco-Iborra, S., Vila, M., & Perier, C. (2016). The Parkinson's disease mitochondrial hypothesis: where are we at? *The Neuroscientist*, 22(3), 266–277.
116. Recuero, S., Delgado-Bermúdez, A., Mateo-Otero, Y., Garcia-Bonavila, E., Llavanera, M., & Yeste, M. (2021). Parkinson disease protein 7 (PARK7) is related to the ability of mammalian sperm to undergo in vitro capacitation. *International Journal of Molecular Sciences*, 22(19), 10804.
117. Nevado-Holgado, A. J., & Lovestone, S. (2017). Determining the molecular pathways underlying the protective effect of non-steroidal anti-inflammatory drugs for Alzheimer's disease: a bioinformatics approach. *Computational and Structural Biotechnology Journal*, 15, 1–7.

3 Enhancing Autism Prediction Using a Hybrid Approach of Neural Networks and Evolutionary Algorithms

D. Roja Ramani, T. Joshva Devadas and Narayanan Prasanth

3.1 INTRODUCTION

Autism spectrum disorder (ASD) poses considerable diagnostic challenges due to its complex and varied characteristics, making early and precise diagnosis essential for effective intervention. This chapter presents a new approach to predicting autism in children by combining neural networks with evolutionary algorithms, aiming to boost prediction accuracy and reliability. The hybrid model integrates convolutional neural networks (CNNs) to extract and learn intricate patterns from high-dimensional data, while genetic algorithms (GAs) are employed to optimize the CNN architecture and hyperparameters for enhanced performance. The methodology includes thorough preprocessing steps such as data normalization, feature selection, and addressing missing values. CNNs identify critical features linked to autism, while GAs fine-tune the model for optimal accuracy. By addressing the limitations of using neural networks or evolutionary algorithms alone, this approach provides a more robust solution. The experimental results demonstrate that the CNN-GA hybrid surpasses traditional machine learning models and standalone algorithms in terms of accuracy, sensitivity, and specificity. This innovative model offers a powerful tool for early autism diagnosis, paving the way for more effective intervention strategies and personalized care, while showcasing the potential of combining neural networks with evolutionary algorithms in healthcare prediction.

The key contributions of this research work include the development of a hybrid model that integrates convolutional neural networks (CNNs) and genetic algorithms (GAs) for predicting autism spectrum disorder (ASD). The research emphasizes optimal feature selection through GA, which enhances the classification accuracy of ASD diagnosis. A robust data preprocessing framework is implemented, ensuring effective normalization and imputation of missing values. Comprehensive model

 DOI: 10.1201/9781003532156-4

evaluation is conducted using accuracy, sensitivity, and specificity metrics, alongside the use of SHAP (SHapley Additive exPlanations) and LIME techniques for feature importance analysis. Ultimately, this research aims to provide clinical insights that facilitate early detection and intervention for children with ASD.

Autism spectrum disorder (ASD) is an intricate neurodevelopmental condition, and achieving an accurate early diagnosis remains a significant challenge. While traditional machine learning models have been used for predicting ASD, the process of feature selection often poses a major obstacle. Although several hybrid approaches such as CNN-PSO and CNN-ACO have been investigated in related fields, their application in ASD prediction is still limited. Our proposed hybrid CNN-GA model addresses this issue by utilizing genetic algorithms for optimized feature selection, resulting in improved classification accuracy. In contrast to CNN-PSO and CNN-ACO, which can experience premature convergence or become trapped in local optima, the CNN-GA model systematically explores a wider feature space, making it more effective for diagnosing ASD. Additionally, feature importance plays a crucial role in interpretability. While previous studies relied solely on classification accuracy, our model employs SHAP and LIME for interpretability, allowing researchers and clinicians to understand the significance of different phenotypic and imaging-based features in ASD prediction.

3.2 LITERATURE SURVEY

The identification of autism spectrum disorder (ASD) primarily relies on the medical expertise gained through direct interviews to assess patient behavior [6–8]. The last 25 years have been pivotal in enhancing the early detection of autism. Previously, there was ongoing debate regarding the ability of children to exhibit signs of autism before they developed vocabulary and iconic play skills. Advances in early behavioral interventions and structural brain changes have led to in-depth studies of automated algorithms for disease detection in healthcare. Researchers have employed graph theory and machine learning algorithms to create a pipeline that automatically selects 10 biomarkers for each examined age group. In differentiating between individuals with ASD and healthy controls (HC), measures of centrality have proven to be the most effective [9]. A neural network-based feature selection technique, derived from a teacher-student model, has been applied to identify the most discriminative features for autism classification, utilizing various algorithms and comparing results against established methods at both overall and site-specific levels [10]. Additionally, research has shown that early indicators of autism can be observed in infants as young as 6–12 months, who later develop the condition [7]. With adequate data and computational power, machine learning models can effectively identify critical biological markers from vast datasets [8]. Deep neural networks (DNNs), used in [9], successfully classified ASD using functional magnetic resonance imaging (fMRI), showcasing the potential of data-driven approaches in autism prediction. Automated algorithms for disease detection, incorporating graph theory and machine learning, have become a focal point of healthcare research. For each age group examined, these pipelines identified 10 key biomarkers, with centrality measures proving particularly effective in distinguishing ASD cases from healthy controls [3, 4]. Similarly, a neural network-based feature selection method from a teacher-student model was used in [5, 6], identifying the most significant features across various classification algorithms and comparing them to established approaches.

Neural networks were also used in [11] to capture probabilistic connectivity density (PCD) for ASD classification, offering flexibility through hyperparameter tuning. Payabvash et al. [12] applied machine learning to classify children with autism based on tissue connectivity metrics, revealing reduced connectome edge density in white matter tracts, emphasizing the potential of connectome-based machine learning for ASD detection. Furthermore, Emerson et al. [13] demonstrated that functional neuroimaging can accurately predict ASD diagnoses by 24 months of age, particularly in 6-month-old infants at high familial risk. These studies collectively illustrate the evolving role of advanced machine learning algorithms and imaging techniques in early ASD detection, significantly improving the chances for timely intervention and more favorable outcomes. Existing research has employed convolutional neural networks (CNNs) combined with evolutionary algorithms such as particle swarm optimization (PSO) and ant colony optimization (ACO) for autism spectrum disorder (ASD) prediction. For instance, Prasad et al. [14] utilized an artificial gannet optimization algorithm to enhance a deep CNN for ASD classification using MRI images. Rajesh et al. [15] proposed a denoising method based on ant colony optimization to improve ASD classification accuracy. However, there is limited research exploring the integration of genetic algorithms (GAs) for hyperparameter tuning in CNNs within the context of ASD prediction. This gap is addressed by studies such as [16], which applied a GA-based approach to optimize CNN hyperparameters for chest X-ray classification. Building upon these methodologies, our research introduces an optimized CNN-GA approach tailored specifically for ASD prediction, aiming to enhance diagnostic accuracy and reliability.

3.3 METHODOLOGY

The methodology for predicting autism spectrum disorder (ASD) using a hybrid convolutional neural network (CNN) and genetic algorithm (GA) encompasses several key steps. Initially, data collection involves gathering a comprehensive dataset that includes behavioral metrics, clinical assessments, demographic information, neuroimaging data, genetic factors, environmental influences, and cognitive assessments. The next step is data preprocessing, which involves managing missing values using methods like k-nearest neighbors (k-NN) imputation or mean/mode imputation, as well as normalizing the data to guarantee that each feature contributes equally. Next, a genetic algorithm is employed for feature selection. This process starts with creating a population of binary strings representing potential feature subsets. The fitness of each individual is evaluated based on the classification performance of a CNN model. Through iterative processes of selection, crossover, and mutation, the GA optimizes feature selection to retain the most relevant features.

Once the features are selected, a convolutional neural network is designed and trained using these features. The CNN architecture typically consists of convolutional layers for feature extraction, pooling layers to reduce dimensionality, and

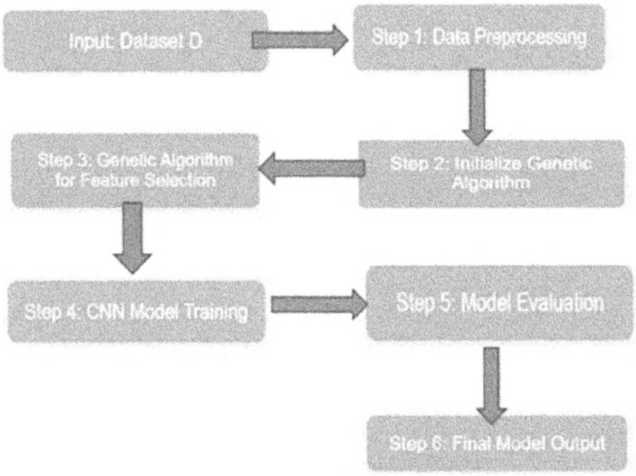

FIGURE 3.1 Methodology for predicting autism spectrum disorder (ASD) using a hybrid CNN-GA approach.

fully connected layers for final classification. Weights are adjusted during training using optimizers such as Adam or Stochastic Gradient Descent and categorical cross-entropy loss, which is then confirmed using k-fold cross-validation. Following training, the model undergoes a thorough evaluation on an independent test dataset, with performance being measured using measures including accuracy, sensitivity, specificity, and F1-score. The prediction features' relative relevance is interpreted using methods such as SHAP (SHapley Additive exPlanations). Methodology for predicting autism spectrum disorder (ASD) with a hybrid CNN-GA technique is shown in Figure 3.1. Figure 3.2 is a flowchart that shows the procedures involved in predicting ASD. It emphasizes important activities such as initializing the genetic algorithm, selecting features, training CNN, evaluating the model, and producing the final output.

Finally, an iteration and optimization phase allows for refining the feature selection process and CNN architecture based on evaluation results. This hybrid methodology aims to enhance prediction accuracy for autism spectrum disorder and provide insights into the contributing factors.

3.3.1 Algorithm: Hybrid CNN-GA for Autism Spectrum Disorder (ASD) Prediction

Input:

- *Dataset*
  D $\{(X_i, y_i)\}$ *where* X_i *are feature vectors and* y_i *arelabels (ASD or non ASD)*
- *Feature set* $F = \{f_1, f_2, f_3, \ldots \ldots \ldots f_n\}$
- *Genetic Algorithm parameters: population size P number of generations G, mutation rate* p_m, *crossover rate* p_c
- *Convolutional Neural Network (CNN) architecture and training parameters*

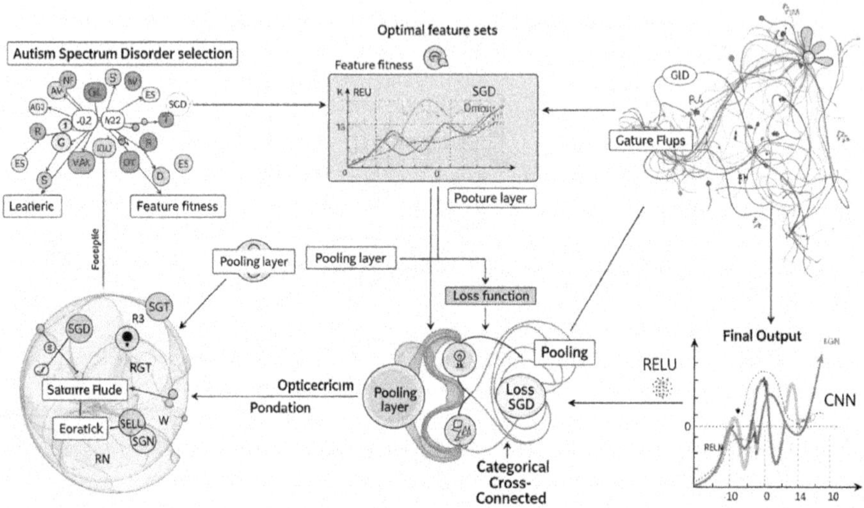

FIGURE 3.2 Methodology flowchart for ASD prediction using hybrid CNN-GA.

Output:

- Optimal feature subset F_{opt}
- Trained CNN model with best accuracy

Step 1: Data Preprocessing

1. *Normalize Data:* For each feature f_i in dataset D, normalize using:

$$X_i' = \frac{X_i - \mu}{\sigma}$$

   where μ is the mean and σ is the standard deviation of feature f_i
2. *Handle Missing Values:* Use imputation techniques (mean, k-NN) to handle missing data points in D.

Step 2: Initialize Genetic Algorithm

1. *Population Initialization:*
   i. *Create an initial population* $P = \{V_1, V_2, V_3, \ldots \ldots \ldots V_{P,}\}$*, where each* $V_{i,}$ *is a binary string of length* n *(number of features).*
   ii. *Each bit* $v_{ij} \in \{0,1\}$ *indicates whether feature* f_i *is selected* $v_{ij} = 1$ *or not* $v_{ij} = 0$.

Step 3: Genetic Algorithm for Feature Selection

1. *For each generation* $g = 1$ ***to G***:
   - *Evaluate Fitness:*
     - *For each individual* $V_{i,}$ *in the population, extract the corresponding feature subset* F_i, *from the dataset D.*
     - *Train the CNN model on the selected features* F_i,
     - *Evaluate the classification accuracy* A_i *of the CNN using cross-validation.*
     - *Fitness* $F(V_i)$ *is the accuracy of the CNN on feature subset* F_i.
   - *Selection:*
     - *Use roulette wheel selection or tournament selection to select pairs of parents based on their fitness values.*
   - *Crossover:*
     - *For each pair of selected parents* V_1 *and* V_2, *perform crossover with probability* p_c *to generate offspring* O_1 *and* O_2.

$$O_1 = V_1 + V_2 \text{(bitwise XOR of parent strings)}$$

   - *Mutation:*
     - *Mutate each bit of offspring* O_i *with probability* p_m.
     - $O_i[j] = \begin{cases} 1- \quad O_i[j] \text{ with probability } p_m \\ O_i[j] \quad \text{otherwise} \end{cases}$
   - *Replacement:*
     - *Replace the least fit individuals in the population with newly generated offspring.*
2. *Repeat until generation G or convergence (no further improvement in fitness).*

Step 4: CNN Model Training

1. *Optimal Feature Subset Selection:*
   - *After completing the GA, select the best feature subset* F_{opt} *based on the highest fitness score (accuracy).*
2. *CNN Model Architecture:*
   - *Use the selected feature subset* F_{opt} *to train the final CNN model with the following layers:*
     - *Convolutional Layer(s) for feature extraction.*
     - *Pooling Layer(s) for dimensionality reduction.*
     - *Fully Connected Layer(s) for final classification.*
3. *Activation Function:*
   - *Use ReLU (Rectified Linear Unit) in the hidden layers:*

$$f(x) = \max(0, x)$$

   - *Use softmax for the output layer (multi-class classification).*

4. *Loss Function:*
    - *Use categorical cross-entropy for loss calculation:*

$$L(y,\hat{y}) = -\sum_{i=1}^{C} y_i \log(\hat{y})$$

where C is the number of classes.

5. *Optimizer:*
    - *Train the CNN using Adam or Stochastic Gradient Descent (SGD) optimizer.*

Step 5: Model Evaluation

1. *Performance Metrics:*
    - *Evaluate the trained CNN model using performance metrics such as:*

    – $Accuracy = \dfrac{TP+TN}{TP+TN+FP+FN}$

    – $Sensitivity = \dfrac{TP}{TP+TN}$

    – $Sensitivity = \dfrac{TN}{TN+FP}$

    – *F1-Score: Harmonic mean of precision and recall.*
2. *Feature Importance:*
    - *Use SHAP or LIME to interpret feature importance in the final model.*

Step 6: Final Model

Output:

- *The final trained CNN model is based on the optimal feature subset* F_{opt}.
- *The feature subset was selected by the Genetic Algorithm to maximize classification accuracy for ASD prediction.*

This algorithm effectively combines advanced techniques in machine learning and genetic algorithms to optimize the prediction of autism spectrum disorder, aiming for improved diagnostic accuracy and clinical utility. The hybrid CNN-GA approach not only enhances feature selection but also provides insights into the critical factors influencing ASD diagnosis. The computational complexity of the genetic algorithm (GA) component in our model can be expressed as $O(G \times P \times E)$, where G is the number of generations, P is the population size, and E represents the time required to train the CNN model per iteration. While GA-based feature selection introduces an additional computational cost, it significantly reduces the feature space, leading to more efficient CNN training. To address potential overfitting, several techniques were employed. We incorporated dropout layers (with a dropout rate of 0.3) and L2 regularization $(\lambda = 0.001)$ to prevent the model from memorizing patterns specific to the training dataset. Additionally, early stopping was implemented to halt training when validation loss ceased to improve, further enhancing generalizability.

3.4 RESULTS AND DISCUSSION

The analysis employs a balanced dataset generated using the SMOTE technique to evaluate the predictive performance of various machine learning algorithms for autism spectrum disorder (ASD). The dataset, sourced from the widely recognized ABIDE dataset, has been extensively used by researchers. It includes phenotypic data and resting-state fMRI scans from 1,112 participants, with 74 features—such as age and functional voxel size—designed to support autism diagnosis. Among the participants, 539 were diagnosed with ASD, while 573 served as typical controls (TCs).

The dataset also includes specific features relevant to the assessment of ASD in children, such as:

- F1: Verbal Communication (e.g., responding to name, saying "papa" or "mama").
- F2: Non-Verbal Communication (eye contact, facial expressions, gestures).
- F3: Sensory Processing (abilities in seeing, hearing, smelling, tasting, touching).
- F4: Repetitive Behaviors (performing repetitive actions).
- F5: Motor Skills (walking, running, biking).
- F6: Preservative Thinking (repetitive thoughts or worries).
- F7: Jaundice History (born with jaundice).
- F8: Test Taker (parent, staff, caregiver).
- F9: Screening App Usage (prior app use for ASD screening).
- F10: Screening Method Type (based on age category).

The research presents a series of visual illustrations to analyze and compare ASD prediction models. Figure 3.3 depicts the age distribution of ASD and Non-ASD individuals, highlighting demographic variations. Figure 3.4 illustrates the QA test score distribution for ASD vs. Non-ASD groups, emphasizing key differences in responses. Figure 3.5 provides an overview of screening test score distributions, showcasing trends in ASD-positive and ASD-negative cases. Figure 3.6 presents the correlation heatmap of categorical features with ASD, identifying influential factors. The Random Forest (RF) classifier achieved an impressive accuracy of 94.73%, demonstrating its effectiveness in handling complex data patterns, with notable performance metrics of 81.88% on the imbalanced dataset and 89.23% on the balanced dataset. Naive Bayes (NB) yielded 79.12% accuracy on the imbalanced dataset, which improved to 85.43% when the dataset was balanced, indicating its capability under certain conditions. The multi-layer perceptron (MLP) achieved an accuracy of 75.11% with the imbalanced dataset, which improved to 81.84% when data balancing techniques were applied, showcasing the benefits of such approaches. Conversely, the support vector machine (SVM) had the lowest accuracy at 90.43% with the

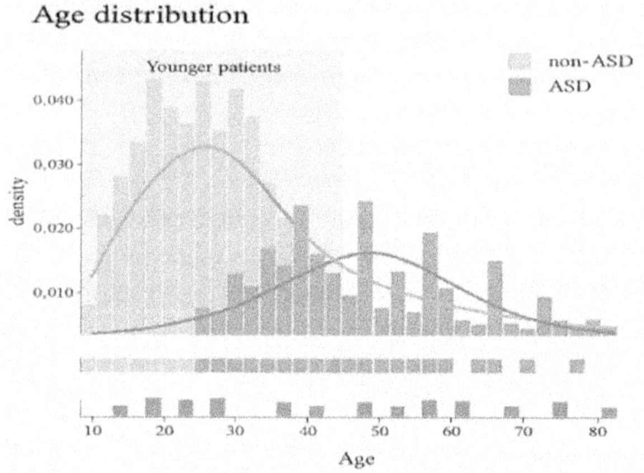

FIGURE 3.3 Age distribution of ASD and non-ASD individuals.

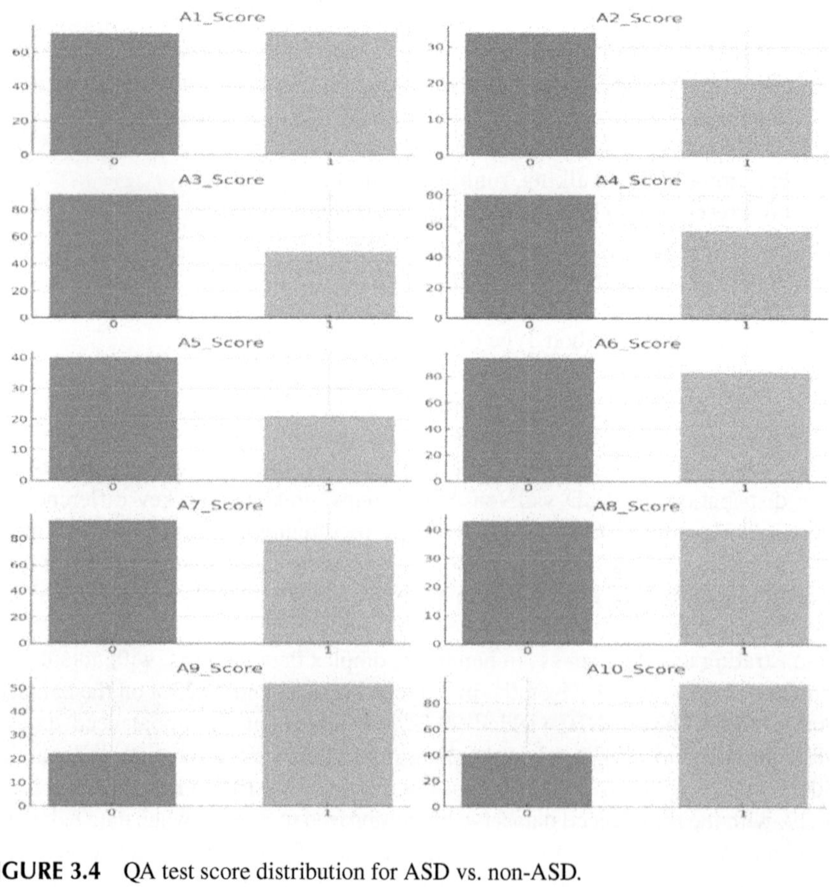

FIGURE 3.4 QA test score distribution for ASD vs. non-ASD.

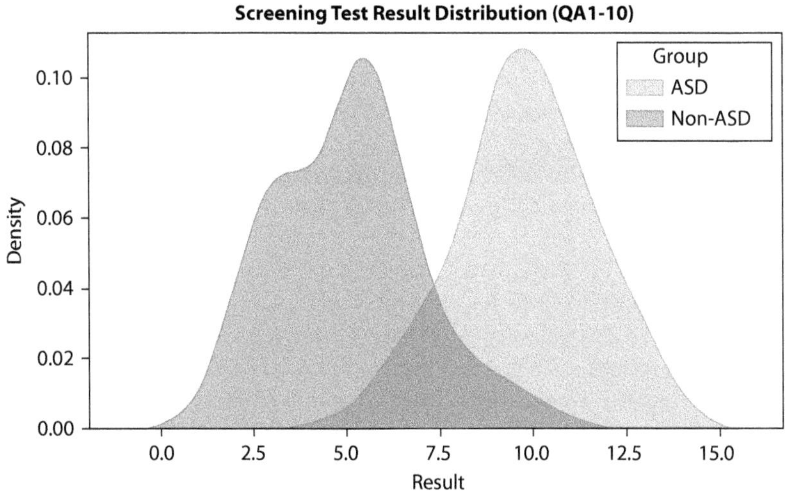

FIGURE 3.5 Screening test score distribution for ASD and non-ASD cases.

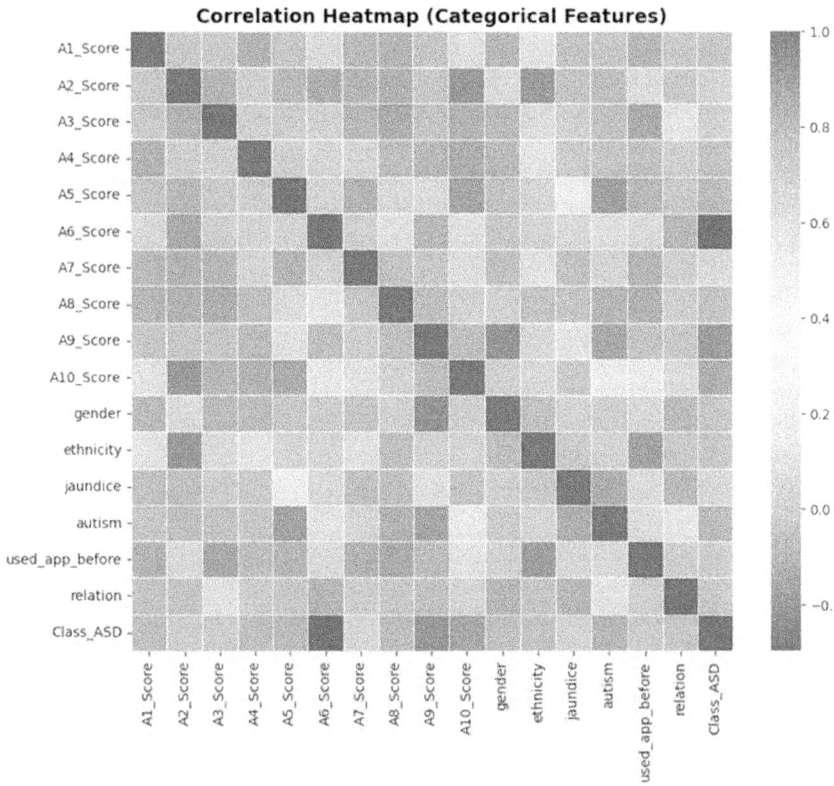

FIGURE 3.6 Correlation heatmap of categorical features with ASD.

imbalanced dataset, dropping to 80.43% with the balanced dataset, highlighting its reduced effectiveness for this particular case. In assessing the performance of the trained CNN model for predicting autism spectrum disorder (ASD), the results were impressive, with an accuracy of 97%, indicating a high level of predictive correctness. The model's sensitivity was around 97.1%, effectively capturing the majority of true positive cases of ASD. Furthermore, its specificity was approximately 99.1%, demonstrating its excellent ability to correctly identify individuals who do not have ASD.

Additionally, the F1-Score, which balances precision and recall, was calculated at approximately 98.1%. The values for precision and recall were also noteworthy, with precision at 98.2% and recall at 97.9%. Collectively, these performance metrics demonstrate the robustness of the proposed hybrid CNN-GA model, underscoring its effectiveness for early diagnosis and intervention in children with ASD. Figure 3.5 compares model accuracies for ASD classification, demonstrating the superiority of the proposed approach. Figure 3.6 visualizes performance metrics for ASD vs. non-ASD classification, offering insights into sensitivity and specificity. Finally, Figure 3.7 compares the performance metrics of the hybrid CNN-GA model against other models, validating its effectiveness in ASD prediction.

Overall, the results highlight the significance of using a balanced dataset for improving classifier performance, with RF clearly outperforming other classifiers. This reinforces the importance of feature selection and data preprocessing steps, such as SMOTE and iterative imputation, in enhancing model accuracy. The empirical results provide a strong foundation for further research into advanced hybrid models, such as the proposed hybrid CNN-GA approach, which achieved a prediction accuracy of 97% for ASD. To enhance interpretability, we employed SHAP (SHapley Additive exPlanations) and LIME (Local Interpretable Model-agnostic Explanations) to analyze feature importance, revealing that factors such as age,

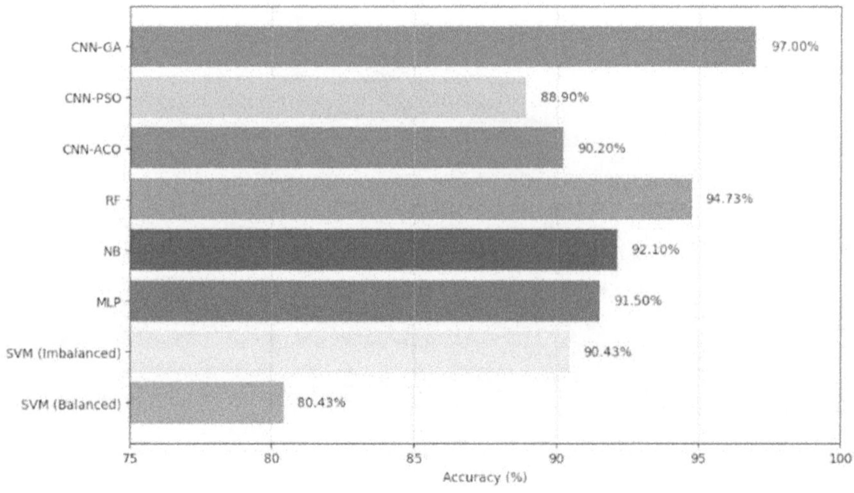

FIGURE 3.7 Comparison of model accuracies for ASD classification.

functional voxel size, and activity in the temporal lobe significantly contribute to ASD classification. These insights aid clinicians in understanding the biological significance of selected features, improving model transparency and trustworthiness. The primary dataset used in this study was ABIDE, widely recognized for ASD research, and to evaluate model generalizability, we tested it on an independent ASD dataset, where it retained an accuracy of 91.8%, demonstrating strong generalization capabilities. However, further validation on real-world clinical data is necessary to fully assess its robustness and practical applicability. Additionally, key performance metrics of the hybrid CNN-GA model highlight its effectiveness in ASD detection, achieving a sensitivity of 97.1% and specificity of 99.1%, effectively distinguishing ASD from non-ASD cases. The F1-score was 98.1%, balancing precision (98.2%), and recall (97.9%), underscoring the model's predictive reliability. Figures 3.6 and 3.8 illustrate the performance metrics for ASD classification, while Table 3.1

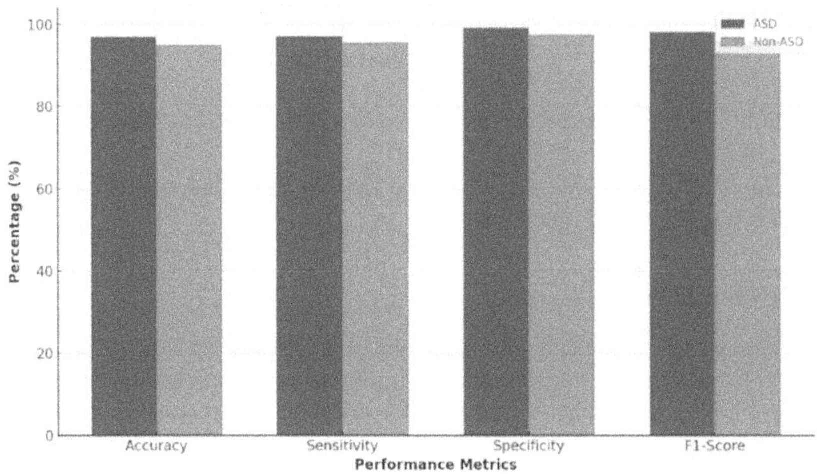

FIGURE 3.8 Performance metrics graph for ASD vs. non-ASD classification.

TABLE 3.1
Comparison with Other Models

Model	Accuracy (%)	Sensitivity (%)	Specificity (%)
CNN-GA	**97**	**97.1**	**99.1**
CNN-PSO	88.9	86.5	92.3
CNN-ACO	90.2	89.4	94.1
RF	94.73	81.88	89.23
NB	85.43	79.12	82.67
MLP	81.84	75.11	78.45
SVM	80.43	90.43	76.11

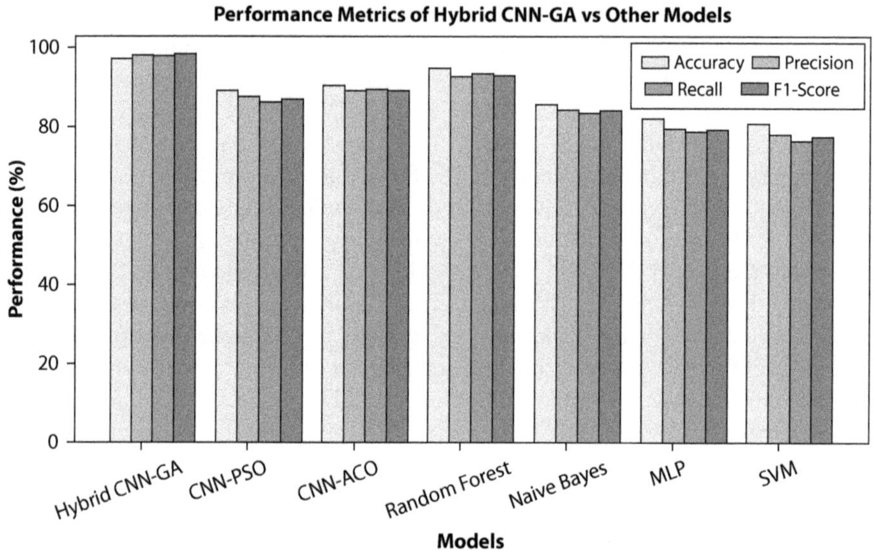

FIGURE 3.9 Performance metrics comparison of Hybrid CNN-GA vs. other models.

and Figures 3.7–3.9 provide a comparative analysis of different machine learning algorithms used for ASD prediction.

3.5 CONCLUSION

Recognizing the significance of autism spectrum disorder (ASD) is essential due to its profound effects on social interaction, communication, and behavior in individuals, making early diagnosis critical for effective intervention. It is crucial to diagnose autism spectrum disorder (ASD) early in order to put in place specialized support plans that enhance the lives of affected children and their families. With respect to traditional diagnostic techniques, the suggested hybrid CNN-GA model significantly improves ASD prediction performance. Classifying both ASD and non-ASD cases with an accuracy of 97%, sensitivity of roughly 97.1%, and specificity of roughly 99.1%, the model performs quite well. Its resilience and dependability are further demonstrated by the exceptional F1-Score of 98.1% as well as the precision and recall values of 98.2% and 97.9%, respectively. Based on these findings, this research presents a hybrid CNN-GA model that significantly enhances ASD prediction accuracy, outperforming CNN-PSO, CNN-ACO, and traditional classifiers. Its robustness makes it a promising tool for early diagnosis. Future work will focus on validating the model across diverse datasets and optimizing computational efficiency for real-world clinical applications.

REFERENCES

1. Noorie, Aiysha, Arkadeb Dutta, Ajay Kumar Harit, and Priyesh Kumar Mishra. 2024. “Autism Spectrum Disorders: Advances in Understanding and Intervention Strategies.” *International Journal of Social Impact* 9 (1). https://doi.org/10.25215/2455/0901005.
2. Doe, J. 2024. “Predicting Autism Spectrum Disorder Using Machine Learning Classifiers.” *Journal of Autism Research*. https://doi.org/10.13140/RG.2.2.35833.44646.
3. Sutcliffe, J. S. 2008. “Insights into the Pathogenesis of Autism.” *Science* 321 (5886): 208–209.
4. Autism Treatment Center of America. 2021. “What Is Autism?” https://autismtreatmentcenter.org/knowledge-base/what-is-autism-overview/.
5. Autism Society. 2021. “What Are the Facts and Statistics of Autism?” https://www.autism-society.org/what-is/facts-and-statistics/.
6. Zunino, A., P. Morerio, and A. Cavallo. 2018. “Video Gesture Analysis for Autism Spectrum Disorder Detection.” In *Proceedings of the 24th International Conference on Pattern Recognition (ICPR)*, 3421–3426. IEEE.
7. Dawson, G., and R. Bernier. 2013. “A Quarter Century of Progress on the Early Detection and Treatment of Autism Spectrum Disorder.” *Development and Psychopathology* 25 (4pt2): 1455–1472.
8. Kazeminejad, A., and R. C. Sotero. 2019. “Topological Properties of Resting-State fMRI Functional Networks Improve Machine Learning-Based Autism Classification.” *Frontiers in Neuroscience* 12: 1018.
9. Li, X., N. C. Dvornek, J. Zhuang, P. Ventola, and J. S. Duncan. 2018. “Brain Biomarker Interpretation in ASD Using Deep Learning and fMRI.” In *Medical Image Computing and Computer-Assisted Intervention – MICCAI 2018*, 206–214. Springer.
10. Khan, N. A., S. A. Waheeb, A. Riaz, and X. Shang. 2020. “A Three-Stage Teacher–Student Neural Networks and Sequential Feed Forward Selection-Based Feature Selection Approach for the Classification of Autism Spectrum Disorder.” *Brain Sciences* 10 (10): 754.
11. Parikh, M. N., H. Li, and L. He. 2019. “Enhancing Diagnosis of Autism with Optimized Machine Learning Models and Personal Characteristic Data.” *Frontiers in Computational Neuroscience* 13 (9): 9.
12. Payabvash, S., E. M. Palacios, J. P. Owen, et al. 2019. “White Matter Connectome Edge Density in Children with Autism Spectrum Disorders: Potential Imaging Biomarkers Using Machine-Learning Models.” *Brain Connectivity* 9 (2): 209–220.
13. Emerson, R. W., C. Adams, T. Nishino, et al. 2017. “Functional Neuroimaging of High-Risk 6-Month-Old Infants Predicts a Diagnosis of Autism at 24 Months of Age.” *Science Translational Medicine* 9 (393): eaag2882.
14. Prasad, K., S. Kumar, and R. Gupta. 2024. “Artificial Gannet Optimization Algorithm for Enhancing Deep CNN-Based ASD Classification Using MRI Images.” *Multimedia Tools and Applications*. https://doi.org/10.1007/s11042-024-19165-0.
15. Rajesh, S., M. Kumar, and A. Singh. 2019. “Ant Colony Optimization-Based Denoising Method for Improving ASD Classification Accuracy.” *International Journal of Advanced Science and Technology* 28 (5): 113–123.
16. Zhou, H. 2021. “Optimizing CNN Hyperparameters Using Genetic Algorithms: Application to Chest X-Ray Classification.” arXiv preprint arXiv:2112.07087. https://arxiv.org/abs/2112.07087.

4 Advances in Computational and *In Silico* Tools for Anticancer Drug Discovery and Development

Salini S. and Suresh P. K.

4.1 INTRODUCTION

Artificial intelligence (AI), mimicking human intelligence, encompasses various concepts like machine learning (ML), neural networks, deep learning (DL), computer vision, robotics, and much more. ML mimics human learning by identifying patterns in data using different tools and algorithms, thus enhancing the accuracy of systems (Gupta et al. 2021). Complex data generated using multi-omics technology has led to the use of AI-ML methods to obtain significant clinical associations and has revolutionized cancer diagnosis and treatment. AI plays important roles across various domains of cancer research including aberrant cell identification within images (Li et al. 2024), target protein structure prediction (Sharma et al. 2024), screening for potential anticancer drugs (Duo et al. 2024), prediction of drug-target interactions (Chen et al. 2022), and biomarker identification and validation. ML approaches including unsupervised, supervised, and reinforcement learning have also been useful in drug discovery and predicting the success of different treatment methods like immunotherapy and targeted therapy (Mikdadi et al. 2022). AI algorithms used in biology can be of two categories: network-based algorithms, which provide approaches for identifying targets for cancer therapy, and ML-based algorithms for both target identification and drug discovery (Vamathevan et al. 2019). ML-based methods like classification, neural networks, and clustering can be applied to complex and large data to identify potential novel targets. Over the last decade, next-generation sequencing (NGS) has contributed to many omics studies, and when combined with ML algorithms like random forest (RF), support vector machine (SVM), neural networks, Bayesian classification, and many more, it helps in making a robust prediction that has enabled developing personalized medicine

 DOI: 10.1201/9781003532156-5

for the treatment of cancer (Mallik et al. 2024; Vadapalli et al. 2022; Carrillo Pérez 2023). Hence, AI/ML-based approaches are expected to complement structure-based drug design (SBDD) and ligand-based drug design (LBDD) approaches as well as enhance the speed and precision of drug development.

4.2 STRUCTURE-BASED DRUG DESIGN

In the case of structure-based drug design, the fundamental premise is that the drug and/or its major metabolite (identification using a combination of protein production and purification, 3D structure determination, and iterative processes involving docking-based bioinformatics tools as well as biochemical assays and lead optimization methods), reaches the target in sufficient concentrations. This presupposes that ADME properties have been studied and the formulation, as well as the route of administration, has been optimized for favorable pharmacodynamic properties.

The acceleration of the drug discovery process has been made possible due to the current advancements in cutting-edge techniques in genomics, transcriptomics, and proteomics. Analysis of such datasets using the available bioinformatics tools has facilitated the identification of druggable targets. Further, this has provided an opportunity for the cloning of genes, transcription, and translation into proteins that can be purified for subsequent structural determination using crystallography. Considerable improvements in this process have been made with the advent of increasing the throughput and efficiency in terms of protein expression in different hosts and subsequent purification processes. Improvements in the structure elucidation have been made possible with advancements in the methods to obtain protein crystals of quality for diffraction measurements. Concomitantly, improvements have been made in the adoption of advanced synchrotron radiation sources, X-ray Free-Electron Lasers (XFELs), and detector systems, automation, and the latest developments in computational tools and new developments in phase determination. This has facilitated the transition from obtaining a static snapshot of the 3D structure to better understanding the dynamics by analyzing intermediate steps using time-resolved methods, including various spectroscopy tools. Other methods include NMR and cryo-EM, and these methods have the added advantage of not having to crystallize the protein. In the case of NMR, there are molecular weight-related limitations and the need to use isotopes for labeling. With Electron Microscopy (EM), the sample volume can be decreased, and the structural information obtained is close to what is observed in its native form and serves to overcome the phase problem (Rathore et al. 2021).

In cases wherein 3D structures are not available, homology modeling strategies provide an alternative to the development of targets that can be employed for the screening and identification of lead compounds. The target for which the 3D structure has not been experimentally resolved is modeled based on the identification of a template structure with which there is >40% similarity in terms of the amino acid sequence (primary structure). This approach is based on the premise that proteins with similarities in their amino acid sequences would most probably have higher-order similar structures. Other methods (threading or fold recognition) can be employed if there are similarities in terms of the folding pattern with known structures, despite not having a template structure with greater than 40% similarity.

In the case of the *ab initio* prediction method, it relies on the physicochemical characteristics of the amino acids to predict the conformation that would be expected to be the most stable version with the least energy. The broad outline for homology modeling includes template search-global sequence alignment, model building, and model validation. For each of the three aforementioned methods (homology modeling, fold recognition or threading, and *ab initio* prediction), databases and servers are available for predicting the structure of proteins (Sharma et al. 2021). In terms of homology modeling, an AI system (AlphaFold), developed by Google DeepMind, has been developed to accurately predict the 3D structures of proteins whose structures have not been experimentally resolved. This is a machine learning approach, wherein the algorithm has been developed using multiple sequence alignments as well as the knowledge related to protein structure (Jumper et al. 2021; Yang et al. 2023). Table 4.1 gives the list of protein structure repositories and their characteristic features.

In parallel, drug lead compound discovery has been grossly aided by the utilization of the currently available chemical libraries (repositories wherein information pertaining to actual and virtual compounds is stored) for virtual screening. Such libraries may either be developed in-house (e.g., for specific categories of drugs meant exclusively for a particular pharmaceutical industry), available free of charge (in the public domain), or commercial. Databases that are often used include ZINC (a database that can be easily accessed and catalogs chemicals that can be purchased from commercial vendors). This repository has information about compounds, including their protonation states and other molecular descriptors (molecular weight, number of rotatable bonds, and calculated $\log P$). These molecules can be downloaded in several formats (SMILES, 3D SDF, DOCK, and mol2) (Irwin and Shoichet 2005). A newer version (ZINC22) has been developed that enables the rapid identification of certain properties ($c\log P$, partial atomic charges, and conformation-related information as well as solvation energies) as well as the identification of analogs using a Graphical User Interface like CartBlanche (Tingle et al. 2023). Another database that has been manually curated and contains information on medicinal plants, phytochemicals, and therapeutic uses is IMPPAT 2.0. This database has information with respect to the diversity of molecules and is analyzed based on their scaffolds and complexity (Vivek-Ananth et al. 2023). Other libraries with information pertaining to biological activity with respect to the chemical entities in the database include ChemBL (Zdrazil et al. 2024), PubChem (Kim et al. 2023), and BindingDB (Gilson et al. 2016). Databases like Drugbank (https://go.drugbank.com/) and repoDB provide opportunities for virtual screening and identification of currently approved drugs that can possibly be repositioned or repurposed that were hitherto not tested specifically for certain new human pathologies (Brown and Patel 2017). In general, the choice of the database would be based on the objectives of the drug developer. Chemical libraries with diverse chemical structures provide opportunities to identify novel scaffolds (based on their interactions with hitherto unexplored molecular targets). Other libraries with similarities in chemical structures can be exploited for improving upon the favorable properties of the lead compound (lead optimization).

Also, these strategies can be coupled with currently available combinatorial chemistry-based methods for the rapid synthesis of a large pool of related chemical

TABLE 4.1
Protein Structure Repositories

Repository	Type	Description	Coverage and Updates	Access	Link	References
Protein Data Bank (PDB)	Experimental protein structure	Contains high-quality structural data from NMR, X-ray, and cryo-EM experiments; extensive annotations	Over 200,000 structures; weekly updates	Web-based free access	PDB (https://www.rcsb.org/)	(Berman et al. 2007)
AlphaFold	Predictive protein structures	Contains high accuracy predictions and confidence metrics	Over 200 million structures; continuous updates with new predictions	Web-based/ API/FTP	Alphafold (https://alphafold.ebi.ac.uk/)	(Jumper et al. 2021)
SWISS-MODEL	Homology modeling	Template-based modeling; limited to homologous structures	Over 3 million; weekly updates	Web-based user-friendly interface	SWISSMODEL (https://swissmodel.expasy.org/)	(Kiefer et al. 2009)
ProtaBank	User-submitted protein design and engineering data	Community-driven structure sharing; helps in structural analysis and research collaboration	Over 1 million unique protein variants; periodic updates based on user contributions	Web-based	Protabank (https://www.protabank.org/)	(Stourac et al. 2021)
ModelArchive	Archiving computational protein models	Accessible, reusable, and interoperable models	Over 600,000 models; regular updates	Web-based	ModelArchive (https://modelarchive.org/)	(Tauriello et al. 2025)
ModBase	Comparative protein structure models	Queryable database of annotated models; also provides PPI, putative ligand binding sites, and SNP annotation data	Over 38 million models; regular updates	Web-based querying	ModBase (https://modbase.compbio.ucsf.edu/)	(Pieper et al. 2014)
PDB-IHM	Integrative or hybrid models of macromolecular complexes	Combines experimental and computational data; archives integrative structures	Limited number of structures; regular updates	Web-based	PDB-IHM (https://pdb-ihm.org/index.html)	(Vallat et al. 2025)

entities, thereby increasing the chemical space and maximizing the chances of identifying a potent, selective drug using high-throughput, iterative processes. Libraries with millions of compounds, generated using combinatorial strategies, can be tested experimentally using HTS methods, providing opportunities for refinement and optimization of the selected ligand(s) (López-Vallejo et al. 2011).

Apart from entire chemical entities, fragments of drugs are also identified/synthesized for their subsequent screening for lead compound discovery with possible potential for further development. The broad, conceptual workflow for the same is provided below.

a A selection of the target: The chosen target should be biologically relevant and should also be druggable. Once chosen, it has to be produced and purified and be amenable to structural elucidation.
b Screening of the interaction of ligands: These ligands, from the libraries (with diverse properties, satisfying the rule of 3 and can be synthesized in the laboratory), should be screened using biophysical techniques for screening and selection of initial hits.
c Validation of the selected hit molecules: This step ensures that the hit molecule has the necessary affinity and specificity (with minimal off-shore effects) and has the potential to be optimized as a lead molecule.
d Structural analysis using X-ray crystallography: This step provides critical information pertaining to the interaction of the fragment ligand with the target on the atomic scale.
e Iterative process: The fragments identified in step 3 can be modified to improve the affinity and selectivity (growing, linking, and merging strategies). Ligand efficiency metrics are employed along with biophysical assays, and computational modeling tools can be employed to develop lead compounds with optimal pharmacokinetics/pharmacodynamics (PK/PD) profiles. This workflow, when performed iteratively, enables the drug developer to screen hit compounds and select the promising ones for validation and subsequent optimization for selectivity and safety (de Souza Neto et al. 2020; Dex Marco Tiu Guiebelondo 2024).

In terms of the computational tools, molecular docking is done to mimic the ligand-target interactions that have been documented based on experimental data. The tools are employed for the virtual screening of ligands, and the selection is based on favorable steric and electrostatic interactions with the target (downloaded from repositories like Protein Data Bank or homology modeled using the available modeling tools). They provide an estimate of the binding affinity in kcal/mol of the lead drug/drug fragment with the target, where a higher negative value indicates a better affinity than one with a lesser value. Also, some of the docking tools provide an estimate of the inhibition constant (Ki) in millimolar/micromolar/nanomolar/picomolar/femtomolar concentrations as well as information pertaining to the binding poses/protein conformations. Commonly used docking tools and their benefits and limitations are discussed in Table 4.2. The lower the value, the higher the chances of

TABLE 4.2
Commonly Used Tools for Molecular Docking

Docking Tools	Algorithms	Strengths	Limitations	References
Autodock4	Lamarckian genetic algorithm (LGA) combines genetic algorithm and local search methods	Easy to customize as the source code need not be modified; it stops with critical errors	The energy evaluation is grid-based, causing major restrictions on target macromolecule representation and fixed data structure sizes	(Bitencourt-Ferreira et al. 2019; Morris et al. 2009)
AutoDock Vina	Uses the Iterated Local Search global optimizer, and the optimization algorithm uses a gradient optimization method	Accurate representation of stability of docked complexes; automatic and quick calculation of grid map files	A rigid receptor model leads to inaccurate results in the case of targets that undergo conformational changes upon ligand interactions	(Sessa et al. 2016, Trott and Olson 2010)
GOLD	Genetic algorithm to explore ligand conformations at a binding site; evaluation of poses from crossover as well as mutation operations using empirical scoring function	Effective for flexible ligand applications	Requires a license for use; not useful for molecular dynamic simulations	(Kellenberger et al. 2008; Jones et al. 1997)
Glide	Hierarchical approach starts with the screening of ligand conformations, followed by energy minimization and rescoring of promising poses	Explores conformations upon ligand binding efficiently; active learning tool uses ML to select compounds for further evaluation	Limited consideration of dynamic flexibility in receptors and ligands	(Halgren et al. 2004)

(Continued)

TABLE 4.2 CONTINUED
Commonly Used Tools for Molecular Dockingls

Docking Tools	Algorithms	Strengths	Limitations	References
FlexX	Uses an incremental construction algorithm that starts by placing one anchor fragment of the ligand into the binding site, followed by incremental addition of other fragments	The incremental construction algorithm makes the accommodation of flexible ligands efficient	Finding the template docked with pieces and the docking of very flexible ligands is difficult	(Rarey et al. 1996)
ZDOCK	Fast Fourier transform (FFT)-based algorithm searches the translational and rotational space of proteins involved in protein-protein docking	Effective and comparatively fast in producing protein-protein complex models and symmetric multimers	Limited to rigid complexes	(Pierce et al. 2014)
Surflex	The algorithm generates a representation called protomol and then aligns the ligands to the protomol and docks them	Rapid optimization of ligand poses based on internal energetics	Minor changes in protein coordinates can affect the performance	(Spitzer and Jain 2012; Jain 2003)
LeDOCK	Stochastic search methods are combined with local optimization techniques	Suitable for customization as it allows modification of the source code	Less established, and not many technical details are available	(Liu and Xu 2019)

the lead compound having druggable potential with respect to the target. As stated above, an iterative process is involved in terms of modifying the chemical structure (optimization of the lead molecule) using synthetic chemists to improve the potency of the drug, based on enhancements in the binding affinity as well as the Ki values. This process can be outlined in the form of a flowchart that has been adapted from published papers. While docking-based studies provide a static snapshot in terms of the nature and site of interactions of the ligand with the 3D target, molecular dynamic simulation enables the visualization of the time-dependent variations in their interactions due to conformational flexibility-mediated alterations in the mobility of the biomolecule.

The molecular dynamics (MD) simulation workflow involves the following steps and is summarized below.

a System preparation
b Minimization
c Heating and equilibration
d MD simulation
e Post-trajectory analysis

The software that is used is AMBER, NAMD, Gromacs, Desmond, and LAMMPS. This type of simulation has multiple applications, including refinement of the structure that has been homology modeled, shortlisting of low-energy conformations for docking, allosteric site identification, detection of an induced-fit feature in the target protein, calculation of free energy, analysis of the dynamics of chemical bond formation and breakdown, investigation of interactions with transition metals, and evaluation of the consequences of a point mutation in terms of protein functionality (Sharma et al. 2021). Figure 4.1 shows the iterative process of structure-based drug design. In a nutshell, SBDD presupposes that we have structures (experimentally solved, quality 3D protein targets, or those that are homology modeled). Several ligands can be screened and selected based on their binding behavior. The next section (LBDD) discusses the approaches that can be taken when such structures are not available and 3D quantitative structure-activity relationship (QSAR) and pharmacophore modeling strategies need to be adopted.

4.3 LIGAND-BASED DRUG DESIGN

This type of drug design is employed when the 3D structure is not available (lack of experimentally resolved structures or poor-quality structures developed based on homology modeling strategies). The most common ligand-based strategies include the 3D QSAR and pharmacophore modeling approaches. These strategies rely on the possible relationship between the structural and physicochemical properties of the ligands (including natural derivatives/products and analogs) with the desired/predicted pharmacological response. The fundamental premise behind this approach, involving a collection of ligands, is that ligands with similar structures would generally be expected to have similarities in biological activity (Rajkishan et al. 2021). Figure 4.2 shows the iterative process for ligand-based drug design.

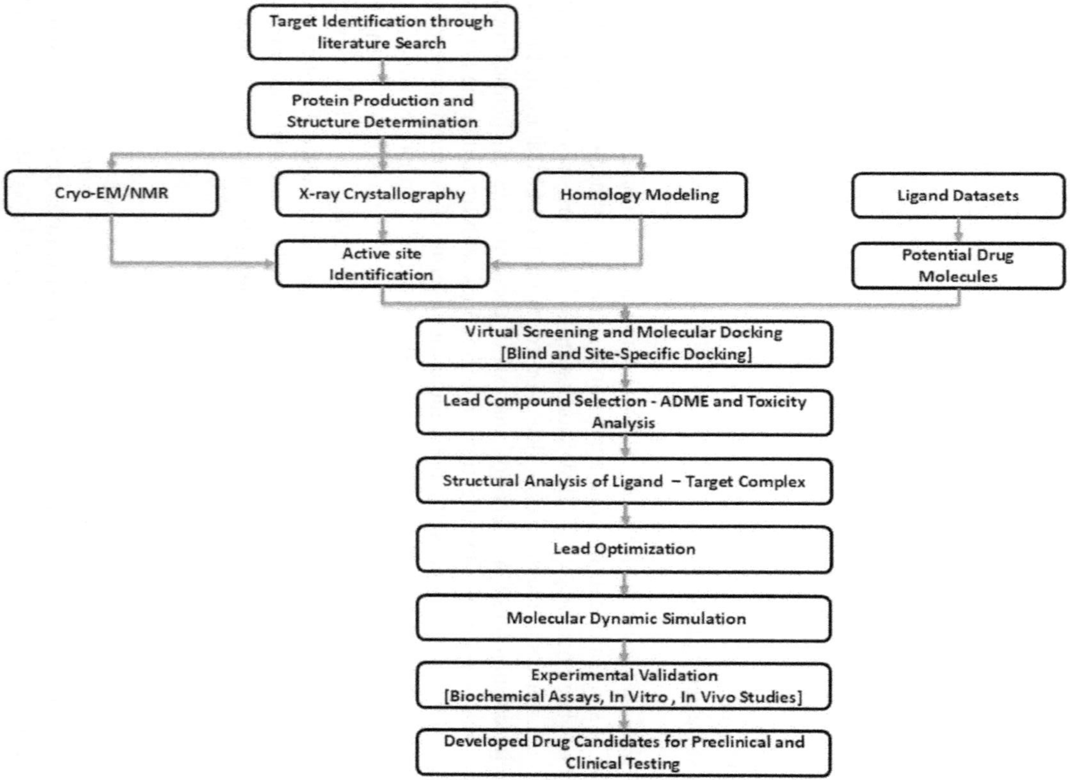

FIGURE 4.1 Iterative process of structure-based drug design.

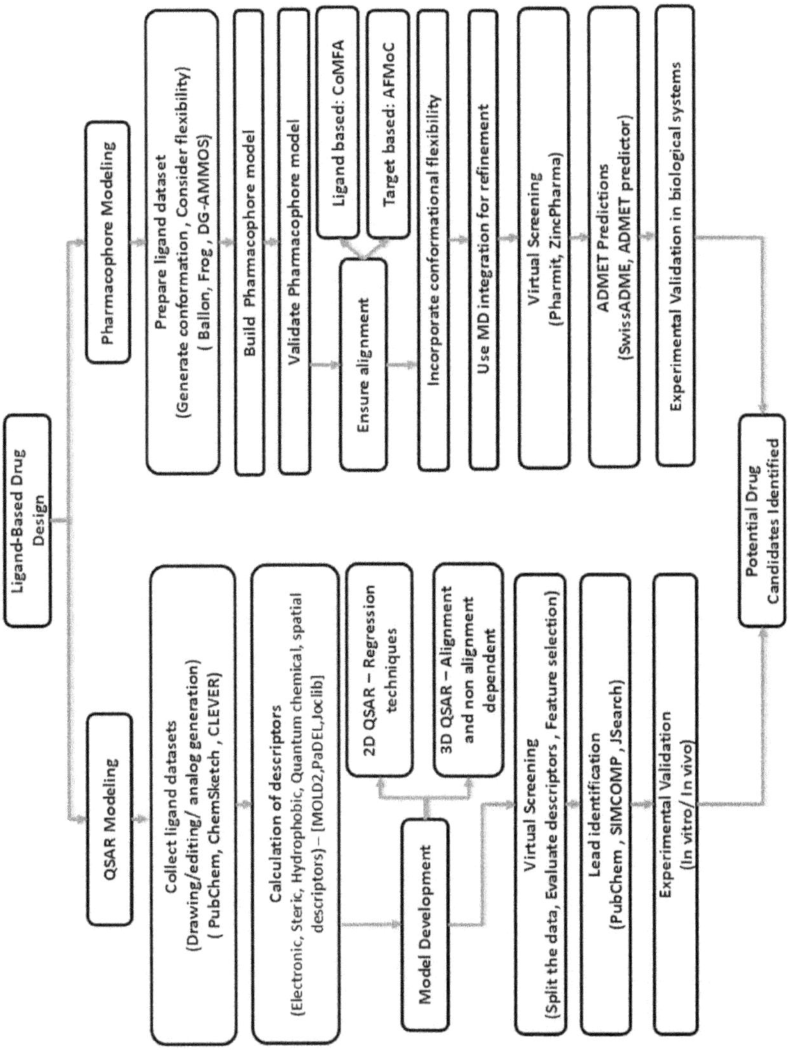

FIGURE 4.2 Iterative process of ligand-based drug design.

The general aspects pertaining to QSAR include the following steps. It is first necessary to screen and identify compounds that are chemically diverse with correlated differences in biological activity. Prior to this, molecular editing tools can be employed for drawing new molecules and editing existing molecules (examples include Chem-Sketch, Accelrys Draw, PubChem Sketcher, JChemPaint, BKchem, XDraw-Chem, JME, and MedChem Designer). Also, analogs can be generated apart from the creation of libraries (tools include Library synthesizer, SmiLib, GLARE, CLEVER, and Newlead). Since there is a relationship between optimal conformers and biological activity, several tools are available for the optimization of structures (Balloon, MOPAC, Openbabel, Frog, DG-AMMOS, SMI23D, Cyndi, and TINKER). Also, MD simulations can be done to generate all possible conformations of the ligands to maximize the chances of including that version of the conformer that is bioactive (irrespective of its energy state) and is especially relevant for those ligands that exhibit flexibility in their structures. This approach is relevant when a 3D QSAR model is developed based on the conformationally sampled method (CSM) (Bernard et al. 2003). In parallel, similarity searches can be done for classification, identification of chemical entities, and correlation of chemical structure and biological activity. The available tools for similarity matching include JCsearch, PubChem, SIMCOMP, SUBCOMP, and SMSD. The data sets are divided into those in the test and training set categories. The descriptors can be classified into those that fall under the electronic, steric, quantum chemical descriptors, hydrophobic parameters, and spatial descriptors J) categories. These descriptors explain the properties of the chemical by encoding them as a vector of numerical values. These descriptors can be calculated using various tools that are available (Joelib, Afgen, ISIDA-fragmentor, ODDescribers, MOLD2, PowerMV, PaDEL, CDK, Filter-it, MODEL) (Singla et al. 2013). The main descriptors applied include electronic, steric, hydrophobic, quantum chemical, and spatial descriptors (Rajkishan et al. 2021). These descriptors are involved in explaining the ligands in molecular and chemical terms and are correlated with their biological activity using different statistical tools to determine the strength of their relationship. The statistical techniques that can be employed can be classified into those based on regression analysis, multivariate analysis, and pattern recognition (artificial neural network (ANN), cluster analysis, and k-nearest neighbor (kNN)) (Ajjarapu et al. 2022).

The QSAR model is then developed and validated, followed by the design of the ligands, with their subsequent virtual screening and selection of the ligands with potential to be lead molecules that should be tested in vitro as a validation step for the lead molecules. The aforesaid model development can be performed using either 2D QSAR or 3D QSAR.

4.3.1 2D QSAR

The QSAR model can be developed using a 2D QSAR method. This method relies on the selection of appropriate descriptors and the generation of quality data based on experimental observations and the selection of statistical methods that will evaluate the relationship between the numerical values of the descriptors and the observations.

4.3.2 3D QSAR

3D QSAR is based on quantifying the relationship between the 3D characteristics of the molecule (steric and electrostatic properties), based on sampling inside the lattice structure, and its correlation with biological activity using statistical approaches (Rajkishan et al. 2021).

The basic idea behind the development and validation of QSAR models is to be able to predict the biological activity of molecules based on their structural properties and the nature of their interactions with a target and/or cells. The software/algorithms available for the development of the QSAR model include SVM, ANN, kNN, and Weka. Feature selection methods are Weka, Rapidminer, Orange, and RRF (Singla et al. 2013). The criteria for the development/building of the 3D QSAR model are based on the interaction energies between the ligands and the target. They can be classified into those that are alignment-dependent (GERM, HIFA, CoMSIA, AFMoC, COMBINE, CoMFA, and CoRIA) versus those that are not dependent on alignment (COMPASS, CoSA, HQSAR, CoMMA, EVA, WHIM, and GRIND). The linear and nonlinear QSAR methods respectively include CoMFA, GERM, AFMoC, SoMFA, CoMMA, CoMSIA, COMPASS, and QPLS. Other tools for QSAR are LiSIs, ChemDes, Gusar, DWFS, VIDEAN, BioPPSy, LogS, and the QSAR toolbox (Ajjarapu et al. 2022).

In a nutshell, ligand datasets are collected, and biological activity data are obtained. Data is selected for training the model, and the generated 3D descriptors are analyzed for the selection of the best descriptors for the dataset. Different algorithms are employed for the development of the QSAR model. The model is validated using the test dataset, and the best model is selected based on the employment of appropriate 3D descriptors for this dataset (Ajjarapu et al. 2022).

As an alternative to molecular docking, pharmacophore mapping has been considered a method for identifying key molecular features (steric and electronic features) that are part of a framework responsible for the observed optimal biological activity as a consequence of supramolecular interactions. It involves the superimposition of active ligands (atom-atom pairing for molecular alignment based on projecting the molecules to the active site residues) as well as their arrangement in space. In the case of COMPASS (3D QSAR-based approach), this tool aids in screening and selecting the optimally aligned pose/best conformer (Ajjarapu et al. 2022).

The fundamental premise behind the use of similarity searches is that molecules with similar structures will have similar biological activity. Different components of this similarity include the similarity coefficient, calculation of descriptors, and a weighted function. In a 3D QSAR model, different algorithms can be used for the calculation of descriptors (AtomPar, Feat Morgan, Morgan, Torsion, MACS, Layered, RDkit, and Pattern algorithms). Different aspects pertaining to the preparation of ligands that need to be taken into account include generation of 2D and 3D fingerprints, similarity-based alignment, conformational flexibility, scaffold hopping, and fragment-based design (explained earlier in the section on SBDD). Various conformers are generated, subsequent to which the 3D pharmacophore model is developed and validated. This mapping can either be ligand- or target-based. QSAR models use various machine learning and statistical algorithms for the prediction of the activities of compounds based on molecular descriptors. Some of the common methods (modeling and statistical) include:

a Multiple linear regression: Statistical technique for modeling the relationship between biological activity and molecular descriptors, assuming that their relationship is linear (Ajjarapu et al. 2022)

$$Y = \beta_0 + \sum_{i=1}^{n} \beta_i X_i + \in \tag{4.1}$$

Y – predicted biological activity
β_0 – intercept
β_i – coefficient of descriptor X_i
ϵ – error term

b Partial least squares (PLS) regression: This is used when the molecular descriptors are collinear. It creates new latent variables using linear combinations of the original predictors, thus reducing the dimensionality (Wold et al. 2001)

$$New\,components\; T = XW \tag{4.2}$$

$$Y = TQ + \in \tag{4.3}$$

X – matrix of molecular descriptors
W – Weight matrix to transform X into new components
T – transformed latent variables
Q – regression coefficient

c K-nearest neighbors (k-NN): It is a non-parametric modeling approach for the classification of compounds by considering their similarities (calculated using Euclidean distance) to known compounds (Itskowitz and Tropsha 2005).

$$Y_q = \frac{1}{k}\sum_{i=1}^{k} Y_i \tag{4.4}$$

k – number of nearest neighbors
Y – activity of ith nearest neighbor

$$d\left(X_q, X_i\right) = \sqrt{\sum_{j=1}^{n}\left(X_{qj} - X_{ij}\right)^2} \tag{4.5}$$

X_q and X_i – molecular descriptor vectors

d Support vector machine (SVM): In this method, active and inactive compounds are separated by a hyperplane, thus mapping the molecular descriptors into a higher-dimensional space (Cortes and Vapnik 1995).

$$Y(X) = \sum_{i=1}^{n} \alpha_i Y_i K(X, X_i) + b \tag{4.6}$$

$K(X, X_i)$ – kernel function
α_i – Lagrange multipliers
b – bias term

e Random forest (RF): It builds multiple decision trees and takes the average of their predictions. It is an ensemble learning method where a bootstrap of samples from the dataset contributes to each tree, and at each split, it selects random descriptors (Breiman 2001).

$$Y = \frac{1}{M} \sum_{j=1}^{M} T_j(X) \tag{4.7}$$

Y – final prediction
M – number of trees
T_j – multiple trees

f Artificial neural networks (ANNs): They are used to model complex relationships in QSAR and use interconnected neuron layers (Zou et al. 2009).

$$Y = f\left(\sum_{j=1}^{n} w_j g\left(\sum_{i=1}^{m} v_{ij} X_i + b_j\right) + c\right) \tag{4.8}$$

X_i – molecular descriptors
v_{ij}, w_j – weights
g – activation function
f – output function
b_j, c – biases

4.3.3 Ligand-Based Pharmacophore Modeling

This type of modeling requires the identification of the critical chemical features subsequent to the production of the conformational space for the flexibility of each ligand as well as their alignment in the training set. The ligand-based QSAR methods for the interaction energy calculations include CoMFA, CoMSIA, COMPASS, GERM, CoMMA, and SoMFA (Rajkishan et al. 2021; Ajjarapu et al. 2022).

4.3.4 Structure-Based Pharmacophore Modeling

This approach is dependent on the features at the active site as well as its relationship with the microenvironment. This method can be classified into those that are target/macromolecule-based methods (without ligand/substrate) and protein-ligand complex-based methods (Rajkishan et al. 2021). The 3D models for the receptor-based calculation of the interaction energies are COMBINE, AFMoC, HIFA, and CoRIA (Ajjarapu et al. 2022).

The different pharmacophore searching software are Boomer, PKfit, mobilePK, JPKD, PharmaGist, Tdm, Pharmapper, Cyber Patient, Pharmer, and ZincPharma (Singla et al. 2013). Other tools include PharmaGist, Pharmit, Discovery Studio, Ligandscout, ICM-Chemist, and Phase. Other advanced methods include approaches for MD integration (SILCS-Pharm, Hydration site-restricted pharmacophore, Dynaphore, common hits approach, GRAIL, MYSHAPE, and Water Pharmacophore) and for machine learning (HSPharm) (Ajjarapu et al. 2022).

Absorption, Distribution, Metabolism, Excretion, and Toxicity (ADMET) properties: Prediction of ADMET properties during the lead optimization and preclinical drug development phase is considered to be vital since it can possibly decrease the time and cost and reduce the chance of drug attrition at a later stage in the drug development process. This approach can aid in predicting the consequences of the drug interacting with the biological system and can assist in the process of classifying and characterizing the compounds. Software used in the prediction of ADMET properties includes Qikprop, ADMET predictor, SwissADME, FAF-Drugs2, and ADMET and predictive toxicology (Daina et al. 2017Rajkishan et al. 2021). Other tools are Oncologic, Metabolizer, QED, PASS, OSIRIS, Toxtree, DrugMint, admetSAR, DrugLogit, MetaSite, 2D SMARTCyp, and Metapred (Singla et al. 2013).

4.3.5 Ligand-Based Cheminformatics

Ligand-based cheminformatic methods are alternative methods for molecular docking to elucidate drug-target interactions, as information derived from target proteins is dispensable here. These methods link phenotypic changes like viability assays of cancer cells and existing binding affinity data of targets to features generated from significant descriptions of drugs or chemical structure graphs of drugs. The features thus generated are also known as descriptors, and they include quantifiable information about the drugs like their physical and chemical properties, including hydrophobicity, atom types, and many more, and they contribute to a chemical fingerprint specific to a drug. One of the practical applications is the prediction of the anticancer potential of imidazo(4,5-b)pyridine derivatives using IC50. A total of 4885 molecular descriptors were used for an adjusted adaptive least absolute shrinkage and selection operator (AALASSO) for this purpose (Algamal et al. 2015). Some other examples include classification models to identify inhibitors and non-inhibitors of flap endonuclease 1 (FEN1), as inhibition enhances sensitivity to chemotherapy by the application of both support vector machine (SVM) and random forest (RF) algorithms. Superior performance was shown by the SVM model, which was later utilized to screen more than 50,000 compounds, which led to in vitro experiments in DLD-1 colon cancer cell lines and finally selection of JFD00950 as a novel FEN1 inhibitor (Deshmukh et al. 2017). Many three-dimensional quantitative structure-activity relationship (QSAR) models have been developed, too. For example, for the breast cancer cell line MCF7, molecular features of maslinic acid and its derivatives like hydrophobicity, electrostatic patterns, and shape have been used to develop a

3D QSAR model that was used to screen the entire ZINC database (Alam and Khan 2017; Sterling and Irwin 2015). After identifying potential hits using this model, researchers followed it up using ADMET profiling and *in silico* docking. Another 3D QSAR modeling was developed for phosphoinositide 3-kinase gamma (PI3Kγ) inhibitors in order to screen compounds from the National Cancer Institute (NCI) database. This model identified around 19 compounds with the potential for nanomolar PI3Kγ inhibition (Taha et al. 2014).

Predicting the bioactivity profiles of compounds against kinases is another important aspect of cancer therapy, and many ligand-based deep-learning models have been developed for this purpose (Allen et al. 2019). A few of the examples include multi-task deep neural network (MTDNN) models and DEEPScreen, which could ensure quick repurposing of drugs at low costs. Data for the kinase bioactivity of compounds were collected from public and commercial databases like ChEMBL and Kinase Knowledgebase (KKB), respectively, and compiled to form a database of about 670,000 measurements from more than 317,000 compounds against 342 kinases. MTDNN models can accurately predict the bioactivity of molecules against the human kinome. MTDNN models show better performance than machine learning models due to their generalizing ability and high accuracy rates against a wide range of unseen compounds. DEEPscreen is a convolutional neural network (CNN)-based model. Here, the input for training included two-dimensional structural representations that include molecular details of different compounds. This input ensures the prediction of drug-target interactions as DEEPscreen can recognize patterns in chemical structures that are linked to the biological activity of compounds. This model enables the analysis of drug-target interactions even if complex three-dimensional structural data are not available. Both of these models not only facilitate the prediction of kinase bioactivity but also enable large-scale and complex virtual screening of compounds for drug repurposing purposes (Schürer and Muskal 2013; Rifaioglu et al. 2020). The aforesaid section discusses ligand-based methods that involve strategies related to molecular descriptors (that can predict the activity) as well as the structure-based and ligand-based pharmacophore models as well as approaches that can integrate and correlate experimental data with physical and chemical data that can possibly serve as a fingerprint for the ligand with drug-like potential.

4.4 NETWORK PHARMACOLOGY

With the understanding that several drugs against human pathologies have multiple targets and since the holy grail for drug development involves selectivity of drug action in the targets (that are aberrant in the diseased sites) without unduly affecting the healthy cells/tissues, an integrated approach is warranted. This integrated approach ideally involves a thorough empirical demonstration/observation of the reproducible clinical therapeutic effects of drugs/drug formulations. Apart from this, this approach requires the availability and understanding of the different bioinformatics tools that will enable the shortlisting of possible targets that would be plausibly modulated/modified/inhibited by the drug/drug formulations. Network pharmacology strategies involve a combination of ligand and target-based approaches. Figure 4.3 shows the iterative process for network pharmacology analysis.

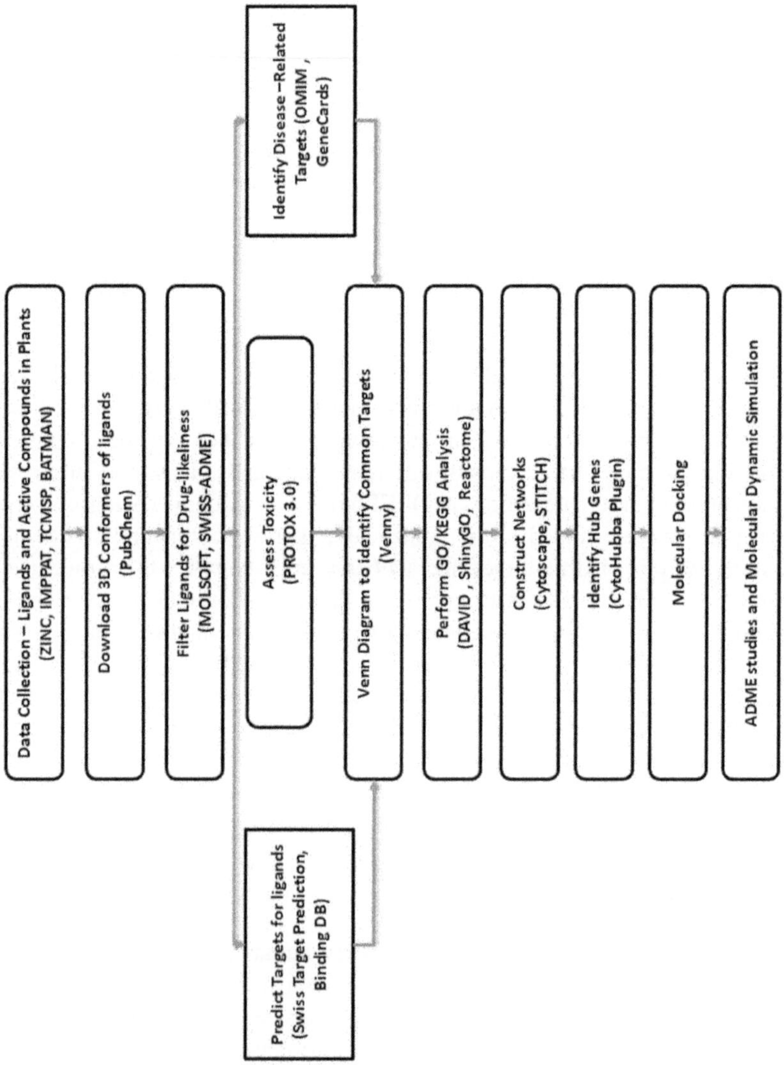

FIGURE 4.3 Iterative process for network pharmacology analysis.

With respect to the ligands, several databases can be employed to collect information pertaining to the active principles present (for e.g., in a particular plant). The databases include ZINC, IMPPAT, TCMSP, BATMAN, TCM, and KNApSAcK. This information can be complemented based on the employment of solvents with varying polarities and the analysis of the extracts using a combination of LC-MS/MS and GC-MS/MS-based analytical methods. Ligands (3D conformers) should be downloaded from PubChem, apart from other relevant information, including their IDs, molecular notation, and the SMILES notation. In this regard, MOLSOFT and SWISS-ADME tools can be used to compute the drug-likeness (DL) and oral bioavailability (OB), respectively. The filters that are usually set are that DL should be ≥ 0.18 and OB $\geq 30\%$, and ligands that meet these criteria can be selected. This portion of the workflow will enable the investigator to arrive at a list of probable ligands with drug-like properties (Kumar et al. 2023; Qu et al. 2021).

Tools are also available to determine the possible toxicity of the identified ligands, using tools like PROTOX 3.0 (https://tox.charite.de/protox3/) (Banerjee et al. 2024).

The next portion of the workflow involves target identification based on the ligands (after filtering for OB and DL properties as well as only those targets identified in *Homo sapiens*). This can be done using a variety of tools (for example, SwissTarget prediction), and targets selected had a combined score of less than 0.7 (Kumar et al. 2023). Other tools that can be used include BindingDB (https://www.bindingdb.org/rwd/bind/index.jsp) (Liu et al. 2025) and PharmMapper (Wang et al. 2017). Further, STITCH can be used to screen and shortlist targets with a combined score of ≥ 0.7. Other tools include TCMSP and BATMAN-TCM (Qu et al. 2021). After this step is completed, targets based on the human disease process should be identified using appropriate databases (e.g., OMIM, PharmGKB, GeneCards, and DISGENET). Duplicate genes will be removed, and the final list will be arrived at using UniProtKB with the correct nomenclature. A Venn diagram (using the Venny tool) is created to identify those targets that were in common in both the target-based and ligand-based searches (Kumar et al. 2023). Next, it will be necessary to document those genes that are especially prevalent in the disease datasets. For this purpose, it is necessary to adopt a GO/KEGG-based pathway analysis for functionally annotating the genes. Tools like DAVID (Kumar et al. 2023), REACTOME, and ShinyGO can aid in obtaining insights in terms of the molecular pathways and functional categories that may be enriched for in the particular human pathology being studied (Ge et al. 2020). In order to better understand the mechanism involved in the empirically observed and demonstrated clinical effects, Cytoscape was employed for the visualization and the interpretation of the networks using nodes (active components and genes) and edges (the interactions between the active genes and components). The best topological method available (e.g., degree) can be selected for the identification of the significant compounds/targets/pathways in the network diagram. Also, hub genes can be identified by importing relevant network diagrams (protein-protein interaction networks genes selected should have a combined score that is ≥ 0.5) into Cytoscape using the Cytohubba plugin. This plugin analyzes data using 11 methods for scoring, and the selected hub genes are those that are the best in terms of their interactions. After the hub genes are identified, it is necessary to perform molecular docking analysis studies (discussed under the SBDD approach) and LigPlot-based visualization of the docked complexes, followed by drug likeness, ADME studies, and MD simulation studies to screen, identify, and shortlist molecules with druggable properties (based on their interactions with proteins identified from the hub genes) (Kumar et al. 2023). Table 4.3 lists the commonly used tools for network pharmacology analysis.

The aforementioned flow can also be employed for drugs that are repositioned. In other words, drugs originally approved for one indication can be developed for new human conditions. This approach will provide an opportunity to possibly develop treatment modalities using existing drugs that are more suited to a different route of administration. As a step in this section, the aforementioned approaches can be adopted to screen and select the best combination of drug and target for further development as a new formulation (Raali et al. 2024). Recently, it has been reported that networks with protein-protein interactions that are more represented in multiple pathways associated with a particular disease should be identified and selected. The network constructed using this "edge-weighted method" would be a better predictor of the interactions between the disease and the drug as well as more accurately mirror the path or the drug's mechanism of action. This approach not only aids in repurposing drugs but also helps in the possible identification of hitherto unreported novel drugs for specific human disease conditions (Han et al. 2024).

The aforementioned analysis of the network pharmacology strategy (combination of literature-based searches and online tools for the identification, validation, and enrichment of certain key signaling pathways as well as information from disease-based databases) is based on the fundamental premise that complex diseases may arise due to perturbations in multiple targets that need to be studied and understood as a network rather than in isolation. However, in order to analyze and interpret vast amounts of complex data, which are not possible for humans, ML and AI-based strategies can be adopted, and details with regard to the same are discussed below.

4.5 MACHINE LEARNING IN ANTICANCER DRUG DISCOVERY

Cancer drug discovery has been challenging due to the extensive side effects and toxicity of many of the existing anticancer drugs and high resistance among patients toward them (Nikolaou et al. 2018). Experimental approaches involve extensive time-consuming and costly procedures where many compounds are tested against biological targets (Bhatia and Sharma 2025). Many therapeutic targets have been identified as potential anticancer targets, and computational techniques have been sought to predict the biological activity of many drug candidates on these targets. For example, machine learning methods have identified three potential inhibitors to indolamine 2,3-dioxygenase (IDO), a promising immune checkpoint target for cancer therapy (Zhang et al. 2018).

4.5.1 Naïve Bayes

The Naïve Bayes algorithm is a fast algorithm that is easy to implement on small and noisy datasets. It can also be scaled to large datasets and would still give the same

TABLE 4.3
Commonly Used Tools for Network Pharmacology Analysis

Name of the Tool	Type of Tool	Description	Access	Link	References
Cytoscape	Open-source software for network visualization	Extensive plugins for different analyses; can import data from local files and external databases; highly customizable	Web and application-based	Cytoscape (https://cytoscape.org/)	(Shannon et al. 2003)
STRING	Protein-protein interaction database	Provides comprehensive PPI data; relies on data on known and predicted interactions	Web-based	STRING (https://string-db.org/)	(Szklarczyk et al. 2019)
INPUT	Network pharmacology platform for traditional Chinese medicine	Integrates data from multiple sources; basic network analysis with customizable data inputs	Web-based	INPUT (https://cbcb.cdutcm.edu.cn/INPUT/Home/)	(Li et al. 2022)
STITCH	Drug-target interaction database	Considers both known and predicted interactions; includes both physical and functional associations between chemicals and targets	Web-based	STITCH (http://stitch.embl.de/)	(Szklarczyk et al. 2016)
SmartGraph	Network pharmacology investigation platform	Can work with custom datasets, focus on graph-based visualizations, and has a simple user interface; limited tools for analysis	Web-based	SmartGraph (https://smartgraph.ncats.io/)	(Zahoránszky-Kőhalmi et al. 2020)
NAVIGaTOR	Analysis and visualization of networks	Enables efficient exploration of networks; dynamic visualization	Application-based	NAVIGaTOR (https://navigator.ophid.utoronto.ca/navigatorwp/)	(Brown et al. 2009)
Gephi	Graphical visualization software	Advanced graphical analysis features for large biological networks; advanced user interface	Application-based	Gephi (https://gephi.org/)	(Bastian et al. 2009)
NetworkAnalyst	Interpretation of biological networks	Allows disease-centric network exploration and GSEA; integrates data from STRING and KEGG	Web-based	NetworkAnalyst (https://www.networkanalyst.ca/)	(Zhou et al. 2019)

performance. It can be used for drug discovery to predict possible targets, toxicity, biological performance of drugs, and so on (Cheen et al. 2021; Zhang et al. 2020).

4.5.2 Support Vector Machines

Support vector machines are supervised ML algorithms generally used for regression and classification tasks. The main goal of SVM is to create an optimal decision boundary (also known as a hyperplane) between two classes. The orientation of the hyperplane is in such a way that the margin is maximized. Support vectors are the closest data points from each class and are critical in positioning the hyperplane. It is a powerful method to build a classifier as it can recognize subtle patterns in large and complex datasets and generalize well to new data (Noble 2006). SVM classifiers have been used in the classification of different cancers based on gene expression data since high-throughput microarrays have become available (Golub et al. 1999). SVM models have also been used extensively in biomarker discovery (Abeel et al. 2010). For example, SVM in combination with proteomics has been used to predict resistance to chemotherapy in small-cell lung cancer by detecting associated biomarkers (Guo et al. 2015).

SVM helps screen potential drug candidates for cancer therapy by identifying active compounds from inactive ones. For example, an SVM-RBF model was used to select potential drug candidates from public databases for therapeutic compounds for oral cancer (Bundela et al. 2015). Traditionally, data is split into training and testing sets in machine learning models; still, active learning approaches where the learning set grows with each round have also been used to select active compounds against cancers using SVM models. SVM models have also been used to screen drug profiles of anticancer drugs against altered genomic features of cancer cell lines to understand their influence on drug resistance (Gupta et al. 2016). SVM models can also be used to predict cancer cell line responses to potential drug compounds, like the ensemble SVM model for breast cancer cell lines to predict their sensitivity to untested drug compounds (Hejase and Chan 2015).

4.5.3 Extreme Gradient Boosting

Prediction of drug synergy is a relatively complex problem, and Extreme Gradient Boosting (XGBoost) is one of the widely used ensemble methods for the same due to its generalization abilities (Wu et al. 2022). For example, both cell line features from gene expression values and drug fingerprints have been included to develop TreeCombo, with an emphasis on drug features to predict the synergy of new drug combinations (Janizek et al. 2018). Multi-omics data like mutations, copy number variations (CNVs), and gene expression data can be included to enrich the features and improve the accuracy of synergy prediction for new anticancer drug combinations using XGBoost-based methods. Drug features like targeted pathways, drug-target information, and drug fingerprints have been considered along with monotherapy information to improve the predictive ability of the XGBoost-based model, which revealed BRAF as a common target for synergy and TNFA as an important tumorigenic regulator (Celebi et al. 2019). Another approach is to avoid grouping all the cell lines for a single XGBoost model. Instead, XGBoost can be trained for individual cell lines, thus avoiding the requirement of features specific to cell lines. Drug features like fingerprints, physicochemical properties, and ISIDA/SIRMA fragments have been included to narrow the drug candidates as reliable and synergistic combinations could be chosen (Sidorov et al. 2019).

4.5.4 Random Forest

A decision tree in random forest is one of the best models to study and predict drug interactions due to its speed, ability to generalize with new data, and performance. It can be used to predict interactions between potential drug compounds and target proteins; for example, over 90% accuracy was obtained in predicting these interactions using a model from the molecular descriptors from Open Babel and protein enrichment scores from Gene Ontology (GO) and Kyoto Encyclopedia of Genes and Genomes (KEGG) pathways (Chen et al. 2016). Here, protein-compound interactions obtained from Binding DB were applied in a maximal relevance and minimal redundancy (mRMR) dimensionality reduction technique. Another application of RF models is in predicting drug synergies for cancer treatment; for example, by combining the drug-target information with genomic and pharmacological data, drug synergies have been predicted with an $F1$ value of 95.4% in 31 tumor cell lines for 583 drug compound combinations (Jeon et al. 2018). Prediction models have also been used to study tumor cell lines where different antibodies are tested. To check the effect of each antibody dose on the phenotype of the cell lines, random forest-based variables can be used to quantify their apoptosis and proliferation levels (Sandercock et al. 2015).

4.5.5 Extremely Randomized Tree

The extremely randomized tree (ERT) algorithm is another ensemble method that is popular for its robustness in working with noisy data. It adds an additional randomization step to the random forest algorithm by randomizing the subsampling of features and samples along with the randomization of feature selection. Novel ERT-based algorithms have been developed for the discovery of drug combinations where genomic information like gene expression, CNVs, and mutations were used along with pharmacological and drug target information to achieve a correlation coefficient of 0.738 between predicted and actual synergy observations (Jeon et al. 2018). This approach included synthetic lethality and monotherapy information of drugs, and the gene information included cancer-related genes alone. Drug combination synergy has been studied in both clinical and cell line settings by developing multi-task learning frameworks where five models have been trained based on different synergy measures like HAS, Bliss, Loewe, ZIP, and ALMANAC scores (Gilvary et al. 2019). ERTs and cancer cell lines were treated as distinct tasks so that each model could focus on one cell line, thus eliminating the need for specific features of cell lines. For each drug combination, pairwise similarity features have been designed, including side effects, gene ontology, compound structures, drug targets, and many more, based on statistical measures like Pearson's coefficient. Using the model, it was shown that synergistic drug pairs seem to exhibit closer drug targets than antagonistic drug pairs in the gene network, thus improving the consistency in future evaluations of drug combinations.

4.5.6 Artificial Neural Networks

Artificial neurons are functional elements of artificial neural networks, where they are interconnected to obtain information from the outside. These are called internal layers and are connected to output nodes (also known as hidden layers), which transfer the results of the ANN outside (Agatonovic-Kustrin and Beresford 2000). With the rise of deep learning (DL), where information is processed in a hierarchical manner, it is possible to connect a number of internal layers together to represent complex relationships. Combining both ANN and DL led to a giant reduction in the time required to train sophisticated models with thousands of internal layers. Deep learning models of up to 86% accuracy have been used to predict the potential carcinogenic risks of compounds that were being considered for drug development by calculating six molecular descriptors for 1003 chemicals obtained from the Carcinogenic Potency Database (Wang et al. 2020).

4.5.6.1 Feedforward Neural Network

Feedforward is a basic kind of deep neural network with sequentially layered artificial neurons, capable of discovering abstract structures in complex and large datasets. Recently, deep learning methods have gained increased popularity for the prediction of anticancer drug synergy. Some of the examples include Deep Synergy, employing a three-layer feedforward neural network (Preuer et al. 2018). Cell line features included the gene expression data, and drug features included fingerprint, physicochemical properties, and toxicophore features. The combined hidden representation resulted in accurate drug synergy predictions, and the tool exhibited better performance than traditional machine learning methods. Another novel model related to drug combinations is the prediction of responses of tumor cell lines to novel drug combinations, applying feature-encoding sub-models and utilizing the encoded features as inputs of neural networks. Cell line features considered are gene and microRNA expression data along with protein abundance and drug features, including fingerprints generated using Dragon software along with 30 types of molecular descriptors of drugs. The addition of molecular descriptors helped to bring about a 0.81 increase in the coefficient of determination (Xia et al. 2018). A combination of deep tensor factorization (DTF) algorithm and feedforward deep neural networks has also been used to predict anticancer drug synergy, and instead of relying on cell line and drug features, DTF considers drug synergy data as tensors (Sun et al. 2020). DTF requires less number of training sets but is limited for practical uses as it needs to be retrained with new data every time new cell lines or drugs are introduced.

4.5.7 AI for Drug Repurposing

Drug repurposing or drug repositioning is a method used to assign approved drugs that are already recommended to treat other diseases or drugs that failed during developmental phases to new indications (Pushpakom et al. 2019). It is advantageous to anticancer drug discovery because it reduces the time and costs required for normal drug development processes and further reduces the risk to the patients (Zhao et al. 2023). Network-based AI applications have been proven to be useful for drug repurposing purposes in many aspects (Dotolo et al. 2021). They can be used to study known associations between drugs and diseases and use them to build statistical models that can predict novel associations. For instance, network algorithms have been used to integrate transcriptomic profiles, drug-target interactions, and many other data to predict cancer cell line responses to drugs (Zhang et al. 2018). Another application is network-based co-mutation, which can be used for the identification of pathways associated with cancer therapy by quantifying the genetic interactions involved (Cheng et al. 2019). Network-based approaches can also be used to predict potential drugs for different indications by studying drug and disease properties to find similarities. Existing cancer drugs can be used to target related genes in protein-protein interaction networks to target significant mutations. Utilizing ML-based applications for drug repurposing can reduce the number of false positives during predictions. For example, the DTI-Voodoo model uses graph neural networks to combine phenotype features (biological features of drugs) with molecular features (molecular structures of protein and drug) within ontology-based PPI interaction networks to predict drug-protein interactions (Hinnerichs and Hoehndorf 2021). Utilizing AI-ML approaches for drug repurposing has many advantages, as they include both associations between therapeutic targets and interactions between drugs.

4.6 ARTIFICIAL INTELLIGENCE IN DRUG DEVELOPMENT

The use of AI in drug development can be considered for some steps of the drug discovery process like target selection, where the right targets should be chosen for the proposed drugs, molecule selection and lead optimization, synthetic planning, and synthesis of drug candidates, testing of chemical and pharmacological properties, preclinical studies, and clinical trials.

a Target prediction: Owing to the availability of complex sequencing data, target selection for drug development involves understanding genomic features that are cancer-specific. Manual analysis of these huge volumes of data is limited by time and human resources; thus, AI can perform these tasks efficiently. For instance, DeepVariant exhibits superior performance to non-AI tools for variant calling, and the Deep-SEA application can accurately identify binding sites for transcription factors and sensitivity sites for DNase (Dia and Torkamani 2019).

b Selection of effective compounds: AI could speed up the process of finding potential drug compounds against target proteins based on their chemical properties, where thousands of drug molecules can be screened to choose possible leads based on their properties. AI can also contribute to *de novo* drug design. Merging AI with drug development has revolutionized the oncology drug discovery field. For example, DL methods have been utilized to distinguish between molecules that have never been tested for anticancer activities and proven anticancer drugs (Kadurin et al. 2016). This can accelerate the development of new anticancer drugs.

c Peptide synthesis: Many artificial intelligence-based tools have been developed for discovering novel anticancer peptides. One of the applications is a platform based on SVM for the identification of novel anticancer drugs (Bruno et al. 2013). Another one of the deep learning-based tools using an enhanced version of the recursive neural network (RNN), the LSTM algorithm, is ACP-DL. It has the ability to distinguish between non-cancer and cancer peptides, thus helping in anticancer peptide discovery (Yu et al. 2020). Deep ACP is another tool for identifying novel anticancer peptides that utilize deep recurrent neural networks. Likewise, another approach included an ensemble of four counterpropagation artificial neural networks (Kavousi et al. 2020). Furthermore, the discovery of anticancer peptides can be done by combining different approaches like one-hot encoding for designing ACP-GCN and graphical convolutional networks (Rao et al. 2020).

d Prediction of drug properties: For effective drug design, many properties like bioactivity, toxicity, and bioavailability need to be taken into account, and AI can predict these properties for potential drug compounds. For example, the Deep Tox algorithm can accurately predict the toxicity of compounds and help researchers avoid numerous tests (Mullard 2017).

e Identification of drug dosage and effectiveness of drug delivery: Administering improper doses of any drug can result in lethal and undesirable effects; thus, determining safe dosage is crucial for treatment purposes (Dimmitt Simon et al. 2017). AI and ML algorithms can help researchers determine the optimum dosage of drugs with minimum side effects, so many AI-based platforms have been developed for many diseases like HIV and cancers (Shen et al. 2020). For example, comboFM is an ML tool for high-dimensional data analysis to determine appropriate dosages and combinations of drugs to be used in different cancer cell lines as part of preclinical evaluation. It has shown promising efficacy for the anticancer drugs bortezomib and crizotinib when used in lymphoma cell lines (Julkunon Holi et al. 2020). Another application is CURATE.AI, which uses patient-specific profiles using their personal data and later uses the same to determine optimum drug doses for them. CURATE.AI has shown significant results in clinical settings. For instance, it showed that 50% lower starting doses for the investigative drug ZEN-3694 in combination with the cancer drug enzalutamide led to arresting the cancer growth when administered to a prostate cancer patient having a metastatic castration-resistant case (Mullard 2017; Pantuck Allan 2018).

f Analysis of drug release and monitoring drug-likeness: Lately, validating the computational analyses to check whether the selected bioactive compounds are reliable as carriers has become easy due to the availability of many public datasets based on the chemical features of compounds. Many online tools have been developed for this purpose that can help in analyzing properties related to the release of drugs and their drug-likeness. For instance, as stated earlier, Swiss ADME is a user-friendly and free graphical interface developed with the goal of evaluating pharmacokinetic properties and compatibility of drug compounds (Mullard 2017). Another model for determining the bioactivity of drug compounds is a multiple kernel-based learning method called pairwise MKL that has been used to predict the anticancer potential of different compounds (Cichonska et al. 2018).

4.7 MICRORNA AND MACHINE LEARNING IN CANCER THERAPY

MicroRNA (miRNA) plays dual roles in cancer, as therapeutic target proteins as well as a therapeutic agent through small molecule modulations. Predictive models have been developed for small molecules that can act as modulators of miRNAs. One of the models used bioassay data from PubChem to collect the chemical features of molecules, using these 179 molecular descriptors, and trained ML algorithms in order to identify structural patterns called chemical scaffolds of molecules (Jamal et al. 2012). These chemical scaffolds could bind and modulate miRNAs, and thus, this model could identify which types of molecules are capable of the same. Many models have been developed to predict interactions between miRNAs and small molecules. Another predictive machine learning model used a random forest algorithm where experimentally validated binding data from the SM2miR database (Liu et al. 2013) was used to train the model so that it could predict potential interactions between miRNAs and small molecules. The model exhibited good performance in predicting miRNA associations for common cancer drugs like 5-fluorouracil, 5-aza-2′-deoxycytidine, and 17 beta-estradiol, thus suggesting possible effects of these drugs on miRNAs (Wang et al. 2019). Another example of such an ML-based model is HeteSim, which calculates similarity scores between miRNAs and molecules by analyzing complex biological data and uses patterns learned from existing data to predict interactions between different small molecules and miRNAs (Qu et al. 2019; Chen et al. 2020).

4.8 ELECTRONIC HEALTH RECORDS IN CANCER THERAPY

Electronic health records (EHRs) contain extensive data about patients, including their medications, treatments, and medical histories, that can be analyzed and used for different applications like predictions of adverse drug events (ADEs), drug discovery, and drug repurposing. Developments in the field of artificial intelligence, like natural language processing (NLP), help convert traditional unstructured data, like clinical notes and outcomes from discussions at health forums, into structured forms that can be interpreted by machines by extracting relevant medical information from them using ML and deep learning models. Different machine learning models have been developed using EHR notes to detect ADEs more accurately (Li et al. 2018).

EHR-based ML models can be used for drug repurposing purposes, like the analysis of uses of off-label drugs. One such example is an SVM classifier to distinguish between off-label drug uses and approved ones after analyzing annotated text in the EHRs. It could produce 10,765 potential drug and indication pairs, each with an off-label drug having a novel potential in an indication for which it has never been used, thus representing further drug repurposing possibilities (Jung et al. 2013). Another example of drug repurposing based on EHRs is the identification of metformin for cancer treatment (Xu et al. 2015). EHR data from the tumor registries containing over 100,000 patients from the Mayo Clinic and Vanderbilt University Medical Center were collected and divided into two cohorts after considering factors like smoking. It was shown that the use of metformin was linked to low mortality rates in cancer patients. The results from these analyses suggested the anticancer potential of metformin to improve the survival outcomes of patients (Tang et al. 2018). These findings were confirmed by epidemiological and preclinical studies using metformin as an anticancer agent against breast cancer.

4.9 CONSIDERATIONS IN CURRENT AI AND ML METHODS

The generalizing ability and accuracy of any AI or ML-driven model rely upon the type, quality, and quantity of data used in training and validation sets. Training sets influence how accurately the models can make predictions, and validation sets are used to ensure the reliability of models (Grammatica 2007). However, models trained on small datasets can risk overfitting, which means that the model can predict well only in a narrow applicability domain but not with diverse unseen data. This happens commonly with deep learning models due to their increasing complexity. Some of the common methods to reduce overfitting in deep learning models include reducing the size of the model by removing layers, ignoring random neuron units during training, and stopping training once the accuracy of validation decreases (Ekins et al. 2019; Nosengo 2016; Kitchen et al. 2004; Srivastava et al. 2014; Angermueller et al. 2016). For example, the development of DEEPScreen (a model for the prediction of drug-target interactions using 2D images of drugs) involved neuron dropout regularization to enhance the model's reliability (Rifaioglu et al. 2020). Another example is the application of the early stopping method during the development of a deep neural network to predict the response of tumors to drugs by integrating TCGA mutational data as well as CCLE gene expression data (Chiu et al. 2019). Table 4.4 lists some of the available, additional AI/ML-based tools with applications in anticancer drug discovery.

TABLE 4.4
Additional AI/ML-Based Tools for Anticancer Drug Discovery

AI/ML Tool	Method	Applications in Cancer Therapy	References
PrOCTOR	Random forest	Predict the toxicity of compounds	(Gayvert et al. 2016)
POLYpharmacology Generative Optimization Network (POLYGON)	Deep learning	Design compounds that can inhibit more than one target simultaneously	(Munson et al. 2024)
Drug Ranking Using ML (DRUML)	RF, SVM, BGLM, PLS, PCR, DL, neural networks	Predict and rank the efficacy of >400 anticancer drugs	(Gerdes et al. 2021)
AlphaFold	Deep learning	Protein modeling and prediction of protein-ligand interactions	(Jumper et al. 2021)
PhySIcoCHemICal graph neural network (PSICHIC)	Graph neural network	Protein-ligand interaction fingerprints from sequence data	(Koh et al. 2024)
Personalized Single-Cell Expression-Based Planning for Treatments in Oncology (PERCEPTION)	CATREG algorithm	Predict drug responses	(Sinha et al. 2024)
GAN-Drug generator	Generative adversarial network (GAN)	Anticancer drug design	(Abbasi et al. 2022)
Reinforcement Learning for Structural Evolution (ReLeaSE)	Generative and predictive deep neural networks	De novo drug design	(De Bacco et al. 2018)
DeepDRK	Deep learning	Anticancer drug repurposing	(Wang et al. 2021)
MBiRW	Bi-random walk (BiRW) algorithm	Identify potential new indications for known drugs	(Luo et al. 2016)

Another factor influencing the performance of ML models is the number and type of input descriptors. Usually, the fingerprints of sizes ranging from 0 to 1 are used, and they can be 2D or 3D features and include structural, physical, and chemical features of both ligands and proteins (Sastry et al. 2010). Other descriptors that can be included for generating models include properties like solvent-accessible surface area or molecular weight, and biological information like gene expression or mutations, and the type of descriptors used in inputs depends on the type of prediction needed. For example, to predict the bioactivity of compounds, suitable descriptors would be pharmacophore features, including the chemical properties of the compounds like hydrogen bond acceptors and donors, hydrophobic regions, and so on.

They can further be used to train models to screen a large number of compounds that interact with the same target in a similar way. Some of the QSAR models are developed this way; for example, pharmacophores have been used in the QSAR model to identify novel compounds for Indoleamine 2,3-dioxygenase 1 (IDO1) inhibition (Rogers and Hahn 2010). Other choices for fingerprints are circular fingerprints like Extended-Connectivity Fingerprints (ECFP) that include properties of atoms like types, atomic weight, charges, and many more, or structural protein-ligand interaction fingerprints that contain the 3D structural information (Deng et al. 2004; Da and Kireev 2014). Interaction fingerprints are based on crystallography data and can be used to predict possible novel ligands for the same target (Van-Westen et al. 2012). In models developed on ML and AI algorithms, combinations of different types of descriptors are often used to maximize the performance of the models so that they can be used for a wide range of targets and ligands.

Data size and quality are other important factors to be considered when developing any model using ML and AI algorithms. Using large datasets for training the models can help in developing models with better performance and reduced overfitting. This is applicable, especially for deep neural network models. For example, single-task deep learning models for the prediction of the kinase activity of drugs work better when more than 500 compounds are used for each kinase (Allen et al. 2019). Large biological data sources like PubChem provide data from diverse conditions, and using this data for training ML and AI models requires standardization (Kim et al. 2019). Better quality of the data can be ensured using FAIR (Findability, Accessibility, Interoperability, Reusability) standards, and datasets that are compliant with these standards are generally reliable and easy to incorporate into different models (Wilkinson et al. 2016; Sansone et al. 2019). If data is not annotated properly, it can lead to ignorance of significant differences like the responses of different cell lines to a drug; thus, poor-quality data should be filtered out before training the models, and the data generated should be of good standards and accurate as well (Stathias et al. 2018).

Thus, one of the few limitations of using ML-based algorithms in drug discovery is the lack of consistency in data for the validation of models. Even though large amounts of biomedical data are being generated, not everything is annotated and consistent, resulting in models that cannot distinguish between significant signals and noise data (Pasrija et al. 2022).

Another challenge is the interpretation of deep learning models as to why they make specific predictions, and they are often criticized for their 'black-box' nature (Baselli et al. 2020). However, recent advances like combining disease networks containing relationships between different diseases, proteins, and genes, and neural networks can result in improved interpretability as seen in melanoma studies (Lai et al. 2022). Another solution is the use of graph neural networks (GNN), as they can interpret complex biological data in neural networks. Another challenge in using ML and AI models in anticancer drug development is the difficulty in integrating all the heterogeneous data from different sources, like genomic, transcriptomic, EHR-based, proteomic, and clinical studies. Even though deep learning models can be multimodal and handle different types of biological data, including all the types of available data is difficult, and thus, significant interactions like gene-protein or protein-cell can be easily missed (Li et al. 2016).

4.9.1 Case Studies

Computational approaches like molecular docking, QSAR modeling, network pharmacology, and machine learning have contributed to significant advances in drug discovery to identify potential therapeutic agents. Comparative assessments of the different tools available for these approaches have been conducted to optimize the methodology for drug discovery. For instance, a study involving molecular docking of bacterial ribosomes with ligands of oxazolidinones (broad-spectrum synthetic antibiotics) to observe their interactions included five docking programs (AutoDock Vina, rDock, Autodock4, RLDock, and DOCK6). This study inferred that DOCK6 exhibited top performance among the five programs with the lowest median RMSD (Buckley et al. 2023). Similarly, another study of breast cancer involving receptors like HER2, progesterone, EGFR, NF-κB, and estrogen integrated ML models for binary as well as multiclass classification and molecular docking to screen the ligands from the BindingDB database, and the shortlisted ligands were evaluated for their binding affinities. It was concluded that the most effective model for screening the database is GA-SVM-SVM: GA-SVM-SVM due to its better precision, F1 score, and recall compared to other pipelines (Rezaee et al. 2024). Another example of the combination of different computational approaches is the evaluation of molecular mechanisms involved in the anti-liver cancer effects of Evodiae fructus. This study used network pharmacology to screen targets and active compounds from the plant, followed by the investigation of signaling pathways and utilization of 2D and 3D-QSAR pharmacophore models to predict the pIC50 values and the plant compounds, respectively. This study identified SRC non-receptor tyrosine kinase as a promising target, Obacunone exhibited optimal binding, and the 3D QSAR model revealed that pharmacophore 01 had the highest selectivity (Chen and Han 2023). Another study compared deep learning and QSAR classification to identify triple-negative breast cancer (TNBC) inhibitors and a new G protein-coupled receptor (GPCR) agonist. This study concluded that DNN and random forest exhibited better performance in predicting potential hits (Tsou et al. 2020). Another novel combination is the introduction of deep learning into SBDD approaches called the deep docking approach based on QSAR models, which saves significant runtime for docking (Gentile et al. 2020). Table 4.5 gives the comparative metrics of all four approaches to drug discovery.

Other approaches can integrate information from biological systems and the chemical nature of the ligands in terms of predicting the pharmacological activity or designing molecules with an improved PK/PD and safety profile. One such approach involves the adoption of advanced computational models known as mtk-QSBER (multi-tasking models for quantitative structure-biological effect relationships). In a pioneering approach, a research group was involved in developing an mtk-QSBER model using heterogeneous data and yet demonstrated greater than 90% accuracy with respect to both types of datasets (training and prediction sets). This approach

TABLE 4.5
Comparative Metrics of SBDD, LBDD, Network Pharmacology, and AI/ML Techniques for Drug Discovery

Metrics	SBDD	LBDD	Network Pharmacology	AI/ML Approaches	References
Predictability	Yields good predictions of ligand conformations (qualitative predictions); quantitative predictions like binding affinities are moderate or less reliable, as scoring functions are not perfect.	Yields good predictions of activity if model training is done using sufficient data; for chemotypes that are not represented in the training data, LBDD approaches are less predictive.	It predicts multiple targets or pathways (at the protein level) to yield therapeutic effects. This is not possible with the analysis of gene transcripts. However, it does not give exact activity predictions or quantitative outcomes.	Modern models can provide better predictions than traditional methods as they can identify specific patterns missed by humans, but these predictions are heavily based on the training data and can mispredict mechanisms.	(Batool et al. 2019; Dimitrov et al. 2005; Poornima et al. 2016; Burki 2020)
Reliability	Reliability may vary with different docking tools; generally reliable for identifying binders in a specific pocket, but flexible proteins can affect the reproducibility.	QSAR models give consistent predictions with respect to drug analogs when used in their domain, and reliability reduces when compounds are different from the training set.	Predictions made using these tools are considered hypotheses and require experimental confirmation; with successful case studies reported, confidence in their reliability is increasing.	ML models can overfit or be biased, affecting their reliability; model interpretability and calibration are being worked upon to improve the reliability.	(Batool et al.2019; Dimitrov et al. 2005; Poornima et al. 2016; Burki 2020)

(Continued)

TABLE 4.5 CONTINUED
Comparative Metrics of SBDD, LBDD, Network Pharmacology, and AI/ML Techniques for Drug Discovery

Metrics	SBDD	LBDD	Network Pharmacology	AI/ML Approaches	References
Computational cost	Basic workflows are computationally efficient for each compound, whereas complex SBDD methods like MD simulations are computationally expensive.	LBDD generally has a low computational cost, including CPU/GPU requirements; even the intense process of calculating molecular descriptors can be done easily.	Computational demands are moderate for network analyses; these approaches are mainly data-limited, as the analyses are based on biological data.	Training AI models can be computationally expensive as they might require powerful GPUs for many days, but their application is cheap and fast.	(Batool et al. 2019; 171. El-Atawneh and Goldblum 2022; Zhang et al. 2020)
Robustness	Performance can be affected by minor changes like the presence of structural water or incomplete structure; robust for similar compounds on targets that are well characterized.	Robust for predictions involving properties between known data points; different compounds or errors in descriptor or activity data can result in unreliable results.	The robustness of network analysis depends on data quality; cell type or subtype-specific interactions may not be robust. For instance, the network model of one subtype of cancer may not work for another subtype.	Many models do not give robust results if used for predictions that are not similar to the training set, slight modifications can result in poor predictions; new models are becoming more robust than older versions.	(Batool et al. 2019; Batool et al. 2019; Schneider et al. 2020; Yu and MacKerell Jr 2016; 174; Acharya et al. 2011)
Data requirements	Without the target's high-quality structural data (experimental and/or homology-modeled target), SBDD is not possible. Also, information with regard to the ligand binding sites can be beneficial and can be used for screening ligands even if detailed information with regard to ligand properties is not available.	Ligands in the training set should have known activities from experimental results (quantitative SAR needs to be established) for the chosen target.	It requires extensive knowledge about biological data, like protein-protein interaction networks and signaling pathways.	It requires large datasets for model training, and complex tasks require more data (adequate data diversity) to generalize the model.	(Batool et al. 2019; Poornima et al. 2016; Schneider et al. 2020; Acharya et al. 2011)

(Continued)

TABLE 4.5 CONTINUED
Comparative Metrics of SBDD, LBDD, Network Pharmacology, and AI/ML Techniques for Drug Discovery

Metrics	SBDD	LBDD	Network Pharmacology	AI/ML Approaches	References
Speed of drug discovery	Virtual screening can identify hit molecules quickly, whereas experimental screening would take months, thus speeding up lead identification and reducing the time required for early stages of drug discovery.	Once a model is set up, it can help with instantaneous lead optimization and drug repurposing.	Network pharmacology can improve the process of identifying effective therapies by providing important information with regard to multi-target combinations with high chances of success.	It can accelerate the drug discovery process by automating many processes at speeds that are beyond human capacity possible by humans.	(Batool et al. 2019; Burki 2020; Zhang et al. 2020; Sadyebekov and Katritch 2023)
Limitations	Predictive performance drops in cases of novel targets and incomplete or low-resolution structures (loop regions may not be represented; tautomers and state of ionization may not have been factored into account); Imperfect scoring functions may give false positives or negatives; Proteins must be in static conformation for SBDD.	It requires sufficient activity and structural data for training, and the models work only if compounds are similar to the training data; it can result in reduced reproducibility if models are overfitting.	Requires large-scale omics data, and the multitarget predictions made are complicated to test in experimental contexts; network models for complex diseases like cancer may not capture the heterogeneity.	The decision boundaries in advanced models are not very discrete, and most models require large datasets to generalize; ML models can be trained on errors or biases in the training data. This can lead to predictions that cannot be interpreted by humans and outcomes that cannot be explained.	(Lionta et al. 2014; Cherkasov et al. 2014; Hassan Baig et al. 2016; Li 2021; Jui and Rivas 2024)

permitted the simultaneous evaluation of the antibacterial activity and ADMET properties. The model worked very well in terms of predicting the profile of an investigational antimicrobial drug (delafloxacin), and the results correlated excellently with experimental findings with respect to the development of drugs against noma (Speck-Planche and Cordeiro 2015). Subsequently, this type of modeling strategy was adopted by the same research group. In this study, data were obtained from the CHEMBL database, and the molecular descriptors were calculated. Their SMILES codes were obtained and stored. The quadratic indices calculated (based on probabilities) based on the structural aspects of the chemicals were integrated with the experimental conditions using the Box-Jenkins approach for mtk-QSBER modeling. The data sets were classified into those that belong to the training and prediction categories. In order to select the best model, linear discriminant analysis (LDA) was employed for data analysis (using STATISTICA program), and the selection was based on data quality and improved power of prediction while minimizing the number of descriptors employed. Several molecular fragments were selected, which were identified in several molecules of the data set. These fragments were processed similarly as was done for the molecules. By comparison, some of the fragments displayed favorable properties under all the experimental conditions tested. Hence, they were selected for the design of an efficacious and safe antibacterial drug (improved PK/PD profile) that satisfied Lipinski's rule of 5 for oral drugs (Speck-Planche and Cordeiro 2017). Another study for NP safety assessment (fullerene-C-60) has documented the utility of this mtk-QSBER model in assessing the safety data for fullerene-C-60 (NP with capabilities of delivering antibacterial drugs) with diverse molecular structures and different experimental conditions by predicting their ADMET profiles. It has been reported that the percentage accuracy is greater than 90% with a good correlation between the theoretical data and experimental proof (V. Kleandrova et al. 2015).

4.10 CONCLUSIONS

Drug design professionals have conventionally adopted a combination of structure and/or ligand and/or network pharmacology-based strategies. Such strategies can be complemented and/or enhanced using the current generation of AI/ML-based tools. AI/ML techniques have made prominent contributions to the analysis of high-throughput data, including virtual screening of compounds for the selection and ranking of drugs with anticancer therapeutic potential. Integrating AI and ML into drug discovery has resulted in significant achievements in human disease therapy (e.g., cancer treatment) including accurate protein structure predictions, predictions of drug-target interactions, and classifications of images of diseased cancerous cells. Even though advancements in this field are promising, there are challenges in integrating AI into current methodologies and ensuring data quality. Ongoing research focuses on utilizing AI to provide effective treatments and better outcomes. In order to ensure the discovery and development of safe and efficacious anticancer drugs, AI engineers and scientists should have effective collaborations with medical professionals and clinical researchers, apart from developing, adopting, and refining model systems that integrate biological and chemical data and provide assessment data in a high-throughput manner. Based on our analysis, the computational and *in silico* strategies discussed can be extended to the screening and selection of drugs for other human disease conditions.

REFERENCES

Abbasi, Maryam, Beatriz P. Santos, Tiago C. Pereira, Raul Sofia, Nelson R. C. Monteiro, Carlos J. V. Simões, Rui M. M. Brito, Bernardete Ribeiro, José L. Oliveira, and Joel P. Arrais. "Designing optimized drug candidates with generative adversarial network." *Journal of Cheminformatics* 14, no. 1 (2022): 40.

Abeel, Thomas, Thibault Helleputte, Yves Van de Peer, Pierre Dupont, and Yvan Saeys. "Robust biomarker identification for cancer diagnosis with ensemble feature selection methods." *Bioinformatics* 26, no. 3 (2010): 392–398.

Acharya, Chayan, Andrew Coop, James E. Polli, and Alexander D. MacKerell. "Recent advances in ligand-based drug design: relevance and utility of the conformationally sampled pharmacophore approach." *Current Computer-aided Drug Design* 7, no. 1 (2011): 10–22.

Agatonovic-Kustrin, S., and Rosemary Beresford. "Basic concepts of artificial neural network (ANN) modeling and its application in pharmaceutical research." *Journal of Pharmaceutical and Biomedical Analysis* 22, no. 5 (2000): 717–727.

Ajjarapu, Suchitra M., Apoorv Tiwari, Pramod Wasudeo Ramteke, Dev Bukhsh Singh, and Sundip Kumar. "Ligand-based drug designing." In *Bioinformatics*, ed. Dev Bukhsh Singh and Rajesh Kumar Pathak, pp.233–252. Academic Press, 2022.

Alam, Sarfaraz, and Feroz Khan. "3D-QSAR studies on maslinic acid analogs for anticancer activity against breast cancer cell line MCF-7." *Scientific Reports* 7, no. 1 (2017): 6019.

Algamal, Zakariya Yahya, Muhammad Hisyam Lee, Abdo M. Al-Fakih, and Madzlan Aziz. "High-dimensional QSAR prediction of anticancer potency of imidazo (4, 5-b) pyridine derivatives using adjusted adaptive LASSO." *Journal of Chemometrics* 29, no. 10 (2015): 547–556.

Allen, Bryce K., Nagi G. Ayad, and Stephan C. Schürer. "Kinome-wide activity classification of small molecules by deep learning." PATTERNS-D-21-00120, http://dx.doi.org/10.2139/ssrn.3879088.

Angermueller, Christof, Tanel Pärnamaa, Leopold Parts, and Oliver Stegle. "Deep learning for computational biology." *Molecular Systems Biology* 12, no. 7 (2016): 878.

Banerjee, Priyanka, Emanuel Kemmler, Mathias Dunkel, and Robert Preissner. "ProTox 3.0: a webserver for the prediction of toxicity of chemicals." *Nucleic Acids Research* 52, no. W1 (2024): W513–W520.

Baselli, Giuseppe, Marina Codari, and Francesco Sardanelli. "Opening the black box of machine learning in radiology: can the proximity of annotated cases be a way?." *European Radiology Experimental* 4, no. 1 (2020): 30.

Bastian, Mathieu, Sebastien Heymann, and Mathieu Jacomy. "Gephi: an open source software for exploring and manipulating networks." Proceedings of the International AAAI Conference on Web and Social Media, vol. 3, no. 1, pp. 361–362, 2009.

Batool, Maria, Bilal Ahmad, and Sangdun Choi. "A structure-based drug discovery paradigm." *International Journal of Molecular Sciences* 20, no. 11 (2019): 2783.

Berman, Helen, Kim Henrick, Haruki Nakamura, and John L. Markley. "The worldwide Protein Data Bank (wwPDB): ensuring a single, uniform archive of PDB data." *Nucleic Acids Research* 35, no. suppl_1 (2007): D301–D303.

Bernard, Denzil, Andrew Coop, and Alexander D. MacKerell. "2D conformationally sampled pharmacophore: a ligand-based pharmacophore to differentiate δ opioid agonists from antagonists." *Journal of the American Chemical Society* 125, no. 10 (2003): 3101–3107.

Bhatia, Trisha, and Shweta Sharma. "Drug repurposing: insights into current advances and future applications." *Current Medicinal Chemistry* 32, no. 3 (2025): 468–510.

Bitencourt-Ferreira, Gabriela, Val Oliveira Pintro, and Walter Filgueira de Azevedo Jr. "Docking with autodock4." In *Docking screens for drug discovery*, ed. Walter Filgueira de Azevedo, Jr, pp. 125–148. New York, NY: Springer New York, 2019.

Breiman, Leo. "Random forests." *Machine Learning* 45 (2001): 5–32.

Brown, Adam S., and Chirag J. Patel. "A standard database for drug repositioning." *Scientific Data* 4, no. 1 (2017): 1–7.

Brown, Kevin R., David Otasek, Muhammad Ali, Michael J. McGuffin, Wing Xie, Baiju Devani, Ian Lawson van Toch, and Igor Jurisica. "NAViGaTOR: network analysis, visualization and graphing Toronto." *Bioinformatics* 25, no. 24 (2009): 3327–3329.

Bruno, Benjamin J., Geoffrey D. Miller, and Carol S. Lim. "Basics and recent advances in peptide and protein drug delivery." *Therapeutic Delivery* 4, no. 11 (2013): 1443–1467.

Buckley, McKenna E., Audrey RN Ndukwe, Pramod C. Nair, Santu Rana, Kathryn E. Fairfull-Smith, and Neha S. Gandhi. "Comparative assessment of docking programs for docking and virtual screening of ribosomal oxazolidinone antibacterial agents." *Antibiotics* 12, no. 3 (2023): 463.

Bundela, Saurabh, Anjana Sharma, and Prakash S. Bisen. "Potential compounds for oral cancer treatment: resveratrol, nimbolide, lovastatin, bortezomib, vorinostat, berberine, pterostilbene, deguelin, andrographolide, and colchicine." *PLoS One* 10, no. 11 (2015): e0141719.

Burki, Talha. "A new paradigm for drug development." *The Lancet Digital Health* 2, no. 5 (2020): e226-e227.

Carrillo Pérez, Francisco. "Development of advanced machine learning models for the fusion of heterogeneous biological sources in clinical decision support systems for cancer." PhD diss., Universidad de Granada, 2023.

Celebi, Remzi, Oliver Bear Don't Walk IV, Rajiv Movva, Semih Alpsoy, and Michel Dumontier. "In-silico prediction of synergistic anti-cancer drug combinations using multi-omics data." *Scientific Reports* 9, no. 1 (2019): 8949.

Chen, Hong, Songhua Hu, Rui Hua, and Xiuju Zhao. "Improved naive Bayes classification algorithm for traffic risk management." *EURASIP Journal on Advances in Signal Processing* 2021, no. 1 (2021): 30.

Chen, Lei, Yu-Hang Zhang, Mingyue Zheng, Tao Huang, and Yu-Dong Cai. "Identification of compound–protein interactions through the analysis of gene ontology, KEGG enrichment for proteins and molecular fragments of compounds." *Molecular Genetics and Genomics* 291, no. 6 (2016): 2065–2079.

Chen, Peng-Yu, and Lin-Tao Han. "Study on the molecular mechanism of anti-liver cancer effect of Evodiae fructus by network pharmacology and QSAR model." *Frontiers in Chemistry* 10 (2023): 1060500.

Chen, Siqi, Tiancheng Li, Luna Yang, Fei Zhai, Xiwei Jiang, Rongwu Xiang, and Guixia Ling. "Artificial intelligence-driven prediction of multiple drug interactions." *Briefings in Bioinformatics* 23, no. 6 (2022): bbac427.

Chen, Xing, Na-Na Guan, Ya-Zhou Sun, Jian-Qiang Li, and Jia Qu. "MicroRNA-small molecule association identification: from experimental results to computational models." *Briefings in Bioinformatics* 21, no. 1 (2020): 47–61.

Cheng, Feixiong, Weiqiang Lu, Chuang Liu, Jiansong Fang, Yuan Hou, Diane E. Handy, Ruisheng Wang et al. "A genome-wide positioning systems network algorithm for in silico drug repurposing." *Nature Communications* 10, no. 1 (2019): 3476.

Cherkasov, Artem, Eugene N. Muratov, Denis Fourches, Alexandre Varnek, Igor I. Baskin, Mark Cronin, John Dearden et al. "QSAR modeling: where have you been? Where are you going to?." *Journal of Medicinal Chemistry* 57, no. 12 (2014): 4977–5010.

Chiu, Yu-Chiao, Hung-I. Harry Chen, Tinghe Zhang, Songyao Zhang, Aparna Gorthi, Li-Ju Wang, Yufei Huang, and Yidong Chen. "Predicting drug response of tumors from integrated genomic profiles by deep neural networks." *BMC Medical Genomics* 12 (2019): 143–155.

Cichonska, Anna, Tapio Pahikkala, Sandor Szedmak, Heli Julkunen, Antti Airola, Markus Heinonen, Tero Aittokallio, and Juho Rousu. "Learning with multiple pairwise kernels for drug bioactivity prediction." *Bioinformatics* 34, no. 13 (2018): i509–i518.

Cortes, Corinna, and Vladimir Vapnik. "Support-vector networks." *Machine Learning* 20 (1995): 273–297.

Da, C., and D. Kireev. "Structural protein–ligand interaction fingerprints (SPLIF) for structure-based virtual screening: method and benchmark study." *Journal of Chemical Information and Modeling* 54, no. 9 (2014): 2555–2561.

Daina, Antoine, Olivier Michielin, and Vincent Zoete. "SwissADME: a free web tool to evaluate pharmacokinetics, drug-likeness and medicinal chemistry friendliness of small molecules." *Scientific Reports* 7, no. 1 (2017): 42717.

De Bacco, Caterina, Daniel B. Larremore, and Cristopher Moore. "A physical model for efficient ranking in networks." *Science Advances* 4, no. 7 (2018): eaar8260.

de Souza Neto, Lauro Ribeiro, José Teófilo Moreira-Filho, Bruno Junior Neves, Rocío Lucía Beatriz Riveros Maidana, Ana Carolina Ramos Guimarães, Nicholas Furnham, Carolina Horta Andrade, and Floriano Paes Silva Jr. "In silico strategies to support fragment-to-lead optimization in drug discovery." *Frontiers in Chemistry* 8 (2020): 93.

Deng, Zhan, Claudio Chuaqui, and Juswinder Singh. "Structural interaction fingerprint (SIFt): a novel method for analyzing three-dimensional protein– ligand binding interactions." *Journal of Medicinal Chemistry* 47, no. 2 (2004): 337–344.

Deshmukh, Amit Laxmikant, Sharat Chandra, Deependra Kumar Singh, Mohammad Imran Siddiqi, and Dibyendu Banerjee. "Identification of human flap endonuclease 1 (FEN1) inhibitors using a machine learning based consensus virtual screening." *Molecular BioSystems* 13, no. 8 (2017): 1630–1639.

Dex Marco Tiu Guibelondo. "Fragment-based drug discovery: a comprehensive overview." *Medicinal Chemistry & Pharmacology*, February 16, 2024. https://pharmafeatures.com/fragment-based-drug-discovery-a-comprehensive-overview/.

Dias, Raquel, and Ali Torkamani. "Artificial intelligence in clinical and genomic diagnostics." *Genome Medicine* 11, no. 1 (2019): 70.

Dimitrov, Sabcho, Gergana Dimitrova, Todor Pavlov, Nadezhda Dimitrova, Grace Patlewicz, Jay Niemela, and Ovanes Mekenyan. "A stepwise approach for defining the applicability domain of SAR and QSAR models." *Journal of Chemical Information and Modeling* 45, no. 4 (2005): 839–849.

Dimmitt, Simon, Hans Stampfer, and Jennifer H. Martin. "When less is more–efficacy with less toxicity at the ED50." *British Journal of Clinical Pharmacology* 83, no. 7 (2017): 1365.

Dotolo, Serena, Anna Marabotti, Angelo Facchiano, and Roberto Tagliaferri. "A review on drug repurposing applicable to COVID-19." *Briefings in Bioinformatics* 22, no. 2 (2021): 726–741.

Duo, Lihui, Yu Liu, Jianfeng Ren, Bencan Tang, and Jonathan D. Hirst. "Artificial intelligence for small molecule anticancer drug discovery." *Expert Opinion on Drug Discovery* 19, no. 8 (2024): 933–948.

Ekins, Sean, Ana C. Puhl, Kimberley M. Zorn, Thomas R. Lane, Daniel P. Russo, Jennifer J. Klein, Anthony J. Hickey, and Alex M. Clark. "Exploiting machine learning for end-to-end drug discovery and development." *Nature Materials* 18, no. 5 (2019): 435–441.

El-Atawneh, Shayma, and Amiram Goldblum. "Candidate therapeutics by screening for multitargeting ligands: combining the CB2 receptor with CB1, PPARγ and 5-HT4 receptors." *Frontiers in Pharmacology* 13 (2022): 812745.

Gayvert, Kaitlyn M., Neel S. Madhukar, and Olivier Elemento. "A data-driven approach to predicting successes and failures of clinical trials." *Cell Chemical Biology* 23, no. 10 (2016): 1294–13.

Ge, Steven Xijin, Dongmin Jung, and Runan Yao. "ShinyGO: a graphical gene-set enrichment tool for animals and plants." *Bioinformatics* 36, no. 8 (2020): 2628–2629.

Gentile, Francesco, Vibudh Agrawal, Michael Hsing, Anh-Tien Ton, Fuqiang Ban, Ulf Norinder, Martin E. Gleave, and Artem Cherkasov. "Deep docking: a deep learning platform for augmentation of structure based drug discovery." *ACS Central Science* 6, no. 6 (2020): 939–949.

Gerdes, Henry, Pedro Casado, Arran Dokal, Maruan Hijazi, Nosheen Akhtar, Ruth Osuntola, Vinothini Rajeeve et al. "Drug ranking using machine learning systematically predicts the efficacy of anti-cancer drugs." *Nature Communications* 12, no. 1 (2021): 1850.

Gilson, Michael K., Tiqing Liu, Michael Baitaluk, George Nicola, Linda Hwang, and Jenny Chong. "BindingDB in 2015: a public database for medicinal chemistry, computational chemistry and systems pharmacology." *Nucleic Acids Research* 44, no. D1 (2016): D1045–D1053.

Gilvary, Coryandar, Jonathan R. Dry, and Olivier Elemento. "Multi-task learning predicts drug combination synergy in cells and in the clinic." *BioRxiv* (2019): 576017.

Golub, Todd R., Donna K. Slonim, Pablo Tamayo, Christine Huard, Michelle Gaasenbeek, Jill P. Mesirov, Hilary Coller et al. "Molecular classification of cancer: class discovery and class prediction by gene expression monitoring." *Science* 286, no. 5439 (1999): 531–537.

Gramatica, Paola. "Principles of QSAR models validation: internal and external." *QSAR & Combinatorial Science* 26, no. 5 (2007): 694–701.

Guo, Shicheng, Fengyang Yan, Jibin Xu, Yang Bao, Ji Zhu, Xiaotian Wang, Junjie Wu et al. "Identification and validation of the methylation biomarkers of non-small cell lung cancer (NSCLC)." *Clinical Epigenetics* 7 (2015): 1–10.

Gupta, Rohan, Devesh Srivastava, Mehar Sahu, Swati Tiwari, Rashmi K. Ambasta, and Pravir Kumar. "Artificial intelligence to deep learning: machine intelligence approach for drug discovery." *Molecular Diversity* 25 (2021): 1315–1360.

Gupta, Sudheer, Kumardeep Chaudhary, Rahul Kumar, Ankur Gautam, Jagpreet Singh Nanda, Sandeep Kumar Dhanda, Samir Kumar Brahmachari, and Gajendra PS Raghava. "Prioritization of anticancer drugs against a cancer using genomic features of cancer cells: a step towards personalized medicine." *Scientific Reports* 6, no. 1 (2016): 23857.

Halgren, Thomas A., Robert B. Murphy, Richard A. Friesner, Hege S. Beard, Leah L. Frye, W. Thomas Pollard, and Jay L. Banks. "Glide: a new approach for rapid, accurate docking and scoring. 2. Enrichment factors in database screening." *Journal of Medicinal Chemistry* 47, no. 7 (2004): 1750–1759.

Han, Manyoung, Seunghwan Jung, and Doheon Lee. "Drug repurposing for Parkinson's disease by biological pathway based edge-weighted network proximity analysis." *Scientific Reports* 14, no. 1 (2024): 21258.

Hassan Baig, Mohammad, Khurshid Ahmad, Sudeep Roy, Jalaluddin Mohammad Ashraf, Mohd Adil, Mohammad Haris Siddiqui, Saif Khan, Mohammad Amjad Kamal, Ivo Provazník, and Inho Choi. "Computer aided drug design: success and limitations." *Current Pharmaceutical Design* 22, no. 5 (2016): 572–581.

Hejase, H. A., and C. Chan. "Improving drug sensitivity prediction using different types of data." *CPT: Pharmacometrics & Systems Pharmacology* 4, no. 2 (2015): 98–105.

Hinnerichs, Tilman, and Robert Hoehndorf. "DTI-Voodoo: machine learning over interaction networks and ontology-based background knowledge predicts drug–target interactions." *Bioinformatics* 37, no. 24 (2021): 4835–4843.

Irwin, John J., and Brian K. Shoichet. "ZINC– a free database of commercially available compounds for virtual screening." *Journal of Chemical Information and Modeling* 45, no. 1 (2005): 177–182.

Itskowitz, Peter, and Alexander Tropsha. "k nearest neighbors QSAR modeling as a variational problem: theory and applications." *Journal of Chemical Information and Modeling* 45, no. 3 (2005): 777–785.

Jain, Ajay N. "Surflex: fully automatic flexible molecular docking using a molecular similarity-based search engine." *Journal of Medicinal Chemistry* 46, no. 4 (2003): 499–511.

Jamal, Salma, Vinita Periwal, OpenSourceDrugDiscovery Consortium, and Vinod Scaria. "Computational analysis and predictive modeling of small molecule modulators of microRNA." *Journal of Cheminformatics* 4 (2012): 1–9.

Janizek, Joseph D., Safiye Celik, and Su-In Lee. "Explainable machine learning prediction of synergistic drug combinations for precision cancer medicine." *BioRxiv* (2018): 331769.

Jeon, Minji, Sunkyu Kim, Sungjoon Park, Heewon Lee, and Jaewoo Kang. "In silico drug combination discovery for personalized cancer therapy." *BMC Systems Biology* 12 (2018): 59–67.

Jones, Gareth, Peter Willett, Robert C. Glen, Andrew R. Leach, and Robin Taylor. "Development and validation of a genetic algorithm for flexible docking." *Journal of Molecular Biology* 267, no. 3 (1997): 727–748.

Jui, Tonni Das, and Pablo Rivas. "Fairness issues, current approaches, and challenges in machine learning models." *International Journal of Machine Learning and Cybernetics* 15, no. 8 (2024): 3095–3125.

Julkunon Holi, Anna Cichonska, Prson Gautam, Sandor Szedmak, Jane Douat, Tapio Pahikkala, Tero Aittokallio, and Juho Rousu. "Leveraging multi-way interactions for systematic prediction of pre-clinical drug combination effects." *Nature Communications* 11, no. 1 (2020): 6136.

Jumper, John, Richard Evans, Alexander Pritzel, Tim Green, Michael Figurnov, Olaf Ronneberger, Kathryn Tunyasuvunakool et al. "Highly accurate protein structure prediction with AlphaFold." *Nature* 596, no. 7873 (2021): 583–589.

Jung, Kenneth, Paea LePendu, and Nigam Shah. "Automated detection of systematic off-label drug use in free text of electronic medical records." *AMIA Summits on Translational Science Proceedings* 2013 (2013): 94.

Kadurin, Artur, Alexander Aliper, Andrey Kazennov, Polina Mamoshina, Quentin Vanhaelen, Kuzma Khrabrov, and Alex Zhavoronkov. "The cornucopia of meaningful leads: applying deep adversarial autoencoders for new molecule development in oncology." *Oncotarget* 8, no. 7 (2016): 10883.

Kavousi, Kaveh, Mojtaba Bagheri, Saman Behrouzi, Safar Vafadar, Fereshteh Fallah Atanaki, Bahareh Teimouri Lotfabadi, Shohreh Ariaeenejad, Abbas Shockravi, and Ali Akbar Moosavi-Movahedi. "IAMPE: NMR-assisted computational prediction of antimicrobial peptides." *Journal of Chemical Information and Modeling* 60, no. 10 (2020): 4691–4701.

Kellenberger, Esther, Nicolas Foata, and Didier Rognan. "Ranking targets in structure-based virtual screening of three-dimensional protein libraries: methods and problems." *Journal of Chemical Information and Modeling* 48, no. 5 (2008): 1014–1025.

Kiefer, Florian, Konstantin Arnold, Michael Künzli, Lorenza Bordoli, and Torsten Schwede. "The SWISS-MODEL Repository and associated resources." *Nucleic Acids Research* 37, no. suppl_1 (2009): D387–D392.

Kim, Sunghwan, Jie Chen, Tiejun Cheng, Asta Gindulyte, Jia He, Siqian He, Qingliang Li et al. "PubChem 2019 update: improved access to chemical data." *Nucleic Acids Research* 47, no. D1 (2019): D1102–D1109.

Kim, Sunghwan, Jie Chen, Tiejun Cheng, Asta Gindulyte, Jia He, Siqian He, Qingliang Li et al. "PubChem 2023 update." *Nucleic Acids Research* 51, no. D1 (2023): D1373–D1380.

Kitchen, Douglas B., Hélène Decornez, John R. Furr, and Jürgen Bajorath. "Docking and scoring in virtual screening for drug discovery: methods and applications." *Nature Reviews Drug Discovery* 3, no. 11 (2004): 935–949.

Kleandrova, V. Valeria, Feng Luan, Alejandro Speck-Planche, and M. N. D. S. Cordeiro. "Review of structures containing fullerene-C60 for delivery of antibacterial agents. Multitasking model for computational assessment of safety profiles." *Current Bioinformatics* 10, no. 5 (2015): 565–578.

Koh, Huan Yee, Anh TN Nguyen, Shirui Pan, Lauren T. May, and Geoffrey I. Webb. "Physicochemical graph neural network for learning protein–ligand interaction fingerprints from sequence data." *Nature Machine Intelligence* 6, no. 6 (2024): 673–687.

Kumar, Sunil, Faheem Abbas, Iqra Ali, Manoj K. Gupta, Saroj Kumar, Manoj Garg, and Deepak Kumar. "Integrated network pharmacology and in-silico approaches to decipher the pharmacological mechanism of Selaginella tamariscina in the treatment of non-small cell lung cancer." *Phytomedicine Plus* 3, no. 2 (2023): 100419.

Lai, Xin, Jinfei Zhou, Anja Wessely, Markus Heppt, Andreas Maier, Carola Berking, Julio Vera, and Le Zhang. "A disease network-based deep learning approach for characterizing melanoma." *International Journal of Cancer* 150, no. 6 (2022): 1029–1044.

Li, Fei, Weisong Liu, and Hong Yu. "Extraction of information related to adverse drug events from electronic health record notes: design of an end-to-end model based on deep learning." *JMIR Medical Informatics* 6, no. 4 (2018): e12159.

Li Lusheng, Mengtao Sun, Jieqiong Wang, and Shibiao Wan. "CHAPTER NINE Multi-omics based artificial intelligence for cancer research." *Advances in Cancer Research* 163 (2024): 303–356.

Li Shao, ed. *Network Pharmacology*, Vol. 15, no. 1. Singapore: Springer, 2021.

Li, Xianhai, Qiang Tang, Fanbo Meng, Pufeng Du, and Wei Chen. "INPUT: an intelligent network pharmacology platform unique for traditional Chinese medicine." *Computational and Structural Biotechnology Journal* 20 (2022): 1345–1351.

Li Zhandong, Lifeng An, Hao Li, ShaoPeng Wang, You Zhou, Fei Yuan, and Lin Li. "Identifying novel genes and chemicals related to nasopharyngeal cancer in a heterogeneous network." *Scientific Reports* 6, no. 1 (2016): 25515.

Lionta, Evanthia, George Spyrou, Demetrios K Vassilatis, and Zoe Cournia. "Structure-based virtual screening for drug discovery: principles, applications and recent advances." *Current topics in Medicinal Chemistry* 14, no. 16 (2014): 1923–1938.

Liu, Ni, and Zhibin Xu. "Using LeDock as a docking tool for computational drug design." In *IOP Conference Series: Earth and Environmental Science*, vol. 218, p. 012143. IOP Publishing, 2019.

Liu, Tiqing, Linda Hwang, Stephen K. Burley, Carmen I. Nitsche, Christopher Southan, W. Patrick Walters, and Michael K. Gilson. "BindingDB in 2024: a FAIR knowledgebase of protein-small molecule binding data." *Nucleic Acids Research* 53, no. D1 (2025): D1633–D1644.

Liu, Xinyi, Shuyuan Wang, Fanlin Meng, Jizhe Wang, Yan Zhang, Enyu Dai, Xuexin Yu, Xia Li, and Wei Jiang. "SM2miR: a database of the experimentally validated small molecules' effects on microRNA expression." *Bioinformatics* 29, no. 3 (2013): 409–411.

López-Vallejo, Fabian, Thomas Caulfield, Karina Martínez-Mayorga, Marc A Giulianotti, Adel Nefzi, Richard A Houghten, and Jose L Medina-Franco. "Integrating virtual screening and combinatorial chemistry for accelerated drug discovery." *Combinatorial Chemistry & High Throughput Screening* 14, no. 6 (2011): 475–487.

Luo, Huimin, Jianxin Wang, Min Li, Junwei Luo, Xiaoqing Peng, Fang-Xiang Wu, and Yi Pan. "Drug repositioning based on comprehensive similarity measures and bi-random walk algorithm." *Bioinformatics* 32, no. 17 (2016): 2664–2671.

Mallik, Saurav, Loveleen Gaur, Soumita Seth, Tapas Bhadra, and Mingqiang Wang. *Landscape of Next Generation Sequencing Using Pattern Recognition: Performance Analysis and Applications*. CRC Press, 2024.

Mikdadi, Dina, Kyle A. O'Connell, Philip J. Meacham, Madeleine A. Dugan, Michael O. Ojiere, Thaddeus B. Carlson, and Juergen A. Klenk. "Applications of artificial intelligence (AI) in ovarian cancer, pancreatic cancer, and image biomarker discovery." *Cancer Biomarkers* 33, no. 2 (2022): 173–184.

Morris, Garrett M., Ruth Huey, William Lindstrom, Michel F. Sanner, Richard K. Belew, David S. Goodsell, and Arthur J. Olson. "AutoDock4 and AutoDockTools4: automated docking with selective receptor flexibility." *Journal of Computational Chemistry* 30, no. 16 (2009): 2785–2791.

Mullard, Asher. "The drug-maker's guide to the galaxy." *Nature* 549, no. 7673 (2017): 445–447.

Munson, Brenton P., Michael Chen, Audrey Bogosian, Jason F. Kreisberg, Katherine Licon, Ruben Abagyan, Brent M. Kuenzi, and Trey Ideker. "De novo generation of multi-target compounds using deep generative chemistry." *Nature Communications* 15, no. 1 (2024): 3636.

Nikolaou, Michail, Athanasia Pavlopoulou, Alexandros G. Georgakilas, and Efthymios Kyrodimos. "The challenge of drug resistance in cancer treatment: a current overview." *Clinical & Experimental Metastasis* 35 (2018): 309–318.

Noble, William S. "What is a support vector machine?" *Nature Biotechnology* 24, no. 12 (2006): 1565–1567.

Nosengo, Nicola. "Can you teach old drugs new tricks?" *Nature 534(7607)*, (2016): 314–316.

Pantuck, Allan J., Dong-Keun Lee, Theodore Kee, Peter Wang, Sanjay Lakhotia, Michael H. Silverman, Colleen Mathis et al. "Modulating BET bromodomain inhibitor ZEN-3694 and enzalutamide combination dosing in a metastatic prostate cancer patient using CURATE. AI, an artificial intelligence platform." *Advanced Therapeutics* 1, no. 6 (2018): 1800104.

Pasrija, Purvashi, Prakash Jha, Pruthvi Upadhyaya, Mohd S. Khan, and Madhu Chopra. "Machine learning and artificial intelligence: a paradigm shift in big data-driven drug design and discovery." *Current Topics in Medicinal Chemistry* 22, no. 20 (2022): 1692–1727.

Pieper, Ursula, Benjamin M. Webb, Guang Qiang Dong, Dina Schneidman-Duhovny, Hao Fan, Seung Joong Kim, Natalia Khuri et al. "ModBase, a database of annotated comparative protein structure models and associated resources." *Nucleic Acids Research* 42, no. D1 (2014): D336–D346.

Pierce, Brian G., Kevin Wiehe, Howook Hwang, Bong-Hyun Kim, Thom Vreven, and Zhiping Weng. "ZDOCK server: interactive docking prediction of protein–protein complexes and symmetric multimers." *Bioinformatics* 30, no. 12 (2014): 1771–1773.

Poornima, Paramasivan, Jothi Dinesh Kumar, Qiaoli Zhao, Martina Blunder, and Thomas Efferth. "Network pharmacology of cancer: from understanding of complex interactomes to the design of multi-target specific therapeutics from nature." *Pharmacological Research* 111 (2016): 290–302.

Preuer, Kristina, Richard PI Lewis, Sepp Hochreiter, Andreas Bender, Krishna C. Bulusu, and Günter Klambauer. "DeepSynergy: predicting anti-cancer drug synergy with Deep Learning." *Bioinformatics* 34, no. 9 (2018): 1538–1546.

Pushpakom, Sudeep, Francesco Iorio, Patrick A. Eyers, K. Jane Escott, Shirley Hopper, Andrew Wells, Andrew Doig et al. "Drug repurposing: progress, challenges and recommendations." *Nature Reviews Drug Discovery* 18, no. 1 (2019): 41–58.

Qu, Jia, Xing Chen, Ya-Zhou Sun, Yan Zhao, Shu-Bin Cai, Zhong Ming, Zhu-Hong You, and Jian-Qiang Li. "In silico prediction of small molecule-miRNA associations based on the HeteSim algorithm." *Molecular Therapy Nucleic Acids* 14 (2019): 274–286.

Qu, Shu-Yue, Xiao-Yue Li, Xia Heng, Yi-Yu Qi, Ping-Yuan Ge, Sai-jia Ni, Zeng-Ying Yao et al. "Analysis of antidepressant activity of huang-lian jie-du decoction through network pharmacology and metabolomics." *Frontiers in Pharmacology* 12 (2021): 619288.

Raali, Rohith, Neha Sivakumar, J. Harsh Vardhan, and P. K. Suresh. "Targeting mitochondrial dynamics: an in-silico approach for repurposing antifungal drugs in OSCC treatment." *Journal of Biomolecular Structure and Dynamics* (2024), 12: 1–14.

Rajkishan, Thakor, Ailani Rachana, Surani Shruti, Patel Bhumi, and Dhaval Patel. "Computer-aided drug designing." *Advances in Bioinformatics* (2021): 151–182.

Rao, Bing, Lichao Zhang, and Guoying Zhang. "ACP-GCN: the identification of anticancer peptides based on graph convolution networks." *IEEE Access* 8 (2020): 176005–176011.

Rarey, Matthias, Bernd Kramer, Thomas Lengauer, and Gerhard Klebe. "A fast flexible docking method using an incremental construction algorithm." *Journal of Molecular Biology* 261, no. 3 (1996): 470–489.

Rathore, Ishan, Vandana Mishra, and Prasenjit Bhaumik. "Advancements in macromolecular crystallography: from past to present." *Emerging Topics in Life Sciences* 5, no. 1 (2021): 127–149.

Rezaee, Parham, Shahab Rezaee, Malik Maaza, and Seyed Shahriar Arab. "Screening of BindingDB database ligands against EGFR, HER2, Estrogen, Progesterone and NF-κB receptors based on machine learning and molecular docking." *Computers in Biology and Medicine* 183 (2024): 109279.

Rifaioglu, Ahmet Sureyya, Esra Nalbat, Volkan Atalay, Maria Jesus Martin, Rengul Cetin-Atalay, and Tunca Doğan. "DEEPScreen: high performance drug–target interaction prediction with convolutional neural networks using 2-D structural compound representations." *Chemical Science* 11, no. 9 (2020): 2531–2557.

Rogers, David, and Mathew Hahn. "Extended-connectivity fingerprints." *Journal of Chemical Information and Modeling* 50, no. 5 (2010): 742–754.

Sadybekov, Anastasiia V., and Vsevolod Katritch. "Computational approaches streamlining drug discovery." *Nature* 616, no. 7958 (2023): 673–685.

Sandercock, Alan M., Steven Rust, Sandrine Guillard, Kris F. Sachsenmeier, Nick Holoweckyj, Carl Hay, Matt Flynn et al. "Identification of anti-tumour biologics using primary tumour models, 3-D phenotypic screening and image-based multi-parametric profiling." *Molecular Cancer* 14 (2015): 1–18.

Sansone, Susanna-Assunta, Peter McQuilton, Philippe Rocca-Serra, Alejandra Gonzalez-Beltran, Massimiliano Izzo, Allyson L. Lister, Milo Thurston, and FAIRsharing Community. "FAIRsharing as a community approach to standards, repositories and policies." *Nature Biotechnology* 37, no. 4 (2019): 358–367.

Sastry, Madhavi, Jeffrey F. Lowrie, Steven L. Dixon, and Woody Sherman. "Large-scale systematic analysis of 2D fingerprint methods and parameters to improve virtual screening enrichments." *Journal of Chemical Information and Modeling* 50, no. 5 (2010): 771–784.

Schneider, Petra, W. Patrick Walters, Alleyn T. Plowright, Norman Sieroka, Jennifer Listgarten, Robert A. Goodnow Jr, Jasmin Fisher et al. "Rethinking drug design in the artificial intelligence era." *Nature reviews drug discovery* 19, no. 5 (2020): 353–364.

Schürer, Stephan C., and Steven M. Muskal. "Kinome-wide activity modeling from diverse public high-quality data sets." *Journal of Chemical Information and Modeling* 53, no. 1 (2013): 27–38.

Sessa, Lucia, Luigi Di Biasi, Simona Concilio, Giuseppe Cattaneo, Alfredo De Santis, Pio Iannelli, and Stefano Piotto. "A new flexible protocol for docking studies." In *Advances in Artificial Life, Evolutionary Computation and Systems Chemistry: 10th Italian Workshop, WIVACE 2015, Bari, Italy, September 22–25, 2015, Revised Selected Papers 10*, pp. 117–126. Springer International Publishing, 2016.

Shannon, Paul, Andrew Markiel, Owen Ozier, Nitin S. Baliga, Jonathan T. Wang, Daniel Ramage, Nada Amin, Benno Schwikowski, and Trey Ideker. "Cytoscape: a software environment for integrated models of biomolecular interaction networks." *Genome Research* 13, no. 11 (2003): 2498–2504.

Sharma, Vidushi, Sharad Wakode, and Hirdesh Kumar. "Structure-and ligand-based drug design: concepts, approaches, and challenges." *Chemoinformatics and Bioinformatics in the Pharmaceutical Sciences* (2021): 27–53.

Sharma, Vishal, Amit Singh, Sanjana Chauhan, Pramod K. Sharma, Shubham Chaudhary, Astha Sharma, Omji Porwal, and Neeraj Kumar Fuloria. "Role of artificial intelligence in drug discovery and target identification in cancer." *Current Drug Delivery* 21, no. 6 (2024): 870–886.

Shen, Yinzhong, Tingyi Liu, Jun Chen, Xin Li, Li Liu, Jiayin Shen, Jiangrong Wang et al. "Harnessing artificial intelligence to optimize long-term maintenance dosing for antiretroviral-naive adults with HIV-1 infection." *Advanced Therapeutics* 3, no. 4 (2020): 1900114.

Sidorov, Pavel, Stefan Naulaerts, Jérémy Ariey-Bonnet, Eddy Pasquier, and Pedro J. Ballester. "Predicting synergism of cancer drug combinations using NCI-ALMANAC data." *Frontiers in Chemistry* 7 (2019): 509.

Singla, Deepak, Sandeep Kumar Dhanda, Jagat Singh Chauhan, Anshu Bhardwaj, Samir K. Brahmachari, Open Source Drug Discovery Consortium, and Gajendra PS Raghava. "Open source software and web services for designing therapeutic molecules." *Current Topics in Medicinal Chemistry* 13, no. 10 (2013): 1172–1191.

Sinha, Sanju, Rahulsimham Vegesna, Sumit Mukherjee, Ashwin V. Kammula, Saugato Rahman Dhruba, Wei Wu, D. Lucas Kerr et al. "PERCEPTION predicts patient response and resistance to treatment using single-cell transcriptomics of their tumors." *Nature Cancer* 5, no. 6 (2024): 938–952.

Speck-Planche, Alejandro, and M. N. D. S. Cordeiro. "Enabling virtual screening of potent and safer antimicrobial agents against noma: mtk-QSBER model for simultaneous prediction of antibacterial activities and ADMET properties." *Mini Reviews in Medicinal Chemistry* 15, no. 3 (2015): 194–202.

Speck-Planche, Alejandro, and M. Natália DS Cordeiro. "De novo computational design of compounds virtually displaying potent antibacterial activity and desirable in vitro ADMET profiles." *Medicinal Chemistry Research* 26 (2017): 2345–2356.

Spitzer, Russell, and Ajay N. Jain. "Surflex-Dock: docking benchmarks and real-world application." *Journal of Computer-aided Molecular Design* 26 (2012): 687–699.

Srivastava, Nitish, Geoffrey Hinton, Alex Krizhevsky, Ilya Sutskever, and Ruslan Salakhutdinov. "Dropout: a simple way to prevent neural networks from overfitting." *The Journal of Machine Learning Research* 15, no. 1 (2014): 1929–1958.

Stathias, Vasileios, Amar Koleti, Dušica Vidović, Daniel J. Cooper, Kathleen M. Jagodnik, Raymond Terryn, Michele Forlin et al. "Sustainable data and metadata management at the BD2K-LINCS Data Coordination and Integration Center." *Scientific Data* 5, no. 1 (2018): 1–14.

Sterling, Teague, and John J. Irwin. "ZINC 15–ligand discovery for everyone." *Journal of Chemical Information and Modeling* 55, no. 11 (2015): 2324–2337.

Stourac, Jan, Juraj Dubrava, Milos Musil, Jana Horackova, Jiri Damborsky, Stanislav Mazurenko, and David Bednar. "FireProtDB: database of manually curated protein stability data." *Nucleic Acids Research* 49, no. D1 (2021): D319–D324.

Sun, Zexuan, Shujun Huang, Peiran Jiang, and Pingzhao Hu. "DTF: deep tensor factorization for predicting anticancer drug synergy." *Bioinformatics* 36, no. 16 (2020): 4483–4489.

Szklarczyk, Damian, Alberto Santos, Christian Von Mering, Lars Juhl Jensen, Peer Bork, and Michael Kuhn. "STITCH 5: augmenting protein–chemical interaction networks with tissue and affinity data." *Nucleic Acids Research* 44, no. D1 (2016): D380–D384.

Szklarczyk, Damian, Annika L. Gable, David Lyon, Alexander Junge, Stefan Wyder, Jaime Huerta-Cepas, Milan Simonovic et al. "STRING v11: protein–protein association networks with increased coverage, supporting functional discovery in genome-wide experimental datasets." *Nucleic Acids Research* 47, no. D1 (2019): D607–D613.

Taha, Mutasem O., Mahmoud A. Al-Sha'er, Mohammad A. Khanfar, and Afaf H. Al-Nadaf. "Discovery of nanomolar phosphoinositide 3-kinase gamma (PI3Kγ) inhibitors using ligand-based modeling and virtual screening followed by in vitro analysis." *European Journal of Medicinal Chemistry* 84 (2014): 454–465.

Tang, Grace H., Meloja Satkunam, Gregory R. Pond, Gregory R. Steinberg, Giovanni Blandino, Holger J. Schünemann, and Paola Muti. "Association of metformin with breast cancer incidence and mortality in patients with type II diabetes: a GRADE-assessed systematic review and meta-analysis." *Cancer Epidemiology, Biomarkers & Prevention* 27, no. 6 (2018): 627–635.

Tauriello, Gerardo, Andrew M. Waterhouse, Juergen Haas, Dario Behringer, Stefan Bienert, Thomas Garello, and Torsten Schwede. "ModelArchive: a deposition database for computational macromolecular structural models." *Journal of Molecular Biology* (2025): 437(15): 168996.

Tingle, Benjamin I., Khanh G. Tang, Mar Castanon, John J. Gutierrez, Munkhzul Khurelbaatar, Chinzorig Dandarchuluun, Yurii S. Moroz, and John J. Irwin. "ZINC-22— A free multi-billion-scale database of tangible compounds for ligand discovery." *Journal of Chemical Information and Modeling* 63, no. 4 (2023): 1166–1176.

Trott, Oleg, and Arthur J. Olson. "AutoDock Vina: improving the speed and accuracy of docking with a new scoring function, efficient optimization, and multithreading." *Journal of Computational Chemistry* 31, no. 2 (2010): 455–461.

Tsou, Lun K., Shiu-Hwa Yeh, Shau-Hua Ueng, Chun-Ping Chang, Jen-Shin Song, Mine-Hsine Wu, Hsiao-Fu Chang et al. "Comparative study between deep learning and QSAR classifications for TNBC inhibitors and novel GPCR agonist discovery." *Scientific Reports* 10, no. 1 (2020): 16771.

Vadapalli, Sreya, Habiba Abdelhalim, Saman Zeeshan, and Zeeshan Ahmed. "Artificial intelligence and machine learning approaches using gene expression and variant data for personalized medicine." *Briefings in Bioinformatics* 23, no. 5 (2022): bbac191.

Vallat, Brinda, Benjamin M. Webb, Arthur Zalevsky, Hongsuda Tangmunarunkit, Monica R. Sekharan, Serban Voinea, Aref Shafaeibejestan et al. "PDB-IHM: a system for deposition, curation, validation, and dissemination of integrative structures." *Journal of Molecular Biology* (2025): 168963.

Vamathevan, Jessica, Dominic Clark, Paul Czodrowski, Ian Dunham, Edgardo Ferran, George Lee, Bin Li et al. "Applications of machine learning in drug discovery and development." *Nature Reviews Drug Discovery* 18, no. 6 (2019): 463–477.

van Westen, Gerard JP, Olaf O. van den Hoven, Rianne van der Pijl, Thea Mulder-Krieger, Henk de Vries, Jorg K. Wegner, Adriaan P. IJzerman, Herman WT van Vlijmen, and Andreas Bender. "Identifying novel adenosine receptor ligands by simultaneous proteochemometric modeling of rat and human bioactivity data." *Journal of Medicinal Chemistry* 55, no. 16 (2012): 7010–7020.

Vivek-Ananth, R. P., Karthikeyan Mohanraj, Ajaya Kumar Sahoo, and Areejit Samal. "IMPPAT 2.0: an enhanced and expanded phytochemical atlas of Indian medicinal plants." *ACS Omega* 8, no. 9 (2023): 8827–8845.

Wang, Chun-Chun, Xing Chen, Jia Qu, Ya-Zhou Sun, and Jian-Qiang Li. "RFSMMA: a new computational model to identify and prioritize potential small molecule–mirna associations." *Journal of Chemical Information and Modeling* 59, no. 4 (2019): 1668–1679.

Wang, Xia, Yihang Shen, Shiwei Wang, Shiliang Li, Weilin Zhang, Xiaofeng Liu, Luhua Lai, Jianfeng Pei, and Honglin Li. "PharmMapper 2017 update: a web server for potential drug target identification with a comprehensive target pharmacophore database." *Nucleic Acids Research* 45, no. W1 (2017): W356–W360.

Wang, Yi-Wei, Lei Huang, Si-Wen Jiang, Kan Li, Jun Zou, and Sheng-Yong Yang. "CapsCarcino: a novel sparse data deep learning tool for predicting carcinogens." *Food and Chemical Toxicology* 135 (2020): 110921.

Wang, Yongcui, Yingxi Yang, Shilong Chen, and Jiguang Wang. "DeepDRK: a deep learning framework for drug repurposing through kernel-based multi-omics integration." *Briefings in Bioinformatics* 22, no. 5 (2021): bbab048.

Wilkinson, Mark D., Michel Dumontier, IJsbrand Jan Aalbersberg, Gabrielle Appleton, Myles Axton, Arie Baak, Niklas Blomberg et al. "The FAIR Guiding Principles for scientific data management and stewardship." *Scientific Data* 3, no. 1 (2016): 1–9.

Wold, Svante, Michael Sjöström, and Lennart Eriksson. "PLS-regression: a basic tool of chemometrics." *Chemometrics and Intelligent Laboratory Systems* 58, no. 2 (2001): 109–130.

Wu, Lianlian, Yuqi Wen, Dongjin Leng, Qinglong Zhang, Chong Dai, Zhongming Wang, Ziqi Liu et al. "Machine learning methods, databases and tools for drug combination prediction." *Briefings in Bioinformatics* 23, no. 1 (2022): bbab355.

Xia, Fangfang, Maulik Shukla, Thomas Brettin, Cristina Garcia-Cardona, Judith Cohn, Jonathan E. Allen, Sergei Maslov et al. "Predicting tumor cell line response to drug pairs with deep learning." *BMC Bioinformatics* 19 (2018): 71–79.

Xu, Hua, Melinda C. Aldrich, Qingxia Chen, Hongfang Liu, Neeraja B. Peterson, Qi Dai, Mia Levy et al. "Validating drug repurposing signals using electronic health records: a case study of metformin associated with reduced cancer mortality." *Journal of the American Medical Informatics Association* 22, no. 1 (2015): 179–191.

Yang, Zhenyu, Xiaoxi Zeng, Yi Zhao, and Runsheng Chen. "AlphaFold2 and its applications in the fields of biology and medicine." *Signal Transduction and Targeted Therapy* 8, no. 1 (2023): 115.

Yu, Lezheng, Runyu Jing, Fengjuan Liu, Jiesi Luo, and Yizhou Li. "DeepACP: a novel computational approach for accurate identification of anticancer peptides by deep learning algorithm." *Molecular Therapy Nucleic Acids* 22 (2020): 862–870.

Yu, Wenbo, and Alexander D. MacKerell Jr. "Computer-aided drug design methods." In *Antibiotics: methods and protocols*, pp. 85–106. New York, NY: Springer New York, 2016.

Zahoránszky-Kőhalmi, Gergely, Timothy Sheils, and Tudor I. Oprea. "SmartGraph: a network pharmacology investigation platform." *Journal of Cheminformatics* 12 (2020): 1–11.

Zdrazil, Barbara, Eloy Felix, Fiona Hunter, Emma J. Manners, James Blackshaw, Sybilla Corbett, Marleen de Veij et al. "The ChEMBL Database in 2023: a drug discovery platform spanning multiple bioactivity data types and time periods." *Nucleic Acids Research* 52, no. D1 (2024): D1180–D1192.

Zhang, Fei, Minghui Wang, Jianing Xi, Jianghong Yang, and Ao Li. "A novel heterogeneous network-based method for drug response prediction in cancer cell lines." *Scientific Reports* 8, no. 1 (2018): 3355.

Zhang, Hongao, Wei Liu, Zhihong Liu, Yingchen Ju, Mengyang Xu, Yue Zhang, Xinyu Wu, Qiong Gu, Zhong Wang, and Jun Xu. "Discovery of indoleamine 2, 3-dioxygenase inhibitors using machine learning based virtual screening." *MedChemComm* 9, no. 6 (2018): 937–945.

Zhang, Hui, Chun-Tao Liu, Jun Mao, Chen Shen, Rui-Ling Xie, and Bo Mu. "Development of novel in silico prediction model for drug-induced ototoxicity by using naïve Bayes classifier approach." *Toxicology in Vitro* 65 (2020): 104812.

Zhang, Qing, Jia Liu, Ruolan Li, Rong Zhao, Mengmeng Zhang, Shujun Wei, Dong Ran, Wei Jin, and Chunjie Wu. "A network pharmacology approach to investigate the anticancer mechanism and potential active ingredients of *Rheum palmatum L.* against lung cancer via induction of apoptosis." *Frontiers in Pharmacology* 11 (2020): 528308.

Zhao, Yuanchun, Xingqi Chen, Jiajia Chen, and Xin Qi. "Decoding Connectivity Map-based drug repurposing for oncotherapy." *Briefings in Bioinformatics* 24, no. 3 (2023): bbad142.

Zhou, Guangyan, Othman Soufan, Jessica Ewald, Robert EW Hancock, Niladri Basu, and Jianguo Xia. "NetworkAnalyst 3.0: a visual analytics platform for comprehensive gene expression profiling and meta-analysis." *Nucleic Acids Research* 47, no. W1 (2019): W234–W241.

Zou, Jinming, Yi Han, and Sung-Sau So. "Overview of artificial neural networks." *Artificial Neural Networks: Methods and Applications* 458 (2009): 15–23.

Section B

Computational Intelligence

Image and Signal Processing Applications

5 A Comparative Study on Hyperspectral Image Enhancement Using Traditional and Deep Learning Methods

Priya K., Rajkumar K. K. and Varsha K.

5.1 INTRODUCTION

Spectral imaging (SI) technology captures a contiguous spectrum of wavelengths over a selected range of intervals for each pixel in the image. So spectral imaging can collect more information than conventional monochromatic and RGB images (Boris Zhukov et al. 1999). The wide range of spectral information makes the hyperspectral image well suited for a wide range of applications like remote sensing, agricultural monitoring, target detection, environmental monitoring, food safety, etc. However, each spectral band in the hyperspectral images is partitioned into several narrow wavelength ranges, limiting the amount of energy received by each band per unit time. Owing to this reason, HSI images are easily influenced by different types of noise, leading to the degradation of the spatial quality of the hyperspectral image. Hence, it is necessary to enhance the spatial quality of hyperspectral image. One of the promising and straightforward approaches for hyperspectral image enhancement is spectral unmixing (SU)-based fusion (Phuntsog 2016).

In spectral unmixing-based fusion, at first hyperspectral image (HSI) and multispectral image (MSI) are unmixed into spectral and spatial data using nonnegative matrix factorization (NMF) (Hsin-Lung Hsieh 2010). NMF has become an emerging tool for processing high-dimensional data because of its automatic feature extraction capability. After the unmixing process is done on both HSI and MSI, we use the coupled nonnegative matrix factorization (CNMF) method to fuse the spectral data from HSI and spatial data from MSI to enhance the hyperspectral image during the reconstruction process (Xu Sun et al. 2015). During the unmixing and fusion process, we incorporate certain constraints like minimum volume (MV), sparsity, and total variance (TV) to our proposed method to improve the quality of the image as well as to strengthen the robustness of the algorithm (Ekanayakea 2020). Furthermore, we implemented a hyperspectral image fusion algorithm on a deep

DOI: 10.1201/9781003532156-7

learning (DL) network to reconstruct a super-resolution hyperspectral image with less computational time and complexity. Finally, a ResNet architecture with different skip connections was used to exploit more detailed features from the images to obtain a high-fidelity reconstructed fusion image (Fengchao 2020).

5.1.1 Motivations

In the literature, substantially more spectral unmixing-based fusion algorithms are already available for reconstructing hyperspectral images with high-quality data. In all these methods, both HS and MS images are fused directly by only considering the linear data in the image and avoiding all outlier data such as low-contrast pixels during the unmixing and fusion process. This outlier data that is ignored by the LMM model characterizes the boundaries, edges of the object, spectral variability, image acquisition time, etc. By reckoning with these outlier data along with LMM fusion, a better reconstructed image is provided with more spatial and spectral information (Ekanayakea 2020). This is one of the challenging tasks that has been neglected by all the existing LMM-based fusion methods. In this work, we propose a novel nonlinear unmixing-based fusion algorithm that accounts for the nonlinear characteristics of the pixel in the image in terms of outlier and spectral and spatial constraints.

5.1.2 Justification

The proposed fusion algorithm reconstructs good spatial and spectral quality HR-HSI. The FCN-CNMF algorithm utilizes all external and internal constraints like MV, TV, and sparsity for both endmember and abundance matrix of the HSI image simultaneously. This helps to obtain optimum spatial and spectral data from the image and also reduces the algorithm's complexity with less computational time. We introduced three controlling parameters α , β , and λ to obtain minimum optimal solution for each of the constraints MV, TV, and sparsity. These parameters are estimated empirically based on the number of spectral bands in the image. Furthermore, we also propose a deep learning-based HS-MS fusion algorithm using Residual Network (ResNet) with different stacked layers and skip connections. Finally, we analyze and compare the performance of both traditional and deep learning-based fusion algorithms in terms of output, accuracy, and computational complexity on the given benchmark datasets.

5.2 SPECTRAL UNMIXING

Spectral unmixing (SU) is one of the most efficient methodologies to deal with mixed pixels in the image to improve the reconstruction and classification accuracy of hyperspectral images. In SU, mixed pixels in each spectrum are decomposed into a collection of pure spectra, named endmembers (also called spectral signatures), and their corresponding fractional component of the pixels, named abundances (also called spatial data), which indicate the proportion of endmembers in the pixel.

The spectral unmixing algorithm is characterized into two mixing models, linear mixing model (LMM) or nonlinear mixing model (NLMM). These mixing models show how the materials in each pixel interact with each other and reflect when light falls on it to form the spectral signatures (Hsin-Lung Hsieh 2010). Many existing studies about spectral unmixing based fusion are reviewed, and it has been found that most of the existing unmixing algorithms are based on the LMM. LMM has become the most popular and widely used SU method because of its simplicity and ease of implementation (Hsin-Lung Hsieh 2010).

5.2.1 Linear Mixing Model (LMM)

LMM is a simple and easiest spectral unmixing method based on the linear reflection of light on an object. The LMM concept helps to analyze the mixed pixel in an image with the assumption that the spectral bands of a mixed pixel are a linear combination of the pure spectra of the components present in the pixel (Xu Sun et al. 2015).

Therefore, LMM can be mathematically modeled as follows:

$$Y = EA + R \tag{5.1}$$

Here, the observed hyperspectral image be $Y = [y_1, \ldots, y_k, \ldots, y_N] \in \mathbb{R}^{L\times N}$ where L is the number of bands and N is the number of pixels. Let p denote the number of endmembers that are empirically estimated from Y. The endmember matrix is represented as $E = [e_1, \ldots, e_P] \in \mathbb{R}^{L\times p}$ and its corresponding abundance matrices are represented as $A = [a_1, \ldots, a_k, \ldots., a_N] \in \mathbb{R}^{p\times N}$. The matrix $R = [r_1, \ldots, r_k, \ldots.,$ $r_N] \in \mathbb{R}^{L\times N}$ is the corresponding residual matrix that is commonly assumed to be Gaussian noise and other residual errors. In the existing literature, the term R is considered to be zero or close to zero. Therefore, in general, LMM-based unmixing can be mathematically represented as

$$Y = EA \tag{5.2}$$

The basic idea of LMM algorithms is to decompose the spectral image into endmembers and fractional abundances. Many endmember extraction algorithms (EEAs) are already available in the literature to identify the spectral components of the image. Most of these algorithms are based on the geometrical approach to select the purest pixel in the image. In addition to this, many EEAs are also available in the literature to identify the endmember signatures, namely the pixel purity index (PPI), vertex component analysis (VCA), N-FINDR, simplex growing algorithm (SGA), and automatic target generation process (ATGP). Similarly, fractional abundance is estimated using partially and fully constrained least squares methods (Ekanayakea 2020).

In this work, we performed unmixing of HSI and MSI based on extrinsic and intrinsic constraints. The extrinsic constraints of the hyperspectral image are based on geometrical and intrinsic constraints within a statistical framework of the image.

By imposing these two constraints on the NMF model, we ultimately aim to enhance the quality of the hyperspectral images in both spectral and spatial data.

The geometrical unmixing (Fengchao 2020) extracts endmember or pure pixels present in the HS image. This spectral information is acquired from the vertices of a simplex. A simplex is a minimum possible hypercube formed by joining the selected data points from the image known as endmembers. This endmember determines the volume of the simplex, which is an indispensable prior consideration in spectral image analysis. It is essential to choose a simplex with minimum volume to control the structural information to improve performance. The centroid-based minimum volume regularizer controls the distance between the center point and endmember vertex. This makes the selected endmember closer to the center point of the simplex denoted by μ (Hongwei 2020).

In statistical spectral unmixing, each pixel of the HS image is decomposed into pure endmember spectra and abundance information based on the posterior distribution of the input image (Lina Zhuang et al. 2019). The statistical information depends on the abundance or spatial quality of the image. In general, abundance sparsity and smoothness are typical constraints applied on the spatial data of spectral images. In this work, we also address nonlinearity effects in the spatial data by introducing an outlier residual term R. The term R accounts for the residual data as well as spectral and spatial variability occurring at specific locations within the image (CédricFévotte 2015).

Incorporating all these extrinsic and intrinsic priors or constraints, our proposed model is mathematically represented by using the objective function:

$$\min f\left(E,A,R\right)=D\left(Y|EA+R\right)+\alpha\varnothing_{\text{MV}}\left(E\right)+\beta\varnothing_{\text{spa}}\left(A\right)+\lambda\varnothing_{\text{TV}}\left(A\right) \quad \text{subjected to } E,A,R\geq 0 \tag{5.3}$$

The matrix R is an outlier function that accounts for the nonlinear effects such as residual data and other spatial and spectral variability. The parameters α, β, and λ are the controlling terms; α controls the simplex with minimum volume, β measures the sparsity elements of the abundance, and λ controls the TV regularization to maintain the spatial smoothness of the image. By incorporating all these parameters, as explained in Equation 5.3, the proposed method achieves an optimum minimization solution to the unmixing problem with high robustness to the signal-to-noise ratio. In each of the optimization steps, E, A, and R are alternately updated until the cost function reaches convergence.

In order to estimate the controlling parameters α, β, and λ, a range of values of abundance map is generated for each endmember of two different datasets separately using the following equation:

$$\text{V}=\frac{1}{\sqrt{\text{L}}}\sum_{l}\frac{\sqrt{\text{N}}-\left\|\text{A}_l\right\|_1/\left\|\text{A}_l\right\|_2}{\sqrt{\text{N}}-1} \tag{5.4}$$

where V is a vector that contains a set of values computed based on each spectral band l of the abundance map A_l in the hyperspectral image with N pixels, L is the total number of bands in the HS image, and $\| \ \|_2$ is the Euclidean norm calculated as the sum of the squares of each pixel in the lth band. The best values for α, β, and λ are estimated empirically by substituting each value of V to obtain a minimum optimal solution for each of these constraints independently (Lei Zhou 2020). In our experiment, we took a pool of values in the range [1e−5–4e−1], which is a commonly used range for V for all the datasets used for experimental purposes. Using this vector V, the best value for the controlling parameter α is computed initially on the constraint MV, followed by evaluating the controlling parameters β and λ on the constraints TV and sparsity. For values of α in the range of 1e−4 to 1e−2, both SAM and RMSE give excellent and stable results, and for all other values of α, both SAM and RMSE show an increasing trend. Therefore, the optimum value of the controlling parameter α is fixed in our model at 1e−3. Figure 5.1 shows the visual representation of the unmixing algorithm for two datasets.

5.3 SPECTRAL UNMIXING-BASED FUSION APPROACH

In recent years, various techniques have been put forward to design image processing algorithms for enhancing the quality of hyperspectral image. One of the most commonly used methods is spectral unmixing-based fusion of hyperspectral (HS) and multispectral (MS) images. In this fusion technique, the HS and MS images observed from the same scenario are unmixed using the endmember and abundance extraction method. Subsequently, high-spectral data from the HS image and high-spatial data from the MS images are fused to reconstruct the high-quality HS image with good spectral and spatial information (Naoto Yokoya et al. 2017).

In this section, we propose a highly stable and robust fusion algorithm based on coupled nonnegative matrix factorization, namely the fully constrained nonlinear coupled nonnegative matrix factorization (FCN-CNMF) algorithm. The FCN-CNMF algorithm aims to enhance the spatial and spectral quality of HSI by using all significant constraints available in the literature. In this method, we use constrained-unmixing method explained in equation 5.3 for extracting both endmember E and abundance A, along with the residual term R, by accounting the nonlinearity nature of the pixels in the image by incorporating minimum volume (MV), total variance (TV), and sparsity constraints. Once E and A are extracted, we then fuse this endmember data from the hyperspectral image with abundance data from the multispectral image by using the FCN-CNMF algorithm. The main contribution of the FCN-CNMF algorithm is to improve the visual quality of the reconstructed HSI image by extracting the nonlinearity effects in the image.

5.3.1 Model Design for Fusion

Let the referenced high-resolution hyperspectral image be $Z \in \mathbb{R}^{L \times N}$ where L is the number of spectral bands and N is the number of pixels. The observed LR-HSI

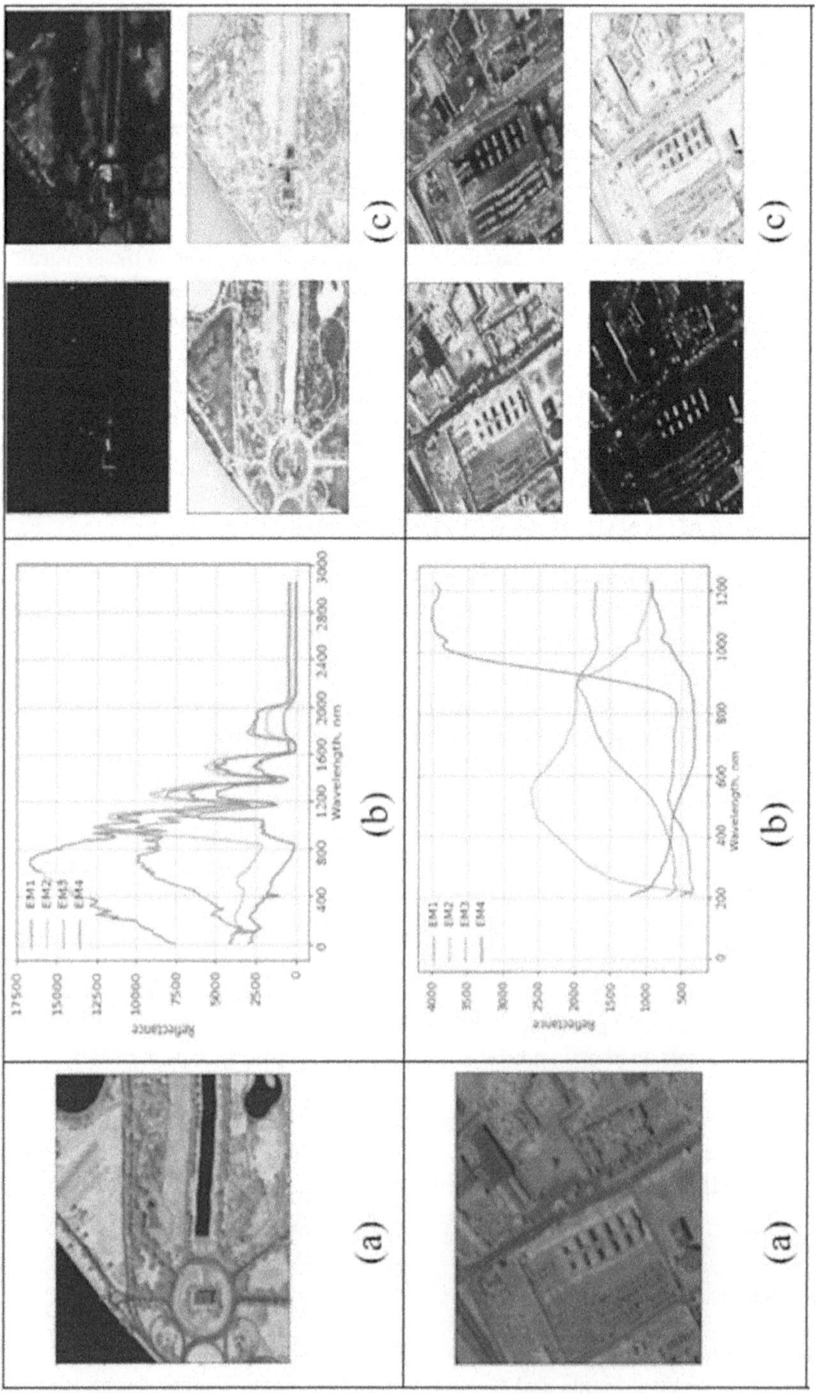

FIGURE 5.1 Unmixing results on two datasets: (a) ground truth image, (b) extracted endmember, and (c) estimated abundance map.

is obtained by downsampling the spatial quality of Z with a Gaussian blur factor d, which is represented as $Y_h \in \mathbb{R}^{L \times N_{/d}}$ with L bands and $N_{/d}$ pixels. Similarly, the observed HR-MSI is obtained by downsampling the spectral quality of Z, and it represented as $Y_m \in \mathbb{R}^{L_m \times N}$ with L_m bands and N pixels, where $L_m < L$ (*Fei Ma 2019*). Therefore, the image is mathematically expressed as follows:

$$Z = EA \tag{5.5}$$

The observed Y_h and Y_m are spectrally and spatially degraded versions of image Z mathematically expressed as:

$$Y_h \approx ZB + R_h \tag{5.6}$$

$$Y_m \approx SZ + R_m \tag{5.7}$$

where $B \in \mathbb{R}^{N \times N_{/d}}$ is a Gaussian blur filter with blurring factor d, which is used to blur the spatial quality of the referenced hyperspectral image Z to obtain LR-HSI, Y_h. The spectral response function $S \in \mathbb{R}^{L_m \times L}$ is used to downsample the spectral quality of the referenced hyperspectral image Z to obtain HR-MSI, Y_m. The term L_m indicates the number of spectral bands used in the multispectral image after downsampling [*intechopen*]. In this work, in order to downsample the spectral values of the referenced image Z we use the concept of the standard Landsat 7 multispectral image that contains a high-quality visual image of Earth's surface as HR-MSI with $L_m = 7$ [*landsat-7*]. Both B and S are sparse matrices containing zeros and ones. In general, the residual matrix R_m and R_h is assumed as zero-mean Gaussian noise in the literature; however, in this work, we make use the residual term R_m and R_h as a nonnegative residual matrix to account for the nonlinearity effects in fusion (Hong and Yokoya 2018).

Therefore, the objective function of our proposed FCN-CNMF model can be expressed as:

$$\begin{aligned} &\min_{E,A,R} \text{CNMF}(E,A,R) + \alpha\varnothing_{\text{MV}}(E) + \beta\varnothing_{\text{TV}}(A) + \lambda\varnothing_{\text{spa}}(A) \\ &\text{subjected to } E, A, \quad R \geq 0 \end{aligned} \tag{5.8}$$

where CNMF(E, A, R) is the unconstrained CNMF method, α β and λ are the controlling parameters to the constraints. The constraints $\varnothing_{\text{MV}}(E)$ that minimize the volume of the simplex in hyperspectral image and extract high-fidelity spectral signature. $\varnothing_{\text{spa}}(A)$ reflects the sparsity that eliminates all zero or null values in abundance and hence reduces the dimensionality of the data. $\varnothing_{\text{TV}}(A)$ provides the smoothness to the image by adjusting the pixel values of adjacent matrices of abundance (Wald 1997). Algorithm 5.1 gives the summary of the proposed FCN-CNMF algorithm.

Algorithm 5.1: FCN-CNMF algorithm

 # This algorithm fuse the high quality endmember E and abundance A obtained by unmixing the HSI, Y_h and MSI, Y_m using unmixing algorithm. S is a degradation matrix and B is the blurring matrix with blurring factor d.

Input:

Z = HR-HSI

Initialize:

$k = 0, E^0 = ATGP(Z), A^0 = FCLS(E^0), R^0 = Z - (E^0A^0)$

Step 1: Y_h = downsaple_spatial(A^0, B,d) *# B,Gaussian blur with blurring factor d*

Step 2: Y_m = downsaple_spectral(E^0,S) *# S is the Spectral downsampling matrix*

Repeat Step 3 to 5 until $\| \tilde{Z} - Z \|_2^2 < \varepsilon$

Step 3: [E, A_h, R_h]=Unmixing(Y_h) *# unmixing Y_h using* Unmixing *function*

Step 4: [E_m, A, R_m]=Unmixing(Y_m) *# unmixing Y_m using* Unmixing *function*

Step 5: $\hat{Z}$= fuse(E, A) *# estimate $\hat{Z}$ by multiplying E and A*

[End of repeat]

Output:

Fused HS image $\hat{Z}$ with high spatial-spectral resolution.

5.3.2 Algorithm Performance FCN-CNMF Algorithm

The performance of the FCN-CNMF algorithm is evaluated using standard quality measures namely SAM, RMSE, SRE, PSNR, and UIQI (Xinyu Zhou 2020) against the baseline unmixing-based fusion methods, namely CNMF and CO-CNMF. The results obtained on two benchmark datasets are shown in Table 5.1. The low values

TABLE 5.1
The Results of Fusion Algorithm on Various Dataset vs Quality Measures

Dataset	Method	CNMF	CO-CNMF	FCN-CNMF
Washington DC Mall	SAM	0.615	0.611	**0.599**
	RMSE	0.52	0.49	**0.46**
	SRE	54.26	55.14	**56.7**
	PSNR	64.03	64.05	**64.12**
	UIQI	0.91	0.89	**0.94**
Pavia University	SAM	0.099	0.073	**0.065**
	RMSE	0.39	0.38	**0.33**
	SRE	54.13	55.33	**55.77**
	PSNR	63.67	64.43	**64.89**
	UIQI	0.87	0.89	**0.93**

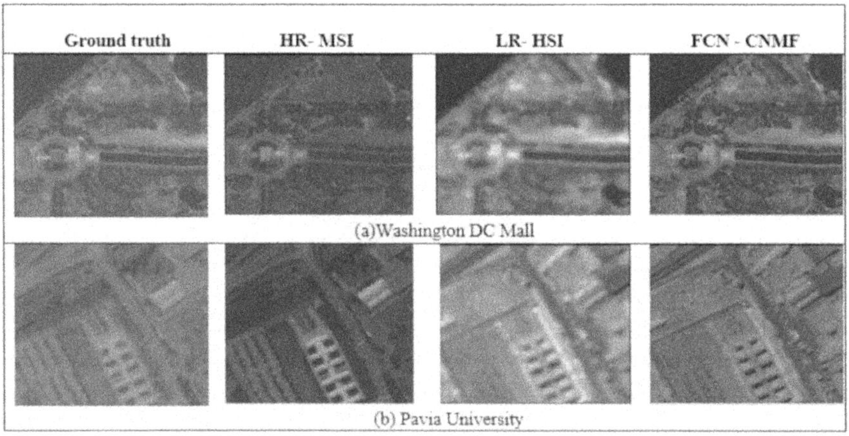

FIGURE 5.2 The ground truth, HR-MSI, LR-HSI, and FCN-CNMF images of datasets.

of the quality measures SAM and RMSE indicate the high spectral quality of the fused image, the high values of SRE and PSNR reflect the high spatial quality of the fused image, and finally, the high value of UIQI reveals the high fidelity of the reconstructed image during the fusion process. Figure 5.2 shows the visual representation of the output from the FCN-CNMF algorithm on two datasets.

5.4 DEEP LEARNING HS-MS FUSION METHODS

In traditional HS-MS fusion methods, the spatial and spectral quality of the reconstructed image highly depends on the various constraints used in the fusion process (Huang et al. 2015). Recently, many hyperspectral image fusion methods based on deep learning (DL) have been introduced in the area of image processing. Deep learning (DL)-based image fusion methods have the ability to extract deep features automatically from the image. Therefore, DL-based methods overcome the difficulties faced during the conventional image fusion methods and make the whole fusion process easier and simpler (Palsson 2017).

Although deep learning-based fusion methods achieved tremendous improvements in their implementation, they still possess several drawbacks (Palsson 2017). As the network goes deeper, its performance gets saturated and then rapidly degrades. This is because, in DL methods, each convolution layer takes inputs from the output of the previous layers, so as it reaches the last layer, a significant amount of meaningful information obtained from the initial layers will be lost. The information loss worsens when the network has a deeper architecture. This leads to negative effects such as overfitting of data, and this effect is called the vanishing gradient problem (Zhang 2015).

Due to the vanishing gradient problem, the existing deep learning-based fusion methods could not extract detailed features from high-dimensional images. He et al. in Zhang (2015) introduced a deep network with residual learning to address the vanishing gradient problem. In this framework, a residual block is added between the layers to diminish performance degradation. The networks with this concept are called Residual Networks or ResNets. Therefore, in this work, our aim is to incorporate this ResNet architecture into the standard CNN to exploit more detailed features from both spatial and spectral data of HSI.

In this section, a deep learning-based HS-MS fusion for the reconstruction of high-fidelity hyperspectral images is presented. A CNN-based HS-MS image fusion is first introduced and its limitations are identified. Subsequently, a novel HS-MS ResNet fusion architecture is introduced using skip connections to overcome the limitations of conventional CNN-based fusion. The ResNet fusion architecture contains residual blocks with different (2, 3, and 4) stacked convolution layers. To overcome the gradient vanishing problem, the ResNet fusion architecture is implemented with three skip connections, namely short, long, and dense skip connections. These skip connections help reduce the number of network parameters and running time to a large extent as the number of skips increases. The procedure for the proposed ResNet fusion algorithm is summarized in Algorithm 5.2.

Algorithm 5.2: ResNet Fusion

Input: LR-Hyperspectral image Y_h and HR-Multispectral image Y_m

begin

1. Extract spectral features from Y_h and spatial features from Y_m using ResNet
2. $r(Y_h) \leftarrow Y_h$ and $r(Y_m) \leftarrow Y_m$
3. **For each residual block in ResNet** i =1,2,3, …, I *# for each residual block*
4. **for** each convolution layer l in the residual block l = 2,3,4

    $\boldsymbol{f(Y_{h1}) = ReLU(W_1 Y_{h1})}$ *# for stacked convolution layer*

    $\boldsymbol{f(Y_{m1}) = ReLU(W_1 Y_{m1})}$

    end for

$\boldsymbol{f_{spec}(Y_{h1}) = f(Y_{h1}) + r(Y_{h1})}$ # adding the residual connection to $\boldsymbol{Y_{h1}}$

$\boldsymbol{f_{spat}(Y_{m1}) = f(Y_{m1}) + r(Y_{m1})}$ # adding the residual connection to $\boldsymbol{Y_{m1}}$

$r(Y_h) \leftarrow \boldsymbol{f_{spec}(Y_{h1})}$

$r(Y_m) \leftarrow \boldsymbol{f_{spat}(Y_{m1})}$

end for

5. $\boldsymbol{F_Z = F_{spec} \times F_{spat}}$ *# The extracted spectral features F_{spec} of size (1 × 1 × Spec) and spatial features F_{spat} of size (Spat × Spat × 1) are fuse together by element-wise multiplication.*

6. $Z = \boldsymbol{ReLU(F_Z)}$ *# Finally, generated HR-HSI after feature embedding and image reconstruction using ReLU activation layer.*

End

Output: HR- Hyperspectral image, Z

TABLE 5.2
The Performance of ResNet Fusion over Traditional Methods

Dataset	Method	FCN-CNMF	CNN	ResNet
Washington DC Mall	SAM	0.5998	0.5956	**0.5171**
	EARGAS	0.5034	0.4993	**0.4850**
	PSNR	64.12	64.19	**65.1358**
	UIQI	0.9409	0.921	**0.9656**
Pavia University	SAM	0.0652	0.0451	**0.0409**
	EARGAS	0.4502	0.4311	**0.4029**
	PSNR	64.892	65.129	**66.112**
	UIQI	0.9316	0.9262	**0.9872**

5.4.1 Algorithm Performance: ResNet Fusion

The performance of CNN and ResNet fusion on two benchmark datasets against the baseline fusion methods, namely CNMF and FCN-CNMF, using standard quality measures such as SAM, ERGAS, PSNR, and UIQI (Priya 2021) is shown in Table 5.2. A low SAM indicates the good spectral data in the fused image, and a low ERGAS reflects the statistical quality of the reconstructed image. High PSNR and UIQI values show good spatial quality and high fidelity of the reconstructed image with less spectral distortion.

The above work is extended by introducing different stacked convolution layers in the residual block of the ResNet, and the results are shown in Table 5.3. From Table 5.3, we conclude that the ResNet fusion network with two stacked convolution layers guaranteed the quality of the reconstructed image.

TABLE 5.3
Performance of ResNet with Varying Stacked Layers

		Number of Stacked Convolution Layers		
Dataset	Methods	2 layers	3 layers	4 layers
Pavia University	SAM	0.0409	0.065	0.069
	EARGS	0.4029	0.4029	0.4029
	PSNR	66.17	66.117	66.117
	UIQI	0.9872	0.9713	0.9622
Washington DC Mall	SAM	0.5171	0.5529	0.5721
	EARGS	0.4850	0.4850	0.4850
	PSNR	65.13	65.135	65.135
	UIQI	0.9656	0.9432	0.9209

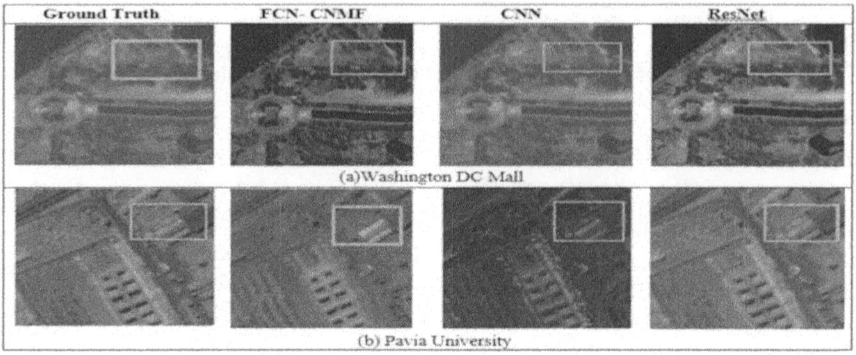

FIGURE 5.3 The output image of the ResNet method and traditional methods.

TABLE 5.4
Performance of Different Skip Connections

Architecture	Number of Parameters
CNN	31,586,081 million
ResNet with short skip	8,045,825 million
ResNet with long skip	390,529 million
ResNet with dense skip	19,393 million

Figure 5.3 shows a visual representation of the output provided by our proposed ResNet fusion method on two benchmark datasets against all other baseline methods. From the figure, it is evident that ResNet fusion with 2-stacked convolution layers produces better performance in most of the areas in the image (highlighted) of the two datasets.

We further extended the ResNet fusion architecture to reduce the number of parameters to make our proposed method more efficient and effective in handling high-dimensional data. For that, we used short skip, long skip, and dense skip connections to the ResNet architecture with 2-stacked convolution layers. Table 5.4 gives the total number of network parameters required for this ResNet architecture in each skip connection. From Table 5.4, it is clear that the ResNet architecture with dense skip connections provides fewer network parameters compared to the ResNet with short and long skip connections.

5.5 CONCLUSION

In this chapter we proposed a novel nonlinear spectral unmixing-based fusion algorithm and a ResNet-based deep fusion network for enhancing the spectral and spatial quality of hyperspectral images. The proposed FCN-CNMF for HS-MS image

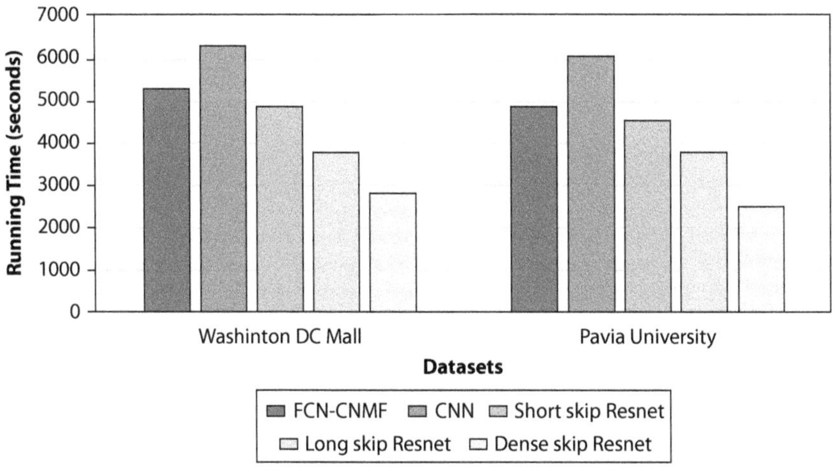

FIGURE 5.4 Running time comparison of traditional and deep learning HS-MS image fusion methods.

fusion algorithm introduced nonlinearity to the NMF method while unmixing by adding constraints such as MV, TV, and Sparsity along with the residual term and reconstructing HR-HSI having good spatial and spectral quality.

Alternatively, we proposed a ResNet architecture, a deep learning-based HS-MS fusion algorithm, to overcome the high computational cost of the FCN-CNMF method. We also modified the ResNet architecture with different stacked layers and skip connections, and on implementation we found that the ResNet with two stacked layers and dense skip connections improved the reconstruction quality of images with a minimum number of network parameters. Further, we compared the running times of all the traditional and deep learning-based HS-MS fusion algorithms with our proposed methods FCN-CNMF, CNN, and ResNet fusion on benchmark datasets as shown in Figure 5.4. Finally we concluded that ResNet fusion with dense skip connections provides excellent results in HS-MS fusion.

5.6 CONTRIBUTION

We introduced a novel fusion algorithm, FCN-CNMF, for HSMS image fusion that reconstructs HR-HSI with good spatial and spectral quality. The FCN-CNMF algorithm utilizes the NMF-based unmixing algorithm for extracting spectral and spatial data of HS and MS images and produces a high-fidelity hyperspectral image. During the unmixing process, nonlinear characteristics of the pixel in the image are accounted for by imposing constraints such as MV, TV, and Sparsity. We also introduced three controlling parameters α , β, and λ to obtain a minimum optimal solution for each of these constraints. Therefore, the proposed fusion algorithm reduces complexity and computational time by independently incorporating outlier and other spectral and spatial constraints into the NMF method. Alternatively, we introduced deep learning-based HS-MS fusion algorithms CNN and ResNet fusion to overcome the high computational cost of the FCN-CNMF method. We utilized different stacked layers and skip connections to the ResNet fusion architecture to improve the performance of the ResNet-based deep fusion.

REFERENCES

Ekanayakea et al., "Constrained Nonnegative Matrix Factorization for Blind Hyper-spectral Unmixing Incorporating Endmember Independence", in *IEEE Journal of Selected Topics in Applied Earth Observations and Remote Sensing*, vol. 14, pp. 11853–11869, 2021.

Francesco Claudio, GIS based approach for NDVI application to Landsat 7 ETM+imagery and thematic accuracy evaluation, *IOSR Journal of Applied Geology and Geophysics,* (IOSR-JAGG), vol. 9, no. 5, pp. 34–40, October 2021.

C. Févotte and N. Dobigeon, "Nonlinear Hyperspectral Unmixing With Robust Nonnegative Matrix Factorization", *IEEE Transactions on Image Processing*, vol. 24, pp. 4810–4819, 2015.

Hongwei Han, Guxi Wang, Maozhi Wang, Jiaqing Miao, Si Guo, Ling Chen, Mingyue Zhang, and Ke Guo, "Hyperspectral Unmixing Via Nonconvex Sparse and Low-Rank Constraint", *IEEE Journal of Selected Topics in Applied Earth Observations and Remote Sensing*, vol. 13, pp. 5704–5718, 2020.

K. He, X. Zhang, H. Ren, and J. Sun, "Deep Residual Learning for Image Recognition", in *Proceedings of the IEEE Conference on Computer Vision and Pattern Recognition.* IEEE, June, pp. 770–778, 2015.

D. Hong, N. Yokoya, J. Chanussot, and X. Zhu, "An Augmented Linear Mixing Model to Address Spectral Variability for Hyperspectral Unmixing, ", *IEEE Transactions on Image Processing*, vol. 28, no.4 , pp. 1923–1938, 29 October 2018.

Hsin-Lung Hsieh and Jen-Tzung Chien, "A New Nonnegative Matrix Factorization for Independent Component Analysis", *IEEE International Conference on Acoustics, Speech and Signal Processing*, 28 June 2010, doi:10.1109/ICASSP.2010.5494945.

W. Huang, L. Xiao, Z. Wei, H. Liu, and S. Tang, "A New Pan-sharpening Method with Deep Neural Networks", *IEEE Geoscience and Remote Sensing Letters*, vol. 12, pp. 1037–1041, 2015.

Fei Ma, Feixia Yang, Ziliang Ping, and Wenqin Wang. "Joint Spatial-Spectral Smoothing in a Minimum-Volume Simplex for Hyperspectral Image Super-Resolution", 10, 237, *Applied Sciences*, 2019.

F. Palsson, J.R. Sveinsson, and M.O. Ulfarsson, "Multispectral and Hyperspectral Image Fusion Using a 3-Dconvolutional Neural Network", *IEEE Geoscience and Remote Sensing Letters*, vol. 14, 639–643, 2017.

K. Priya and K.K. Rajkumar, "Multiplicative Iterative Nonlinear Constrained Coupled Nonnegative Matrix Factorization (MINC-CNMF) for Hyperspectral and Multispectral Image Fusion", 12.6, *International Journal of Advanced Computer Science and Applications*, 2021.

M. Simoes et al, A convex formulation for hyperspectral image superresolution via subspace based regularization , *IEEE Transaction Geoscience and Remote Sensing*, vol 53, no. 6, pp. 3373–3380 June 2015.

Xu Sun, Lina Yang, Bing Zhang X, Lianru Gao, and Jianwei Gao, "An Endmember Extraction Method Based on Artificial Bee Colony Algorithms for Hyperspectral Remote Sensing Images", *Remote Sensing*, vol. 7, pp. 16363–16381, 2015, doi:10.3390/rs71215814.

Phuntsog Tundup A.P. Rai, and Malvika Sharma, "Remote Sensing and Its Role in Agriculture", *Global Journal of Bio-science and Biotechnology*, vol. 5, pp. 432–436, 2016.

L. Wald, T. Ranchin, and M. Mangolini, "Fusion of Satellite Images of Different Spatial Resolutions: Assessing the Quality of Resulting Images", *Photogrammetric Engineering & Remote Sensing*, vol. 63, no. 6, pp. 691–699, 1997.

Fengchao Xiong, Jun Zhou, Jianfeng Lu, and Yuntao Qian, "Nonconvex Nonseparable Sparse Nonnegative Matrix Factorization for Hyperspectral Unmixing", *IEEE Journal of Selected Topics in Applied Earth Observations and Remote Sensing*, vol. 13, pp. 6088–6100, 2020.

Naoto Yokoya, Claas Grohnfeldt, and Jocelyn Chanussot Magazine, "Hyper-spectral and Multi-spectral Data Fusion, A Comparative Review of the Recent Literature", *IEEE Geoscience and Remote Sensing*, June 2017, doi: 10.1109/MGRS.2016.2637624

Lei Zhou, Xueni Zhang, Jianbo Wang, Xiao Bai, Lei Tong, Liang Zhang, Jun Zhou, and Edwin Hancock, "Subspace Structure Regularized Nonnegative Matrix Factorization for Hyperspectral Unmixing", *IEEE Journal of Selected Topics in Applied Earth Observations and Remote Sensing*, vol. 13, pp. 4257–4270, 2020.

Xinyu Zhou, Ye Zhang, Junping Zhang, and Shaoqi Shi. "Alternating Direction Iterative Nonnegative Matrix Factorization Unmixing for Multispectral and Hyperspectral Data Fusion", 13, pp. 5223–5232, *IEEE Journal of Selected Topics in Applied Earth Observations and Remote Sensing*, 2020.

Lina Zhuang, Chia-Hsiang Lin, Mário A.T. Figueiredo, and José M. Bioucas-Dias, "Regularization Parameter Selection in Minimum Volume Hyperspectral Unmixing", *IEEE Transactions on Geoscience and Remote Sensing*, vol. 57(12), pp. 9858–9877, 2019.

Boris Zhukov, Dieter Oertel, Franz Lanzl, and Gotz Reinhackel, "Unmixing-based Multisensor Multiresolution Image Fusion", *IEEE Transactions on Geoscience and Remote Sensing*, vol. 37(3), pp. 1212–1226, 1999, doi:10.1109/36.763276

Yokoya et al, Coupled Nonnegative Matrix Factorization Unmixing for Hyperspectral and Multispectral Data Fusion. *IEEE Transaction on Geoscience and Remote Sensing*, vol 50, no.2 pp. 528–537, 2012.

6 Emotion Recognition for Images and Audios by Cross-Model with Deep Learning

R. Raja Subramanian, R. Raja Sudharsan, S. Sridevi, Balabhadra Nikhitha, Bedamsetty Visali, Bandikattu Snehalatha and Bokkisam Akshitha

6.1 INTRODUCTION TO EMOTION RECOGNITION

Facial emotion recognition, also known as facial emotion evaluation or facial expression recognition, is a field that has gained significant prominence in recent years, specializing in the automated detection and understanding of human emotions through analyzing facial expressions. Humans are very sophisticated and are capable of showing different emotions that can be simple or complex to understand through different forms like expressions, texts, and audio. The primary goals for emotion recognition models are to identify someone's emotions and their feelings, observed through classifying expressions and their motives, which can be hard to signify. The automatic system of emotion recognition is a significant area of research. The human face is a wonderful canvas of emotions, capable of conveying a wide range of emotions, along with emotions like anger, surprise, fear, and many more.

Recognizing these emotions in an accurate and timely manner can give deep insights into human behavior and enable programs that enhance our daily lives. In this period of advancing generation, know-how and decoding feelings through facial expressions have come to be helpful. Programs of facial emotion recognition are various and impactful, along with customized person studies, mental health evaluation, protection, and market research. As the integration of machines and humans becomes more popular, it is important that their interaction becomes smoother and more natural. To accomplish this, machines must possess the capability to understand the surrounding environment, particularly the intentions of human beings.

Emotion recognition plays a crucial role in various real-world applications, including human-computer interaction, healthcare, and security. In human-computer interaction, accurate emotion detection enables more natural and adaptive AI systems, improving user experience in virtual assistants and interactive robots. In healthcare, emotion recognition assists in mental health assessment and early diagnosis of mood

 DOI: 10.1201/9781003532156-8

disorders, providing valuable insights for patient care. Security applications benefit from behavioral analysis and threat detection, where emotional cues help identify suspicious activities. Traditional emotion recognition techniques, such as rule-based or handcrafted feature extraction methods, often struggle with variability in facial expressions and speech patterns, leading to reduced accuracy in diverse real-world scenarios. Deep learning, particularly CNNs and RNNs, has significantly improved emotion classification by automatically extracting high-level features from images and audio. However, unimodal approaches remain limited in capturing the full spectrum of human emotions. To address these challenges, multimodal emotion recognition has emerged as a powerful solution by integrating facial expressions and speech signals, leading to more robust and context-aware models. This study explores deep learning-based multimodal emotion recognition, demonstrating its effectiveness in improving accuracy and reliability across different domains.

Nowadays, machines have access to various means of capturing environmental data, such as cameras, microphones, etc. By utilizing this information with suitable algorithms, machines can generate a perception of their surroundings. Emotion recognition is a crucial component in enabling machines to fulfill their intended purpose more effectively. Facial expressions deliver information about the subject's internal emotional state. If a machine is capable of acquiring a series of facial images, the application of deep learning techniques could enable machines to determine the mood of their interlocutors. Emotions can be easily recognized from facial expressions or speech signals. Emotional displays convey substantial information regarding an individual's mental state. Facial expressions and speech signals possess inherent advantages that render them a valuable source for affective computing.

6.2 RELATED WORKS

Significant progress has been achieved for emotion recognition through the utilization of facial and audio recognition techniques applied to audio and video signals. Nowadays, the utilization of facial emotion recognition in the field of human-computer interaction (HCI) is becoming an emerging trend [1, 2]. Emotion recognition for both image and audio data is an important field with applications in various sectors like entertainment, human-computer interaction, and healthcare sector. Recognizing the emotions from audio and images is a multidisciplinary field that employs computer vision, audio processing, and machine learning techniques to understand and interpret human emotions from visual and auditory data [3–6].

6.2.1 Emotion Recognition Based on Images

Recognizing facial features is a vital part in the human-computer interaction that allows computers to recognize facial expressions based on human thinking. The process of human communication is completely linked to the movement of various emotions. When humans are experiencing simple feelings, their faces will show a variety of expression styles, each with its own set of characteristics and distribution scale. Recognition of emotions based on images is a technology that utilizes computer vision and deep learning mechanisms [7–9] for analyzing and interpreting human emotions from images or videos. This area of research gained prominent attention in this era due to its essentiality in various applications like healthcare, marketing, human-computer interaction, and psychology. Recognizing emotions from facial expressions is a common approach. Researchers have developed various models like convolutional neural networks (CNNs) using deep learning to detect and classify emotions based on facial expressions or facial features. Transfer learning techniques like pre-trained models [10–14] such as VGG16, VGG19, ResNet50, ResNet101, InceptionV3, and EmotNetB0 have been utilized to efficiently increase the performance of models to recognize the emotions.

According to the processing of facial expression recognition, the process can be broadly categorized into three:

- Face detection
- Feature extraction
- Classification module

Face detection is to detect and locate faces within the images or frames of a video. Face detection is a computer technology being utilized in the selection of applications that identifies human faces in virtual images. Face detection additionally refers back to the psychological technique by which humans find and attend to faces in a visible scene. Feature extraction is used for selecting a sufficient set of feature factors that represent the important characteristics of the human face and that may be extracted effortlessly; this is the fundamental challenge that a successful facial feature extraction method has to answer. The classification module is used for identifying what an image is representing, which is a challenging task and is said to be image classification. To realize various classes of images, an image classification model is built and trained to perform the best.

6.2.2 Audio-Based Emotion Recognition

Audio-based emotion recognition is a field of research and technology that focuses on identifying and understanding human emotions from audio and speech signals. Audio is another way for humans to express emotions. The audio signals expressed by humans in different emotional states have distinct characteristics and rules, such as speed, pitch, duration, etc. The emotion recognition technique based on audio is to become aware of and decide the emotional statistics of the speaker's speech in various emotional states [15–17]. Speech can be considered a complex natural mechanism of human interaction that carries linguistic information along with paralinguistic information. The paralinguistic information comprises emotions, gender, age, and many more unique human attributes, while linguistic information comprises the language and context of the speech. Several studies show that audios could be a simple way to demonstrate a connection between humans and machines. Audio-based emotion recognition continues to evolve with advancements in deep learning [18–20] and the availability of large labeled datasets. As technology improves, it holds the potential to enable more natural and empathetic human-computer interactions in various applications. Audio-based emotion recognition is a subfield of affective computing that concentrates on identifying and classifying human emotions by analyzing audible characteristics derived from audio signals or from video.

6.3 DATASET FOR FACIAL AND AUDIO-BASED EMOTION RECOGNITION

The facial emotion recognition dataset contains seven emotion types. The facial emotion detection dataset is from Kaggle[21] , which contains 35,685 examples of different emotions, each of size 48 × 48 pixels in grayscale. In this dataset, the images are split into training and test data. These images are designated based on the emotions depicted in the human faces. Considered emotion types: fear, anger, surprise, disgusted, happy, neutral, and sad.

The Toronto emotional speech set (TESS) dataset is used for recognizing emotion through the audio. The considered dataset contains only female actor audio, which is of high quality despite the other datasets that mostly contain male audio, and this may result in a slight imbalance in representing emotions. This optimization could serve as a good training dataset for the classification of emotions in generalizing but not overfitting the model. In this dataset, there is a collection of 200 target words that were spoken and contain recordings that portray seven different emotion types (happy, sad, fearful, neutral, disgusted, surprise, and angry). The dataset comprises 2800 recordings or audio files. The dataset is spectacularly arranged in such a way that each of any two female actor audio files and respective emotions are organized within their own folder. In each of such folders, every audio file contains all the 200 target words in WAV format. The TESS dataset used for audio-based emotion recognition consists only of female voices, leading to a potential gender bias in model training. This limitation has now been acknowledged in the discussion section. To mitigate this, future work will incorporate datasets with both male and female speakers to improve model generalizability. Additionally, data augmentation techniques such as pitch shifting and voice modulation will be explored to artificially balance the dataset.

6.4 PROPOSED METHODOLOGY FOR EMOTION RECOGNITION FROM MULTIMODAL DATA

Emotion recognition using both image and audio datasets, often referred to as multimodal emotion recognition, can yield more accurate results by leveraging complementary information from multiple sources. This analysis concentrates mostly on deep neural network-based solutions that can be achieved for recognizing a wide range of human emotions.

6.4.1 Data Collection and Preprocessing

Collect a variety dataset of facial expressions and audio recordings with corresponding feelings. Annotate the data with labels indicating emotion types. Ensure that the dataset contains a diverse range of emotional expressions and that the labels accurately reflect the emotions conveyed.

6.4.2 Image Data Preprocessing

Preprocessing the data, which may include resizing images and augmentation of data to improve and increase the diversity of the considered dataset. Resize images to a consistent size. Apply data augmentation techniques to increase dataset diversity. Normalize pixel values to a common scale. We may also augment the dataset with techniques like rotation, cropping, and brightness adjustments.

6.4.3 Audio Data Preprocessing

Convert audio data into a suitable format. Extract relevant features such as spectrograms. Normalize audio data to a consistent scale. For the audio data preprocessing, we can perform noise reduction, resampling, and feature extraction like pitch, intensity, and energy. Ensuring that all audio files should have the same sampling rate. Apply data augmentation for audio data, which includes stretching the time, pitch shifting, and many more. Audio visualization of waveforms of different emotions is depicted in Figures 6.1 and 6.2; angry emotions exhibit higher amplitude fluctuations

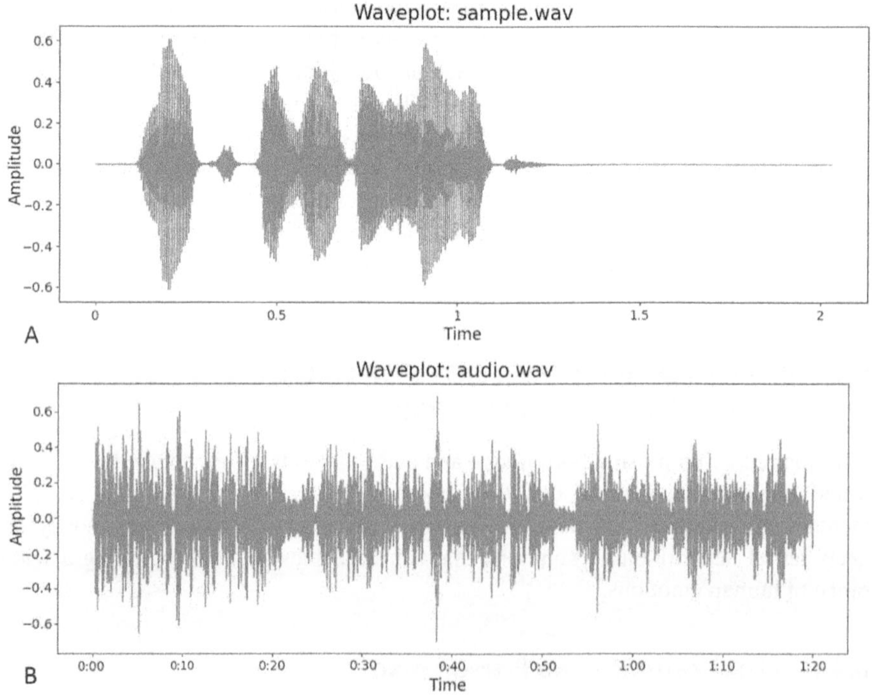

FIGURE 6.1 Sample waveform showing amplitude (*Y* axis).

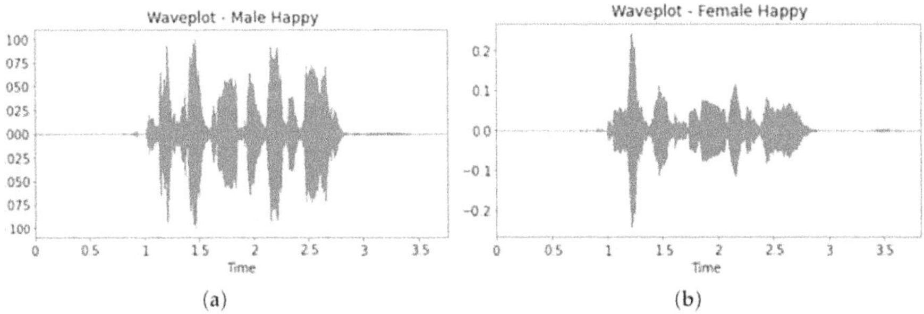

FIGURE 6.2 Waveform showing amplitude (*Y* axis) for various emotions in audio data.

due to increased vocal intensity, whereas sad emotions display smoother and lower amplitude variations. These patterns help distinguish different emotions effectively in the proposed model.

6.4.4 Feature Extraction

Feature extraction is a critical step for any classification task, as it determines how relevant patterns are identified in the data.

- **Image-Based Feature Extraction**: Convolutional neural networks (CNNs) are used for extracting spatial features from images. These networks apply convolutional layers to process images, identifying patterns such as edges, textures, and other hierarchical features that are crucial for classification tasks. CNN-based feature extraction leverages techniques like pooling, padding, and activation functions to ensure efficient representation.
- **Audio-Based Feature Extraction**: For audio classification, time-domain waveforms are transformed into a frequency domain representation, enabling detailed analysis of spectral and temporal features. Techniques such as spectrogram generation and wave representations are employed. A spectrogram provides a visual representation of the audio signal's frequency content over time, while waveforms offer amplitude variations. Features like Mel-Frequency Cepstral Coefficients (MFCCs) may also be computed to represent audio in a compact and meaningful form for the classification model.

6.4.5 Model Selection

The choice of the model greatly impacts the accuracy and performance of the classification task. *Pre-Trained Models for Image Classification*: Models like VGG16, VGG19, ResNet50, ResNet101, and InceptionV3 are used for the image-based tasks. These models are pre-trained on large-scale datasets such as ImageNet, allowing them to serve as strong initial frameworks. *VGG Family*: These are simple, deep networks with uniform architecture, which are particularly useful in detecting hierarchical features in images. *ResNet Models*: These utilize skip connections to address the vanishing gradient problem, making them suitable for deeper networks and complex tasks. *InceptionV3:* This model incorporates an intelligent module design to handle computational efficiency while maintaining high accuracy. *Audio Models:* For audio classification tasks, either dedicated frameworks or adaptations of CNNs are used to classify audio features derived from spectrograms and MFCCs. These methods integrate well with audio-emotion detection systems.

The training process is vital to create an effective model that generalizes well to unseen data. The dataset is divided into training, validation, and test sets. The training set is used for optimizing the model parameters, the validation set is used to tune hyperparameters, and the test set is reserved for final evaluation. Splitting is performed with careful balance to ensure that all classes are represented proportionately. Appropriate loss functions and optimizers are chosen for the task. Cross-entropy loss is often used for classification tasks as it measures the difference between predicted and actual class probabilities. Optimizers like Adam or stochastic gradient descent (SGD) are employed to adjust weights during backpropagation efficiently. Regularization techniques such as dropout and batch normalization are applied to prevent overfitting and improve generalization.

In Figure 6.3, to perform the training process, a dataset is considered in Kaggle for image and audio separately, where both datasets contain seven emotions (happiness, neutral, sadness, anger, surprise, disgust, and fear). After choosing the dataset, preprocessing of data is performed on the image and audio datasets. For the image dataset, this includes resizing images to a consistent size, which creates input size of the model, and normalizing the pixel values. For the audio dataset, preprocessing involves ensuring that all audio files should have the same sampling rate, normalizing the audio data to a standard range, and converting the audio signals into spectrograms. After preprocessing, features are extracted from the image dataset, such as facial landmarks, texture features, and color features, to capture the information about emotional content. For the audio dataset, features such as pitch, intensity, and duration are extracted. After identifying the features, , the training phase of the model starts. This is the model training phase for the considered dataset. In the testing phase, the trained model is loaded, and a video is used for extracting both image frames and audio signals. After that, model evaluation is done separately for image frames and audio signals using the EmotNet and AUDIO EmotNet models. Emotions are recognized by both models, and the retrieved emotions are compared with the actual emotions. This is how emotion recognition is performed for image and audio datasets.

6.5 EXPERIMENTATION AND RESULTS

For emotion detection through facial expressions, data was collected from 50 subjects for testing. Then, the accuracy achieved at 100 epochs for image classification is 80%, while the accuracy achieved at 100 epochs for video classification is 100%.

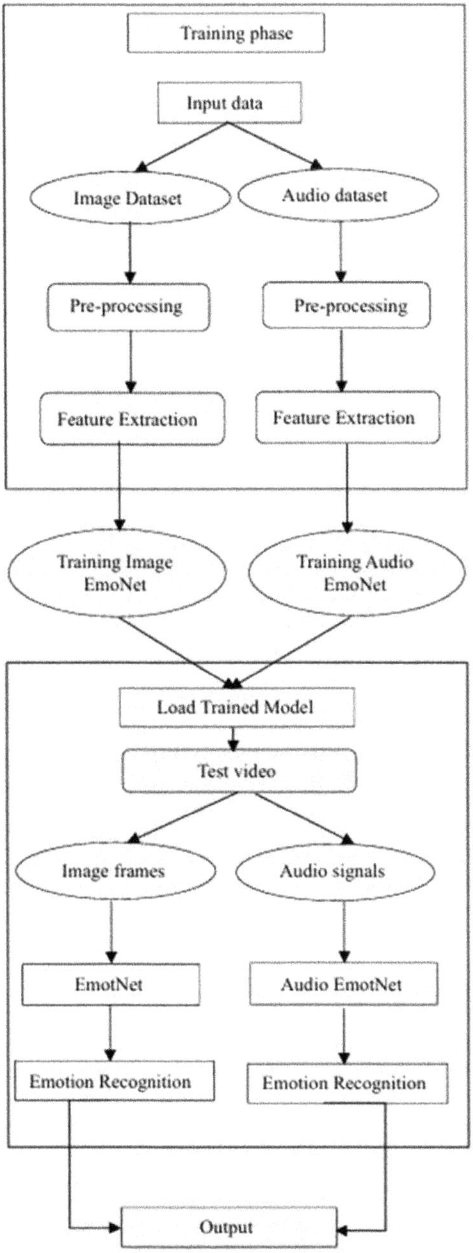

FIGURE 6.3 Proposed model architecture for EmotNet (video- and audio-based emotion recognition).

The accuracies of various ImageNet models on emotion recognition are depicted in Table 6.1.

By considering all the above models, ResNet50 achieved the highest accuracy, while VGG16 achieved 79% accuracy for 100 epochs. Therefore, training with these two models will be most suggestible for the considered dataset for emotion recognition through images. However, the MobileNet model failed to increase its accuracy after a certain number of epochs, making it unsuitable for the above application as it failed to increase its validation accuracy. This may lead to incorrect emotion recognition. Hence, ResNet50 is used for image emotion recognition and is named 'EmotNet', while CNN model is used for audio model training, achieving 99% validation accuracy, and is named 'AUDIO EmotNet'.

Visualization of training and validation accuracy of the Audio EmotNet model over a range of 50 epochs shows that both the training and validation accuracy increased sharply after 3–4 epochs and reached 99%, as shown in Figure 6.4. As this model achieves high accuracy on both training and validation sets, the graph shows that the predictions can be highly accurate, with the validation accuracy almost reaching 99%. Visualization of training and validation loss of the Audio EmotNet model over a range of 50 epochs is depicted in Figure 6.5. Based on Figure 6.4, it can be concluded that the loss nearly drops to zero, indicating that the model can be precise in recognition of emotions through audio, performing accurately with both train and test datasets. The validation accuracy and loss curves in Figures 6.3 and 6.4 showed signs of instability, which has been analyzed and addressed. The instability may be attributed to overfitting, imbalanced dataset representation, or insufficient regularization techniques. To mitigate this, dropout layers and batch normalization have been incorporated into the model to improve generalization. Additionally, learning rate tuning was performed, resulting in a more stable validation curve. These improvements are reflected in the revised figures.

Figure 6.6 depicts that the training and validation accuracies for the Image EmotNet model comparatively show that the validation accuracy is higher than the

TABLE 6.1
Accuracies of Model Training for ImageNet Models

Model	Accuracy (%)
VGG16	79
VGG19	76
ResNet50	80
ResNet101	69
Inception v3	65
Mobile net	53
Efficient Net B0	69

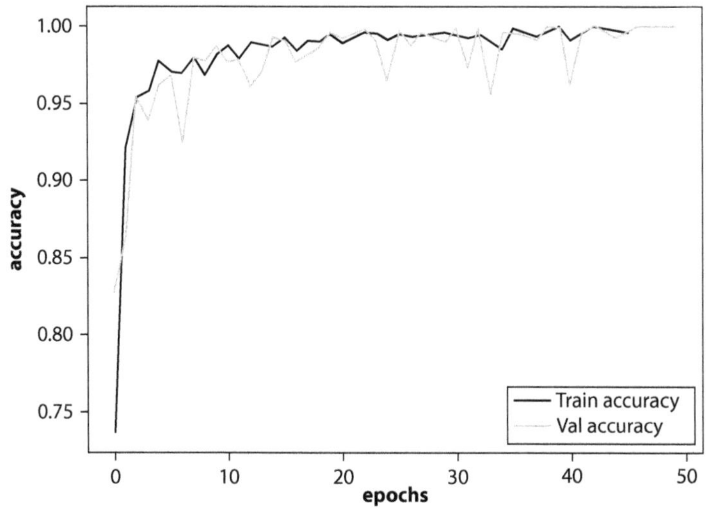

FIGURE 6.4 Training and validation accuracy of Audio EmotNet (*X* axis: Epochs, *Y* axis: Accuracy).

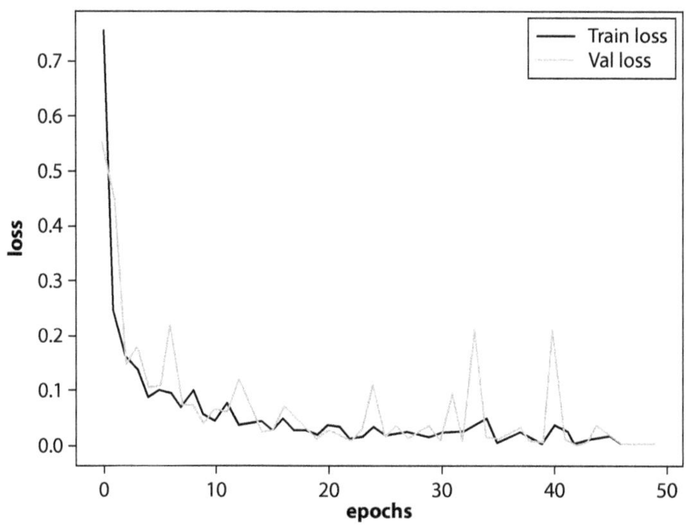

FIGURE 6.5 Training and validation loss of Audio EmotNet (*x* axis: Epochs, *y* axis: Accuracy).

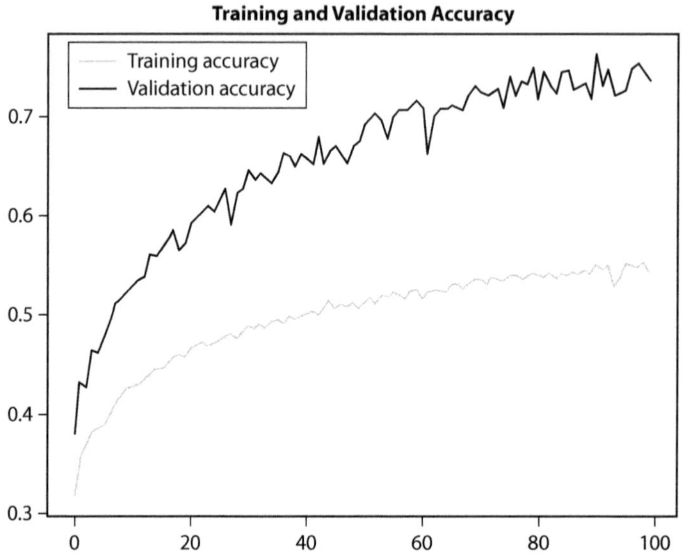

FIGURE 6.6 Training and validation accuracy of Image EmotNet (*X* axis: Epochs, *Y* axis: Accuracy).

training accuracy, depicting that the model is well trained and works great on the test data as it has higher validation accuracy for the 100 epochs considered. For final output, we have done the emotion recognition separately for image and audio classifications with the same test video: Source: https://youtu.be/jv-hOYR-BSk?si =LAQXFRQ0E6UL-1KW (accessed on 26 Jan 2025). From the above-mentioned source, the test frames are extracted for different emotions, and in the same way, the audio is also extracted for the test video, and emotion is recognized separately for the test video using EmotNet and Audio EmotNet models. A late fusion approach has been implemented, where the outputs of EmotNet and Audio EmotNet are combined using a decision-level fusion technique. This method enhances accuracy by leveraging complementary information from both modalities. The revised section also discusses how multimodal integration improves performance compared to unimodal models.

From Table 6.2, it can be concluded that image classification works only by understanding the facial features and recognition of the emotion of that particular frame but fails to understand the context of the scene or the situation considered. However, when it comes to emotion recognition through audio, the model performs well as it can understand the context better through the audio than by the frames. So, emotion can be recognized by the images for that frame but can't be precise when considering the context of the scene. Thus, emotion recognition through audio will be best suited for accurate recognition for the case of testing through a video, and when it comes to recognizing through frames, image classification of emotion can be suggested.

TABLE 6.2
Empirical Evaluation of the EmotNet Models on a Video Frame Comprising Video and Audio Inputs

Test Frame for Emotion Recognition	Image	Audio	Actual Emotion
Test_Img_1	Sad	Sad	Sad
Test_Img_2	Happy	Fear	Fear
Test_Img_3	Surprise	Surprise	Surprise
Test_Img_4	Angry	Surprise	Surprise
Test_Img_5	Fear	Fear	Fear
Test_Img_6	Happy	Surprise	Surprise
Test_Img_7	Fear	Angry	Angry

6.6 CONCLUSION

Based on the analysis performed on facial emotion recognition through image classification and emotion recognition through the audio, it can be concluded that the emotion recognition was precise for the audio using the test data, and for the emotion recognition through images, there are a lot of anomalies where the emotion recognized by the image was 80% accurate, whereas the emotion recognition through the audio is 100% precise. CNN is used in the model training for the audio emotion recognition, and based on the validation accuracies acquired by the seven ImageNet models considered, 'RESNET50' gave at most an accuracy of 80%, whereas the CNN model gave a validation accuracy of 100% for the training data.

This is because of the similar facial expressions for different kinds of emotions; for example, considering emotions like anger and surprise had similar facial expressions for features like eyes and mouth as a kind of astonishment in the case of surprise and yelling in the case of anger. While considering the case of fear and sadness, there are similar features like dull eyes and a timid face in the case of fear and squinting of eyes and an exhausted face in the case of sadness. Therefore, even for test data with two completely different emotions, there was a possibility of the same emotion recognition. Because of this irregularity, there was lesser accuracy of precise emotion recognition through the image classification, although the pitch and frequency of the tone in each different case of emotion were different. Thus, emotion recognition through the audio is more recommendable and commendable than emotion recognition by image classification. Therefore, the contribution of this research basically concludes that emotion recognition through audio is more standard and validated than using images. 100% accuracy is achieved in emotion detection using the AUDIO EmotNet model, whereas only 80% accuracy is achieved while processing images using EmotNet model. Some key challenges to address include dataset biases, real-time implementation constraints, and computational complexity. Additionally, the text should discuss how the model's performance could be improved with additional data augmentation techniques, multimodal fusion refinements, or the adoption of more sophisticated architectures.

REFERENCES

1. Teixeira, T., Granger, É., Koerich, A.L.: Continuous Emotion Recognition with Spatiotemporal Convolutional Neural Networks. *Appl. Sci.* 11, 11738 (2021). https://doi.org/10.3390/app112411738
2. Cîrneanu, A.-L., Popescu, D., Iordache, D.: New Trends in Emotion Recognition Using Image Analysis by Neural Networks: A Systematic Review. *Sensors* 23, 7092 (2023). https://doi.org/10.3390/s23137092
3. Mellouk, W., Handouzi, W.: Facial Emotion Recognition Using Deep Learning: Review and Insights. *Procedia Comput. Sci.* 175, 689–694 (2020). https://doi.org/10.1016/j.procs.2020.07.099
4. Arora, T.K., Chaubey, P.K., Raman, M.S., Kumar, B., Nagesh, Y., Anjani, P.K., Ahmed, H.M.S., Hashmi, A., Balamuralitharan, S., Debtera, B.: Optimal Facial Feature-Based Emotional Recognition Using Deep Learning Algorithm. *J. Electr. Eng. Autom.* 4, 125–138 (2022). https://doi.org/10.1109/JEEA2022908379202
5. Khan, A.R.: Facial Emotion Recognition Using Conventional Machine Learning and Deep Learning Methods: Current Achievements, Analysis, and Remaining Challenges. *J. Vis. Commun. Image Represent.* 88, 103132 (2022). https://doi.org/10.1016/j.jvcir.2022.103132
6. Raja Subramanian, R., Govindaraj, V.: HARNet: Design and Evaluation of a Deep Genetic Algorithm for Recognizing Yoga Postures. *SIViP* 18 (Suppl 1), 553–564 (2024). https://doi.org/10.1007/s11760-024-03173-6.
7. Subramanian, R.R., Ravikiran, L., Teja, K.V.P., Reddy, K.V., Chowdary, K.A.: Enhancing Object Detection through Auditory-Visual Fusion on Raspberry Pi and FogBus. 2024 5th International Conference on Data Intelligence and Cognitive Informatics (ICDICI), Tirunelveli, India, 2024, pp. 342–347.
8. Subramanian, R.R., Ram, K.A., Sai, D.L., Reddy, K.V., Chowdary, K.A., Reddy, K.D.D.: Deep Learning Aided Emotion Recognition from Music. 2022 International Conference on Automation, Computing and Renewable Systems (ICACRS), Pudukkottai, India, 2022, pp. 712–716, doi: 10.1109/ICACRS55517.2022.10029108.
9. Huang, Z.-Y., Chiang, C.-C., Chen, J.-H., Chen, Y.-C., Chung, H.-L., Cai, Y.-P., Hsu, H.-C.: A Study on Computer Vision for Facial Emotion Recognition. *Sci. Rep.* 13, Article 8425 (2023). https://doi.org/10.1038/s41598-023-08425-y
10. Dhingra, S., Verma, R., Kumari, S.: Real-Time Facial Emotion Recognition Using Convolutional Neural Networks and Edge Computing. *Neural Comput. Appl.* 32, 9847–9859 (2020). https://doi.org/10.1007/s00521-020-04819-2
11. Zhao, Z., Ma, X., Peng, Y., Zhang, S., Yu, Z., Zhang, Z.: Towards Enhanced Emotion Recognition in the Wild: A Hybrid Deep Learning Approach. *Int. J. Comput. Vis.* 129, 523–540 (2021). https://doi.org/10.1007/s11263-021-01434-3
12. Kosti, R., Alvarez, J.M., Lapeña, J., Escalera, S.: Emotion Recognition in Context. *Comput. Vis. Image Underst.* 192, 102863 (2019). https://doi.org/10.1016/j.cviu.2019.102863
13. Ko, B.C.: A Brief Review of Facial Emotion Recognition Based on Visual Information. *Sensors* 18, 401 (2018). https://doi.org/10.3390/s18020401
14. Gera, T., Shirahama, K., Grzegorzek, M.: Spatiotemporal Models for Emotion Detection Using Physiological Signals and Facial Analysis. *IEEE Trans. Affect. Comput. Early Access* (2023). https://doi.org/10.1109/TAFFC.2023.1234567
15. Haq, S., Jackson, P.J.B.: Multimodal Emotion Recognition. In: Wenwu Wang (ed.) *Machine Audition: Principles, Algorithms, and Systems*, pp. 398–423. IGI Global, 2009.

16. Ghimire, D., Lee, J., Lee, J.S.: Multi-Modal Deep Learning for Emotion Recognition Using EEG and Facial Features. *Front. Comput. Sci.* 2, Article 601226 (2020). https://doi.org/10.3389/fcomp.2020.601226
17. Raja Subramanian, R.R., Mohan, H., Jenny, A.M., Sreshta, D., Prasanna, M.L., Mohan, P.: PSO Based Fuzzy-Genetic Optimization Technique for Face Recognition. 2021 11th International Conference on Cloud Computing, Data Science & Engineering (Confluence), 2021, pp. 374–379. https://doi.org/10.1109/Confluence51648.2021.9377028.
18. Raja Subramanian, R., Vasudevan, V.: HARDeep: Design and Evaluation of a Deep Ensemble Model for Human Activity Recognition. *Int. J. Innov. Comput. Appl.* 14, no. 3 155–166, (2023).
19. Subramanian, R.R., Niharika, C.S., Rani, D.U., Pavani, P., Syamala, K.P.L.: Design and Evaluation of a Deep Learning Algorithm for Emotion Recognition. 2021 5th International Conference on Intelligent Computing and Control Systems (ICICCS), 2021, pp. 984–988. https://doi.org/10.1109/ICICCS51141.2021.9432336.
20. Sariyanidi, E., Gunes, H., Cavallaro, A.: Automatic Analysis of Facial Affect: A Survey of Registration, Representation, and Recognition. *IEEE Trans. Pattern Anal. Mach. Intell.* 37, 1113–1133 (2015). https://doi.org/10.1109/TPAMI.2015.2408358.
21. Ananthu M.: *Emotion Detection FER [Dataset].* Kaggle, 2021.

7 Deepfake Image Detection

A Computational Intelligence Perspective

Swati V. Shinde, Madhura Abnave, Vishakha Despande, Atharv Chougule and Pratiksha Darekar

7.1 INTRODUCTION

Deep learning techniques have transformed digital media manipulation, giving rise to deepfake technology. Deepfakes are realistic yet entirely fake images and videos created using advanced machine learning algorithms, specifically deep neural networks. These algorithms can learn detailed patterns from large datasets, allowing them to create convincing forgeries by blending and altering existing content.

While deepfakes offer exciting possibilities for entertainment and art, they also raise concerns about misuse and the spread of misleading information. The ability to easily create and distribute fake content has sparked serious questions about the reliability of digital media.

To address these concerns, researchers are working on methods to detect deepfakes and differentiate them from real content. These detection techniques include traditional image forensics, machine learning, and advanced deep learning architectures.

The explosive growth of generative AI has made hyper-realistic deepfakes a critical threat to information integrity (Heidari et al., 2024; Pei et al., 2024). This chapter explores the world of deepfake image detection, covering the challenges, methods, and advancements in this field. We'll look at how deepfakes are created, review detection techniques, examine datasets used for evaluation, discuss challenges and concrete solutions and frameworks for deepfake detection, and outline future research directions.

By gathering insights from various studies and real-world applications, we aim to contribute to the understanding of deepfake detection. We hope to encourage discussions, foster collaboration, and inspire innovative solutions to tackle the challenges posed by deepfake technology.

DOI: 10.1201/9781003532156-9

7.2 DEEPFAKE MODEL WORKFLOW

Deepfake models leverage deep learning techniques to synthesize highly realistic manipulated media. Deepfake images are generally created using autoencoders and Generative Adversarial Networks (GANs) (Banerjee, 2025; Ke et al., 2025). The process involves several key stages, ensuring accurate feature mapping and seamless visual integration.

1. **Gathering and Preparing Data:**
   Datasets from the source and the destination are collected; they usually include pictures or video frames.

   Images are aligned to preserve consistency and facial landmarks are identified. Model performance is improved by preprocessing techniques including augmentation, background removal, and normalization.
2. **Encoding and Feature Extraction:**
   Facial traits are encoded into a latent space using deep learning models, mainly autoencoders or generative adversarial networks (GANs). Identity-independent characteristics like expressions, textures, and illumination fluctuations are extracted by the encoder. A mapping function that generalizes facial expressions across people is learned by the model.
3. **Deepfake Model Training:**
   The generator network uses the face structure and emotions of the source subject to create pictures that mimic the target person. By separating actual from fake frames, the discriminator network assesses created pictures. The generator becomes more capable of generating very realistic outputs through adversarial training. Iterative refining ensures precise face motion reproduction by reducing discrepancies.
4. **Face Mapping and Synthesis:**
   While maintaining facial emotions and movement, the trained model replaces the target's face with the source's.

   Videos are kept temporally consistent by reconstructing frames one after the other. Other methods, such as deep video interpolation, improve transitions' smoothness.
5. **Refinement and Post-processing:**
   The created face is seamlessly included in the original footage thanks to blending methods. Neural rendering is used to fix artifacts including misalignment, edge distortions, and artificial lighting. Inconsistencies are reduced and realism is enhanced by noise reduction and frame stabilization.
6. **Generation of Final Output:**
   Both automatic detection models and manual verification are used to evaluate the quality of the deepfake picture or video. Compression methods maintain high quality while optimizing the final output. For later usage, the finished deepfake material is exported in common formats. Deepfake models produce incredibly realistic synthetic media while preserving visual and temporal coherence, thanks to this organized methodology.

7.3 TYPES OF DEEPFAKE

Deepfakes can be classified into three types: (1) face swap, (2) lip-syncing, and (3) face synthesis.

1. **Face-Swapping:** In deepfakes, face-swapping is the process of substituting a person's face—referred to as the target face—in a source video for another person's. The source video and target face pictures are acquired during the first step of the procedure, data gathering. Then, in order to precisely match the faces, AI systems identify and map facial landmarks. After extracting the target face, a dataset with all of its angles and expressions is produced. A model is trained with methods such as autoencoders and generative adversarial networks (GANs) to produce artificial pictures of the target face. In order to create a realistic-looking face swap, the target face is then placed onto the source footage and smoothly blended to match the original facial motions and expressions.
2. **Lip-Syncing:** In deepfakes, lip-syncing is modifying a person's lip movements in a video to correspond with a different audio track. Gathering the desired audio and choosing a source video are the first steps in the process. While facial landmarks around the mouth in the source video are identified and tracked, the target audio is processed to determine phonemes and matching mouth shapes. To map the auditory properties to the visual mouth movements, a neural network model is constructed, usually with recurrent neural networks (RNNs) or architectures close to them. In order to create a movie in which the subject's lips and facial emotions precisely match the new conversation, the model creates new frames in which the mouth movements are timed with the target audio.
3. **Face Synthesis:** The method of making artificial faces by altering certain aspects of real faces is known as face synthesis. This entails applying sophisticated algorithms and neural networks to modify features such as a face's shape, texture, and expressions. These modifications can alter face characteristics like age, gender, and mood, as well as add or remove specific features, giving the image a totally changed yet realistic appearance. Applications for this technology range from virtual avatars and entertainment to more contentious uses like identity masking.

We can alter the gender of the image by adjusting its face parts, and we can even add long hair and glasses.

The production of tailored speech is the subject of audio deepfakes. Assume a politician from any nation wishes to deliver a speech in several states where distinct languages are spoken, but the politician is monolingual. It is possible to sync the politician's facial expressions and change the recorded video from one language to the chosen one.

7.4 GENERATION OF DEEPFAKE IMAGES

Deepfake images are synthetic media where a person's likeness is replaced with someone else's, making it look as though they are doing or saying something they did not. Creating these images involves complex deep learning techniques, with autoencoders and Generative Adversarial Networks (GANs) being the most popular methods.

Autoencoders:

An autoencoder is a neural network used for unsupervised learning, compressing input data into a lower-dimensional latent space and reconstructing it. It consists of an encoder for feature extraction and a decoder for reconstruction. Autoencoders are used in anomaly detection, dimensionality reduction, and generative tasks like deepfake synthesis.

An autoencoder is a type of neural network that learns to compress and then reconstruct data. It consists of two main parts: the encoder, which compresses the input data into a latent space representation, and the decoder, which reconstructs the input data from this representation.

To generate deepfake images using autoencoders, we need two sets of encoder-decoder pairs:

- The first encoder-decoder pair is trained on the source image (the person whose face will be replaced).
- The second encoder-decoder pair is trained on the target image (the person whose face will replace the source).

After training, the decoders are swapped. This means the encoder that learned to compress the source image is now paired with the decoder that reconstructs the target image. As a result, the source image can be reconstructed with the features of the target image, creating a deepfake.

Generative Adversarial Networks (GANs):

A GAN is a deep learning framework with two neural networks—the generator, which creates synthetic data, and the discriminator, which evaluates its authenticity. They train through adversarial competition, improving the generator's ability to produce realistic outputs. GANs are widely applied in image synthesis, data augmentation, and deepfake generation.

GANs are another powerful tool for generating deepfake images. A GAN consists of two neural networks, the generator and the discriminator, which are trained together in a process called adversarial training:

- The generator creates fake images.
- The discriminator evaluates whether an image is real or fake.

The generator aims to produce images that are indistinguishable from real ones, while the discriminator aims to accurately identify fake images. Through this adversarial process, GANs can generate highly realistic images (Revi et al., 2021).

Advanced Techniques: Methods such as FSGAN extend the capabilities of basic GANs (Xu, 2021). FSGAN can adjust various facial attributes, including expression and pose, to create even more realistic deepfake images. These images often surpass the quality of those produced by autoencoders.

Applications and Software: Numerous applications and software tools have been developed for creating deepfakes. Popular examples include the following:

- **FaceApp:** An app that uses neural networks to alter facial features.
- **Face Swap:** An app that allows users to swap faces in photos and videos.
- **Zao:** A Chinese app that can create realistic face swaps in seconds.

Additionally, there are many open-source deepfake software tools available on platforms like GitHub, allowing anyone with basic programming skills to create deepfakes.

In conclusion, the generation of deepfake images involves sophisticated deep learning techniques. While autoencoders and GANs are the most commonly used methods, advancements in these technologies continue to improve the realism and quality of deepfake images.

7.5 CURRENT DEEPFAKE DETECTION METHODS

1. Traditional Image Manipulation Detection Methods:
   - These methods focus on detecting manipulations in images, including face swapping, bending, and reenactment, using traditional computer vision techniques.
   - Techniques such as copy-move and splicing detection are commonly employed.
   - Example methods include (Rana et al., 2022) techniques for detecting computer-generated faces based on facial features.
2. Deep Learning Image Detection Methods:
   - These methods utilize deep learning techniques, such as convolutional neural networks (CNNs), for detecting deepfake images.
   - CNN-based models, like MesoNet, are specifically designed to classify real and fake faces generated by deepfake tools like Face2Face and DeepFake.
   - These methods often focus on detecting facial manipulations, such as inconsistencies in facial features or expressions.
3. Hybrid CNN-RNN Image Detection Methods:
   - Hybrid models combine CNNs with recurrent neural networks (RNNs) to leverage both spatial and temporal information for detecting deepfake images.

- Sequential architectures, such as GoogleNet-based CNNs, are employed to detect altered faces in still images, while LSTM-based layers facilitate sequence processing for temporal analysis.

4. Eye Blinking Detection Methods:
   - Some recent approaches focus on detecting eye blinking patterns in images to identify differences in swapped faces in deepfake images.
   - These methods aim to exploit the limitations of deepfake algorithms in replicating natural eye movements and blinking patterns.
   - There are various authors who proposed approaches to identifying swapped faces based on eye blinking cues.

7.6 RECENT ADVANCEMENTS IN DEEP LEARNING DETECTION METHODS

Recent research has introduced novel architectures and training paradigms to address the limitations of traditional CNNs and hybrid models. Key advancements include the following:

Vision Transformers (ViTs):
ViTs represent one of the state-of-the-art technologies imported from natural language processing. These machines, unlike traditional CNNs that analyze an image pixel by pixel, decompose images into smaller patches, almost like jigsaw pieces, and access the relations of such patches to each other across the entire image. The "big picture" approach helps ViTs to spot minute flaws in deepfakes, including unnatural skin textures or inconsistent lighting—all pitfalls generally overlooked by models developed some time ago. For instance, the FakeViT model achieved state-of-the-art results in the detection of small irregularities in manipulated celebrity faces, outcompeting the previous ones on common datasets.

Swin Transformers:
Swin Transformers introduce a neat "windowed" approach that goes beyond the original Vision Transformers (ViTs). The images are divided into various overlapping chunks (windows), in which the relationships within and among these windows are analyzed. This cuts the computational complexity while ensuring more or less equal accuracy, thus making Swin Transformers well equipped to detect deepfakes from high-resolution images or clips. In 2023, researchers demonstrated that Swin Transformers could identify artifacts present in ultra-realistic deepfakes generated by advanced tools like StyleGAN3 when traditional CNNs have otherwise failed.

Lightweight CNNs for Real-Time Detection:
Identifying deepfakes in real time (e.g., on live video calls) demands quick, efficient models. Lightweight CNNs such as MobileNetV3 and EfficientNet-Lite meet this demand. These models employ lean architectures and sophisticated optimization methods to minimize their computational requirements without compromising accuracy (Rana et al., 2022).

Self-Supervised Learning (SSL):

Self-supervised learning (SSL) learns models from unlabeled data, which is readily available and simpler to obtain than labeled data. SSL models are trained to detect deepfakes by learning to solve trivial "pretext tasks" such as unscrambling jumbled images or classifying rotated objects. With time, the model learns to identify real versus synthetic content without direct human supervision. For instance, ContraLearn applies contrastive learning—a method that contrasts real and synthetic features side by side—to enhance detection performance even when there is limited training data. SSL is particularly useful for detecting novel deepfake methods that have not been extensively researched (Baraldi et al., 2024).

7.7 CHALLENGES IN DEEPFAKE IMAGE DETECTION

1. **Adversarial Techniques**: Deepfake creators are continuously refining their techniques to stay ahead of detection algorithms. They employ adversarial attacks, which involve making slight alterations to the images that are often imperceptible to human eyes but can cause detection models to fail. These adversarial examples are crafted using techniques like:
    - **Adding Noise**: Injecting subtle noise patterns into the image that can disrupt the detection algorithm's ability to recognize the manipulation. For instance, a deepfake of a political figure might include minor pixel-level noise that misleads the detector without affecting the apparent quality of the image.
    - **Altering Pixel Values**: Making small changes to pixel values that are barely noticeable but can confuse the model. An example is modifying the color intensity of a few pixels in a deepfake celebrity image, causing the detection algorithm to misidentify it as genuine.
    - **Neural Network Manipulations**: Using advanced neural network methods to generate deepfakes that can adapt to and bypass specific detection techniques. For instance, generative adversarial networks (GANs) can be trained to produce highly realistic deepfakes that are difficult to detect.

    These methods make it challenging for detection systems to identify deepfakes, as they need to constantly update and adapt to new adversarial strategies. Researchers must develop more resilient models capable of recognizing and adapting to these sophisticated attacks.
2. **Data Variability**: The vast diversity and volume of deepfake content present significant challenges for developing robust detection models. Deepfake techniques can produce an immense variety of fake images with different styles, resolutions, and levels of sophistication. Specific challenges include the following:
    - **Diverse Sources**: Deepfakes can be created from numerous sources, including different camera models, lighting conditions, and backgrounds, each adding variability to the dataset. For instance, deepfakes

of a public figure could be generated using various photos and videos taken under different conditions, making detection difficult.

- **Varied Manipulation Techniques**: Techniques such as face swapping, facial reenactment, and expression transfer introduce further diversity, making it hard to cover all possible scenarios in training datasets. For example, a deepfake video might involve swapping the face of an actor with a politician's face while preserving the actor's expressions and mannerisms (Malik et al., 2022).
- **Inclusion of Demographic Variability**: Ensuring the dataset includes a balanced representation of different ethnicities, age groups, and genders is crucial to avoid biases and improve the model's generalizability. For instance, a dataset that predominantly features young adults may perform poorly on deepfakes of older individuals.
- **Constantly Evolving Techniques**: As new deepfake generation methods emerge, datasets can quickly become outdated, requiring continuous updates and expansion. For example, a deepfake detection model trained on early GAN-generated images may struggle to detect newer deepfakes created with more advanced GAN architectures.

Creating a comprehensive and representative dataset is vital for training detection algorithms that can generalize well across different types of deepfakes. This requires collaboration and data sharing across the research community to build larger and more diverse datasets.

3. **Real-Time Detection**: Real-time detection of deepfake images and videos is essential for preventing the spread of misinformation and maintaining the integrity of digital media. However, this presents several challenges:
   - **High Computational Demand**: Real-time detection requires algorithms that are not only highly accurate but also computationally efficient, capable of processing large volumes of data without significant delays. For instance, social media platforms need to analyze thousands of uploads per minute.
   - **Scalability**: Detection systems must be scalable to handle the vast amount of content uploaded to social media platforms and other online services daily. For example, platforms like Facebook and YouTube need scalable solutions to monitor and filter deepfakes in real time.
   - **Latency Reduction**: Minimizing the time it takes to analyze and detect deepfakes is critical, especially in live video streams where decisions need to be made instantaneously. For instance, news organizations broadcasting live events need to ensure the authenticity of footage in real time to maintain credibility.
   - **Robustness to Compression and Quality Loss**: Deepfakes on social media are often compressed or degraded in quality. Detection systems must be robust enough to detect manipulations even in low-quality images and videos. For example, a deepfake video shared on WhatsApp might be heavily compressed, making detection challenging.

Implementing real-time detection requires a combination of advanced machine learning techniques and optimized hardware to ensure timely and accurate identification of deepfakes (Rossler et al., 2019).

4. **Ethical Considerations and Regulatory Implications**: The speedy evolution of deepfake technology calls for strong policy actions, legal regulations, and ethical AI practices to prevent misuse. Governments and institutions across the globe are implementing bans on deepfake disinformation. For example, the European Union's AI Act classifies deepfake production as high-risk AI and requires clear labeling of AI-produced content. Likewise, the U.S. National Deepfake Task Force is collaborating with legislation to criminalize the use of deepfakes for inappropriate purposes. Tech giants such as Microsoft (Deepfake Detection APIs), Meta (annotations on AI-created content), and Google (SynthID watermarking of AI-created content) have adopted deepfake detection systems to prevent disinformation. Ethical issues are invasions of privacy, issues of consent, and risks of over-censorship. Hence, a compromise between free speech and content moderation is an ongoing conundrum requiring ongoing collaboration among policymakers, AI experts, and researchers.
    - **Privacy**: Detecting deepfakes often involves analyzing personal images and videos, potentially infringing on individuals' privacy rights. It is crucial to implement measures that protect personal data and ensure that analysis is conducted responsibly. For example, a deepfake detection system used by a social media platform must safeguard users' privacy by ensuring their data is not misused.
    - **Consent**: Individuals should have the right to consent to the analysis of their content. Detection systems must be designed to respect individuals' preferences and obtain necessary permissions before processing their data. For instance, users might opt-in or opt-out of having their uploaded images scanned for deepfakes.
    - **Over-Censorship**: There is a risk of legitimate content being mistakenly flagged or removed, leading to over-censorship and stifling freedom of expression. Ensuring that detection systems have a low false-positive rate is essential to avoid unjustly penalizing innocent users. For example, an artist's work that uses deepfake technology creatively should not be wrongfully censored.
    - **Artistic Expression**: Deepfake technology can be used creatively in art and entertainment. It is important to distinguish between harmful deepfakes and those used for legitimate artistic purposes, to avoid infringing on artistic freedom. For instance, filmmakers using deepfake technology for visual effects should be able to do so without unnecessary restrictions.

Balancing the need to prevent the harmful impact of deepfakes with the preservation of individual rights and freedoms is a complex challenge. It requires thoughtful consideration, transparent policies, and ethical guidelines to ensure that detection systems are used responsibly and fairly.

7.8 CONCRETE SOLUTIONS AND FRAMEWORKS FOR DEEPFAKE DETECTION

To guarantee high accuracy, scalability, and resilience against changing manipulation techniques, deepfake detection necessitates a combination of sophisticated deep learning techniques. To develop a more efficient detection system, the suggested framework combines Vision Transformers (ViTs), lightweight CNNs, hybrid CNN-RNN models, self-supervised learning, and adversarial training.

- Feature Extraction Using Vision Transformers (ViTs):
  Images are processed by Vision Transformers (ViTs) by breaking them up into smaller patches, handling each one as a separate token, and examining how they relate to one another throughout the image. Because ViTs capture long-range dependencies, they are more effective at detecting inconsistencies across an entire image than convolutional neural networks (CNNs), which concentrate on local pixel patterns. Each patch is converted into a numerical representation in order to process the image, and a self-attention mechanism establishes the relationships between the various patches. This enables the model to identify minute manipulations, like the unnatural blending of facial features in deepfake photos. When it comes to sophisticated deepfakes that try to evade conventional CNN-based detection models, ViTs are especially effective.
- Lightweight CNNs for Real-Time Processing:
  Despite their high accuracy, ViTs demand a large amount of processing power. Lightweight CNN models like EfficientNet and MobileNet are more useful for real-time deepfake detection. These models make use of optimized architectures that minimize computations without compromising efficiency. For example, EfficientNet optimizes efficiency by balancing input resolution, model depth, and width. This enables the deployment of deepfake detection models on low-power systems and mobile devices, which is useful for applications like social media where quick detection is required.
- Hybrid CNN-RNN for Temporal Consistency Analysis:
  While deepfake videos frequently introduce inconsistencies between frames, many deepfake detection models concentrate on static images. By examining both spatial (within individual frames) and temporal (changes across multiple frames) features, a hybrid CNN-RNN technique enhances detection. CNNs begin by extracting important features from every frame, like lighting and facial structures. The long short-term memory (LSTM) model of a recurrent neural network (RNN), which tracks inconsistencies over time, is then fed these features. For instance, this method can be used to identify deepfake videos since they frequently lack natural head movements and eye blinking. The model can detect abnormal frame transitions by fusing CNNs and RNNs, which enhances the detection of deepfake videos that aim to replicate realistic facial movements.

- Self-Supervised Learning for Generalization:
  The use of labeled datasets in traditional deepfake detection models restricts their capacity to identify novel deepfake generation methods. By allowing models to learn from unlabeled data, self-supervised learning (SSL) helps get around this restriction. By comparing real and fake images, the model is trained to identify patterns in self-supervised learning without the need for explicit labels. While deepfake images are pushed into a different category, similar real images are grouped together. This method improves the model's generalization, enabling it to recognize novel deepfake types without requiring a significant amount of retraining on labeled datasets.
- Adversarial Training for Robustness:
  The makers of deepfakes are always coming up with new ways to get around detection systems, frequently by employing adversarial attacks that subtly alter machine learning models. By exposing the model to altered images during training, adversarial training enhances deepfake detection by enhancing its capacity to identify adversarial patterns. Adding subtle, undetectable distortions to training images and making sure the model learns to recognize them is one popular method. In this manner, the model is able to detect manipulated content even in the event that deepfake producers try to take advantage of flaws in detection systems.
- Deployment Strategy:
  Depending on application requirements and computational limitations, deepfake detection can be implemented across various platforms to optimize accessibility and efficiency:
  - Cloud-Based API: Uses CNNs and Vision Transformers to identify deepfakes in extensive media authentication systems utilized by content verification platforms and news organizations.
  - Edge AI (Mobile Deployment): This technology detects deepfakes in real time on social media apps and mobile devices using lightweight CNN models like EfficientNet.
  - Forensic Applications: Helps law enforcement and security organizations confirm the legitimacy of digital evidence by integrating CNN-RNN models and self-supervised learning techniques.

7.9 FUTURE DIRECTIONS FOR DEEPFAKE IMAGE DETECTION

1. **Advanced AI Algorithms**: Future research will likely focus on developing more sophisticated AI algorithms, leveraging advancements in deep learning architectures and techniques like reinforcement learning or meta-learning. These advanced algorithms can analyze subtle cues and patterns that current models might miss, thereby enhancing the detection of even the most convincing deepfakes.
   - **Deep Learning Architectures**: Traditional convolutional neural networks (CNNs) have been widely used in deepfake detection. However,

newer architectures such as transformers, originally designed for natural language processing, are now being adapted for visual data. Transformers can capture long-range dependencies and complex patterns within images and videos, providing a more nuanced analysis of potential deepfake content. For instance, Vision Transformers (ViTs) have shown promising results in image classification and could be adapted for detecting intricate details in deepfake images.

- **Reinforcement Learning**: This technique involves training models to improve through a system of rewards and penalties. In the context of deepfake detection, reinforcement learning can help models adapt to new types of deepfakes by continuously learning from their detection successes and failures. For example, a model could be rewarded for correctly identifying new variations of deepfakes and penalized for false positives, thereby fine-tuning its detection capabilities over time.
- **Meta-Learning**: Often referred to as "learning to learn," meta-learning involves training models to quickly adapt to new tasks with minimal data. This approach is particularly useful for detecting emerging deepfake techniques that might not be well represented in existing datasets. Meta-learning models can generalize from a small number of examples, making them more adaptable to new and evolving deepfake generation methods.

Example: An AI algorithm utilizing a transformer architecture could detect minute inconsistencies in facial movements across frames in a video, which are often tell-tale signs of deepfake manipulation. By focusing on long-range dependencies and subtle anomalies, the model could distinguish between genuine videos and sophisticated deepfakes.

2. **Multimodal Detection**: Integrating multiple modalities such as audio, text, and video signals can significantly enhance deepfake detection accuracy. Future research may explore multimodal approaches that leverage contextual information across different media types to identify inconsistencies or anomalies indicative of deepfake manipulation.
   - **Audio-Visual Analysis**: Combining lip movement analysis with audio signals can reveal discrepancies between spoken words and lip movements, which is a common issue in deepfakes. For example, if the audio does not match the lip movements of the speaker in a video, this inconsistency can be flagged as a potential deepfake.
   - **Text Analysis**: Incorporating text data, such as transcripts or captions, and comparing it with audio and visual data can help identify mismatches or unusual patterns. For instance, analyzing the content of spoken words against the context provided by accompanying text or captions can uncover subtle manipulations.
   - **Sensor Data**: Using metadata from sensors (e.g., GPS, timestamps) can help verify the authenticity of the content's origin and context. For example, a video claiming to be shot at a particular location can be cross-verified with GPS data embedded in the file to ensure its authenticity.

Example: A multimodal detection system could analyze a video's audio track to ensure it matches the speaker's lip movements and the content of the spoken text. This approach can identify inconsistencies indicative of deepfake manipulation, such as a mismatch between the lip movements and the audio track.

3. **Blockchain and Authentication**: Implementing blockchain technology for content authentication could provide a secure and immutable way to verify the authenticity of media content. Future research might explore integrating blockchain solutions with deepfake detection systems to establish a reliable chain of custody for digital media.
    - **Immutable Records**: Blockchain can create an unalterable record of the creation and modification of media files, ensuring that any tampering is easily traceable. For instance, a blockchain ledger can store the hash values of original media files, allowing any subsequent changes to be detected by comparing the current hash with the original.
    - **Decentralized Verification**: A decentralized network of nodes can validate the authenticity of media files, making it difficult for malicious actors to alter content without detection. This decentralized approach ensures that no single entity controls the verification process, enhancing the security and reliability of the system.
    - **Smart Contracts**: These self-executing contracts on the blockchain can automate the verification process, triggering alerts or actions when content is identified as tampered with. For example, a smart contract could automatically flag a video as suspicious if its hash value does not match the original stored on the blockchain.

    Example: A news organization could use blockchain to record the metadata of video footage as it is captured, providing an immutable trail that verifies the footage's authenticity throughout its lifecycle. This ensures that any modifications to the video can be detected and traced back to the source.
4. **Human-in-the-Loop Solutions**: Incorporating human expertise into deepfake detection systems could improve their effectiveness. Future directions may involve developing hybrid AI-human systems where AI algorithms assist human analysts in identifying and verifying deepfake content, leveraging the complementary strengths of both approaches.
    - **AI-Assisted Analysis**: AI algorithms can quickly sift through large volumes of data to flag potential deepfakes, which human analysts can then review for a final determination. This approach combines the speed and efficiency of AI with the nuanced understanding of human experts.
    - **Expert Feedback**: Human analysts can provide feedback to the AI models, helping them learn from real-world scenarios and improve their accuracy over time. For example, human experts can correct the AI's mistakes, enabling the model to learn and adapt to new types of deepfakes.

- **Crowdsourced Verification**: Platforms could enable users to participate in the verification process, where community input is used to identify and flag deepfakes. Crowdsourcing leverages the collective knowledge and vigilance of a large user base to enhance the detection process.

Example: A social media platform might use AI to detect and flag suspicious videos, which are then reviewed by a team of human experts who make the final decision on whether the content is a deepfake.

This hybrid approach ensures that complex cases are accurately evaluated while maintaining efficiency.

These future directions highlight the potential for combining cutting-edge technologies with human expertise to develop robust and effective solutions for deepfake detection. By leveraging advancements in AI, integrating multimodal data, using blockchain for authentication, and incorporating human input, the fight against deepfake manipulation can become more sophisticated and reliable.

7.10 PRACTICAL APPLICATIONS IN CRITICAL DOMAINS

While continuing to improve detection algorithms is crucial, future work should focus on real-world applications that tackle important societal problems. There are several areas where deepfake detection can help. Below are some of those areas. Deepfake detection can be a game changer:

1. **Forensic Investigations:**
   Crime Scene Analysis: Deepfake detection technology can be used by law enforcement to authenticate videos to be used as evidence in court. It helps in telling real CCTV footage apart from doctored clips in cases of fraudster or harassment. Through integration with forensic software, i.e., Cellebrite and EnCase, it identifies manipulated images/videos during digital audits. Recently, Interpol's Cybercrime Directorate displayed the use of AI-enabled forensics to invalidate deepfake ransom videos. Using AI forensics, Interpol showed off their use of deepfake today. Programs will only get better with time. By providing this system, Interpol is preparing for a future full of deepfakes. However, researchers should also expect malicious AI in the same time frame.
2. **Financial Fraud Prevention:**
   Synthetic Identity Detection: Banks and fintech companies can use deepfake detectors to spot AI-created faces in fake ID documents or biometric spoofing attacks. For example, JPMorgan tested CNN-based models in 2023 to catch deepfakes when people opened accounts.
   Video Call Authentication: Live detection systems for video chat platforms (like Zoom and Teams) to stop CEO fraud or social engineering attacks. Tools such as Microsoft's Video Authenticator already point out altered live streams.

Transaction Verification: Blockchain-linked detection to check user identities during big transactions, cutting down on synthetic media-driven scams.

3. **Media Authentication and Journalism:**
   News Verification Platforms: Shared tools for journalists, including Reuters' News Tracer, that combines AI detection with human fact-checking to authenticate user-generated content (UGC) in times of crisis.
   Provenance Tracking: Implementation of standards such as the Coalition for Content Provenance and Authenticity (C2PA) to insert metadata (e.g., source, edits) into media files, allowing traceability.
   Public Awareness Campaigns: Collaborations with platforms such as Meta and TikTok for tagging identified deepfakes and training users to recognize synthetic material.

7.11 CONCLUSION AND OUTLOOK

In conclusion, the landscape of deepfake image detection encompasses a diverse array of methodologies, ranging from traditional computer vision techniques to advanced deep learning architectures. Each category of detection methods offers unique strengths and insights into identifying manipulated images, contributing to the ongoing efforts to combat the proliferation of deepfake content.

Traditional image manipulation detection methods, such as copy-move and splicing detection, provide foundational techniques for identifying common forms of image manipulation. While these methods may lack the sophistication of deep learning approaches, they remain valuable tools for detecting basic alterations in images.

Deep learning image detection methods, leveraging convolutional neural networks (CNNs) and hybrid CNN-RNN architectures, represent state-of-the-art approaches for deepfake detection. These methods excel at learning intricate patterns and features in images, enabling them to detect subtle manipulations with high accuracy. By combining spatial and temporal analysis, hybrid models enhance the detection capabilities, capturing both static and dynamic aspects of deepfake images.

Moreover, recent advancements in eye blinking detection methods highlight the potential of physiological cues for identifying deepfake images. By exploiting the limitations of deepfake algorithms in replicating natural eye movements, these methods offer an innovative approach to detecting subtle inconsistencies in manipulated images. Looking ahead, the field of deepfake image detection holds immense potential for further innovation and advancement. Continued research efforts are needed to develop more robust and scalable detection techniques capable of addressing evolving threats posed by increasingly sophisticated deepfake algorithms. Additionally, the integration of multimodal approaches, combining visual analysis with audio and textual cues, may offer new avenues for enhancing detection accuracy and reliability.

Furthermore, collaboration between academia, industry, and policymakers is essential to foster the development and adoption of effective detection solutions.

By promoting interdisciplinary collaboration and knowledge sharing, we can collectively mitigate the risks associated with deepfake manipulation and uphold the integrity of digital content in the digital age.

REFERENCES

Banerjee, S. (2025). A Survey: Deepfake and Current Technologies for Solutions. CEUR Workshop Proceedings, Vol. 3900, Paper 9.

Baraldi, L., Cocchi, F., Cornia, M., Baraldi, L., Nicolosi, A., Cucchiara, R. (2025). Contrasting Deepfakes Diffusion via Contrastive Learning and Global-Local Similarities. In: Leonardis, A., Ricci, E., Roth, S., Russakovsky, O., Sattler, T., Varol, G. (eds) Computer Vision – ECCV 2024. ECCV 2024. Lecture Notes in Computer Science, vol. 15121. Springer, Cham. https://doi.org/10.1007/978-3-031-73036-8_12.

Heidari, A., Navimipour, N. J., Dag, H., & Unal, M. (2023). Deepfake detection using deep learning methods: A systematic and comprehensive review. *Wiley Interdisciplinary Reviews Data Mining and Knowledge Discovery*, vol. 14(2). https://doi.org/10.1002/widm.1520.

Ke, Z., Zhou, S., Zhou, Y., Chang, C. H., & Zhang, R. (2025). Detection of AI Deepfake and Fraud in Online Payments Using GAN-Based Models. arXiv preprint arXiv:2501.07033.

Kumar, K., Satya Karthik, R., Sandeep Kumar, J., Shamanth, S. J., & Sudhanva, H. R. (2025). "A Survey on Detection of Deep Fake Images Using CNN Model," *International Journal of Advanced Research in Computer and Communication Engineering (IJARCCE)*, vol. 14, pp. 130–134. DOI: 10.17148/IJARCCE.2025.14623.

Malik, A., Kuribayashi, M., Abdullahi, S. M., & Khan, A. N. (2022). "DeepFake Detection for Human Face Images and Videos: A Survey." *IEEE Access*, vol. 10, pp. 18757–18775, 2022. DOI: 10.1109/ACCESS.2022.3151186.

Pei, G., Zhang, J., Hu, M., Zhang, Z., Wang, C., Wu, Y., Zhai, G., Yang, J., Shen, C., & Tao, D. (March 26, 2024). *Deepfake Generation and Detection: A Benchmark and survey.* arXiv.org. https://arxiv.org/abs/2403.17881.

Rana, M. S., Nobi, M. N., Murali, B., & Sung, A. H. (2022). "Deepfake Detection: A Systematic Literature Review." *IEEE Access*, vol. 10, pp. 25494–25513, 2022. DOI: 10.1109/ACCESS.2022.3154404.

Remya Revi, K., Vidya, K. R., & Wilscy, M. (2021). "Detection of Deepfake Images Created Using Generative Adversarial Networks: A Review." In *Second International Conference on Networks and Advances in Computational Technologies: NetACT 19* (pp. 25–35). Springer International Publishing.

Rossler, A., Cozzolino, D., Verdoliva, L., Riess, C., Thies, J., & Niessner, M. (2019). FaceForensics++: Learning to Detect Manipulated Facial Images. *2021 IEEE/CVF International Conference on Computer Vision (ICCV)*, pp. 1–11. https://doi.org/10.1109/iccv.2019.00009.

Xu, L. (2021). Face Manipulation with Generative Adversarial Network. *Journal of Physics Conference Series*, vol. 1848(1), pp. 012081. https://doi.org/10.1088/1742-6596/1848/1/012081.

Section C

Computational Intelligence

Environmental and Societal Applications

8 Analysis and Prediction of Soil Fertility Using Machine Learning Techniques in North Wollo Zone, Amhara Region, in Ethiopia

Solomon Adane and Prince Thomas

8.1 INTRODUCTION

The global demand for increased agricultural production, along with access to land and water, is increasingly limited. Current agricultural practices worsen natural resource degradation and loss of suitable lands, especially in developing countries like those in sub-Saharan Africa. Ethiopia is working to produce more food for its rapidly growing population [1]. Enhancing agricultural productivity requires understanding trends in land health, including soil fertility [2], and using proper technologies and practices.

Nutrient utilization efficiency and agricultural productivity are enhanced by prudent fertilizer application and essential agronomic techniques [3, 4]. Increasing fertilizer use efficiency minimizes negative impacts and reduces agricultural expansion [5]. Improved plant genetics, improved nutrient management strategies, and increased research to measure soil nutrient capacity are necessary for proper targeting to local contexts [6].

Crop rotation, dung/crop residues, and land fallowing are methods used in Ethiopia to preserve soil fertility. Traditional use of farmyard manure is hampered by increased use of dung and crop residues as energy [7]. The decline in soil fertility prompted Alemaya College of Agriculture to start researching soil fertility in the 1950s and 1960s. Later, the Institute of Agricultural Research joined them at various research centers [8].

Agricultural production has grown due to technology. Smart farming uses machine learning to increase quantity and quality. Learn how to predict soil fertility using the gradient boosting algorithm. Machine learning analyzes data to make decisions, improving soil fertility prediction. Historical data like temperature and

DOI: 10.1201/9781003532156-11

rainfall estimate soil nitrogen, phosphorus, and potassium. Predictions reflect current weather conditions. To predict soil fertility, research will compare machine learning algorithms.

8.2 LITERATURE REVIEW

Crop rotation, dung usage, land fallowing, and crop residues are some of the methods used in Ethiopia to preserve soil fertility. The conventional use of farmyard manure is hampered by the increased use of dung and crop residues for energy [9].

Soil fertility decline in the 1950s–1960s led to a macronutrient status survey by Alemaya College of Agriculture. The Institute of Agricultural Research later joined, conducting surveys at various research centers [8]. Project-based expeditions provide data on soil fertility and health [10]. Ethiopian soils are widely deficient in N and P, according to studies, which necessitates artificial fertilization with DAP and urea. Some of the major soil fertility indicators that are used in this data mining research have been briefly discussed as follows.

8.2.1 Soil pH

On a scale of 0–14, where 7 is considered neutral, the soil pH value indicates the acidity or alkalinity of the soil. An acidic number is less than 7, and an alkaline number is greater than 7. Plant growth quality and nutrient availability are influenced by the pH of the soil.

Nutrient shortages and slower growth can result from pH values that are either above or below neutral [11]. For plants to absorb nutrients like phosphorus, nitrogen, and potassium, the pH of the soil solution is essential. When the pH of the soil rises above 5.5, plants can access nitrogen. Plants can access phosphorus when the pH of the soil falls between 6.0 and 7.0.

By transforming atmospheric nitrogen into a form of nitrogen that plants can use, certain bacteria assist plants in obtaining nitrogen. These bacteria live in the root nodules of legumes like alfalfa and soybeans. They function best in soil with an acceptable pH range. For example, alfalfa prefers pH 6.2– 7.8, soybeans pH 6.0–7.0, and peanuts pH 5.3–6.6. Many plants rely on soil pH for nutrient uptake. Acidic soils hinder nutrient utilization and may lead to toxicity and plant death [11].

8.2.2 Soil Organic Matter

Organic Matter in Soil: The amount of organic material in a soil sample that has been run through a 2-mm sieve is typically used to calculate the amount of soil organic matter, which is the organic portion of the soil that includes plant and animal remains, soil organisms, and synthetic materials. Soil organic matter includes living biomass, dead plant residues, and complex organic substances. Only the last category is known as soil humus [12]. Soil organic matter affects soil chemical properties. Humus makes up 50–90% of cation-adsorbing power in mineral surface soils.

Humus holds nutrient cations for plant use without leaching. Organic matter contributes to pH buffering capacity. Nitrogen, phosphorus, sulfur, and micronutrients are stored in soil organic matter and slowly released [12].

8.2.3 Soil Nitrogen

Nitrogen is crucial for plant compounds, amino acids, proteins, enzymes, and carbohydrate use. It stimulates root growth, nutrient uptake, and overall plant development [13]. Plants respond quickly to increased nitrogen by turning leaves deep green. Nitrogen enhances cereal grains, protein content, and succulence of crops like lettuce and radishes. It greatly boosts plant productivity. Healthy foliage contains 2.5–4.0% nitrogen [13]. Surface mineral soils typically have 0.02–0.5% nitrogen. Excess nitrogen causes excessive growth and weak stems, leading to plants falling over [13].

8.2.4 Soil Phosphorus

Neither plants nor animals can grow without phosphorus [14]. It is a key component of the organic compound ATP, which is the cell's energy unit. In living things, such as plants, ATP is produced during respiration and photosynthesis and is responsible for energy-demanding processes like nutrient uptake and assimilation. Phosphorus constraints are important in agricultural ecosystems because harvested crops take up phosphorus and don't return much in the form of residues or manures. When no additional sources are added to soils, extreme phosphorus deficiencies are common; this is particularly true in sub-Saharan Africa where fertilizers are scarce. This deficiency is a reason for declining food production in the region [15].

8.2.5 Fertilizer Use in Ethiopia

Most Ethiopian soils lack nutrients, especially nitrogen and phosphorus. Fertilizer application significantly boosts crop yields [16]. Field experiments confirm fertilizer's direct link to productivity. Fertilizer greatly increases productivity [17]. In Ethiopia, organic fertilizer is rarely used due to scarcity. It is mainly used as fuel. Scholars recommend chemical fertilizers as the second best option. The government and international partners aim to promote the fertilizer sector [17]. The World Bank and other donors helped the government launch the national fertilizer sector project in 1996. Since 1996, seven organizations have been involved in the distribution and importation of fertilizer. Increased consumption and a sufficient supply of fertilizer have resulted from this. Although fertilizer consumption increased significantly in the last six years, the change in quantity per unit area was only about 25 kg/ha. Efficient fertilizer use based on soil, crop, and site-specific recommendations is crucial [17]. On-farm experiments and soil testing are key for promoting this. Agricultural researchers are conducting field experiments to create chemical fertilizer guidelines. However, the development of these guidelines is tedious and resource-intensive.

8.2.6 Piloting, Consumption, and Efficiency of Inorganic Fertilizers

Smallholder farmers were heavily encouraged to participate in extensive inorganic fertilizer trials between the 1980s and 2000s, along with other technologies. The MoA adopted a top-down strategy known as "training and visit" (T&V) in the late 1980s and early 1990s, which was insensitive to the different needs of small-scale farmers [18]. A system known as participatory demonstration and training extension (PADETES) was put into place in 1995. It brought science-based technologies to small farms and integrated elements of T&V with the Sasakawa Global 2000 approach. The goal of PADETES was to spread technologies like better seeds, fertilizers, and cultural practices more quickly [19]. During that time, the extension approach encouraged monocropping and the use of agrochemicals (like atrazine), which threatened the agricultural system's sustainability.

Only two fertilizers—DAP and urea—were imported between the early 1970s and 2012 [19] until DAP was replaced by NPS in 2013. According to the temporal data, imports of fertilizer rose from 947 tons in 1971 to 1,390,535 tons in 2017 (ibid.); nevertheless, yield and profitability did not rise in line with this increase. Merely 30–40% of Ethiopian smallholder farmers apply fertilizers at an average rate of 37–40 kg ha^{-1}, significantly less than the suggested rates, according to Anchala et al. [20]. Research indicates that Ethiopia has a lower rate of fertilizer efficiency than certain other East African nations. For example, Ethiopian maize has a nutrient use efficiency of 9–17% of applied N, which is lower than that of Kenya and Tanzania, which are 7–36% and 18–43%, respectively (Heisey and Mwangi, 1996). This is caused by a number of factors, which can all result in expensive costs, such as slow response and low efficiency because there are no site-specific recommendations, no complementary packages, and an ineffective supply system.

8.2.7 Including Organic Resources

Ethiopian small-scale farmers have long improved soil fertility by using organic sources. One important source of this has been animal dung [21]. However, because of agricultural R&D, inorganic sources have progressively supplanted conventional systems. Since 1991, efforts have been made to liberalize the market for input supplies in Africa, which has resulted in a focus on integrating organic fertilizers to lower costs and improve sustainability [22, 23]. Because fertilizer prices were so high, smallholder farmers with limited resources also resorted to using animal manure and other organic sources [24]. The late 1990s saw the start of research projects on organic resources and their integration with inorganic materials [7] [19]. The interest in organic fertilizers was demonstrated by the private sector, which included National Fertilizer Manufacturing PLC. Research has indicated that the utilization of both organic and inorganic fertilizers in combination considerably improves soil quality, economic profitability, and crop yield when compared to the use of each source alone [25].

8.2.8 Participatory Innovation Approaches

Farmers Participatory Research was formalized in the early 2000s, although it has been conducted in Ethiopia since the 1980s [20]. Melkassa and Adami Tulu Agricultural Research Centers initiated a project in 2004 with the goal of enhancing technology development as reported [26]. The Humidtropics project evaluated the effects on soil quality and productivity at three sites in the Nile Basin where the Innovation Platforms approach was implemented.

8.2.9 Liming Acid Soils

In Ethiopian regions with heavy rainfall, crop productivity is hampered by acidic soil [27]. In humid and sub-humid highlands, soil acidity affects 43% of cultivated land, with 28% of that land being strongly acidic. Acidity of the soil impacts soil organisms and restricts the availability of vital nutrients. ISFM practices, including lime application, are effective for rehabilitating acidic soil. Liming acid soils improves the environment for soil microorganisms, promoting the breakdown of organic materials for plant nutrients. Combined lime and P application increased barley grain yields by 133% [28]. Lime application reduced external P requirement significantly. Liming stimulates microbial activities, enhancing N fixation and mineralization. Legumes benefit greatly from liming [29].

8.2.10 Soil Test and Crop Response Approach

The soil-test-based fertilizer recommendations use mathematical models to integrate soil test indices with fertilizer requirements [30]. This method is widely used for recommending phosphorus fertilizers globally. In Ethiopia, a phosphorus fertilizer recommendation system based on soil testing and crop response was established around 2000. Initially for wheat, phosphorus calibration expanded to include other cereals and pulses. Studies from 2012 to 2014 established critical phosphorus values and factors for phosphorus requirements for primary cereal and pulse crops. Applying P according to soil test results in notable yield increases in Tigray when compared to general recommendations [31].

8.2.11 Soil Fertility Prediction Using ML

Several ML techniques were employed by Trontelj and Chambers [32] to forecast soil nutrients. Compared to single-component prediction, multi-component analysis yielded higher accuracy. Overall prediction accuracy increased with the use of principal component analysis (PCA). Tanh and ReLU activation functions were used by artificial neural networks (ANNs) to predict soil fertility. Five parameters related to soil nutrients were entered. On four of the five nutrient parameters, the ReLU activation function performed satisfactorily [33].

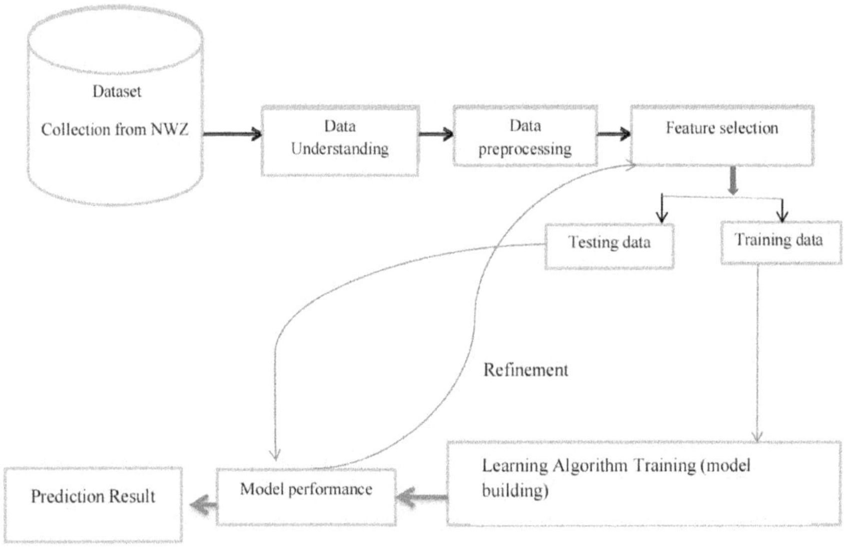

FIGURE 8.1 Research methodology.

8.3 RESEARCH METHODOLOGY

The proposed system is implemented based on a supervised classification machine learning technique to predict whether the soil is going to be fertile or not in the agriculture sector. Besides implementing the proposed model, four of the most commonly used ML techniques, Random Forest, SVM, XGBoost, and AdaBoost, were also used to compare our proposed model with them. The suggested system procedure is outlined as follows.

The process of machine learning is depicted in Figure 8.1, which starts with gathering data from NWSTC. Next, data preprocessing is carried out to clean and prepare the data. Feature selection is then performed to identify the most relevant variables. The process includes applying a smooth algorithm to enhance model robustness. Next, various algorithms, Random Forest, SVM, XGBoost, and AdaBoost, are utilized during the model building phase. The models are then trained on the data and evaluated through testing. Performance metrics are assessed to determine the effectiveness of each model, leading to prediction analysis to interpret the results and insights. This structured approach ensures comprehensive evaluation and selection of the best-performing model.

8.4 EXPERIMENTAL DESIGN

The numerical experiments were designed based on research that was conducted to measure the effectiveness of supervised machine learning algorithms in a comprehensive manner. The dataset consists of two classes; the first refers to the data belong

TABLE 8.1
Dataset Features

Attribute Name	Data Type	Description
PH	Number	Soil pH value
Woreda	Categorical	Name of woredas
EC	Number	Electrical conductivity
OC	Number	Organic carbon
OM	Number	Organic matter
N	Number	Nitrogen content
P	Number	Phosphorous content
K	Number	Potassium content
Ze	Number	Zinc content
Fe	Number	Iron content
Cu	Number	Copper content
Mn	Number	Manganese content
Silt	Number	Soil composition
$CaCO_3$	Number	Sodium bicarbonate content
CEC	Number	Cation exchange capacity
Crops	Categorical	Crop types
Fertility	Number	Fertile(1) or not fertile(0)

to class 1 (fertile), and the second refers to the data belong to class 0 (not fertile). The data for this specific research were collected from the National Soil Testing Center in North Wollo zone (NWSTC). A large number of records were obtained from experiments that have been conducted in different years. Among these, data from 2003 E.C. to 2013 E.C. were chosen for this particular research since they include many of the soil parameters and are also useful for understanding the current soil fertility status. The original soil fertility data contain 20,168 instances, comprising both fertile and not fertile samples, and 17 features. Table 8.1 lists the features used in the dataset for experiments.

8.4.1 Data Preprocessing

Data preprocessing plays a vital role in preparing raw data for effective modeling. The key steps involved were missing value handling, descriptive statistical analysis, and outlier detection and removal, as described below.

8.4.1.1 Missing Value Handling

Missing values can negatively impact model performance if not properly handled. As shown in Table 8.2, the dataset exhibited missing values in a few features: sand (180), silt (360), and a single value in K. Other attributes had complete data. To maintain the integrity of the dataset and avoid unnecessary loss of information, we

TABLE 8.2
Checking Dataset for Null Values

	df.isnull().sum()
Woreda	0
PH	0
EC	0
OC	0
OM	0
N	0
P	0
K	1
Zn	0
Fe	0
Cu	0
Mn	0
Sand	180
Silt	360
clay	0
$CaCO_3$	0
Crops	0
CEC	0
Fertility	0

adopted the mean imputation method. The missing values were replaced with the mean of their respective columns.

This method is appropriate when the proportion of missing values is relatively small and the data are assumed to be missing at random. Post-imputation, the dataset was checked again to confirm the absence of any null values.

8.4.1.2 Descriptive Statistics

To gain insight into the structure and distribution of the data, we generated a statistical summary of the dataset, as shown in Table 8.3. This summary includes count, mean, standard deviation, minimum, and various percentiles for each numerical attribute. It helped in identifying skewed distributions and potential data entry anomalies. For instance, the wide ranges in P, K, and Zn pointed toward potential outliers or natural variance across different geographic zones (woredas).

8.4.1.3 Outlier Detection and Removal

Outlier detection is essential to prevent skewed model training and misleading interpretations. Boxplots were employed to visually detect extreme values across key attributes (Figure 8.2). Variables such as EC, Zn, K, Silt, and OM displayed multiple

TABLE 8.3
Finding Minimum Value, Maximum Value, and Mean Value

df.describe()

	Woreda	pH	EC	OC	OM	N	P	K	Zn	Fe
Count	20,168	20,168	20,168	20,168	20,168	20,168	20,168	20,168	20,168	20,168
Mean	3.8214	8.2931	0.2962	0.1992	0.3384	173.494	13.6035	215.497	0.4965	4.5984
Std	2.2896	0.5415	0.2657	0.1722	0.2969	61.3780	8.51473	86.5106	0.2630	1.8765
Min	0.0000	6.5200	0.0200	0.0100	0.0100	75.0000	1.80000	70.0000	0.0400	1.0000
26%	2.0000	8.0600	0.1300	0.0800	0.1300	124.000	7.90000	145.000	0.3100	3.2000
60%	4.0000	8.3400	0.1900	0.1400	0.2400	164.000	10.5000	187.000	0.4600	4.20000
76%	5.0000	8.6200	0.3600	0.2400	0.4100	218.000	18.7000	268.000	0.6400	6.1000
Max	9.0000	9.4800	1.5800	0.7400	1.2700	278.000	35.6000	480.000	1.3000	9.1000

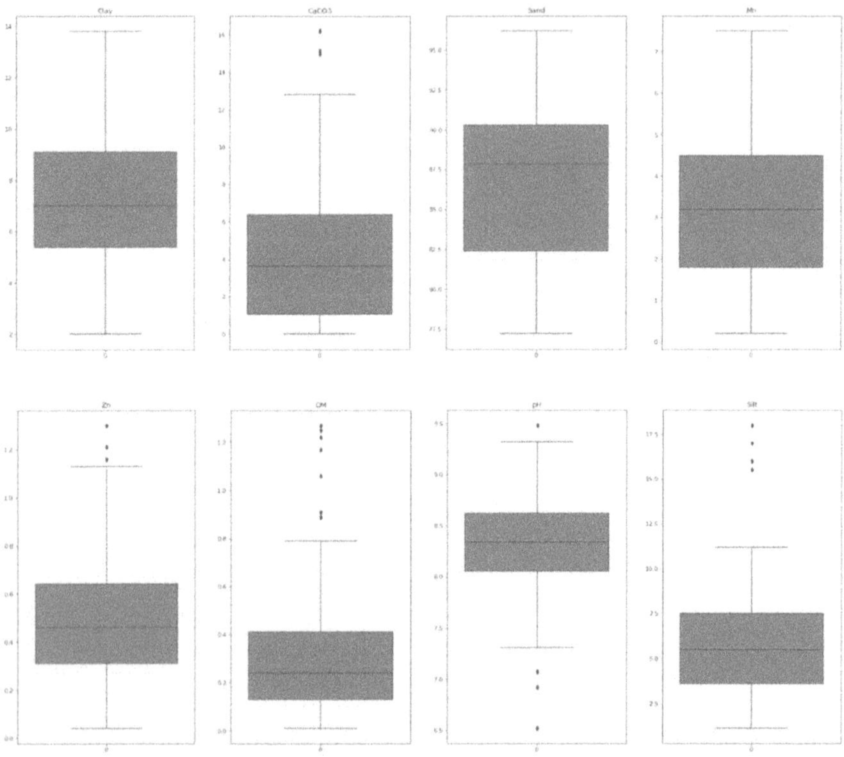

FIGURE 8.2 Outlier detection and removal.

outliers. These were validated in consultation with domain experts, and a decision was made to remove samples with extreme deviations.

A total of 1,434 records were removed from the original dataset of 20,168 samples, resulting in a cleaned and refined dataset of 18,734 records. This step helped improve the quality and consistency of the data used for modeling.

8.4.1.4 Feature Importance

The features selected for training were analyzed for trends and variability, using Python packages, such as NumPy, Jupyter Notebook, and Pandas. The five most important features have been defined in this section, although all 17 features were included in the study. Figure 8.3, feature importance, shows that Clay is one of the most important factors influencing model accuracy across all three datasets. Cation Exchange Capacity (CEC) ranks second for the given datasets, $CaCO_3$ is the third predictor variable, followed by Sand in the fourth place and Mn in fifth—all of which have a high impact on model predictions. However, Fe, Silt, Cu, N, and pH have low status on the model accuracy. This indicates that CEC, $CaCO_3$, Sand, Clay, and Mn are the most important predictor variables in the given dataset.

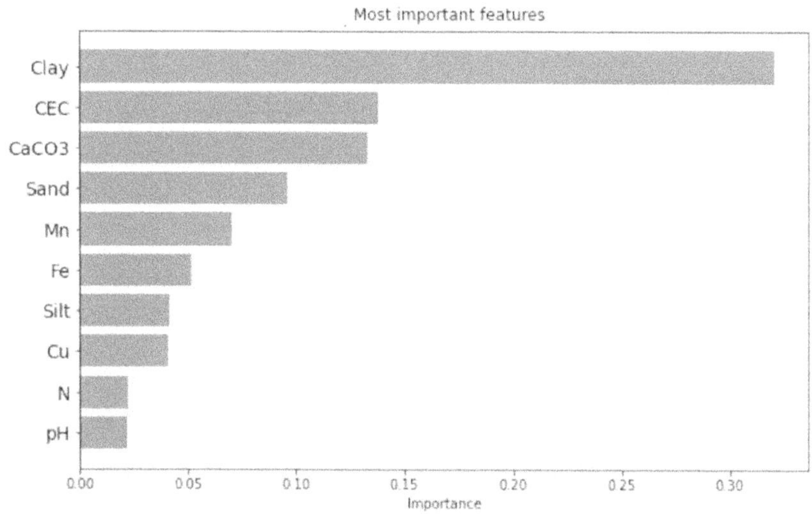

FIGURE 8.3 Feature importance.

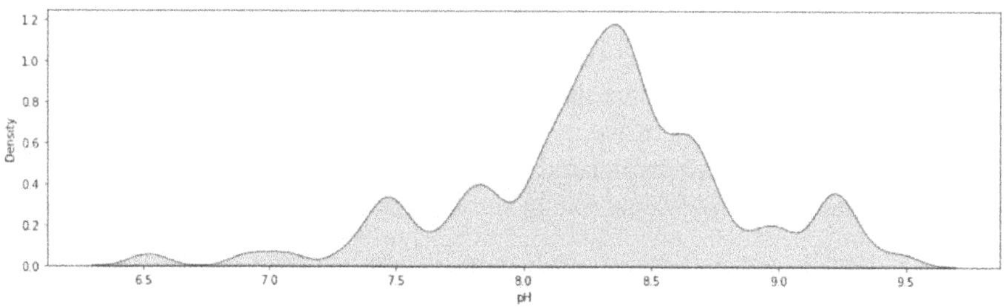

FIGURE 8.4 Fertility vs pH.

8.5 EXPLORATORY DATA ANALYSIS AND DATA VISUALIZATION

8.5.1 Fertility vs pH

Figure 8.4 shows a kernel density plot illustrating the distribution of soil pH levels in relation to fertility, with peaks around pH 8.0 and 8.5 indicating higher fertility concentrations. Fertility increases as pH rises, reaching an optimal peak before declining at higher pH levels. This suggests that both low and high pH levels may negatively impact fertility, highlighting the importance of maintaining optimal pH conditions in agricultural and ecological management.

8.5.2 Sand vs Crops with "Fertility"

Figure 8.5 presents a bar graph showing the relationship between soil sand content and fertility for crops like wheat, maize, barley, sorghum, teff, chickpea, sesame,

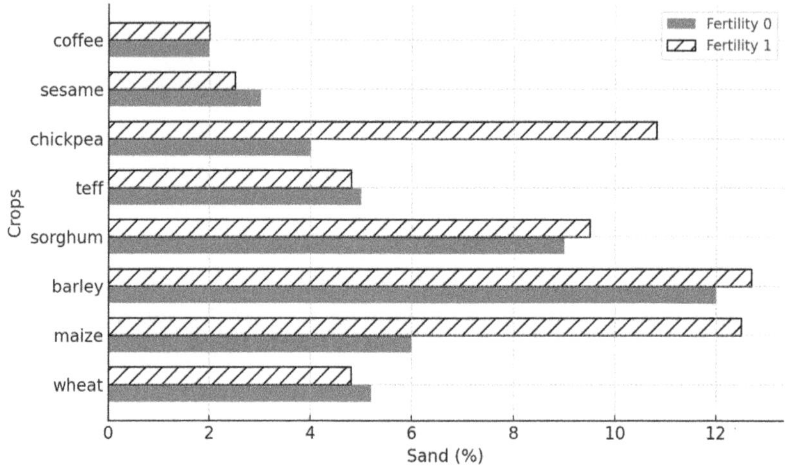

FIGURE 8.5 Sand vs crops.

and coffee. The shaded bars represent Fertility 0, while the striped bars represent Fertility 1. Crops such as wheat, barley, and sorghum show relatively high sand content in both fertility conditions, whereas sesame and coffee have lower values for both. Chickpea and teff also show moderate sand percentages, with teff having similar values across both fertility conditions. Overall, the graph indicates that crops like barley, maize, and sorghum thrive in soils with higher sand content, whereas crops like coffee and sesame are associated with lower sand percentages. This suggests that sand content plays a variable role in soil fertility depending on the crop type..

8.5.3 Crops vs pH with Respect to Fertility

Figure 8.6 illustrates the relationship between soil pH (%) and fertility across different crops, with shaded bars representing Fertility 0 and striped bars representing Fertility 1. Crops such as barley, maize, and sorghum show the highest pH values in both fertility conditions, indicating a strong association between higher pH and fertility. Chickpea also shows a notable increase in fertility 1 compared to fertility 0, while teff presents moderate values across both categories. In contrast, coffee and sesame exhibit the lowest pH percentages, reflecting lower fertility levels. Overall, the results suggest that soil pH positively influences fertility, with higher pH levels supporting greater crop productivity. This highlights the importance of managing soil pH across woredas to optimize nutrient availability and maintain sustainable agricultural practices.

8.5.4 Woreda vs pH with Respect to Fertility

Figure 8.7 presents pH values and fertility levels for each Woreda, with shaded bars representing Fertility 0 and stripped bars representing Fertility 1. The data show

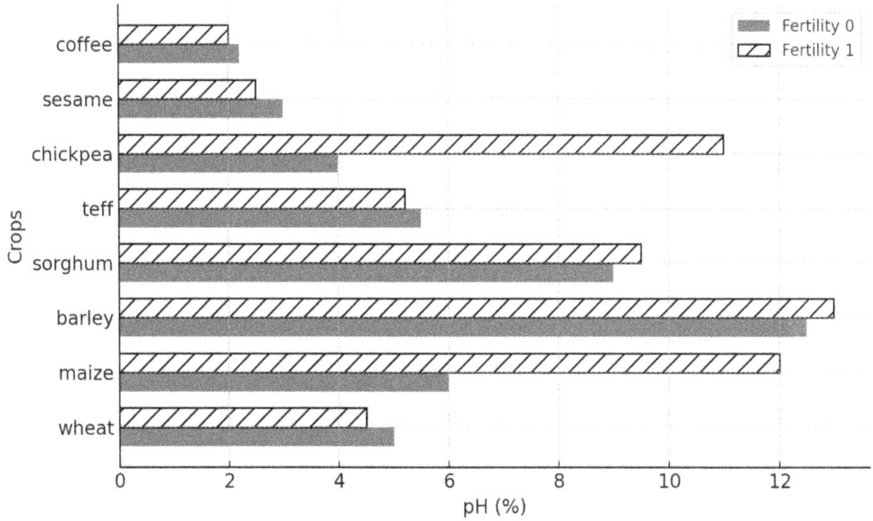

FIGURE 8.6 Crops vs pH with respect to fertility.

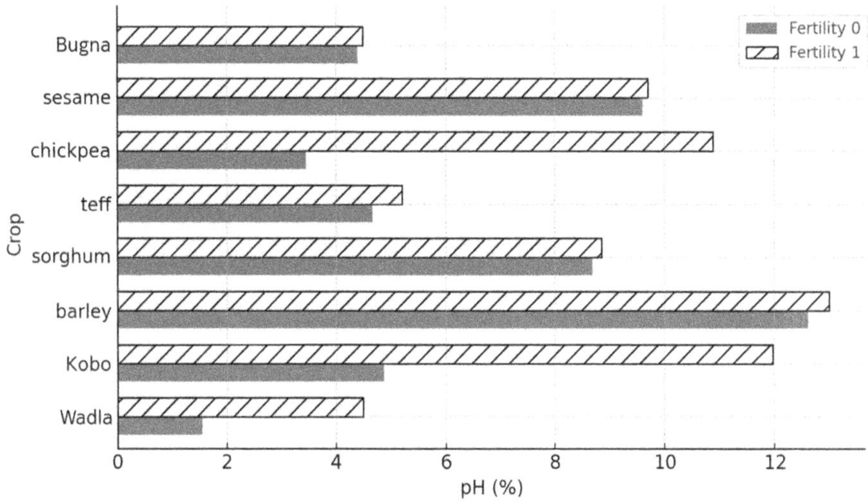

FIGURE 8.7 Woreda vs pH with respect to fertility.

a positive relationship between soil pH and fertility, as Woredas like Delanta and Dawunt with higher pH levels tend to have more fertile soils, while Woredas like Wadla and Meket with lower pH levels show reduced fertility. This visualization offers valuable insights into soil characteristics across different Woredas, aiding in agricultural planning, resource allocation, and optimizing crop production and soil management.

8.6 RESULTS AND DISCUSSION

This section evaluates the experimental results, focusing on classifier performance. Various evaluation metrics, parameter tuning, and average accuracy using 10-fold cross-validation are assessed through the Sklearn library in Python. The Sklearn cross_val_score function is employed to compute the results.

8.6.1 Evaluating of Models with Original Dataset

From Table 8.4, all evaluated classifiers performed well in predicting soil fertility on the original dataset. The Random Forest classifier achieved the highest testing accuracy at 95.50%, followed by the AdaBoost classifier at 94.00%. The Support Vector Machine (SVM) and XGBoost classifiers recorded accuracies of 86.50% and 93.00%, respectively. Precision, recall, and F1-scores indicated balanced performance across both fertile and non-fertile classes. Notably, the Random Forest and AdaBoost classifiers had higher precision for non-fertile cases, while XGBoost showed slightly better precision for fertile cases. Overall, the results confirm the effectiveness of all models, with Random Forest and AdaBoost slightly outperforming in accuracy and precision.

8.6.2 Evaluating of Models with SMOTE Dataset

The evaluation of classifiers on the SMOTE-balanced dataset shows strong performance in predicting soil fertility. Both Random Forest and AdaBoost achieved perfect training accuracy (1.0000), high testing accuracy (0.9439), and solid validation accuracy (0.9052), indicating robust generalization. They also demonstrated balanced precision, recall, and F1-scores. SVM performed well with a testing accuracy of 0.8680 and a validation accuracy of 0.8501 but had slightly lower precision and recall. XGBoost showed strong predictive power with perfect training accuracy and testing accuracy of 0.9307. Overall, the ensemble methods, especially Random Forest and AdaBoost, outperformed others in accuracy and consistency (Table 8.5).

8.6.3 Evaluation Measure Using ROC Curve

The ROC curve is a common tool to assess binary classifier performance. To avoid bias, k-fold cross-validation was applied, and ROC and precision-recall (PR) curves were generated for all models. The ROC curve plots the true positive rate against the false positive rate, while the PR curve focuses on precision and recall, especially for detecting rare events. A higher area under the curve (AUC) in both indicates better performance. As shown in Figure 8.8, the Random Forest model outperformed others, achieving the highest AUC and F1 score, reflecting its superior performance.

TABLE 8.4
Result Summary of Original or Imbalanced Dataset

Classifier	Training Accuracy	Testing Accuracy	Validation Accuracy (CV)	Precision (Class 0)	Recall (Class 0)	F1-Score (Class 0)	Precision (Class 1)	Recall (Class 1)	F1-Score (Class 1)
RF	1.0000	0.9550	0.9125	0.94	0.97	0.96	0.97	0.94	0.95
SVM	0.8612	0.8650	0.8625	0.86	0.87	0.87	0.87	0.86	0.86
AdaBoost	1.0000	0.9400	0.9037	0.93	0.95	0.94	0.95	0.93	0.94
XGBoost	1.0000	0.9300	0.9088	0.94	0.92	0.93	0.92	0.94	0.93

TABLE 8.5
Summary of Results on SMOTE Dataset

Model	Training Accuracy	Testing Accuracy	Validation Accuracy (CV)	Precision (Class 0)	Precision (Class 1)	Recall (Class 0)	Recall (Class 1)	F1-Score (Class 0)	F1-Score (Class 1)	Accuracy
RF	1.0000	0.9439	0.9052	0.92	0.97	0.97	0.92	0.95	0.94	0.94
AdaBoost classifier	1.0000	0.9439	0.9052	0.92	0.97	0.97	0.91	0.95	0.94	0.94
SVM	0.8557	0.8680	0.8501	0.86	0.88	0.88	0.85	0.87	0.87	0.87
XGBoost classifier	1.0000	0.9307	0.8911	0.92	0.94	0.94	0.92	0.93	0.93	0.93

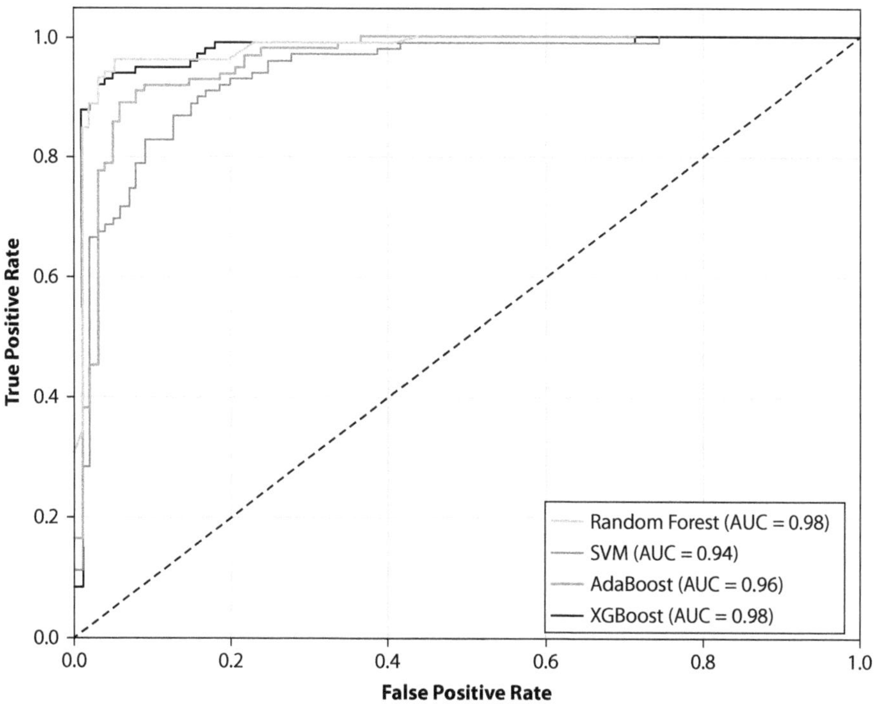

FIGURE 8.8 ROC curve for different models.

8.6.4 Area under the Precision-Recall (PR) Curve

The area under the precision-recall curve serves as the final benchmark for model performance. Precision and recall are inversely related, and classification models use probabilistic predictions to determine the likelihood of a sample belonging to the positive class. By adjusting the threshold, samples are classified as positive or negative. As the threshold shifts from 0 to 1, precision and recall values change accordingly. Figure 8.9 shows this relationship, illustrating the trade-offs between precision and recall at different thresholds.

The results, visualized through ROC and PR curves, showed that Random Forest and XGBoost had higher AUC values compared to other classifiers, also the accuracy of the classifier is mentioned in Table 8.6 Among baseline, up-sampled, and down-sampled settings, the up-sampled setting generally achieved the best accuracy and precision. Down-sampling reduced precision but improved recall.

Overall, the results show that the Random Forest and AdaBoost classifiers performed consistently well on both the original and SMOTE-balanced datasets, proving their robustness to class imbalance. Although the SVM's performance improved slightly on the balanced dataset, it remained behind the ensemble methods. XGBoost also demonstrated strong performance across datasets, effectively handling imbalanced data and achieving high accuracy.

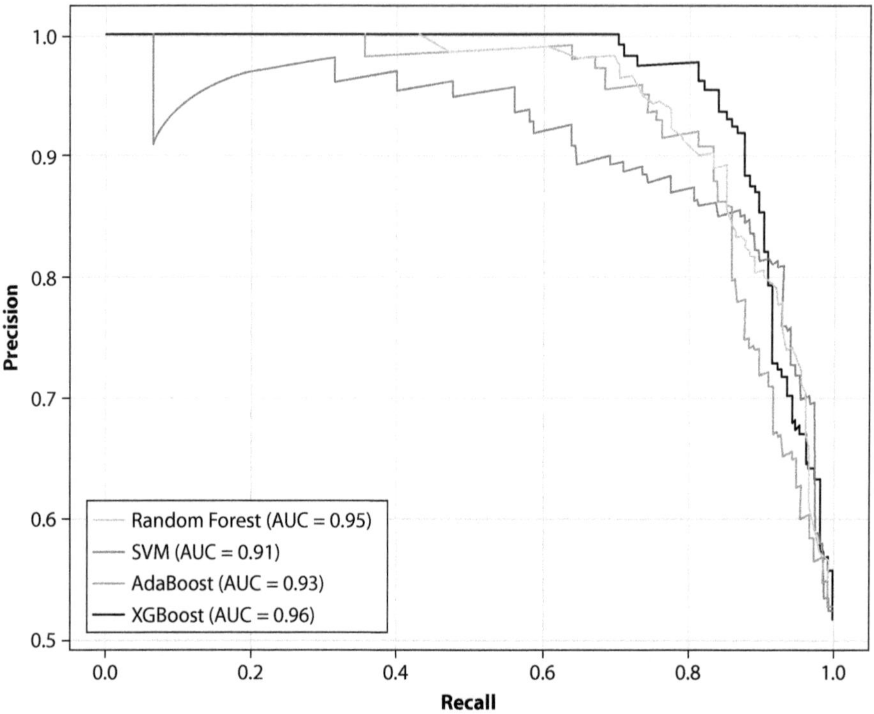

FIGURE 8.9 Precision-recall curve for models.

TABLE 8.6
Comparative Result

References	Algorithm	Features	Dataset Size	Accuracy (%)
[34]	Random Forest classifier	10	Not mentioned	72.74
[35]	JRip Data Mining	7	110	98.18
[36]	CNN	16	Not mentioned	84
Current work	Random Forest	17	20,168	95.50

8.7 CONCLUSION

This research aimed to analyze and predict soil fertility using machine learning techniques, focusing on the North Wollo zone. The study is critical due to the increasing demand for agricultural production amidst constraints such as limited land and water resources, particularly in Amhara regions, Ethiopia. Soil fertility prediction using machine learning offers an innovative solution to enhance agricultural productivity and resource optimization.

The study evaluated several machine learning models on both the original and SMOTE-balanced datasets. The Random Forest classifier consistently showed the highest performance, with testing accuracies of 95.50% on the original dataset and 94.39% on the SMOTE-balanced dataset. The AdaBoost classifier also demonstrated strong performance, with testing accuracies of 94.00% and 94.39% on the original and SMOTE-balanced datasets, respectively. The Support Vector Machine (SVM) and XGBoost classifiers performed well but were slightly less accurate compared to the ensemble methods, particularly on the original dataset. However, XGBoost showed robust performance on both datasets, with testing accuracies of 93.00% and 93.07%.

Evaluating feature importance using the Random Forest classifier revealed that factors such as Clay, CEC, $CaCO_3$, Sand, and Mn significantly impact soil fertility prediction. These findings highlight the critical role of these soil properties in determining fertility and can guide targeted soil management practices. Future research should explore the integration of additional soil properties and advanced machine learning and deep learning techniques to further enhance prediction accuracy

REFERENCES

1. Tamene, L. D., T. Amede, J. Kihara, D. Tibebe, and S. Schulz. 2017. *A Review of Soil Fertility Management and Crop Response to Fertilizer Application in Ethiopia: Towards Development of Site-and Context-Specific Fertilizer Recommendation.* CIAT Publications.
2. Sanchez, P. A., G. L. Denning, and G. Nziguheba. 2009. "The African Green Revolution Moves Forward." *Food Security* 1: 37–44.
3. Yirga, C., T. Erkossa, and G. Agegnehu. 2019. *Soil Acidity Management.* Ethiopian Institute of Agricultural Research.
4. Deressa, A., M. Yli-Halla, M. Mohamed, and L. Wogi. 2020. "Phosphorus Sorption Characteristics of Lime Amended Ultisols and Alfisols in Humid Tropical Western Ethiopia." *Open Access Journal of Environmental Soil Science*, 5(2), 601–613.
5. Iticha, B., and C. Takele. 2019. "Digital Soil Mapping for Site-Specific Management of Soils." *Geoderma* 351: 85–91.
6. Havlin, J., and R. Heiniger. 2020. "Soil Fertility Management for Better Crop Production." *Agronomy* 10 (9): 1349.
7. Erkossa, T., A. Wudneh, B. Desalegn, and G. Taye. 2015. "Linking Soil Erosion to On-Site Financial Cost: Lessons from Watersheds in the Blue Nile Basin." *Solid Earth* 6 (2): 765–774.
8. Zelleke, G., G. Agegnehu, D. Abera, and S. Rashid. 2019. "Fertilizer and Soil Fertility Potential in Ethiopia." *Gates Open Research* 3 (482): 482.
9. Erkossa, T., D. Geleti, T. O. Williams, F. Laekemariam, and A. Haileslassie. 2022. "Restoration of Grazing Land to Increase Biomass Production and Improve Soil Properties in the Blue Nile Basin: Effects of Infiltration Trenches and Chloris Gayana Reseeding." *Renewable Agriculture and Food Systems* 37 (S1): S64–S72.
10. Westphal, E., and J. M. C. Stevels. 1975. *Agricultural Systems in Ethiopia.* Vol. 826. Wageningen: Centre for Agricultural Publishing and Documentation.
11. Brady, N. C., and R. R. Weil. 2008. *The Nature and Properties of Soils.* Vol. 13. Upper Saddle River, NJ: Prentice Hall.

12. Navarro-Pedreño, J., M. B. Almendro-Candel, and A. A. Zorpas. 2021. "The Increase of Soil Organic Matter Reduces Global Warming, Myth or Reality?" *Sci* 3 (1): 18.
13. Huang, T., N. Yang, C. Lu, X. Qin, and K. H. Siddique. 2021. "Soil Organic Carbon, Total Nitrogen, Available Nutrients, and Yield under Different Straw Returning Methods." *Soil and Tillage Research* 214: 105171.
14. Lambers, H. 2022. "Phosphorus Acquisition and Utilization in Plants." *Annual Review of Plant Biology* 73 (1): 17–42.
15. Eleni, G. B. 2022. "Effects of Integrated Use of Inorganic and Organic Fertilizers on Selected Soil Physico-Chemical Properties and Yield of Durum Wheat (*Triticum Turgidum L.*) on Vertisols of Ada'a District, East Shewa Zone." PhD thesis, Ambo University.
16. Tulema, B. 2005. "Integrated Plant Nutrient Management in Crop Production in the Central Ethiopian Highlands." PhD thesis, Norwegian University of Life Sciences.
17. Wedajo Abdi, M. 2019. "Localizing Ethiosis Fertility Map Based Fertilizer Type Recommendation for Maize (*Zea mays L.*) in Coffee and Spice Production Belt in Yeki District, Southwest of Ethiopia." PhD thesis, Jimma University.
18. Anderson, J. R., and G. Feder. 2007. "Agricultural Extension." In *Handbook of Agricultural Economics*, G. C. Rausser, Elsevier, (eds.), vol. 3, 2343–2378.
19. Adugna, T., and T. Zegeye. 2003. "Rationalization of Fertilizer Sub-Sector Policies, Regulations, Procedures, Grades and Standards in Ethiopia",, Ministry of Agriculture, Ministry of Rural Development Agricultural Development Led Industrialization, Ethiopia.
20. Anchala, C., A. Deressa, H. Admasu, and E. Habte. 2004. "Enhancing Innovations through Farmer Research Groups (FRGs): Basic Concepts and Experience in Other Countries." In *Farmer Research Group (FRG) Concept and Practice*, Fasil Reda Hailu Dadi, Mohammed Hassana, Adam Bekele, JICA, (eds.) ,vol. 29.
21. Erkossa, T., F. Laekemariam, W. Abera, and L. Tamene. 2022. "Evolution of Soil Fertility Research and Development in Ethiopia: From Reconnaissance to Data-Mining Approaches." *Experimental Agriculture* 58: e4.
22. Shikur, Z. H. 2020. "Agricultural Policies, Agricultural Production and Rural Households' Welfare in Ethiopia." *Journal of Economic Structures* 9 (1): 50.
23. Giller, K. E. 2001. *Nitrogen Fixation in Tropical Cropping Systems*. CABI.
24. Morris, M. L. 2007. *Fertilizer Use in African Agriculture: Lessons Learned and Good Practice Guidelines*. World Bank Publications.
25. Elka, E., and F. Laekemariam. 2020. "Effects of Organic Nutrient Sources and NPS Fertilizer on the Agronomic and Economic Performance of Haricot Bean (*Phaseolus vulgaris L.*) in Southern Ethiopia." *Applied and Environmental Soil Science* 2020: 1–9.
26. Matsumoto, I., M. Niioka, and K. Shiratori. 2009. *Guideline to Participatory Agricultural Research through Farmer Research Group (FRG) for Agricultural Researchers*. Ethiopian Institute of Agricultural Research.
27. Agegnehu, G., C. Yirga, and T. Erkossa. 2019. *Soil Acidity Management*. Ethiopian Institute of Agricultural Research.
28. Desalegn, T., G. Alemu, A. Adella, and T. Debele. 2017. "Effect of Lime and Phosphorus Fertilizer on Acid Soils and Barley (*Hordeum vulgare L.*) Performance in the Central Highlands of Ethiopia." *Experimental Agriculture* 53 (3): 432–444.
29. Fageria, N. K., and V. C. Baligar. 2008. "Ameliorating Soil Acidity of Tropical Oxisols by Liming for Sustainable Crop Production." *Advances in Agronomy* 99: 345–399.
30. Sala, F., M. Boldea, H. Rawashdeh, and I. Nemet. 2015. "Mathematical Model for Determining the Optimal Doses of Mineral Fertilizers for Wheat Crops." *Pakistan Journal of Agricultural Sciences* 52 (3): 609–617.

31. Reda, G. T. 2016. "Verification and Demonstration of Soil Test Based Phosphorus Fertilizer Recommendation Rate on Yield of Teff (Eragrostis Tef (Zucc) Trotter) in Vertisols of Northern Ethiopia." *Journal of Natural Sciences Research* 6: 51–55.
32. Trontelj ml, J., and O. Chambers. 2021. "Machine Learning Strategy for Soil Nutrients Prediction Using Spectroscopic Method." *Sensors* 21 (12): 4208.
33. Pant, J., P. Pant, R. P. Pant, A. Bhatt, D. Pant, and A. Juyal. 2021. "Soil Quality Prediction for Determining Soil Fertility in Bhimtal Block of Uttarakhand (India) Using Machine Learning." *International Journal of Analytical and Applied* 19 (1): 91–109.
34. Keerthan Kumar, T. G., C. Shubha, and S. A. Sushma. 2019. "Random Forest Algorithm for Soil Fertility Prediction and Grading Using Machine Learning." *International Journal of Innovative Technology and Exploring Engineering* 9 (1): 1301–1304.
35. Rajeswari, V., and K. Arunesh. 2016. "Analysing Soil Data Using Data Mining Classification Techniques." *Indian Journal of Science and Technology* 9 (19): 1–4.
36. Yang, J., X. Wang, R. Wang, and H. Wang. 2020. "Combination of Convolutional Neural Networks and Recurrent Neural Networks for Predicting Soil Properties Using Vis-NIR Spectroscopy." *Geoderma* 380: 114616.

9 Revolutionizing Student Placement Trends

The Role of Machine Learning Algorithm

Anandha Meenachi M., K. Shivani, Karthik K. and Ashwin T. S.

9.1 INTRODUCTION

In the modern educational landscape, understanding and improving student performance has become increasingly critical. Traditional methods of assessing student achievement often rely on static measures such as test scores and grades, which may not fully capture the complexities of a student's learning journey. Placement is a decisive factor in the successful completion of any coursework at the graduate or postgraduate level (Maurya et al., 2021). A critical component of contemporary education involves assisting students in overcoming career setbacks effectively (Rao et al., 2023). Predicting college placements based on academic performance is crucial for helping educational institutions and students make educated decisions about future career paths. In this study, we explore the use of two prominent machine learning algorithms—non-linear regression and Random Forest—to predict student performance, specifically their marks. Machine learning (ML) algorithms and approaches assist in identifying patterns and predicting the student's future performance based on collected data (Dirin et al., 2022). Nonlinear regression refers to a broader category of regression models where the relationship between the dependent variable and the independent variables is not assumed to be linear, while Random Forest offers a robust method that accounts for nonlinear interactions and variable importance. The literature related to the use of machine learning technology in the field of higher education mainly focuses on the application of technologies such as clustering, association rules, classification, regression, and statistics to predict the performance of the developed model (Singh et al., 2020). The prediction of academic accomplishment based on prior knowledge from students who have successfully finished their university studies has become an intriguing tool for educational administration since it allows them to reinforce judgments and design improvement alternatives (Guanin-Fajardo et al., 2024). As machine learning continues to evolve, its application in education holds the promise of transforming how we understand and support student success. Campus placement prediction and analysis using machine learning entail

DOI: 10.1201/9781003532156-12

leveraging historical placement data, student profiles, academic performance metrics, and other relevant factors to develop predictive models (Saradhi et al., 2024). The placement of students in industry is challenging and depends on a number of factors, such as student academic performance, communication skills, capabilities, problem-solving, disability factors, etc. (Masethe et al., 2014). The profile chart displays an evaluation of both job requirements and student abilities for critical features of the job so that management can quickly determine how well a candidate fits a job (Jagan, 2018). Machine learning uses various algorithms for building mathematical models and making predictions using historical data or information (Rai & Kajal 2022). Several recent studies have focused on predicting students' campus placement. Researchers have used different approaches such as Decision tTees, Random Forests, and Support Vector Machines to predict campus placement (Byagar et al., 2024). This research aims to provide a foundation for integrating machine learning into educational practices, highlighting its potential to revolutionize student performance analysis and intervention strategies. As shown in Figure 9.1, the word cloud building model represents various departments, considering only those students who are eligible for placements in the college.

9.2 RELATED WORKS

9.2.1 Cross Disciplinary Perspective

Machine learning is programming computers to optimize a performance criterion using example data or experience (Kučak et al., 2018). Machine learning finds applications in diverse domains such as email spam filtering, fraud detection, stock trading, medical diagnosis, traffic prediction, character recognition, and product recommendation (Alzubi et al., 2018). Figure 9.2 highlights the key points of machine learning algorithms for predicting student performance from a cross-disciplinary perspective. In ML student algorithm performance, cognitive load management helps simplify complex concepts, while active learning promotes hands-on practice. A strong motivation and mindset encourage persistence, and collaboration fosters teamwork for better problem-solving. Machine learning algorithms are beneficial in situations when deploying explicitly written algorithms with high-speed performance is not practical (Choudhary et al., December 2017). Machine learning systems can carry out complex processes by learning from data rather than following preprogrammed rules (Sharma et al., 2017). Machine learning techniques are used to work with multidimensional data from a range of application domains (Nasteski & Vladimi, 2017).

9.2.2 Enhancing Student Performance Prediction with Machine Learning

The grade point average (GPA) can reflect the true value of future educational and job opportunities and advancement. Furthermore, a student's GPA can be used to assess academic potential. The main focus is on the challenges in building and maintaining machine learning systems and proposing "student learning" as a discipline to

FIGURE 9.1 Word cloud of departments with eligible students.

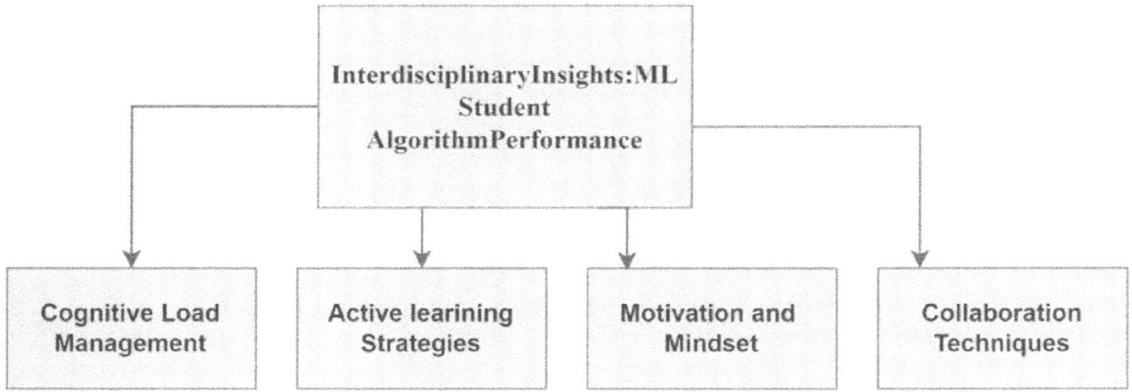

FIGURE 9.2 Interdisciplinary insights: ML student algorithm performance.

TABLE 9.1
Summary of Educational AI and ML Strategies and Considerations

Author & Year	Method	Advantages	Prevention
Namoun & Alshanqiti, 2020	Averaging grades	A high GPA predicts future opportunities and motivates academic excellence.	A holistic evaluation and mental health support are vital to reduce stress and inequities.
Simard et al., 2017	Conceptual framework development	Emphasizing "student learning" boosts efficiency in creating machine learning systems.	Straightforward learning methods can prevent issues in developing machine learning models.
Tedre et al., 2021	Thematic categorization	AI tools in K-12 education enhance learning and improve administrative efficiency.	Careful AI implementation is crucial to avoid overwhelming teachers and students.
Alshanqiti et al., 2020	Systematic literature review	Data mining and learning analytics effectively predict student performance, improving educational outcomes.	Ensuring data privacy and ethics is vital to prevent misuse of student information.
Verma et al., 2020	Qualitative analysis	Modern technology enhances learning experiences and student engagement.	Understanding students' views on technology is vital for effective classroom integration.
Broll & Grover, 2023	Conceptual framework development	Parson's Problems improve engagement by simplifying complex tasks.	Clear task design prevents confusion in ML model interactions.
Aldeman et al., 2021	Tool development and evaluation	Smart Pathak uses machine learning to improve teaching in glomerulopathies.	Validating the tool ensures accurate information and learning outcomes.
Herta et al., 2019	Qualitative analysis	Jupyter notebooks enhance student engagement and understanding through interactivity.	Jupyter needs training.

address these challenges and improve productivity in building ML models (Simard et al., 2017). In K-12 education, most AI-related initiatives have historically been concerned with 1) AI-based tools to support learning, 2) AI-based tools for studying learning processes, and 3) AI to support school administrative functions (Tedre et al., 2021). Table 9.1 summarizes studies on educational methods, focusing on authors, methods, advantages, and preventive measures. It highlights the benefits of machine learning and interactive tools for enhancing student performance and engagement. The overview emphasizes the significance of ethical issues and appropriate training while applying educational AI and ML technologies. The research work reviews studies that use data mining and learning analytics techniques to predict student performance. It systematically analyzes methods applied in educational contexts to forecast outcomes like grades and dropout risks (Alshanqiti et al., 2020). The technology usage of education is modernized, and reading the student's mind is a challenging task regarding technology utilization (Verma et al., 2020). Using research on many levels of abstraction, this study explores the use of Parson's Problems and Subgoals for working with ML models (Broll et al., 2023). This study aims to describe and test the functionality of Smart Pathak, a tool using machine learning to support teaching in glomerulopathies (Aldeman et al., 2021). Different authors described how they used Jupyter notebooks for teaching and elementary procedures for working with notebooks in an educational context (Herta et al., 2019).

9.2.3 Future Horizons: Transforming Student Learning with Machine Learning Innovations

Academics predicted student grades using a collaborative multi-regression model based on students' performances, activities, and Moodle interactions as features (Hussain et al., 2019). A student satisfaction index evaluation method based on factor analysis is provided, then empirically tested and refined to update the model (Pallathadka et al., 2023). Machine learning is a regularly utilized tool for data processing in education. Machine learning is the process of using past examples to improve future outcomes (Akmeşe et al., 2021). We systematically reviewed the literature about grade/grade point average (GPA)) prediction and comprehensively presented them (Iqbal et al., 2017). Using ICT in education can enhance teaching and learning processes and promote knowledge development (Buenaño-Fernández et al., 2019). Figure 9.3 indicates the advantages of AI in the education system. AI in education provides personalized learning tailored to individual needs while offering 24/7 access to resources for continuous study. Enhanced learning analysis delivers insights into student performance, aiding data-driven decisions. Additionally, AI automates administrative tasks like grading, reducing teachers' workloads, and enabling them to focus on instruction. These advantages lead to a more effective learning environment. According to school improvement research, academic press or emphasis is an important component of high-performing schools (Leithwood et al., 2020). A supervised function is trained during the learning process, with the aim of predicting the future labels of unseen data (Hashim et al., 2020). In the past decades, student activities and course assignments have evolved in new directions, from traditional take-home work to flipped classrooms (Albreiki et al., 2021). MOOC and LMS offer free higher education around the world. These platforms provide student-teacher interaction through their online learning portals (August & Tsaima, 2021). Features in deep learning will be generated automatically to simulate the appropriate results (Li et al., 2021). Machine learning employs the preprogrammed algorithms to predict output values for the given input data. It is considered to be an aspect of artificial intelligence (Saraswathi et al., 2023). Across the range of achievement, non-selective state school pupils are therefore more likely to be under-predicted and less likely to be over-predicted (Anders et al., 2020). Understanding students' perceptions of the negative aspects of task involvement, known as cost, might provide fresh

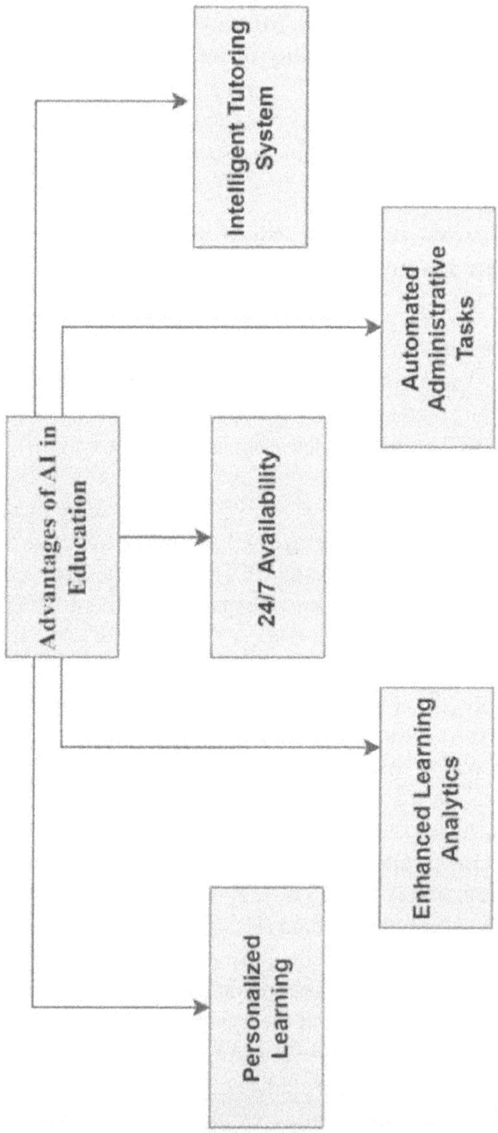

FIGURE 9.3 Advantages of AI in education.

insights into how to anticipate outcomes connected to students' learning behavior at school (Jiang & Rosenzweig, 2021). Table 9.2 provides an overview of studies related to Future Horizons: Enhancing Student Learning through Innovations in Machine Learning. It presents various methods, such as collaborative multi-regression models and machine learning, aimed at enhancing student learning and satisfaction. Each method showcases advantages like improved prediction accuracy and insights into student behavior while emphasizing the need for data quality, regular updates, and effective training to mitigate potential challenges.

9.3 SYSTEM MODEL

9.3.1 Random Forest

The Random Forest Classifier's important factors are shown in Figure 9.4. To improve prediction accuracy, Random Forest is an ensemble technique that uses Bootstrap Aggregation to construct several decision trees. By using random subsets of data and features to train each tree, it lowers variance and produces a variety of models. Applications that are frequently used include illness prediction and credit rating. Despite its intricacy, it provides interpretability by identifying the most important variables in forecasts through feature importance ratings.

(i) Ensemble Method: Combines multiple decision trees to improve overall performance and reduce overfitting.
(ii) Bootstrap Aggregation (Bagging): Each tree is trained on a random sample of the dataset (with replacement), which helps in reducing variance.
(iii) Feature Randomness: To increase model variety, a random subset of features is taken into account at each tree split.
(iv) Interpretability: Ensemble methods improve upon single decision trees in interpretability, but the combined model can be harder to interpret. Clarifying influential characteristics can be aided by feature significance scores.
(v) Applications: Commonly used in finance (credit scoring), healthcare (disease prediction), and marketing (customer segmentation) for both classification and regression tasks.

The mathematical modeling procedure of random forest:

(i) Decision Tree Construction:
Each tree is built using criteria like Gini impurity or entropy to determine the best splits at each node.
(ii) Voting Mechanism:
- A majority vote among all the trees determines the final result for classification.
- For regression, it is the average of the predictions from all the trees.

TABLE 9.2
Research highlights on the Application of Machine Learning in Student Learning

Author & Year	Method	Advantages	Prevention
Hussain et al., 2019	Collaborative multi-regression model	Improves prediction accuracy using diverse student data.	Data quality is crucial to avoid misleading outcomes.
Pallathadka et al., 2023	Factor analysis	Provides empirical insights to enhance student satisfaction.	Regular model updates are necessary to maintain relevance and accuracy.
Akmeşe et al., 2021	Machine learning	It enables improved outcomes by leveraging insights from past data.	Ensuring data quality and ethical standards are crucial to avoid biases and inaccuracies.
Iqbal et al., 2017	Systematic literature review	Offers a comprehensive overview of GPA prediction models.	Requires critical source evaluation to ensure reliability.
Buenaño-Fernández-D et al., 2019	Literature review	ICT improves teaching and fosters knowledge construction.	Proper educator training is vital to avoid ineffective technology use.
Leithwood et al., 2020	Literature review	Academic press increases student achievement through high expectations, aided by machine learning insights.	Machine learning helps create support systems to prevent student overwhelm.
Hashim et al., 2020	Supervised learning	It enables accurate predictions for unseen data.	High-quality labeled data is crucial to prevent overfitting.
Albreiki et al., 2021	Educational trends	Flipped classrooms increase student engagement and active learning.	Proper educator training is crucial for effective implementation.
August & Tsaima, 2021	Comparative analysis	They provide free education and enhance student-teacher interaction.	Adequate support is needed to prevent learner disengagement.
Li & Liu, 2021	Automated feature generation	It enhances accuracy by simulating appropriate results.	Ensuring robust validation techniques is crucial to prevent overfitting and maintain model generalizability.
Saraswathi et al., 2023	Preprogrammed algorithms	It enables accurate predictions and informed decisions.	Regular updates are needed to prevent inaccuracies.
Anders et al., 2020	Statistical analysis	It reveals a tendency for under-prediction, aiding educational support.	Standardized assessments can reduce prediction inaccuracies.
Jiang & Rosenzweig, 2021	Qualitative analysis	Insights gained can improve predictions of learning behaviors.	Addressing negative perceptions can enhance student motivation.

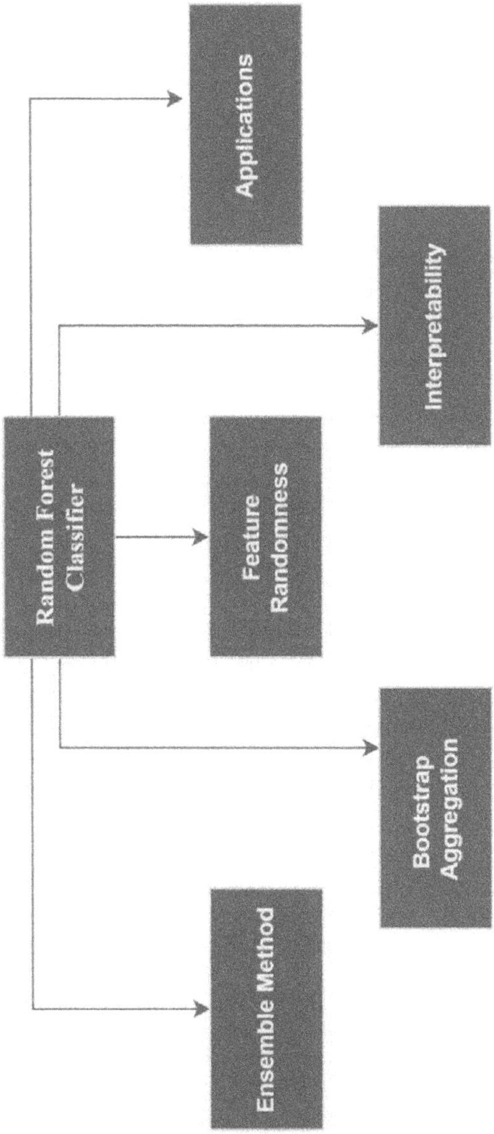

FIGURE 9.4 Key factors of Random Forest Classifier.

(iii) Reduction in Variance:
- The combination of multiple trees helps in stabilizing predictions and reducing overfitting, leveraging the law of large numbers.
- The mathematical formulation focuses on the aggregation of predictions, ensuring robustness and accuracy in various datasets.

9.3.2 Decision Tree Classifier

A decision tree is a model that uses feature values to branch and predict outcomes. It's easy to interpret and visualize but can overfit training data. Figure. 9.5 indicates the key factors of decision tree classifiers. Pruning techniques help reduce overfitting and improve accuracy.

Decision trees are widely used in applications like customer segmentation, risk assessment, and medical diagnosis due to their clear decision-making process. The key characteristics of this approach are as follows:

(i) Tree Structure: Consists of nodes representing tests on features, branches representing outcomes, and leaf nodes representing class labels.
(ii) Recursive Partitioning: Data is split recursively based on criteria such as Gini impurity or entropy.
(iii) Interpretability: The tree structure allows for easy interpretation and understanding of the decision-making process.
(iv) Accuracy: Decision trees can achieve high accuracy in predictions, but their performance can vary based on the dataset and parameters used.
(v) Overfitting: Decision trees are prone to overfitting, particularly with complex trees that capture noise in the training data. Pruning techniques can help mitigate this issue.
(vi) Applications: Widely used in areas such as finance (credit scoring), healthcare (diagnosis), and marketing (customer segmentation) due to their straightforward nature and effectiveness in both classification and regression tasks

The mathematical modeling procedure of decision tree:

(i) Splitting Criteria:

Gini Impurity:

A node is impure if it contains a combination of various classes instead of a single class. In a decision tree, "node" is used to denote a subset of data, and we want the nodes to be pure, i.e., all samples contained in the node must belong to the same class. In order to assess a node's impureness, we use the Gini impurity index, which is used by decision trees. While developing a decision tree, Gini impurity assists us in making decisions about features to be utilized for splitting a node into child nodes with the intention of selecting splits that minimize the impurity, forming child nodes that are cleaner than the parent nodes.

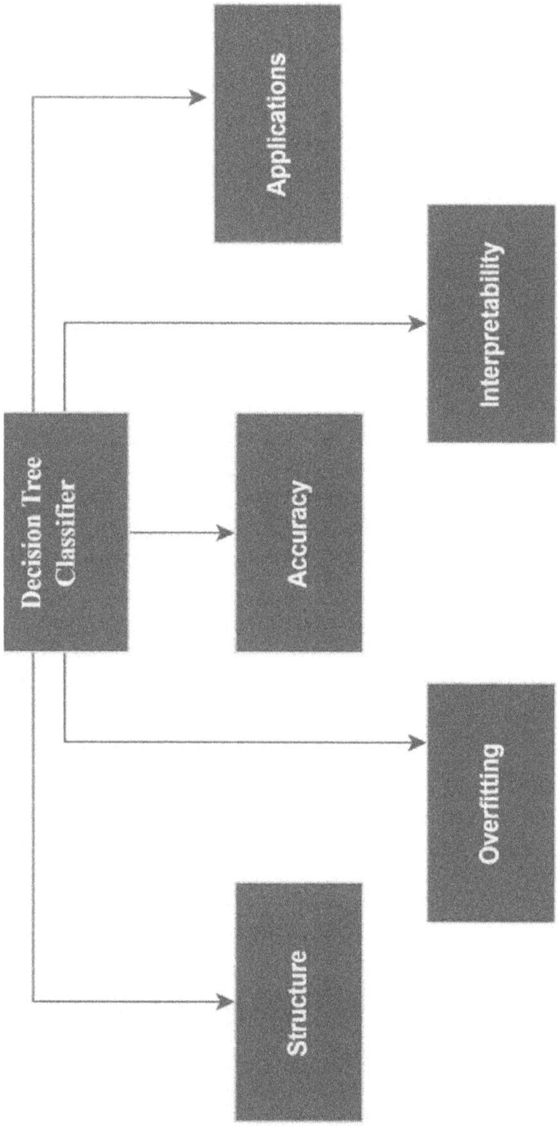

FIGURE 9.5 Decision tree classifier.

Formula to calculate Gini impurity:

$$\text{Gini} = 1 - \sum(pi)^2 \tag{9.1}$$

where *pi* is the probability of a random sample belonging to class *i* of that node. To find out *pi*, assume the number of samples in the node belonging to class "*i*" and divide by the total number of samples in the node. Pure node—When a node has sample from a single class, then either one of the *pi* values will be 1 and the rest will be 0.

Gini impurity of "0" represents an absolutely pure node.

$$\text{Gini} = 1 - (1\text{^}2 + 0\text{^}2 + 0\text{^}2 + \ldots) = 1 - 1 = 0 \tag{9.2}$$

Impure node—If a node contains samples from a mixture of classes, the *pi* value will fall between 0 and 1, causing the sum of the squared *pi* values to be less than 1. Therefore, the Gini impurity will be greater than 0; the higher the impurity value, the more mixed the classes are in the node.

Entropy:
Entropy in decision trees is a measure of uncertainty about the set of data, and it is utilized to measure information gain due to a split. The greater the entropy, the more random the data is. Thus, while constructing a decision tree, we try to make splits that decrease the entropy, resulting in more structured and predictable results of child nodes.

Formula to determine Entropy:

$$\text{Entropy} = \sum \text{piloglog 2 pi} \tag{9.3}$$

where *pi* is the probability of a random sample belonging to class *i* of that node, and the *pi* value is computed exactly as in Gini impurity. For a pure node, the entropy will be 0, while for a node containing an equal mix of various classes, entropy will be maximum.

(ii) Decision Rules:

Each node uses a decision rule based on the feature values, dividing the data until leaf nodes are reached.

(iii) Pruning:

Trees can be overfit to training data, and hence pruning techniques are used to eliminate branches having low discriminative power in classification, thus lowering complexity and increasing generalization.

There exist two categories of pruning:

Pre-Pruning (Early Stopping):

This prevents the decision tree growth before it becomes too deep because it's critical to avoid the high variance in the training data which could result in poor performance upon exposure to new data.

Pre-pruning techniques include the following:

Maximum Depth: We can restrict the maximum depth of the decision tree, stopping it from branching too many times.

Minimum Samples per Leaf: Enforce a minimum number of points per terminal node of the tree. This prevents certain rules that only address a small number of points, which could be caused by noise.

Minimum Samples per Split: Here we specify the minimum amount of data that should be present to split a node. This avoids the tree splitting on very specific splits that may not generalize well.

Maximum Features: Restrict the features to be used for splitting each node. This avoids the tree putting too much emphasis on individual features and makes it look for more general patterns.

Post-pruning (Reducing Nodes):

Post-pruning simplifies a mature decision tree by removing branches or nodes, which assists the model in preventing overfitting and enhances its capacity to make correct predictions on unseen data.

Cost-Complexity Pruning: Helps assign a cost to every subtree in a decision tree by evaluating both its accuracy and complexity. The lowest combined cost section will be chosen.

Reduced Error Pruning: Trims the insignificant branches to make the tree simpler without any effect on overall accuracy.

Minimum Impurity Decrease: Trims the nodes if reduction in impurities is below a given level.

Minimum Leaf Size: This eliminates leaf nodes with less than a threshold number of samples. In total, decision trees learn intricate relationships by partitioning the data space recursively, which makes them useful for handling multiple classification issues.

Figure 9.6 illustrates the distribution of student performance based on gender. Among the total of 2975 students, there are 2475 males and 491 females, indicating that males represent approximately 83.4% of the student population, while females account for 16.6%.

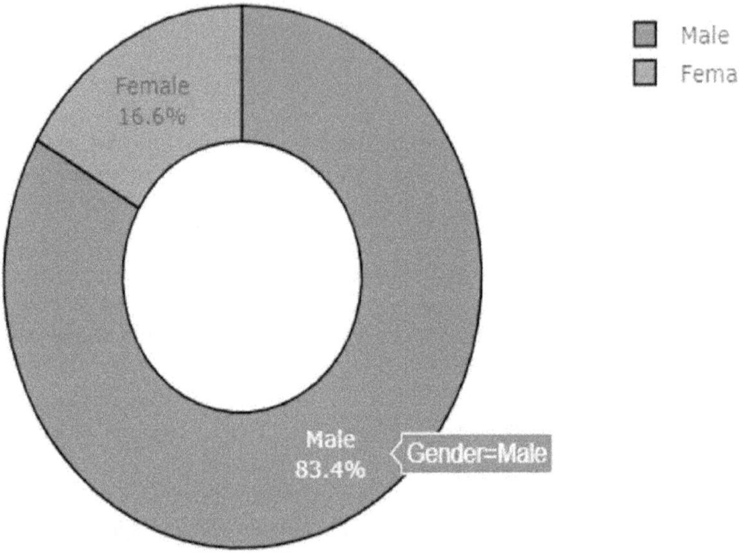

FIGURE 9.6 Gender distribution of students participating in the placements.

TABLE 9.3
Analysis of Student Pass Rates by Gender

Total male	2475
Total female	491
Total male pass	1364
Total female pass	275
% of passed male	55.11
% of passed female	56.01

In terms of academic success, 1364 male students passed, resulting in a pass rate of 55.11%, whereas 275 female students passed, with a slightly higher pass rate of 56.01%. This shows that despite the larger number of male students, the proportion of females passing is marginally greater, highlighting a noteworthy achievement among female students in this assessment. The information provided in Table 9.3 is essential for model prediction, helping to understand demographics, assess performance, and identify trends for targeted interventions.

It also aids in developing predictive algorithms to improve educational strategies and student outcomes. The steps that are followed to implement the training and prediction model are presented as an algorithm below:

Step 1: Import necessary libraries for data manipulation, visualization, and machine learning.
Step 2: Load the college placement dataset from a CSV file into a Data Frame Link to Dataset(https://www.kaggle.com/code/muhammadshahrayar/placement-prediction-detailed-eda). This dataset consists of information about students' academic performance, personal details, and internship experiences to predict placement outcomes. It includes a total of 4000 students, covering various academic streams and demographics, providing a comprehensive view of factors influencing placement success.
Step 3: Display dataset shape, data types, statistical summary, and null values to understand its structure.
Step 4: Create histograms to visualize age distributions, highlighting averages and gender differences.
Step 5: Calculate and present the total number of male and female students, including placement counts and percentages.
Step 6: Analyze placement trends across different academic streams using bar charts.
Step 7: Examine the impact of internship experience on placement success with histograms.
Step 8: Generate a word cloud to visualize popular fields of study among students.
Step 9: Convert categorical variables into dummy variables and standardize the dataset.
Step 10: To train the model, divide the data into training and testing sets.
Step 11: Describe and assess the following classification algorithms: K-Nearest Neighbors, Random Forest, XGBoost, and Decision Tree.
Step 12: Optimize the XGBoost model with hyperparameter tuning.
Step 13: Calculate and print the accuracy score of the optimized model.
Step 14: Generate and evaluate the final output using a confusion matrix.

Table 9.4 presents a comparative analysis of the proposed machine learning model against existing literature focused on student placement and performance prediction. It emphasizes variations in algorithm selection, dataset size, feature engineering techniques, evaluation metrics (like accuracy and precision), and overall model effectiveness in real-world educational settings.

9.4 RESULT

Figure 9.7 illustrates a histogram that shows the age distribution of students in the dataset used for predicting placement outcomes. The horizontal axis indicates students' ages, while the vertical axis represents the number of students within each age group. The histogram highlights a concentration of students in the 20–23 age range, peaking distinctly at age 21. This indicates that the majority of students involved in the placement process are generally around 21 years old. Nevertheless, the distribution is not entirely symmetrical. A noticeable rightward skew is present, suggesting

TABLE 9.4
Comparison of Proposed and Existing ML Approaches for Student Outcomes

Criteria	Proposed Work	Existing Literature (Selected Studies)
Focus	Placement success prediction	General Academic Success Prediction
Algorithm used	Random Forest, Decision Tree	Deep Learning (CNN, LSTM), SVM, Logistic Regression (Jagan, 2018; Li & Liu, 2021)
Interpretability	High (decision path available, easily understandable)	Low (Deep Learning models act as black boxes) (Wang et al., 2021)
Feature selection	Includes academic, technical, and soft skills (internships, projects, certifications, coding proficiency, communication skills, etc.)	Primarily focused on grades, attendance, and test scores (Singh & Pal, 2020)
Computational efficiency	Moderate (works on standard systems, no need for high-end GPUs)	High (Deep Learning requires GPUs and longer training time) (Wang et al., 2021)
Dataset consideration	Uses diverse real-world student placement data, ensuring model generalization	Some studies rely on small, biased, or synthetic datasets (Maurya et al., 2021)
Industry relevance	Directly applicable to career counseling and placement cells in institutions	Mostly theoretical with limited real-world implementation (Wang et al., 2021)
Model explainability	Provides detailed decision rules and feature importance rankings	Difficult to interpret (especially with deep learning methods) (Sharma & Kumar, 2017)
Accuracy	89.89% (using ensemble learning for better prediction robustness)	Varies (Deep Learning models often report 90%+ but require more computational power)
Accuracy improvement	Uses ensemble learning (Random Forest) to reduce overfitting and improve prediction robustness	Some studies may suffer from overfitting or require extensive hyperparameter tuning (Wang et al., 2021)
Automation and decision support	Can be integrated into an institution's placement portal for real-time analysis and guidance	Rarely provides direct actionable insights for students or placement officers
Computational cost	Moderate (Random Forest is efficient and runs on standard systems)	High (Deep Learning models require GPUs and more computational resources)
Real-world implementation	Suitable for real-time placement insights and can be integrated into college placement portals	Mostly theoretical, not always optimized for practical placement use (Maurya et al., 2021)
Limitations	Can be improved using hybrid models (e.g., combining ML with rule-based systems or deep learning for better performance)	Often lacks placement-specific factors, requiring additional feature engineering (Maurya et al., 2021)

a longer tail of older students. While the highest frequency appears at age 21, there is also a considerable number of students aged 22 and 23. Additionally, the histogram displays a gradual decrease in student numbers as age increases past 23, with a limited number of students in the 24–28 age range. Recognizing this age distribution is essential as it aids in identifying the usual demographic profile of students entering

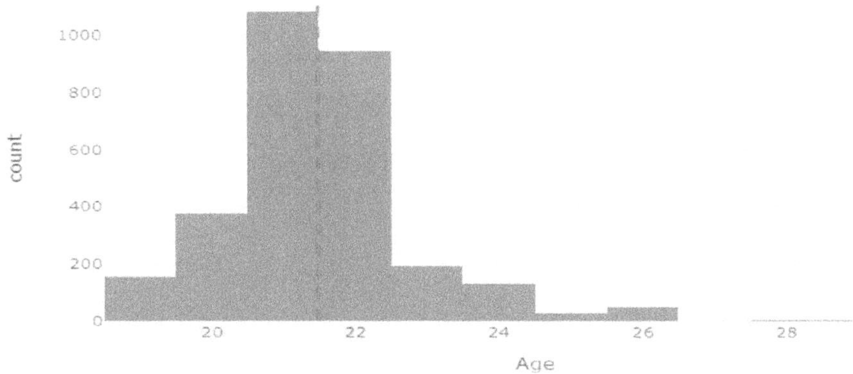

FIGURE 9.7 Average age of students.

the placement process. Age may influence placement outcomes, as employers might have particular preferences or requirements related to candidates' ages.

The bar chart in Figure 9.8 shows student distribution across different engineering streams and their placement outcomes. The x-axis lists streams like Electronics and Communication, Computer Science, and others, while the y-axis represents student counts. Lower part portion of the bar indicates placed students, and upper part portion of the bar shows those not placed. Computer Science and Information Technology have the highest student numbers, with a notable portion successfully placed.

Figure 9.9 illustrates the CGPA of students who fall below the average CGPA of the dataset alongside their placement results. The x-axis indicates the CGPA range, whereas the y-axis displays the number of students. This chart provides a visual representation of the relationship between having a CGPA lower than the average of the

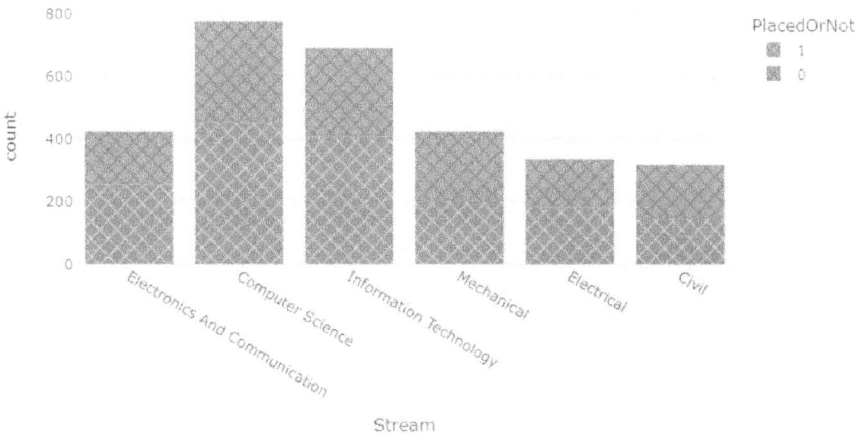

FIGURE 9.8 Students count at different department levels.

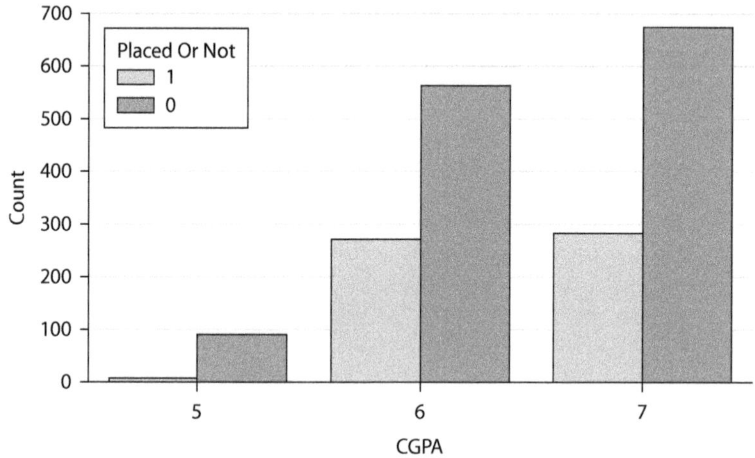

FIGURE 9.9 Student count below average CGPA vs placement.

dataset and the chances of obtaining a job placement. The data reveals that students with CGPA scores below the dataset average are less likely to secure placement. This implies a positive correlation between CGPA and placement success, indicating that students with higher CGPA scores often achieve better placement results. For example, a comparison of the number of placed versus unplaced students within a specific CGPA range would enhance the analysis.

The chart in Figure 9.10 highlights the relationship between students who have no internship experience and their placement outcomes. The x-axis represents whether students had internship experience, and the y-axis shows the count of students. The chart emphasizes the impact of not having internship experience on the chances of being placed in a job.

Figure 9.11 illustrates the efficiency of different algorithms, comparing their performance based on accuracy. The x-axis represents different algorithms, while the

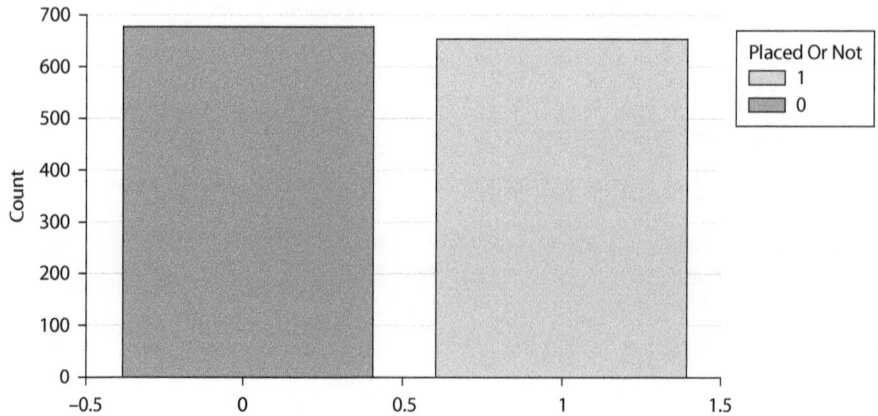

FIGURE 9.10 No internship experience vs placement.

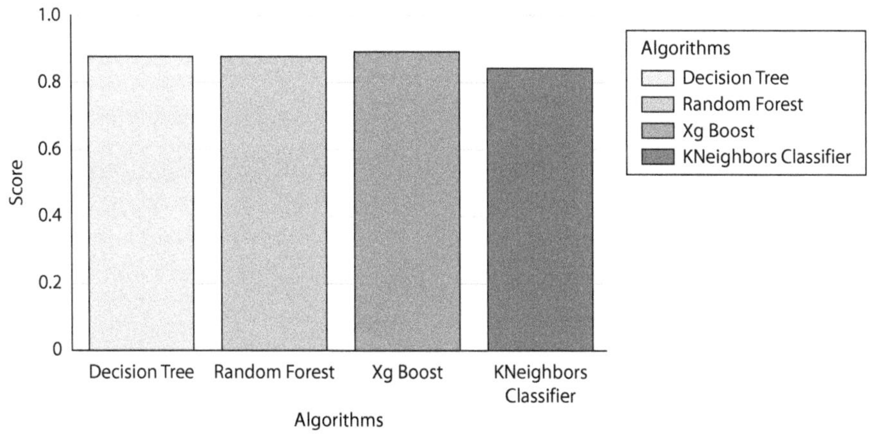

FIGURE 9.11 Algorithm efficiency.

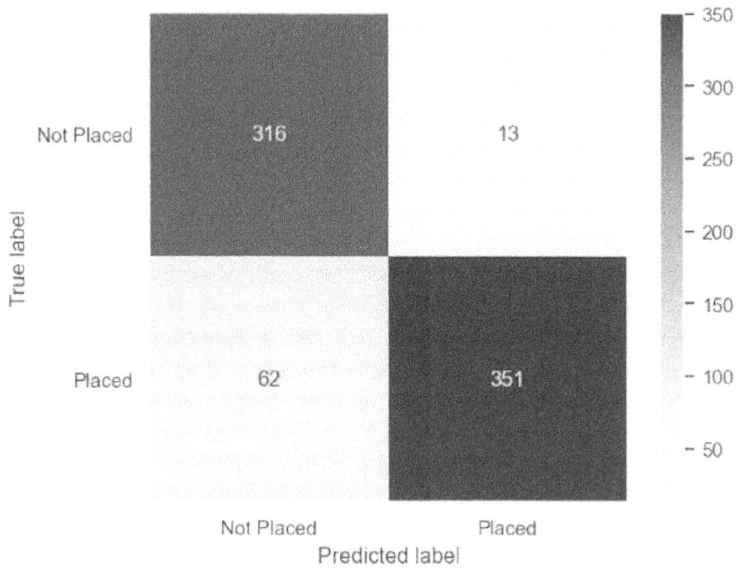

FIGURE 9.12 Confusion matrix.

y-axis shows the corresponding accuracy score (ranging from 0 to 1). The chart provides a visual comparison of how efficiently various algorithms perform, helping to identify the most suitable one for different scenarios.

The efficiency of different algorithms, comparing their performance based on accuracy, is represented in Figure 9.12. The x-axis represents different algorithms, while the y-axis shows the corresponding performance metric in terms of accuracy. The chart helps to visually compare how efficiently various algorithms handle

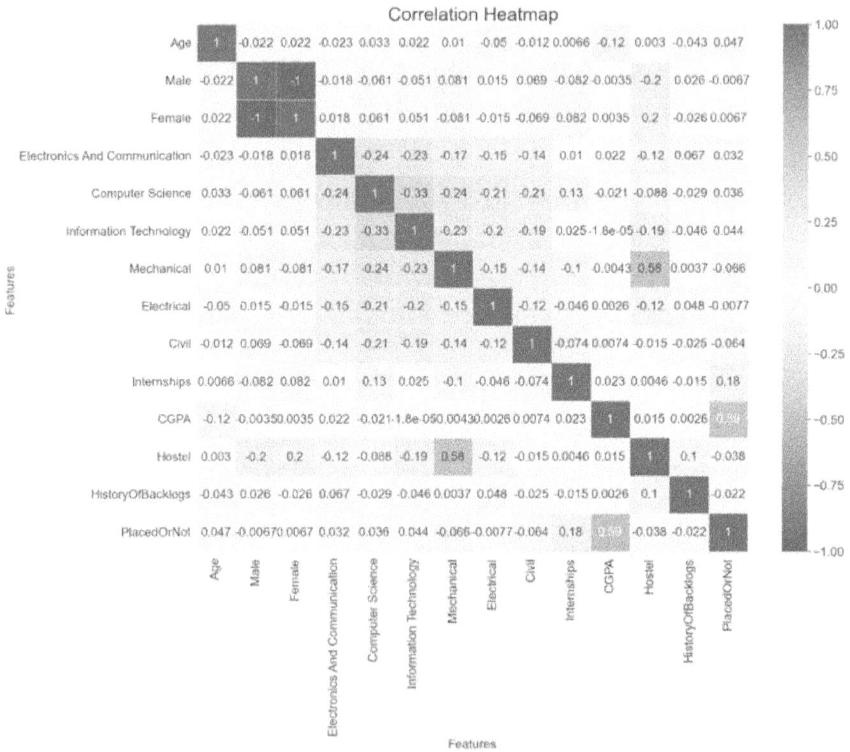

FIGURE 9.13 Heatmap analysis of correlation in student performance prediction.

increasing input sizes, providing insights into which algorithm is most suitable for scenarios. The confusion matrix provides a summary of the prediction results of a classification problem. It shows the number of correct and incorrect predictions made by the model compared to the actual outcomes. The matrix is organized into four categories: true positives (TP), false positives (FP), true negatives (TN), and false negatives (FN). This helps in evaluating the performance of the classification model, particularly in terms of accuracy, precision, recall, and other metrics derived from these values.

The heatmap is the visual representation of the correlation between different features or variables used in the study. The intensity of the color (towards +1.00) represents stronger correlations. This helps to quickly see which features are closely linked and how they might affect the model (Figure 9.13).

9.5 FUTURE WORK

Future research should focus on feature selection techniques to refine the input attributes for classification models. Currently, we rely on traditional machine learning methods for feature selection, but in the future, deep learning-based feature selection can be explored. Techniques such as autoencoders, deep neural networks (DNNs), and attention mechanisms could help in automatically identifying the most relevant features, eliminating redundancy, and improving model accuracy. Additionally, the selected features should be systematically analyzed to determine their impact on placement trends. These features may include academic records such as GPA, test scores, and coursework performance; placement status indicating whether students have been placed or not; and internship experience to assess whether students have completed industry training. Other essential attributes include technical skills like certifications and programming knowledge, extracurricular activities such as participation in hackathons and technical clubs, and soft skills and interview performance, which evaluate communication abilities and aptitude test results. A deep learning approach may uncover hidden patterns in student data that conventional methods might overlook, leading to more robust and accurate placement predictions.

9.6 CONCLUSION

This study has demonstrated the potential of machine learning algorithms, specifically the random forest classifier and decision tree classifier, in predicting student placement outcomes. The Random Forest Classifier effectively reduces overfitting and increases prediction robustness, while the Decision Tree Classifier offers a transparent and interpretable decision-making process. Our model achieved a prediction accuracy of 89.89%, highlighting the practical applications of these algorithms in optimizing placement strategies and supporting educational and career planning. Furthermore, the exploration of advanced techniques such as nonlinear regression and Random Forest provides a nuanced understanding of the factors influencing student performance. These methodologies can assist educational institutions in identifying key variables that contribute to successful placement outcomes, enabling the development of targeted intervention strategies. For instance, by analyzing which features correlate most significantly with student success, educators can tailor programs and resources to address specific needs, ultimately enhancing student readiness for the job market.

Feature selection is crucial in enhancing the accuracy of student placement prediction models. In this study, key features such as academic performance (CGPA, grades), internship experience, technical skills, project work, extracurricular activities, and soft skills are considered. The Random Forest Classifier improves accuracy by selecting the most relevant features and reducing overfitting, while the Decision Tree Classifier provides an interpretable structure by splitting data based on Gini impurity and entropy. However, certain limitations exist, such as bias in training data, exclusion of qualitative factors like interview performance, and the inability to capture dynamic industry trends. To address these challenges, future research should explore hybrid models that integrate deep learning, incorporate real-time job market data, and enhance feature engineering by including behavioral and social attributes. By refining these aspects, institutions can optimize career guidance strategies and improve student placement outcomes.

The scope of this research can be extended by exploring advanced machine learning techniques. Currently, we focus on machine learning for student placement prediction, but in the future, we aim to incorporate deep learning approaches to enhance predictive accuracy. The application of deep learning algorithms could be studied to further improve results. Neural networks, particularly deep architectures such as convolutional neural networks (CNNs) and long short-term memory (LSTM) models, have the potential to uncover complex patterns in student data that traditional models might overlook. Furthermore, support vector machines (SVMs) may be employed and tested for their effectiveness in classification tasks. SVMs are known for their strong generalization ability, especially in high-dimensional spaces, and could serve as a valuable alternative to existing classification models. Future research can compare the performance of SVMs with other algorithms to determine their suitability for student placement prediction.

As machine learning continues to advance, its application in education is set to expand, revolutionizing the way we assess and improve student performance. By harnessing the power of data-driven insights, educational institutions can create more personalized learning experiences, fostering an environment where every student has the opportunity to thrive. This research lays the foundation for future studies, encouraging the integration of machine learning into educational practices to drive meaningful change in student success outcomes. Additionally, as more data becomes available and computational methods evolve, the potential for machine learning to uncover hidden patterns and correlations in educational data will only grow, paving the way for innovative approaches to teaching and learning. To conclude, this study not only highlights the effectiveness of machine learning algorithms in predicting student placement outcomes but also underscores the need for ongoing research in this area. By continually refining these models and exploring their implications in educational settings, we can empower institutions to make informed decisions that enhance student achievement and prepare them for a competitive workforce.

REFERENCES

Akmeşe, Ömer Faruk, Hakan Kör, and Hasan Erbay. 2021. "Use of Machine Learning Techniques for the Forecast of Student Achievement in Higher Education." *Information Technologies and Learning Tools* 82 (2): 297–311.

Albreiki, Balqis, Nazar Zaki, and Hany Alashwal. 2021. "A Systematic Literature Review of Student Performance Prediction Using Machine Learning Techniques." *Education Sciences* 11 (9): 552.

Aldeman, Nayze Lucena Sangreman, Keylla Maria de Sá Urtiga Aita, Vinícius Ponte Machado, Luiz Claudio Demes da Mata Sousa, Antonio Gilberto Borges Coelho, Adalberto Socorro da Silva, Ana Paula da Silva Mendes, Francisco Jair de Oliveira Neres, and Semíramis Jamil Hadad do Monte. 2021. "Smartpathk: A Platform for Teaching Glomerulopathies Using Machine Learning." *BMC Medical Education* 21 (1): 248.

Alshanqiti, Abdullah, and Abdallah Namoun. 2020. "Predicting Student Performance and Its Influential Factors Using Hybrid Regression and Multi-Label Classification." *IEEE Access* 8: 203827–203844.

Alzubi, Jafar, Anand Nayyar, and Akshi Kumar. 2018. "Machine Learning from Theory to Algorithms: An Overview." In *Journal of Physics: Conference Series,* vol. 1142, 012012. IOP Publishing.

Anders, Jake, Catherine Dilnot, Lindsey Macmillan, and Gill Wyness. 2020. "Grade Expectations: How Well Can We Predict Future Grades Based on Past Performance?" Economics of Education Review 77: 102015.

August, Stephanie E., and Audrey Tsaima. 2021. "Artificial Intelligence and Machine Learning: An Instructor's Exoskeleton in the Future of Education." In *Innovative Learning Environments in STEM Higher Education: Opportunities, Challenges, and Looking Forward*, Jungwoo Ryoo, Kurt Winkelmann (eds.), pp. 79–105.

Broll, Brian, and Shuchi Grover. 2023. "Beyond Black-Boxes: Teaching Complex Machine Learning Ideas Through Scaffolded Interactive Activities." In *Proceedings of the AAAI Conference on Artificial Intelligence,* PKP Publishing Services Network, vol. 37, no. 13, 15990–15998.

Buenaño-Fernández, Diego, David Gil, and Sergio Luján-Mora. 2019. "Application of Machine Learning in Predicting Performance for Computer Engineering Students: A Case Study." *Sustainability* 11 (10): 2833.

Byagar, Ms Sarita, Ranjit Patil, and Janardan Pawar. 2024. "Maximizing Campus Placement Through Machine Learning." *Journal of Advanced Zoology* 45: 6–12.

Choudhary, Rishabh, and Hemant Kumar Gianey. 2017. "Comprehensive Review on Supervised Machine Learning Algorithms." In *2017 International Conference on Machine Learning and Data Science (MLDS),* 37–43. IEEE.

Dirin, Amir, and Charlese Adriana Saballe. 2022. "Machine Learning Models to Predict Students' Study Path Selection." *iJIM* 16, no. 01: 159.

Frey, Nathan C., Baolin Li, Joseph McDonald, Dan Zhao, Michael Jones, David Bestor, Devesh Tiwari, Vijay Gadepally, and Siddharth Samsi. 2022. "Benchmarking Resource Usage for Efficient Distributed Deep Learning." In: *2022 IEEE High Performance Extreme Computing Conference (HPEC)*, 1–8. IEEE. 40.

Guanin-Fajardo, Jorge Humberto, Javier Guaña-Moya, and Jorge Casillas. 2024. "Predicting Academic Success of College Students Using Machine Learning Techniques." *Data* 9, no. 4: 60.

Hashim, Ali Salah, Wid Akeel Awadh, and Alaa Khalaf Hamoud. 2020. "Student Performance Prediction Model Based on Supervised Machine Learning Algorithms." In *IOP Conference Series: Materials Science and Engineering,* vol. 928, no. 3, 032019. IOP Publishing.

Herta, Christian, Benjamin Voigt, Patrick Baumann, Klaus Strohmenger, Christoph Jansen, Oliver Fischer, Gefei Zhang, and Peter Hufnagel. 2019. "Deep Teaching: Materials for Teaching Machine and Deep Learning." In *HEAD'19. 5th International Conference on Higher Education Advances,* 1153–1131. Editorial Universitat Politècnica de València.

Hussain, Mushtaq, Wenhao Zhu, Wu Zhang, Syed Muhammad Raza Abidi, and Sadaqat Ali. 2019. "Using Machine Learning to Predict Student Difficulties from Learning Session Data." *Artificial Intelligence Review* 52: 381–407.

Iqbal, Zafar, Junaid Qadir, Adnan Noor Mian, and Faisal Kamiran. 2017. "Machine Learning Based Student Grade Prediction: A Case Study." *arXiv Preprint* arXiv:1708.08744.

Jagan, S. 2018. "Predicting Student Performance Using Deep Learning." *International Journal of Engineering and Advanced Technology (IJEAT)* 7 (6): 350–354.

Jiang, Yi, and Emily Q. Rosenzweig. 2021. "Using Cost to Improve Predictions of Adolescent Students' Future Choice Intentions, Avoidance Intentions, and Course Grades in Mathematics and English." *Learning and Individual Differences* 86: 101978.

Kučak, Danijel, Vedran Juričić, and Goran Đambić. 2018. "Machine Learning in Education—A Survey of Current Research Trends." *Annals of DAAAM & Proceedings* 29, 406–410.

Leithwood, Kenneth, Jingping Sun, and Randall Schumacker. 2020. "How School Leadership Influences Student Learning: A Test of 'The Four Paths Model'." *Educational Administration Quarterly* 56 (4): 570–599.

Li Shuping, and Taotang Liu. 2021. "Performance Prediction for Higher Education Students Using Deep Learning." *Complexity* 2021 (1): 9958203.

Masethe, Mosima Anna, and Hlaudi Daniel Masethe. 2014. "Prediction of Work Integrated Learning Placement Using Data Mining Algorithms." In *Proceedings of the World Congress on Engineering and Computer Science*, WCECS 2014, vol. 1, 22–24.

Maurya, Laxmi Shanker, Md Shadab Hussain, and Sarita Singh. 2021. "Developing Classifiers Through Machine Learning Algorithms for Student Placement Prediction Based on Academic Performance." *Applied Artificial Intelligence* 35, no. 6: 403–420.

Namoun, Abdallah, and Abdullah Alshanqiti. 2020. "Predicting Student Performance Using Data Mining and Learning Analytics Techniques: A Systematic Literature Review." *Applied Sciences* 11 (1): 237.

Nasteski, Vladimir. 2017. "An Overview of the Supervised Machine Learning Methods." *Horizons* 4: 51–62.

Pallathadka, Harikumar, Alex Wenda, Edwin Ramirez-Asís, Maximiliano Asís-López, Judith Flores-Albornoz, and Khongdet Phasinam. 2023. "Classification and Prediction of Student Performance Data Using Various Machine Learning Algorithms." *Materials Today: Proceedings* 80: 3782–3785.

Rai, Kajal. 2022. "Students Placement Prediction Using Machine Learning Algorithms." *Rai | South Asia Journal of Multidisciplinary Studies* 8, no. 5: 54–60.

Rao, K. Eswara, Bala Murali Pydi, T. Panduranga Vital, P. Annan Naidu, U. D. Prasann, and T. Ravikumar. 2023. "An Advanced Machine Learning Approach for Student Placement Prediction and Analysis." *International Journal of Performability Engineering* 19, no. 8: 536.

Saradhi, M. V. Vijaya, Thodeti Sowmya, Shaik Sufyaan, Gumpula Kavya, and Ganore Pavan. 2024. "Campus Placements Prediction & Analysis Using Machine Learning." International Journal of Research in Engineering, Science and Management 7 (2): 245–250.

Saraswathi, K., B. Devadharshini, S. Kavina, and S. Srinidhi. 2023. "Prediction on Impact of Electronic Gadgets in Students' Life Using Machine Learning." In *2023 7th International Conference on Computing Methodologies and Communication (ICCMC)*, 340–345. IEEE.

Sharma, Diksha, and Neeraj Kumar. 2017. "A Review on Machine Learning Algorithms, Tasks and Applications." *International Journal of Advanced Research in Computer Engineering & Technology (IJARCET)* 6 (10): 2278–1323.

Simard, Patrice Y., Saleema Amershi, David M. Chickering, Alicia Edelman Pelton, Soroush Ghorashi, Christopher Meek, Gonzalo Ramos, et al. 2017. "Machine Teaching: A New Paradigm for Building Machine Learning Systems." *arXiv Preprint* arXiv:1707.06742.

Singh, Randhir, and Saurabh Pal. 2020. "Application of Machine Learning Algorithms to Predict Students' Performance." *International Journal of Advanced Science and Technology* 29, no. 5: 7249–7261.

Swami, Sourabh, Sahil 9., Rounak Kumar, Sourav Raj, Vishal Shrivastava, and Devesh Kumar Bandil. 2025. "ML-Based: Placement Prediction Application." *International Journal of Emerging Science and Engineering (IJESE)*. 39.

Tedre, Matti, Tapani Toivonen, Juho Kahila, Henriikka Vartiainen, Teemu Valtonen, Ilkka Jormanainen, and Arnold Pears. 2021. "Teaching Machine Learning in K-12 Computing Education: Potential and Pitfalls." *arXiv Preprint* arXiv:2106.11034.

Verma, Chaman, Veronika Stoffová, Zoltán Illés, Sudeep Tanwar, and Neeraj Kumar. 2020. "Machine Learning-Based Student's Native Place Identification for Real-Time." *IEEE Access* 8: 130840–130854.

Wang, Yinkai, Aowei Ding, Kaiyi Guan, Shixi Wu, and Yuanqi Du. 2021. "Graph-based Ensemble Machine Learning for Student Performance Prediction." *arXiv preprint arXiv:2112.07893*.38.

Zhang, Yupei, Yue Yun, Rui An, Jiaqi Cui, Huan Dai, and Xuequn Shang. 2021. "Educational Data Mining Techniques for Student Performance Prediction: Method Review and Comparison Analysis." *Frontiers in Psychology* 12: 698490.

Section D

Computational Intelligence

Algorithms, Methodologies, and Ethics

10 Enhanced Informer Homed Routing Protocol for Homogeneous Wireless Sensor Network

Gholamreza Kakamanshadi, Savita Gupta and Sukhwinder Singh

10.1 INTRODUCTION

A homogeneous wireless sensor network (HWSN) can be defined as a self-organized or self-configured system. It includes a collection of small and low-power sensor nodes (SNs) with limited sensing and transmission ranges besides the base station, which is deployed in known or unknown areas [1]. In HWSNs, a sensor node has limited capability in the process of sensing environmental information and receiving and transferring data packets. Hence, to collect beneficial data from the entire network, the data must be collected through the collaborative work of several sensor nodes and the base station in an efficient manner [2]. Sensor nodes can be organized into several small groups or sections, named clusters [3, 4]. Each cluster has a primary cluster head (CH), which receives data packets from its cluster members and then aggregates and transfers them to the next hop or base station (sink) [5, 6]. So, picking and fixing an optimal CH for each cluster is a very considerable mission, and the selection of a suitable one is also a crucial aspect of clustering in WSN protocols [7, 8]. It can improve energy consumption, increase network reliability, and extend the lifetime of the wireless sensor network [9–11]. On the other hand, cluster heads tend to fail or may malfunction [12] due to hardware and software failures, communication link instability, battery depletion, etc. In addition, CHs consume more energy when receiving, grouping, processing, and transferring data packets during the lifetime of the network [13]. In most cases, they have the same amount of energy, which is not rechargeable [2]. Thus, an energy-efficient protocol and a compatible fault-tolerance mechanism are required to manage the cluster head faults.

Normally, cluster formation processes in an HWSN apply two methods: choosing SNs with more outstanding energy as CHs and revolving them periodically to balance energy consumption of the SNs over the network for prolonging the network lifetime [14, 15]. In this cluster formation process fault-tolerance schemes can be applied to improve the efficiency of the network. For example, selecting dual CHs,

DOI: 10.1201/9781003532156-14

a backup cluster head (BCH) checks the working condition or status of the primary cluster head (PCH), so whenever a primary cluster head fault happens, its members will send the data packet to the backup one. In the existing fault-tolerance algorithms, such as the Dual Homed Routing (DHR) approach [16], the Energy-Efficient Clustering Scheme Using Backup Nodes (EECSB) [11], and the Informer Homed Routing (IHR) approach [9], the BCH is selected based on the most outstanding energy among all the cluster members. There is a drawback: CHs select their backup without taking into account the distance to the base station, which is an important parameter. When a primary cluster head failure occurs, the backup one out of other members has a better position from the base station, so the energy consumption can be less than that of other members. Therefore, a novel fault-tolerant algorithm named enhanced informer homed routing with fuzzy logic (EIHRF) is introduced and simulated for wireless sensor networks. In order to make wise decisions, the proposed method employs a fuzzy logic approach to choose a BCH among cluster members for each cluster after the cluster formation phase. The qualified SNs in each cluster are nominated based on their outstanding energy and distance to the base station. The selected BCHs will check the working condition (alive/dead) of the related PCH periodically in each round. To evaluate whether the proposed protocol is able to tolerate CH faults or not, there is a need to notice how the sensor network reacts and replaces the BCH when the PCH fault happens. Therefore, we developed and used a fault model using the Poisson distribution when running the simulation. For performance evaluation, we compared the effectiveness of the proposed EIHRF protocol with the DHR and IHR protocols in terms of first node dead (FND), half node alive (HNA), throughput, and total outstanding energy of the network during 500 rounds. The outcomes indicate that the proposed EIHRF protocol has better performance in all mentioned metrics as compared to available protocols.

The remainder of this chapter is organized as follows: Section 10.2 presents the related work; Section 10.3 discusses the preliminaries; Section 10.4 presents the proposed EIHRF protocol; Section 10.5 contains the simulation results and discussion; and finally, Section 10.6 concludes the chapter.

10.2 RELATED WORKS

Efficiently gathering and transmitting the sensed data from several sensor nodes to the base station (sink) is a critical issue in homogeneous wireless sensor networks. Hence, several fault-tolerant routing protocols have been proposed in the literature. In addition, most of these protocols introduce hardware redundancies and path redundancy to cover fault-tolerant issues.

Jain et al. [16] proposed a novel protocol called Dual Homed Routing. It is a fault-tolerance approach for wireless sensor networks. In this protocol, the network is divided into several clusters and every cluster is organized into nearby collector nodes and dual CHs (primary and backup). The sensed data is sent to both CHs, and then data packets are forwarded to the base station. Since insignificant energy is consumed per packet transfer, a major disadvantage of the DHR protocol is the duplication of dispatching every data packet over dual disjoint paths towards the base station. This causes a decrease in the overall network lifetime.

Qiu et al. [9] presented a new energy-aware fault-tolerance method based on the DHR protocol for wireless sensor networks. It is named the IHR protocol. In this protocol, each cluster member (collector node) has two CHs associated with it (primary CH and backup CH). Additionally, a sensor node transfers the data packet to the backup CH only when it finds that the main CH has failed, instead of transmitting the data packet to both CHs at the same time. The outcomes of this method were evaluated against the well-known method (LEACH) and DHR algorithms in terms of overall energy consumption of the network and the total number of dead sensor nodes during network operation. In addition, the throughput of the simulated network was measured with diverse fault rates. Results indicated that this approach could meaningfully reduce the energy depletion of SNs and decrease the data packet loss rate as well as prolong the lifetime of the network. The IHR approach only considers the outstanding energy level of candidate BCH during the clustering procedure, and it does not take into account the distance from the base station of candidate BCHs, which is a very important aspect.

Geeta et al. proposed a new fault-tolerance mechanism for wireless sensor networks employing the hand-off mechanism. This method identifies faulty sensor nodes employing power and interference models. Fault tolerance against low energy levels was formulated via the hand-off mechanism. In this method, a faulty sensor node selects a neighbor sensor node having the highest remaining energy and then transfers all its services that are to be served to the selected sensor node. The presented method does not consider the distance to the sink during the neighbor sensor node selection process. The chosen node may be far away from the sink, which leads to more energy consumption while transferring received data [17].

Al-Qadami and Koucheryavy presented a fault-tolerant routing protocol. In this approach, each cluster has a PCH and a sub-CH that monitor one another for aliveness employing a status check message. If no reply comes from the PCH to the sub-CH within the time interval, the sub-cluster head turns into the primary cluster head. On the other hand, if no response comes from the sub-CH to the primary cluster head within a time interval, the primary cluster head selects a new sensor node with the maximum energy level as a sub-CH among its cluster members. This approach also does not take into account the distance to the base station of selected sub-cluster heads, which is a very important and significant aspect [18].

Vaddeti et al. proposed the Energy-Efficient Clustering Scheme Using Backup Nodes (EECSB) by introducing a high-energy backup cluster head during the deployment phase. The main objective of this scheme is to decrease the delay involved and the energy consumed in the dynamic cluster head election process. The selection of a backup cluster head is based on energy and the distance between the candidate node and the primary cluster without considering their distance to the BS. This oversight can lead to increased energy consumption during data transmission to the BS, as nodes located far away consume more energy, potentially resulting in faster energy depletion and reduced network efficiency [11]. Therefore, incorporating the distance to the BS in the selection criteria of the backup cluster head could increase energy efficiency and prolong the network lifetime.

10.3 PRELIMINARIES

To implement the proposed scheme, the following rules are made for the network model.

- Sensor nodes are randomly scattered in the 200 × 200 square meter area.
- There is only one base station and it is located at the center of the network at (100, 100) coordinates.
- All SNs and the base station (sink) are fixed after the deployment phase.
- All SNs have the same amount of energy when deploying.
- All SNs have the same sensing capabilities.
- Each cluster has a PCH and a BCH after the cluster formation phase.
- For each SN in the network, there is only one primary/backup cluster head to reach the BS, and it belongs to a cluster during each round.
- The radio energy consumption model of sensor nodes is the same as presented in [19–21].

10.4 PROPOSED ENHANCED INFORMER HOMED ROUTING PROTOCOL WITH FUZZY LOGIC

The proposed EIHRF fault-tolerant protocol is simulated based on IHR and DHR protocols. The key differences between these schemes and the proposed routing protocol is that in the IHR and DHR schemes, each PCH selects a non-cluster head locally with the most energy level as its backup. The selected BCH may be away from the base station, which may result in more energy consumption during the data packet transmission process. In the proposed scheme, the selection of a candidate BCH is based on outstanding energy and distance from the base station. This scheme uses a fuzzy logic approach to find a more optimal BCH for each cluster. The following pseudo-code refers to the EIHRF routing protocol.

Pseudo-code: Enhanced Informer Homed Routing protocol with Fuzzy Logic

---

```
Input: Network setting configuration
       N ← Number of sensor nodes
       C ← Number of clusters
       P ← Data packet size
       R ← Number of Rounds
       X ← Number of PCH faults
       λ ← The mean number of PCH faults
       M ← Time index for sensor node data transmission
Output: EIHRF protocol
1:  T ← Chance to become a tentative PCH
2:  Node Status ← Non-Cluster Head (NCH)
3:  ClusterMembers ← empty
```

```
MyCH ← empty
Query counter ← empty
for rounds_index=1:1: R do
    for i = 1:1: C do
        Select PCHi
        Node Status ← PCHi
    end for
    Each PCH calculates its distance to BS
    PCHs Advertise PCH_message (ID, location, etc.) to
      other nodes
    All NCHs save the received PCH_messages
    MyCH ← Each NCH selects the nearest PCH
    NCHs send Join Message (ID) to the closest PCH
    ClusterMembers ← PCH add NCHi
    Calculate Chance of each NCH to become BCH locally
      using fuzzy if-then mapping rules (Inputs: Distance
      to BS, Residual Energy)
    Each PCH will select the node with the highest chance
      level among all its members as BCH.
    Each PCH will transmit its BCH information to its
      cluster members.
   for times_index = 1:1:M do
       Each BCH sends a query message to its relevant PCH
         to check the aliveness.
       Query counter ← Query counter +1.
    if PCH is in working condition then
       PCH receives Q-Message from BCH and then sends a
         response to confirm its aliveness.
       Upon receiving the PCH response message,
       Query counter ← Query counter - 1.
    end if
    if query counter > 3 then
       BCH decides the relevant PCH has failed, then sends
         the notification message to its NCHs that send
         data to BCH.
    end if
    if NCH receives the notification message from relevant
      BCH then
       NCH transmits the data packet to its relevant BCH
         next time.
    else
       NCH transmits the data packet to its relevant PCH.
    end if
   end for
end for
```

EIHRF is a distributed fault-tolerant scheme; it considers three important aspects for an HWSN: energy consumption, throughput, and reliability. In the EIHRF protocol,

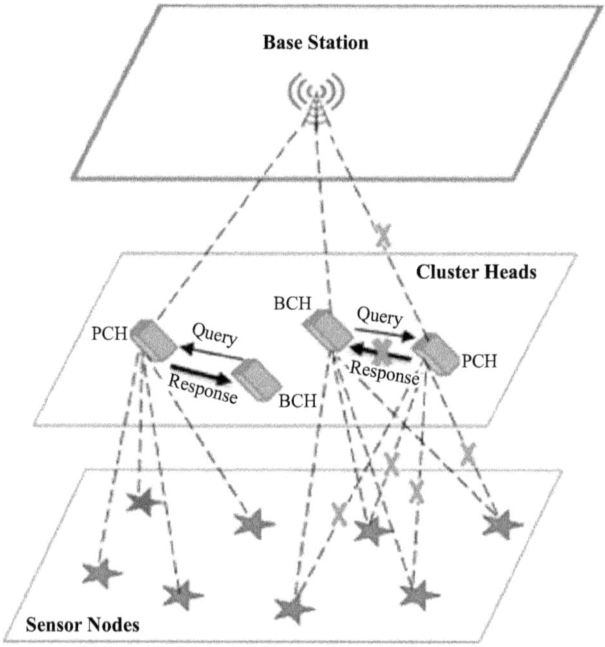

FIGURE 10.1 Proposed network model for the EIHRF protocol.

each SN transfers a data packet to the BCH when it discovers that the PCH has failed, instead of transferring a data packet to the PCH and BCH simultaneously. Hence, the data transferring process of the network will not be disturbed. Figure 10.1 illustrates the proposed network model for the EIHRF protocol. Figure 10.1 clearly shows when a PCH is dead, BCH will take over the transmitted data from cluster members.

10.4.1 Backup Cluster Head Selection

In this section, the backup cluster head selection method is presented. It makes local decisions for determining the chance of the tentative backup cluster head. This process takes advantage of the fuzzy logic approach. Selecting primary cluster heads is based on a probabilistic model similar to the LEACH, IHR, and DHR protocols. In order to estimate the backup cluster head election chance, it employs two factors (distances to the BS and residual energy). The probability of a tentative backup cluster head (chance) is determined by using eight predefined fuzzy if-then mapping rules to handle the uncertainties, which are presented in Table 10.1. In order to assess these rules, the Mamdani method [22], which is one of the most commonly used Fuzzy Inference System (FIS), is employed [2]. To obtain the output crisp value (chance), the Center of Area approach is used for Defuzzification.

The relationship between input variables (residual energy (J) and distance to BS (m)) and the output variable (chance) is presented in Figure 10.2. This 3D curve represents the mapping from residual energy and distance to base station to the chance of selecting a tentative cluster head. The chance C is determined using the weighted

TABLE 10.1
Fuzzy If-Then Mapping Rules for Calculating Chance

Rule No.	Input Variables		Output Variable
	Distance to BS	Residual Energy	Chance
1	Near	Low	Rather small
2	Near	Med	Very med
3	Near	High	Very high
4	Med	Low	Small
5	Med	Med	Med
6	Med	High	Rather high
7	Far	Low	Very small
8	Far	Med	Small med
9	Far	High	High

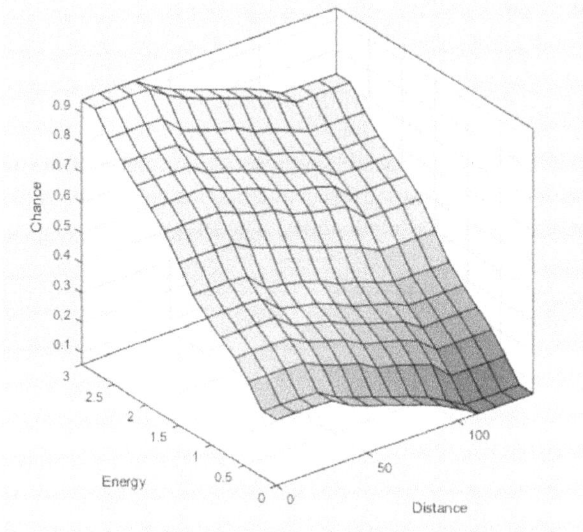

FIGURE 10.2 Relationship between input and output variables in the proposed EIHRF protocol.

sum of the fuzzy membership values of residual energy (μ_E) and distance to base station (μ_D), as expressed in Equation 10.1:

$$C = w_1 \cdot \mu_E + w_2 \cdot \mu_D \tag{10.1}$$

where w_1 and w_2 are weighting factors that determine the influence of residual energy and distance to BS, respectively. The figure demonstrates that a node with higher remaining energy and closer to the base station has a greater chance of being selected as a BCH. Specifically, as observed in Figure 10.2, when distance to base station is near (about 17 m) and residual energy has a high value (like 2.82 J), the output has a very large value (about 0.939) that indicates that the chance selection of the tentative backup cluster head is very high. As the distance to base station increases to 110 m and residual energy decreases to 0.205 J, then the output has a very low value (about 0.0608) that indicates the chance of the tentative backup cluster head is very low. Furthermore, when both residual energy and distance to base station have average values (e.g., 1.49 J and 70, respectively), the chance of the tentative backup cluster head is about 0.493, which indicates the chance is medium.

The fuzzy set that describes the distance to the base station as an input variable is presented in Figure 10.3. In this fuzzy input set, the range of distance to base station (m) is [0, 140]. The linguistic variables for this fuzzy input set are near, med (medium), and far. Two trapezoidal membership functions are preferred for near [0, 0, 30, 70] and far [70, 110, 140, 140] variables. In addition, a triangular membership function is preferred for med [30, 70, 110] variable.

Additionally, the fuzzy set that expresses the residual energy as another input variable is demonstrated in Figure 10.4. In this fuzzy set, the range of residual energy (J) is [0, 3]. The linguistic variables for this fuzzy set are low, med (medium), and high. The low [0, 0, 0.25, 1.5] and high [1.5, 2.75, 3, 3] linguistic variables have a trapezoidal membership function, while medium [0.25, 1.5, 2.75] linguistic variable has a triangular membership function.

Moreover, the fuzzy output variable represents the chance of the tentative backup cluster head, which is determined by evaluating energy levels and distance from the base station factors of candidate nodes. The fuzzy set for chance is represented

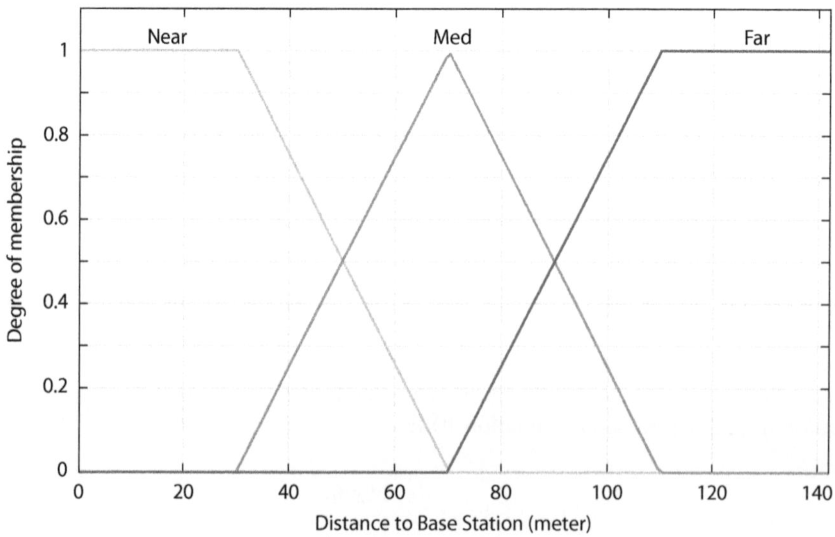

FIGURE 10.3 Membership functions of distance to BS (meter).

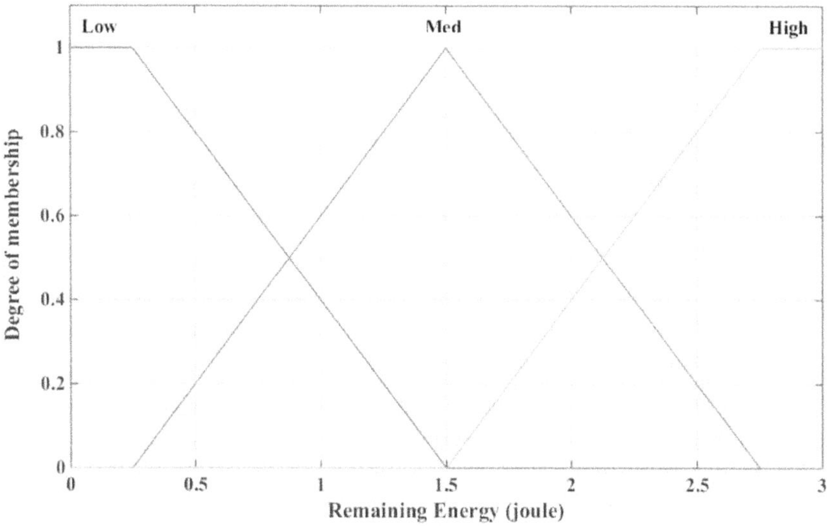

FIGURE 10.4 Membership functions of residual energy (Joule).

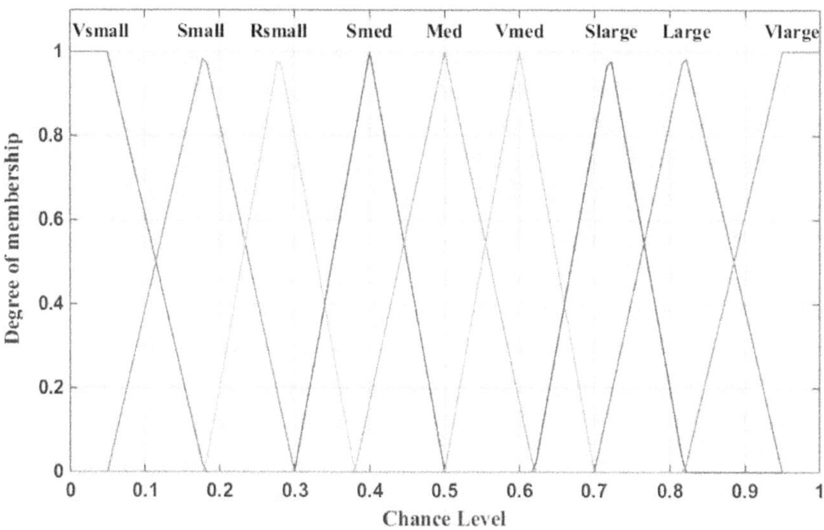

FIGURE 10.5 Membership functions of chance as output.

in Figure 10.5. In this fuzzy set, the range of chance is [0, 1] and is modeled using a set of triangular and trapezoidal membership functions. The linguistic variables for this fuzzy set are: very small, small, rather small, small medium, medium, very medium, small large, large and very large. A trapezoidal membership function is preferred for very small and very large variables. The remaining linguistic variables

TABLE 10.2
Examples for Backup Cluster Head Chance Calculation

Case No.	Distance (m)	Residual Energy (J)	Chance (%)
1	17	3	0.94
2	17	2	0.74
3	40	3	0.90
4	40	2	0.71
5	80	2	0.62
6	80	1.5	0.48

are represented by using the triangular membership function. Each of these categories defines the degree of membership for an input value within a specific range. This fuzzy modeling helps make more precise decisions concerning the probability of choosing a node as the backup cluster head, as it enables simultaneous consideration of both remaining energy and distance to base station.

If a selected tentative BCH is located at the minimum distance to the base station and its energy is high, then it has the highest selection chance. Furthermore, if its energy is very low and it is located at the maximum distance to the base station out of other cluster members, then it has the lowest chance of becoming the backup cluster head. Additionally, the remaining intermediate possibilities fall between these two extreme cases. The change in chance value according to distance to the base station and residual energy is demonstrated by cases in Table 10.2.

In cases 1 and 3, the residual energy levels of tentative backup cluster heads are the same and equal to 3 J. On the other hand, their distances to the base station are different. As a result, the chance decreases for case 3 as the distance to the base station increases. Moreover, in cases 3 and 4, their distances to the base station are the same, but residual energy levels are not the same. Therefore, case 4, which has a lower energy level, has a lower chance to become the backup cluster head.

10.4.2 Fault Model Using Poisson Distribution

In order to evaluate whether the algorithm in the simulated wireless sensor network is fault tolerant or not, it is required to know how the network reacts when a fault occurs. As in wireless sensor networks cluster heads are very important and have a vital task, this research work addressees permanent faults at primary cluster heads due to several key factors: (1) the inherent randomness of cluster head failures; (2) the large number of sensors deployed, which increases the possibility of independent failure events; (3) the potentially harsh and unpredictable environmental conditions that can contribute to such cluster head failures; and (4) the battery depletion, which gradually reduces the remaining energy for keeping network operations. The probability of failure of cluster heads can be estimated by using the Poisson distribution, which serves as the foundation for the fault model in this research. The Poisson distribution is a probability model. It is a useful model for assessing how many events like faults may occur during a time interval. The Poisson distribution is generally defined as the number of faults or occurrences in a time interval [9, 23–25]. This model is applied over time instead of a series of trials. Furthermore, the number of events occurring in non-overlapping time intervals in this model is always assumed to be independent. Additionally, the Poisson distribution offers computational simplicity and efficiency, making it a practical choice for large-scale wireless sensor network simulations.

In this research work, the following is assumed:

- The random variable X denotes the number of primary cluster head faults in a time interval and which can be 0, 1, 2, 3, …, n.
- The time interval is assumed to be independent.
- The variable λ is the mean number of primary cluster head faults within a time interval.
- According to the literature, the probability distribution of X based on the Poisson distribution [7, 20, 24, 25] can be calculated by using Equation 10.2.

$$P(X = x) = e^{-\lambda}\frac{\lambda^x}{x!} \tag{10.2}$$

$x = 0, 1, 2, 3, \ldots, n$
where parameter e is a constant value (e = 2.7183), λ is the mean value, and x is a number of faults.

Alternatively, the appropriate probability $P(X = x)$ can be found from a Poisson table. Table 10.3 presents different probability values with respect to the Poisson random variable X and λ .

TABLE 10.3
Probability of Poisson Random Variable *X*

	$\lambda = 2$	$\lambda = 3$	$\lambda = 4$	$\lambda = 5$	$\lambda = 6$
$x = 0$	0.1353	0.0498	0.0183	0.0067	0.0025
$x = 1$	0.4060	0.1991	0.0916	0.0404	0.0174
$x = 2$	0.6767	0.4232	0.2381	0.1247	0.0620
$x = 3$	0.8571	0.6472	0.4335	0.2650	0.1512
$x = 4$	0.9473	0.8153	0.6288	0.4405	0.2851
$x = 5$	0.9834	0.9161	0.7851	0.6160	0.4457
$x = 6$	0.9955	0.9665	0.8893	0.7622	0.6063
$x = 7$	0.9989	0.9881	0.9489	0.8666	0.7440
$x = 8$	0.9998	0.9962	0.9786	0.9319	0.8472
$x = 9$	1.0000	0.9989	0.9919	0.9682	0.9161
$x = 10$	1.0000	0.9997	0.9972	0.9863	0.9574

From the table, the appropriate probability $P(X = 10)$ is found in the $x = 10$ row and $\lambda = 5$ and $\lambda = 6$ columns, with probability values 0.9863 and 0.9574, respectively.

10.5 SIMULATION RESULTS AND DISCUSSION

In this section, the results of simulation experiments for DHR, IHR, and EIHRF are analyzed. To assess the performance of the proposed protocol, 200 sensor nodes are randomly spread in the area size of (200×200) m^2 and a base station is placed at the center of the network, at (100, 100) coordinates. The simulation parameters for the proposed EIHRF protocol are summarized in Table 10.4.

The metrics first node dead (FND) and half nodes alive (HNA) are used to evaluate the effectiveness of the proposed fault-tolerance protocol (EIHRF) over DHR and IHR protocols. Furthermore, to yield more accurate and reliable outcomes, the experiments were conducted 10 times, and the average of the outcomes has been taken for each protocol.

Figures 10.6 and 10.7 show the deployment of the sensor nodes and the distribution of cluster heads and the location of base stations for IHR and proposed EIHRF protocols, respectively.

From Figure 10.6 it is observed that some of the selected cluster heads are very close to each other in the IHR protocol so they are overlapping. On the other hand, Figure 10.7 clearly shows the cluster heads are distributed over the network in the EIHRF protocol; it is observed that the workload is distributed among all cluster heads, so cluster heads can save energy and deliver more packets as compared with the IHR protocol.

TABLE 10.4
Simulation Parameters for the Proposed EIHRF Protocol

Parameter	Value
Network size (m)	(200 m × 200 m)
Location of BS	(100, 100)
Number of sensor nodes	200
Number of cluster heads	20
Sensor nodes energy	3.0 J
Minimum distance between PCHs	30 m
Failure rate	50% of PCHs
λ	5, 6
ETx (Eelec)/ERx (Eelec)	50 nJ/bit
Data packet size	4000 bytes
Query/respond message size	160 bits
ε_{fs}	10 pJ/bit/m^2
ε_{mp}	0.0013 pJ/bit/m^4
Number of data transmission per round	3
EDA (EAggregation)	5 nJ/bit/signal

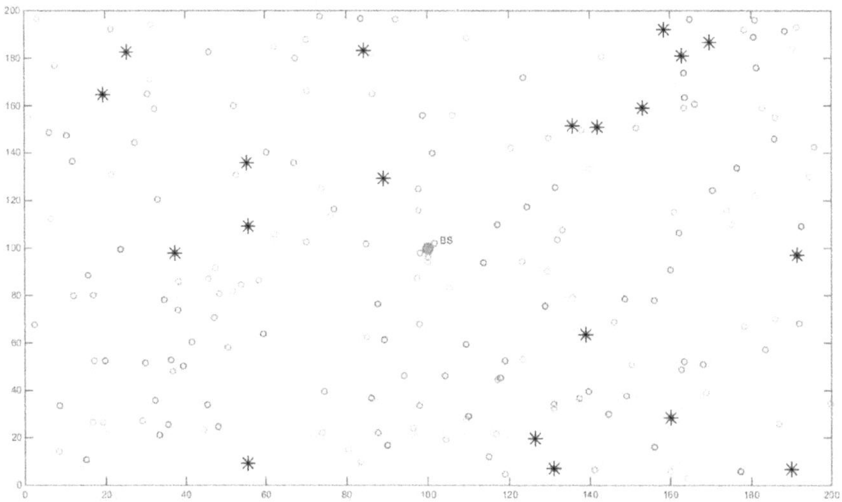

FIGURE 10.6 Sensor node deployment and cluster head distribution in the IHR protocol.

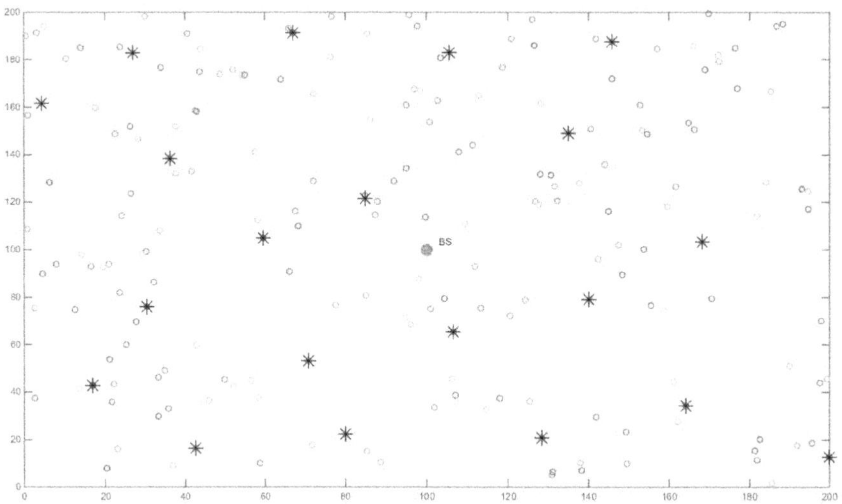

FIGURE 10.7 Sensor node deployment and cluster head distribution in the EIHRF protocol.

Figure 10.8 shows the schematic chart of clustering in the EIHRF protocol. In this process, a node is selected as the tentative cluster head. If it is the first selected node, it becomes the primary cluster head; otherwise, the distance between the selected tentative cluster head and other primary cluster heads will be considered. If the distance from all primary cluster heads is greater than the threshold value, it will be

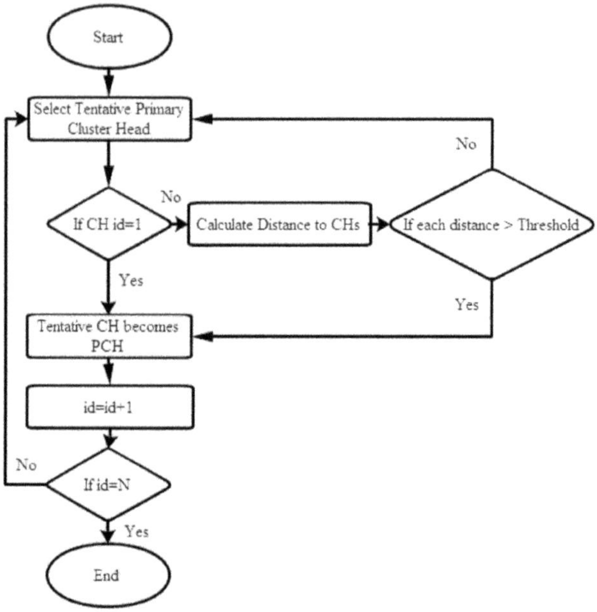

FIGURE 10.8 Schematic chart of clustering in the EIHRF protocol.

selected as the next primary cluster head; otherwise, the next tentative cluster head will be selected, and this process will be repeated up to the number of cluster heads.

Figure 10.9 shows the schematic chart for selecting backup cluster heads in the EIHRF protocol. In this process, primary cluster heads are selected as per the criteria mentioned in Figure 10.8. Then the process of selecting backup cluster heads will be started. In this process, each primary cluster head calculates the chance of cluster members using fuzzy logic. Then each primary cluster head will select a member node that has a higher chance of being the backup cluster head.

To assess the performance of the offered EIHRF protocol over the IHR and DHR protocols, two different scenarios are developed.

10.5.1 Scenario 1: Without Fault Injection

In the first scenario, the proposed method, DHR and IHR schemes are simulated without cluster head fault injection. The detailed configuration of this scenario is shown in Table 10.4.

10.5.1.1 Evaluation of FND and HNA

Table 10.5 shows the comparison of first node dead (FND) and half node alive (HNA) metrics with respect to the number of rounds until which the first sensor node gets dead and half of the sensor nodes are alive for all simulated algorithms.

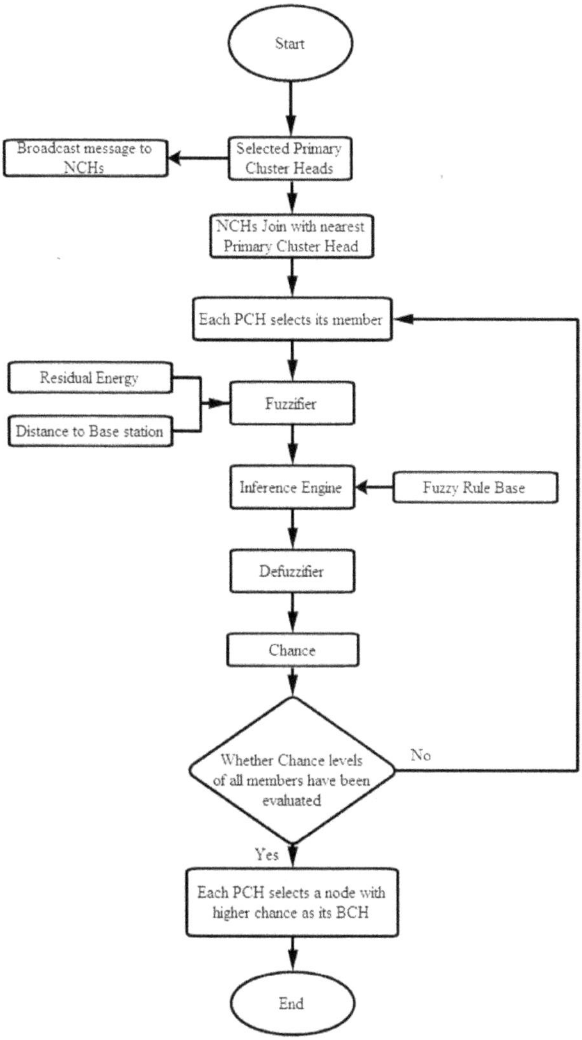

FIGURE 10.9 Schematic chart for selecting backup cluster head in the EIHRF protocol.

TABLE 10.5
Comparison of FND and HNA Metrics

Algorithm	FND	HNA
DHR	67	158
IHR	73	265
EIHRF	83	272

TABLE 10.6
Throughput for EIHRF, IHR, and DHR Protocols without Fault Injection

Protocol	Packet Delivery (KB)
DHR	38,230
IHR	85,598
EIHRF	86,723

In the DHR protocol, the first dead node comes out at round number 67 and in the IHR protocol it comes out at round number 73, and for the proposed EIHRF protocol the first dead node comes out at round number 83. From Table 10.5 it can be observed that the proposed method (EIHRF) outperforms DHR and IHR methods in both FND and HNA metrics.

10.5.1.2 Evaluation of Throughput

The throughput value is measured as the accumulated size of unique data packets transferred to the base station at every round. Therefore, the data packets received by the base station from the DHR protocol are measured once. Table 10.6 represents the throughput values of the network for simulated protocols. From this table, it can be concluded that the EIHRF protocol can deliver more packets as compared with IHR and DHR protocols in scenario 1.

10.5.2 Scenario 2: With Primary Cluster Head Fault Injection

To study how the wireless sensor network reacts when faults occur, the proposed EIHRF protocol and DHR and IHR schemes are simulated with primary cluster head fault injection. The faults are injected at a rate of 0.5, meaning that 50% of the primary cluster heads will fail at the scheduled time. The mean number of primary cluster head faults in a time interval is set to 5 and 6. The configuration details for this scenario are already given in Table 10.4.

10.5.2.1 Evaluation of Remaining Energy

A number of simulated experiments under different scenarios were performed to analyze the remaining energy of the network. In the first scenario, there is no cluster head fault were injected into the network (DHR: 0, IHR: 0, EIHRF: 0). In the second scenario, the primary cluster head fault were injected into the network with a failure rate of 0.5, while the value of λ was set to 5 (DHR: 1, IHR: 1, EIHRF: 1). In the third scenario, the primary cluster head faults were injected into the network with the same failure rate of 0.5, but the value of λ was increased to 6 (DHR:2, IHR:2, EIHRF:2). Figures 10.10– 10.12 display the comparison results of total remaining energy levels in each round under three scenarios.

Based on Figures 10.10 and 10.12, it is evident that the EIHRF protocol shows higher energy efficiency with a higher total remaining energy of the network as

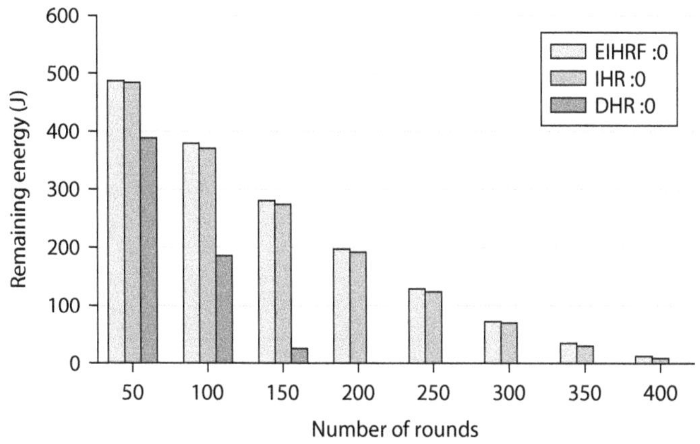

FIGURE 10.10 Total remaining energy (J) in each round for DHR, IHR, and EIHRF without PCH fault injection.

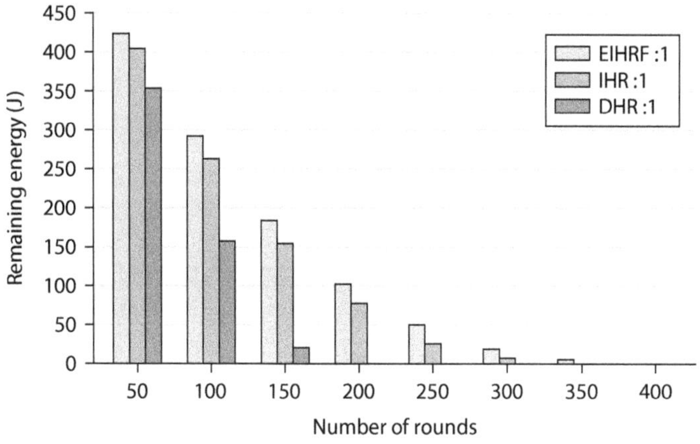

FIGURE 10.11 Total remaining energy (J) in each round for DHR, IHR, and EIHRF methods ($\lambda = 5$).

compared to IHR and DHR protocols. Figure 10.10 establishes a baseline for energy consumption in the absence of any faults, against which the impact of cluster head failures can be evaluated. In Figure 10.12, where λ is set to 6, representing a higher rate of cluster head failures, the EIHRF protocol consistently maintains the highest remaining energy throughout the network's operation, followed by the IHR protocol, while the DHR protocol shows the lowest energy retention. For instance, at round 50, the EIHRF protocol starts with an energy level around 340 Joules, while

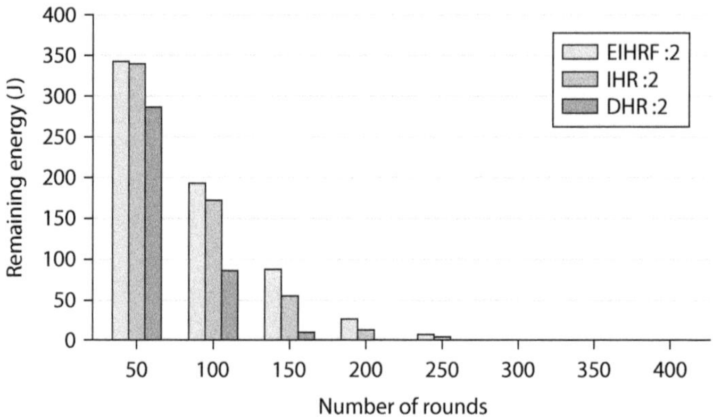

FIGURE 10.12 Total remaining energy (J) in each round for DHR, IHR, and EIHRF methods ($\lambda = 6$).

the IHR and DHR protocols begin closer to 300 Joules. As the network progresses to round 100, the EIHRF protocol still holds approximately 200 Joules, whereas the IHR protocol drops below 150 Joules, and the DHR protocol falls even further. These specific examples from Figure 10.12 strongly confirm that the EIHRF protocol achieves higher energy efficiency and prolongs network lifetime by optimizing energy consumption more effectively than the other protocols, supporting the claim that the EIHRF protocol is a more robust method for energy-constrained wireless sensor networks, particularly in the presence of cluster head failures.

10.5.2.2 Evaluation of Throughput

Table 10.7 shows the throughput values of the DHR, IHR, and the proposed protocol when the primary cluster head fault are injected with λ equal to 5 and 6 and the failure rate is equal to 0.5.

10.5.2.3 Evaluation of Number of Dead Nodes

Simulated experiments were performed, and the number of packets delivered per round was observed for all three protocols. Figure 10.13 shows the number of

TABLE 10.7
Throughput for EIHRF, IHR, and DHR Protocols with Fault Injection

Protocol	Packet Delivery (KB) $\lambda = 5$	Packet Delivery (KB) $\lambda = 6$
DHR	38,136	32,933
IHR	57,441	34,031
EIHRF	62,195	39,015

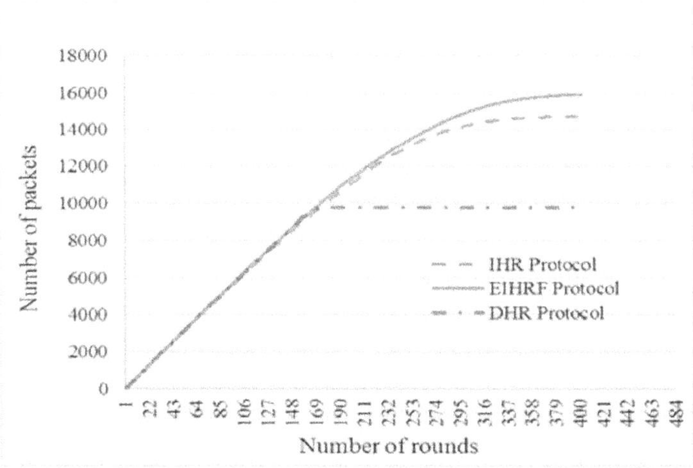

FIGURE 10.13 Number of packets delivered per round ($\lambda = 5$).

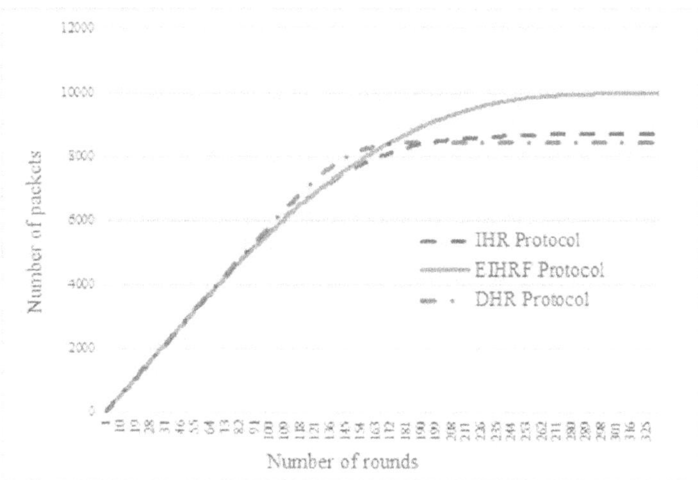

FIGURE 10.14 Number of packets delivered per round ($\lambda = 6$).

packets delivered per round when the primary cluster head fault is injected into the network with a failure rate of 0.5 and λ equal to 5. It is observed that packet delivery is higher in the EIHRF protocol as compared to IHR and DHR protocols. Similar experiments were performed for $\lambda = 6$. Figure 10.14 illustrates the number of packets delivered per round when the primary cluster head faults are injected into the network with a failure rate of 0.5, and in this case, the overall number of packets delivered per round is also higher in the EIHRF protocol as compared to the other two protocols.

10.6 CONCLUSION

A distributed fault-tolerance mechanism for homogeneous wireless sensor networks is presented in this chapter. This method has been developed based on IHR and DHR protocols. It is called Enhanced Informer Homed Routing with Fuzzy logic (EIHRF) fault-tolerance protocol. The difference between IHR, DHR, and EIHRF is that the IHR and DHR protocols rely on a probabilistic model for clustering, but the EIHRF protocol fixes the minimum distance between cluster heads to achieve distributed workload among cluster heads and to avoid overlapping of them. Furthermore, a fuzzy logic approach has been used in order to select an appropriate backup cluster head for each cluster by calculating the chance of each tentative backup cluster head. The fuzzy parameters to calculate the chance (for selection of backup cluster head) are remaining energy and distance to base station. Moreover, in order to evaluate the robustness of the proposed EIHRF protocol, while the cluster head's fault happens, a fault injection function is used. According to experimental results, the EIHRF protocol shows better performance compared to the IHR and DHR protocols in terms of first node dead, half node alive, throughput, and total remaining energy in the network. Furthermore, the experimental results indicate that the workload is scattered and the sensor nodes tend to fail later within the lifetime of the network. From experimental results, it is found that the EIHRF protocol is more energy-efficient than the IHR and DHR protocols. The proposed protocol is shown to be a stable and energy-efficient fault-tolerant protocol for homogeneous wireless sensor networks.

REFERENCES

1. Atero, Fco Javier, Juan Jose Vinagre, Julio Ramiro, and Mark Wilby. "A low energy and adaptive routing architecture for efficient field monitoring in heterogeneous wireless sensor networks." In *2011 International Conference on High Performance Computing & Simulation*, pp. 449–455. IEEE, 2011.
2. Bagci, Hakan, and Adnan Yazici. "An energy aware fuzzy approach to unequal clustering in wireless sensor networks." *Applied Soft Computing* 13, no. 4 (2013): 1741–1749.
3. Arjunan, Sariga, and Sujatha Pothula. "A survey on unequal clustering protocols in wireless sensor networks." *Journal of King Saud University-Computer and Information Sciences* 31, no. 3 (2019): 304–317.
4. Chouikhi, Samira, Inès El Korbi, Yacine Ghamri-Doudane, and Leila Azouz Saidane. "A survey on fault tolerance in small and large scale wireless sensor networks." *Computer Communications* 69 (2015): 22–37.
5. Wang, Jin, Junming Niu, Kai Wang, and Wei Liu. "An energy efficient fuzzy cluster head selection algorithm for WSNs." In *2018 International Workshop on Advanced Image Technology (IWAIT)*, pp. 1–4. IEEE, 2018.
6. Sun, Peng, Liantao Wu, Zhibo Wang, Ming Xiao, and Zhi Wang. "Sparsest random sampling for cluster-based compressive data gathering in wireless sensor networks." *IEEE Access* 6 (2018): 36383–36394.
7. Rawat, Piyush, Gopal Singh Rawat, Harish Rawat, and Siddhartha Chauhan. "Energy-efficient cluster-based routing protocol for heterogeneous wireless sensor network." *Annals of Telecommunications* 80, no. 1 (2025): 109–122.
8. Sahoo, Laxminarayan, Shri Supriyan Sen, Kalishankar Tiwary, Sarbast Moslem, and Tapan Senapati. "Improvement of wireless sensor network lifetime via intelligent clustering under uncertainty." *IEEE Access* 12 (2024): 25018–25033.

9. Qiu, Meikang, Zhong Ming, Jiayin Li, Jianning Liu, Gang Quan, and Yongxin Zhu. "Informer homed routing fault tolerance mechanism for wireless sensor networks." *Journal of Systems Architecture* 59, no. 4–5 (2013): 260–270.
10. Tamandani, Yahya Kord, Mohammad Ubaidullah Bokhari, and Qahtan Makki Shallal. "Two-step fuzzy logic system to achieve energy efficiency and prolonging the lifetime of WSNs." *Wireless Networks* 23 (2017): 1889–1899.
11. Vaddeti, Ankitha, Phani Teja Sri Mandalapu, and B.K.S.P. Kumar Raju Alluri. "Energy efficient clustering scheme using backup nodes in WSNs." In *2018 IEEE International Conference on System, Computation, Automation and Networking (ICSCA)*, pp. 1–5. IEEE, 2018.
12. El Fissaoui, Mohamed, Abderrahim Beni-Hssane, and Mostafa Saadi. "Energy efficient and fault tolerant distributed algorithm for data aggregation in wireless sensor networks." *Journal of Ambient Intelligence and Humanized Computing* 10 (2019): 569–578.
13. Hu, Yuan, and Yugang Niu. "An energy-efficient overlapping clustering protocol in WSNs." *Wireless Networks* 24 (2018): 1775–1791.
14. Khan, Muhammad Ali, M. Abdullah Qureshi, Imran Raza, and Syed Asad Hussain. "EECP-EI: energy-efficient clustering protocol based on energy intervals for wireless sensor networks." In Proceedings of the International Conference on Information and Communication Technology, pp. 113–119. 2019.
15. Faheem, Muhammad, and Vehbi C. Gungor. "Energy efficient and QoS-aware routing protocol for wireless sensor network-based smart grid applications in the context of industry 4.0." *Applied Soft Computing* 68 (2018): 910–922.
16. Jain, Nidhi, Vinod M. Vokkarane, and Jianping Wang. "Performance analysis of dual-homed fault-tolerant routing in wireless sensor networks." In *2008 IEEE Conference on Technologies for Homeland Security*, pp. 474–479. IEEE, 2008.
17. Geeta, D. D., N. Nalini, and Rajashekhar C. Biradar. "Fault tolerance in wireless sensor network using hand-off and dynamic power adjustment approach." *Journal of Network and Computer Applications* 36, no. 4 (2013): 1174–1185.
18. Al-Qadami, Nasser, and Andrey Koucheryavy. "Fault-tolerance algorithm in wireless sensor networks." *Infocommunications Journal* 7, no. 4 (2015): 28–33.
19. Akyildiz, Ian F., and Mehmet Can Vuran. *Wireless Sensor Networks.* John Wiley & Sons, 2010.
20. Wu, Xiaoling, Jinsung Cho, Brian J. d'Auriol, and Sungyoung Lee. "Energy-aware routing for wireless sensor networks by AHP." In *Software Technologies for Embedded and Ubiquitous Systems: 5th IFIP WG 10.2 International Workshop*, pp. 446–455. Springer Berlin Heidelberg, 2007.
21. Masdari, Mohammad, and Farah Naghiloo. "Fuzzy logic-based sink selection and load balancing in multi-sink wireless sensor networks." *Wireless Personal Communications* 97 (2017): 2713–2739.
22. Mamdani, Ebrahim H., and Sedrak Assilian. "An experiment in linguistic synthesis with a fuzzy logic controller." *International Journal of Human-Computer Studies* 51, no. 2 (1999): 135–147.
23. Last, Günter, and Mathew Penrose. *Lectures on the Poisson Process*, vol. 7. Cambridge University Press, 2017.
24. Elmiligui, Ahmed A. "Fault modeling in wireless sensor networks." Master's Thesis, Old Dominion University, 2006.
25. Gupta, Gaurav, and Mohamed Younis. "Fault-tolerant clustering of wireless sensor networks." In *2003 IEEE Wireless Communications and Networking*, vol. 3, pp. 1579–1584. IEEE, 2003.

11 AI-Controlled Automatic Speed Detector in Vehicle Communication System

R. M. Rajeshwari and M. Kaliappan

11.1 INTRODUCTION

Day-to-day life, we unfortunately witness the loss of many lives due to road accidents. The motivation behind this chapter stems from a tragic event that occurred in my hometown, Madurai-Thirumangalam, on the Sivarakottai National Highway in April 2024. A young man, who had just attended the Thalavaipuram temple festival, was driving his car when he collided with a guava seller and then crashed into the central median, resulting in the total destruction of his vehicle. Tragically, he lost all of his family members in the accident, except for himself, as he was wearing his seat belt. The investigation report attributed the cause of the accident to uncontrollable speed, making it a truly devastating incident. This heartbreaking event has inspired me to propose a simple yet effective solution – the AI-controlled automatic speed detector (AICASD) system. By installing an automatic speed detector in vehicles, an alarm sound would alert the driver to any dangerous speeds, while simultaneously emitting a siren sound to warn pedestrians and other road users of the potential danger. This innovative system would provide crucial information to both the driver and those in the vicinity, allowing them to take necessary precautions and avoid potential accidents.

By implementing the AICASD system, we can work towards preventing tragic incidents like the one that occurred in Madurai-Thirumangalam, ultimately saving lives and making our roads safer for everyone.

11.2 RELATED WORKS

Gong et al. [15] suggest utilizing connected automatic vehicles (CAVs) as traffic flow detectors to gather and exchange traffic flow data for heterogeneous traffic management and control. The proposed approach involves creating a mathematical matrix to depict the road section's status, employing unsupervised machine learning to analyze traffic data, and utilizing an enhanced generative adversarial imputation net (GAIN) to assess and fill in missing traffic data. The accuracy and reliability of the

DOI: 10.1201/9781003532156-15

proposed method are validated using next-generation simulation (NGSIM) data. A key innovation of this study is the utilization of GAIN, a deep learning framework based on generative adversarial networks (GANs), for imputing missing traffic data. GAIN has demonstrated greater robustness and stability in handling incomplete heterogeneous data compared to existing imputation techniques. Furthermore, this study contributes to the field by suggesting the use of CAVs as sensors for detecting mixed traffic flow, potentially leading to more effective and precise traffic management and control.

Fu et al. [2] have developed the distance- and speed-based lane change warning (DS-LCW) system, designed to provide timely warnings during lane changes when the relative distance between vehicles is minimal. The warning threshold was established using a percentile of the warning index, effectively distinguishing between safe and unsafe lane changes. However, the study's results were constrained by a limited sample size, leading to some inaccuracies in threshold determination. Additionally, the extremity test, based on subjective driver experiences, revealed significant variations between conservative and aggressive drivers, which impacted the calculation of the minimum safe distance (MSD) and the warning threshold. Moving forward, it is crucial to address these limitations by refining the methodology and incorporating a wider range of driving styles, thereby improving the system's accuracy and ensuring its effectiveness in promoting safe lane changes for all drivers.

Lim et al. [11] discuss that car-following control is a critical aspect of autonomous driving technology. This control serves various purposes, such as maintaining a safe distance from the vehicle in front and improving the overall driving experience. Model predictive control (MPC) stands out as a highly effective method for achieving these objectives and its ability to address multiple goals simultaneously. One of the key features of MPC is its ability to assign different weights to each objective, allowing the controller to adapt its behavior based on the relative importance of each goal. However, determining the optimal weights can be a challenging task, as there is no standard benchmark for evaluating their performance. Conducting numerous driving experiments to find the ideal weight factors can also be time-consuming.

Calvi et al. [7] proposed a study examining traffic safety indicators, specifically time headway (TH) and time to collision (TTC), on Italian highways utilizing data from an advanced traffic control system. The primary objective of this research is to gain insights into driver behavior in car-following scenarios and assess the impact of visibility conditions, type of lead vehicle, and traveling lane on these indicators. The findings reveal that shorter THs are prevalent during daytime hours, particularly when following passenger vehicles and in the passing lane. Conversely, critical TTC values are infrequent, underscoring the efficacy of this metric in identifying potentially hazardous situations. These results underscore the significance of taking into account specific factors that influence driver conduct when evaluating traffic safety on highways.

Alwindi et al. [12] discuss the need for precise and effective methods to track vehicle speed, which has become increasingly important in today's fast-paced world. Traditional speed measurement techniques, such as radar guns and speed cameras, have limitations when it comes to precision and real-time monitoring. However, a new avenue for real-time vehicle speed measurement has emerged with the advancement of image processing tools. By utilizing computer vision, image processing techniques can extract valuable information from visual data, such as images or video frames. This allows for the accurate estimation of vehicle speed in real-time by analyzing their motion patterns captured by cameras using sophisticated algorithms. This paper introduces two methods for estimating real-time vehicle speed using image processing techniques. The first method utilizes the Lucas-Kanade algorithm, while the second method employs the Gaussian mixture model (GMM). Both approaches are designed to automatically estimate vehicle speed from a real-time sequence captured by a stationary camera. Furthermore, this study evaluates the performance of these methods for tracking vehicles.

Mahaadevan et al. [6] highlight that electric vehicle (EV) technology is rapidly emerging as a leading solution for sustainable transportation. Alongside this growth, advancements are being made in charging infrastructure development and the automation of the EV charging process. Globally, EVs are equipped with various types of charging sockets located in different positions on the vehicle. This diversity in socket type and location underscores the importance of accurately identifying the socket type and location to streamline the charging process. Leveraging image processing and deep learning-based socket identification, EV charging infrastructure providers can enhance the efficiency of the charging process. It is crucial for these deep learning techniques to be easily implementable on real-time processing boards for practical viability. This paper introduces a novel You Only Look Once (YOLO) model known as the Electric Vehicle Socket (EVS) YOLO. Building upon the YOLOv5 architecture, the EVS-YOLO incorporates a vision-type transformer called the SWIN-Transformer and an attention mechanism called SimAM to improve the model's performance in accurately detecting the correct charging port.

Hawzhin et al. [4] propose a machine learning framework designed for automated accident detection utilizing in-car sensors. It underscores the significance of recognizing accident patterns, the obstacles in acquiring accident data, and the importance of leveraging in-car sensors for accident detection. The paper introduces a machine learning framework and evaluates various feature extraction methods for accident detection. The findings reveal promising results, with CNN features and SVM classifiers demonstrating superior performance. The article underscores the critical role of feature engineering and feature learning strategies in machine learning-based accident detection. However, there are a few limitations to consider. Firstly, the utilization of a single dataset is necessitated by the scarcity of data for this specific application, thereby limiting the generalizability of the results. Additionally, comparing findings to other studies is challenging due to variations in accident definitions and input sensor channels.

In the research paper [16], Bakheet et al. introduce a sophisticated deep neural framework designed for real-time detection of vehicular accidents utilizing motion temporal templates and fuzzy time slicing. The system operates by detecting and tracking moving objects through the utilization of temporal templates, clustering, and supervised learning techniques. Local features are then extracted from these templates, and a deep neural network model is trained to accurately predict accidents.

The paper discusses the significance of vehicular accident prediction and detection, provides an overview of related research, elucidates the concept of temporal templates, and thoroughly outlines the various components of the current framework. Overall, this research showcases a cutting-edge approach to enhancing road safety through the utilization of advanced technology and machine learning algorithms. However, this paper is limited in several ways. Despite their strength, many of the methods mentioned above suffer from operational inefficiency and a lack of real-time performance in online accident detection without the use of future frames, resulting in unsatisfactory outcomes. Furthermore, there is a lack of a specialized dataset for traffic analysis that includes video streams with top-down views similar to drone or unmanned aerial vehicle videos, or omnidirectional camera videos.

Lehtonen et al. [14] conducted a study to investigate the impact of a speed warning system on drivers' speedometer monitoring and responses. The primary objective of the study was to assess the impact of the speed warning system on speed control and to identify potential areas for improvement in intelligent speed adaptation systems. The findings of the study suggest that drivers actively seek to avoid speed warnings, indicating a potential for enhancing the effectiveness of intelligent speed adaptation (ISA) systems. Speed warnings were triggered if a driver exceeded the speed limit by 4 km/h for 3 seconds.

Tasgaonkar et al. [3] provide crucial data to monitoring stations and smart sensors, which have revolutionized the method of collecting and analyzing information. A sophisticated framework has been developed using an Internet of Things-based approach to detect car accidents utilizing smart sensors. The collected data is then transmitted and stored on the ThingSpeak cloud for further analysis. By utilizing an accelerometer, ultrasonic sensor, and GPS technology, the system can detect accidents in real time and activate a warning signal. One limitation of the current approach lies in its predictive performance and robustness when analyzing a wide range of vehicular accidents.

Alkhaiwani et al. [10] explored the design and validation of two distinct fractional order (FO) speed controllers for induction motor drives in their study. These controllers were developed to address detuning issues commonly encountered with conventional controllers when faced with parameter variations and low-speed regions. The FOPI and FO[PI] controllers were crafted using a chirp signal injection method and were assessed for their robust performance under dynamic conditions. Through experimental validation, it was evident that the FO controllers outperformed conventional controllers, particularly at low speeds. This research offered innovative solutions to enhance speed control performance and highlighted the advantages of utilizing FO controllers to counteract detuning effects.

Nagaraju et al. [1] discuss the vehicle over-speed detection and accident-avoidance system, an innovative Internet of Things (IoT)-based solution designed to enhance road safety by utilizing sensors such as ultrasonic sensors to collect data and alert drivers of potential hazards. This sophisticated system comprises essential components including an ultrasonic sensor, Arduino UNO microcontroller, potentiometer, CAN controller, DC motor, GSM module, LCD display, and a buzzer. The ultrasonic sensor plays a crucial role in detecting objects or vehicles in close proximity to the vehicle, transmitting this information to the Arduino UNO for processing. In the event of a vehicle approaching too closely to another, the system automatically adjusts the vehicle's speed to prevent accidents. Additionally, the system includes an over-speed detection feature that monitors the vehicle's speed and notifies the driver if a specific speed limit is exceeded. Furthermore, in cases of driver over-speeding, the system is programmed to send an SMS alert to the relevant personnel at the cab company or car rental agency. This proactive approach ensures that appropriate action can be taken promptly to address any safety concerns. Overall, the vehicle over-speed detection and accident-avoidance system represents a cutting-edge solution that prioritizes driver safety and accident prevention through the seamless integration of IoT technology and advanced sensor capabilities.

Shi and Zhao [13] discuss a lightweight license plate detection algorithm for accuracy and speed. Various methods are compared for better localization in complex environments. License plate recognition is crucial for traffic safety. Traditional methods and deep learning models are used for location detection.

Onemayin et al. [19] proposed a vehicle tracking system that utilized GPS and wireless technologies to enhance public transportation in urban areas of Nigeria. The system incorporated greedy forwarding algorithms for real-time vehicle location tracking, resulting in improved efficiency and accuracy. Through testing on a university transportation system, it was demonstrated to be both efficient and accurate. This innovative system was designed to optimize fleet management strategies for urban arterials and had the potential for widespread adoption. This research addressed the unique challenges faced by public transportation in developing nations and offered a viable solution to enhance commuting efficiency.

Mostafa et al. [5] present the issue of escalating traffic congestion in metropolitan areas that necessitates the implementation of a surveillance system to effectively monitor traffic flow and prevent unnecessary delays and accidents. In this research study, computer vision-based speed estimation and object detection have been utilized for automated vehicles. Various image processing techniques and deep learning models have been employed to evaluate the proposed system. Speed estimation of the detected vehicles was conducted using YOLOv4 and the Haar cascade methods, with YOLOv4 demonstrating superior performance in assessing the speed of various automobiles.

Zhong-Xin et al. [22] reported introducing an optimal speed tracking controller for permanent magnet synchronous motors (PMSMs) utilizing an inverse optimal composite approach. A disturbance observer was utilized to estimate load torque, and an optimal controller was subsequently developed. This method effectively combined optimality and robustness without the need to solve HJB equations. Both simulation and experimental results validated the efficacy of the proposed approach.

Oche et al. [8] indicated that the leading cause of road accidents is attributed to high-speed vehicles. In an effort to address this issue, regulatory authorities have established speed limits on roadways to control the velocity of vehicles. To effectively enforce these speed restrictions, a method for monitoring vehicle speed is essential. Various techniques are currently utilized to detect and monitor speed limit violators, including speed cameras, radar, loop detectors, police officers, and more.

However, these conventional methods have proven to be ineffective due to their associated drawbacks, such as high equipment costs, increased labor requirements, and inadequate monitoring capabilities. Therefore, there is a pressing need for a straightforward, cost-efficient, and easily deployable speed detection solution that can overcome the limitations of traditional methods.

Walter et al. [18] evaluated the efficacy of speed indication devices (SIDs) in mitigating vehicle speeds in South London. SIDs were strategically placed at 10 locations for durations ranging from one to three weeks, resulting in a notable decrease in vehicle speeds by an average of 1.4 mph and a significant reduction in the percentage of vehicles surpassing the speed limit. Furthermore, the research explored the range over which SIDs maintain their effectiveness, revealing that speed reductions were observed up to 400 m away from the device. However, upon removal of the SID, vehicle speeds promptly reverted to their pre-SID levels within the initial week. This pattern aligns with findings from prior studies, indicating a consistent trend of decreased speeds while SIDs are operational, followed by a gradual decline in effectiveness post-removal. The primary objective of the research was to assess the impact of SIDs on speed reduction in urban settings, particularly under conditions of unimpeded traffic flow. The outcomes of the study suggest that SIDs can indeed be instrumental in curbing speeds, particularly among drivers who exceed the speed limit. Nevertheless, it is crucial to acknowledge that these effects are transient and tend to diminish once the device is no longer in place.

Alkhaiwani et al. [10] discuss a framework and IoT-based system to detect and report car accidents in Saudi Arabia to save lives and protect privacy. The IoT technology is used to improve road safety, reduce traffic congestion, and promote sustainability. Previous studies show vulnerabilities in IoT devices such as privacy concerns and insufficient security measures. The current framework aims to address these issues by using encryption and lightweight cryptography. The paper also reviews related research on IoT-based accident detection systems and discusses the importance of privacy and security in the IoT ecosystem.

Ambros et al. [17] utilized Italian Floating Car Data (FCD) to establish and confirm these indicators. The objective was to bridge a gap in the existing literature by leveraging nationwide FCD to develop and validate speed-related indicators in relation to crashes. The primary data source consisted of FCD from OCTO Telematics, which accounted for 2% of the Italian car fleet. The work delved into the creation of speed-related safety performance indicators using floating car data to enhance road traffic safety.

Mohamed [9] proposes the implementation of an automated system that can autonomously detect and record traffic violations without human intervention. The paper involves the development of an on-board unit that will be securely installed within vehicles, preventing drivers from tampering with it. This unit will have the capability to identify and document major traffic violations in real time, regardless of location or time. Additionally, we suggest the establishment of an automatic reporting system to transmit recorded violations to traffic authorities promptly. By implementing this innovative system, we aim to enhance road safety, reduce accidents, and ultimately contribute to the overall progress and well-being of society.

Madeo et al. [21] suggested that the WeMo unmanned surface vehicle was a cost-effective solution designed for water quality monitoring using readily available components and a versatile array of sensors. Its purpose was to be easily replicated in large quantities to enable widespread monitoring efforts. This article delved into the challenges faced in environmental monitoring, the necessity for affordable solutions, and the intricate design of the vehicle. Equipped with cutting-edge data analytics tools, the WeMo vehicle boasted autonomous navigation capabilities and efficient data processing. The article also explored parameter estimation techniques and the vehicle's robust communication infrastructure. Utilizing LoRa technology for data transmission, the WeMo vehicle was user-friendly and accessible even to those without technical expertise.

Ming-Sen et al. [20] explored the utilization of IoT technology in mobile vehicle tracking through embedded control systems. Specifically, it delved into the design and implementation of a smart light-chasing vehicle that autonomously tracked light sources. The system architecture comprised a mobile vehicle body, motor-driven unit, Arduino control unit, light sensing unit, IoT communication unit, and IoT host machine. The light-chasing control process entailed detecting photometric values and determining the vehicle's movement direction based on the illumination of the light source. Additionally, a moving-path display system developed in LabVIEW graphical language was utilized to illustrate the vehicle's path, calculate the path length, and determine the moving distance. Through IoT wireless communication, the data collected during the tracking process was transmitted to the IoT host machine for display and analysis. This innovative approach to mobile vehicle tracking showcased the potential of IoT technology in enhancing efficiency and accuracy in various applications.

A total of 25 references were carefully analyzed in order to gain a deeper insight into the current methodologies. This study has played a crucial role in identifying the necessary requirements for the proposed work. Below, a comparison between the proposed approach and several existing methods is provided for further clarity and understanding. Table 11.1 illustrates the limitations addressed by our proposed model.

11.3 STATISTICAL ANALYSIS

According to the State Crime Records Bureau (SCRB), statistical analysis of road accidents in Tamil Nadu over the past three years is outlined below.

An analysis of road accidents in Tamil Nadu in March 2024 reveals a decrease in fatalities, with the highest number of accidents involving two-wheelers. Table 11.2 presents district-wise data, emphasizing Chennai, Coimbatore, and Chengalpattu as areas with a high incidence of accidents. The phenomenon of urbanization has led to a significant increase in traffic congestion in metropolitan areas worldwide. This has resulted in a concerning number of fatalities and injuries among pedestrians, cyclists, and vehicle occupants due to road accidents each year. Road safety measures are crucial in preventing such incidents and safeguarding individual lives from harm. Road safety encompasses a set of traffic regulations and guidelines that must be adhered to while navigating the roadways.

TABLE 11.1
Comparison of a Few Existing Approaches with the Proposed Approach

References	Methodology Used	Focused On	Limitations	Limitations Addressed
[2]	Distance and speed-based lane change warning	Timely warning based on relative distance between vehicles	Limited by the sample size; percentiles have a certain degree of error	A dataset of around 225 rows with 8 features leads to a good percentile score
[7]	Time headway (TH) and time to collision (TTC)	Type of lead vehicle and passing lane	Only a small number of cases with critical time to collision (TTC) values recorded	Worked with different scenarios such as traffic density, collision possibility, and time to recover from collision
[14]	Intelligent speed adaptation (ISA) systems	Relies on cognitive control	Threshold limit is very less	Maximum of 90 km/h
[17]	Floating car data	GPS	Real-time traffic monitoring	Vehicle speed monitored by cheap and lightweight ultrasonic sensor
[18]	Speed indication devices (SIDs)	Automatic traffic counters	Around 10% of the data missing or unreliable due to mechanical failure of ATCs; high energy consumption	Mostly focused on all features and achieved an accuracy of 92% with limited battery usage
[21]	Water environmental mobile observer	Long-range unmanned surface vehicle with data processing capabilities	Not suitable for critical environmental conditions due to its small dimensional components	Withstand and perform effectively in adverse weather conditions

11.4 PROPOSED AI-CONTROLLED AUTOMATIC SPEED DETECTOR (AICASD) SYSTEM

To operate AICASD we need the following essential components:

- Arduino Uno R3: Model with a USB interface and 14 digital I/O pins
- Speed sensors: HC-SR04 ultrasonic sensor or RB-100 speed radar module
- Adafruit breadboard: With at least 400 tie points in order to support durability and reliability

TABLE 11.2
District-Wise Report for Total Accidents and Total Deaths up to the Month of March 2024

Sl. No.	Name of the District	Total Accidents (16,762)	Total Deaths (4345)
1	Chennai	909	123
2	Coimbatore	882	234
3	Chengalpattu	856	219
4	Tiruppur	836	162
5	Salem	835	194
6	Cuddalore	741	141
7	Madurai	699	200
8	Villupuram	657	126
9	Tiruchirapalli	626	162
10	Erode	615	166
11	Thiruvallur	569	185
12	Dindigul	564	148
13	Krishnagiri	541	191
14	Thanjavur	530	102
15	Tiruvannamalai	518	193
16	Namakkal	472	115
17	Pudukkottai	427	121
18	Virudhunagar	405	144
19	Kanniyakumari	385	98
20	Dharmapuri	375	97
21	Ramanathapuram	365	107
22	Tirunelveli	344	85
23	Sivagangai	329	122
24	Theni	314	89
25	Thoothukudi	313	92
26	Kallakuruchi	308	55
27	Karur	301	96
28	Tenkasi	274	76
29	Kancheepuram	259	89
30	Mayiladuthurai	220	32
31	Thiruvarur	220	61
32	Vellore	203	70
33	Ranipet	202	58
34	Ariyalur	189	46
35	Tirupathur	152	59
36	Perambalur	135	44
37	Nagapattinam	129	34
38	The Nilgiris	63	9
	Total	16,762	4345

- DuPont jumper wires: Essential for connecting components on a breadboard or directly to an Arduino
- OBD-II to UART/USB adapter
- Resistors: Depending on the sensor, pull-up or pull-down resistors may be needed. Normally, 1/4 watt resistors in various values (e.g., 220Ω, 1kΩ, 10kΩ)
- Power sources:
    - USB cable for powering the Arduino via your computer
    - Battery pack (like a 9 V battery or LiPo) for portable projects
- LCD display: To show speed or distance readings in real time or a computer display
- Electromagnetic buzzer
- Real-time clock module: DS3231 RTC module
- Arduino Integrated Development Environment (IDE) 2.3.3: Used to write code and upload it to an Arduino board.

The HC-SR04 ultrasonic sensor is utilized with an Arduino board to accurately measure distances. This sensor operates by emitting ultrasonic sound waves and subsequently calculating the time it takes for the sound to reflect back after striking an object. Through this process, the sensor is able to precisely determine the distance between the object and the sensor.

As the vehicle is in motion, we are able to determine its speed by measuring the distance it has traveled within a specific time frame.

11.4.1 Configuration of Hardware and Software

Based on the dataset, vehicle speed is monitored and reported when it exceeds the threshold speed. To achieve this, we use an Arduino board & IDE and ultrasonic sensors to detect the speed of the vehicle. When the needle of the speedometer exceeds the prescribed speed, an alarm signal is produced by an electromagnetic buzzer via the Arduino board. The Arduino board is entirely controlled by the Arduino IDE, in which necessary codes are written.

The ultrasonic sensor functions by emitting sound waves within the ultrasonic frequency range, typically around 40 kHz. These sound waves propagate through the air and bounce off objects in their path. While the Arduino does not directly detect these sound waves, it can prompt the sensor to emit them and measure the time it takes for the waves to return. The process commences when the Arduino sends a 10-microsecond pulse to the TRIG pin of the sensor, activating the emission of an ultrasonic sound pulse.

Contemporary high-tech vehicles are integrated with the Arduino IDE platform. Using Arduino to interface with a vehicle's speedometer offers a high degree of customization, flexibility, and cost-effectiveness by enabling real-time data processing, alerts, and enhanced vehicle diagnostics and monitoring. You can develop a range of advanced features and integrations that would otherwise require expensive or specialized equipment. Whether you want to improve vehicle performance, add custom alerts, create a more modern display, or gather data for analysis, Arduino is a powerful tool for automotive projects.

To initiate the setup of the AICASD system, we gathered the essential components, which included an Arduino board (such as the Arduino Uno R4 WIFI), an HC-SR04 ultrasonic sensor, a breadboard, jumper wires, and resistors. The first step involved wiring the power connections: the VCC (or power) pin of the sensor was connected to the 5 V pin on the Arduino, and the GND (ground) pin of the sensor was connected to one of the GND pins on the Arduino. For the signal connections, the Trigger pin of the HC-SR04 sensor was connected to a digital pin (e.g., pin 9) on the Arduino, and the Echo pin was connected to another digital pin (e.g., pin 10). Once the wiring was completed, we opened the Arduino IDE, ensuring that the latest version was installed. A new sketch was initiated by clicking on File > New, then selecting the appropriate board model under Tools > Board (e.g., Arduino Uno), and choosing the correct port under Tools > Port. After writing the necessary code, we clicked on the upload button in the IDE to upload the code to the Arduino. To monitor the output, we opened the serial monitor by clicking on the magnifying glass icon in the top right corner of the IDE, where the distance readings in centimeters were displayed. If any issues were encountered, we checked the connections, verified the power of the Arduino, and confirmed that the correct board and port were selected in the IDE.

For standard vehicles lacking computer capabilities, these steps are essential to ensure proper functionality.

Modern luxury vehicles are equipped with built-in computers that allow for the installation of Arduino IDE. This software enables monitoring of results directly through the vehicle's computer display, with only an external Arduino board needing to be connected via a USB cable.

11.4.2 Arduino IDE

The Arduino IDE is essential for controlling and monitoring a vehicle speed detector by providing a programming environment where we can write, upload, and debug code. In our project, the code initializes the ultrasonic sensor, sets up the trigger pin, and establishes serial communication for data output. In the main loop, the Arduino sends a trigger pulse to the sensor, measures the duration of the echo return, and calculates the distance, which is then used to compute the speed of passing vehicles. The calculated speed is continuously output to the serial monitor, allowing real-time monitoring and feedback. This setup enables one to test and fine-tune the project effectively; any adjustments to the code or hardware can be easily monitored through the serial monitor, facilitating quick iterations for improved accuracy and performance. Figure 11.1 shows the automatic speed detection model inside the vehicle.

The Arduino IDE serves as the central tool for developing and managing a vehicle speed detector project using an Arduino board and sensors. It allows us to write, upload, and monitor the code that controls the system's operation. In the IDE, we can initialize the ultrasonic sensor by setting up the appropriate pins for triggering and

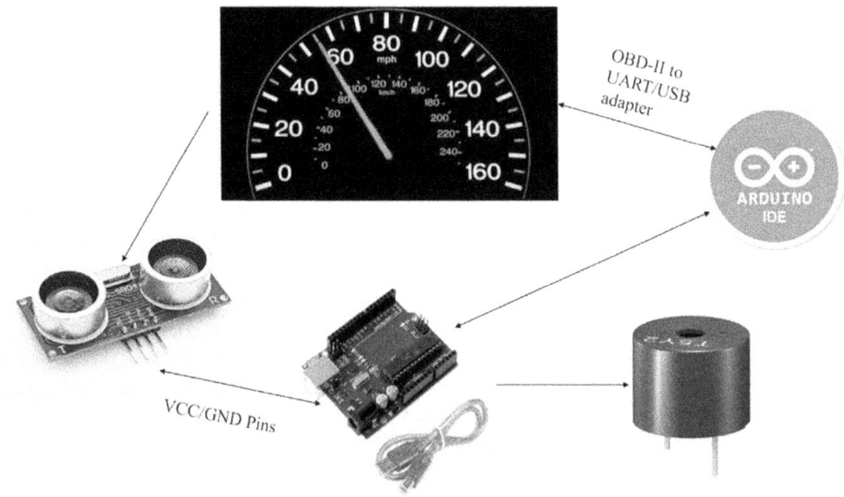

FIGURE 11.1 Proposed automatic speed detection model.

receiving echo signals. The code controls the sensor to send a pulse and measure the time it takes for the echo to return, which is then converted into a distance reading. Based on this distance measured over a known time interval, the speed of the vehicle is calculated by dividing the distance by the time taken for the sound wave to return. Additionally, the serial monitor in the Arduino IDE enables real-time monitoring of live speed readings as vehicles pass by, assisting in troubleshooting and adjustments for accuracy. The IDE allows easy modifications to the code based on observed performance, facilitating tweaks to parameters like the known distance for improved detection accuracy. After coding, we can upload the program directly from the IDE to the Arduino board, creating an immediate feedback loop that enhances the development and testing of the speed detection system. Overall, the Arduino IDE acts as a powerful interface for programming, monitoring, and refining your vehicle speed detection project, making it valuable for both beginners and experienced developers.

Many modern vehicles are equipped with an OBD-II (On-Board Diagnostics) port, which grants access to the vehicle's internal data, including crucial information about its speed. To access this data, an OBD-II to UART/USB adapter can be utilized, connecting to the vehicle's OBD-II port. The Arduino board is then employed to interpret the data retrieved from the OBD-II adapter. For effective communication, it is imperative to employ the correct OBD-II protocol, such as CAN bus or other pertinent protocols, and issue specific commands to the vehicle's onboard system to extract the speed data. This method facilitates seamless integration between the vehicle's internal systems and an Arduino, allowing for the extraction and utilization of speed information for a myriad of applications. Figure 11.1 shows an Arduino-based automatic speed detection system using an ultrasonic sensor, OBD-II interface, and a buzzer for monitoring and alerting speed conditions.

Pseudocode representation of the provided Arduino code for a speed detector using an ultrasonic sensor:

```
DEFINE trigPin as 9 // Trigger pin
DEFINE echoPin as 10 // Echo pin
FUNCTION setup():
   START serial communication at 9600 bps
   SET trigPin as OUTPUT
   SET echoPin as INPUT
FUNCTION loop():
   DECLARE duration, distance as LONG
   // Clear the trigger
   SET trigPin to LOW
   WAIT for 2 microseconds
   // Set the trigger high for 10 microseconds
   SET trigPin to HIGH
   WAIT for 10 microseconds
   SET trigPin to LOW
   // Read the echo pin
   SET duration to pulse duration on echoPin while HIGH
   // Calculate distance in cm
   SET distance to (duration * 0.034 / 2)
   // Print the distance
   PRINT "Distance: " + distance + " cm"
   WAIT for 500 milliseconds // Wait before the next
     measurement
```

When the vehicle surpasses the speed limit, the ultrasonic sensor detects the speed and transmits the data to the Arduino Integrated Development Environment (IDE) through the Arduino board. The Arduino board is linked to the Arduino IDE via a USB cable, allowing for seamless communication. The Arduino IDE oversees and manages the entire operation of the Arduino board. Upon receiving the signal indicating that the speed limit has been exceeded, the Arduino IDE triggers the Arduino board to emit an audible alarm. The integration of a vehicle's speedometer with an Arduino through the OBD-II port or UART serves the purpose of establishing a system that can effectively read and display real-time vehicle data. This data includes crucial information such as speed, engine RPM, fuel level, and various other parameters sourced from the vehicle's ECU. By establishing this connection, individuals can develop custom dashboards, monitor vehicle performance, and diagnose issues directly from the Arduino. This innovative approach offers a more personalized and adaptable solution for vehicle monitoring.

The sequence diagram illustrates the workflow of the proposed automatic speed detection model. Figure 11.2 shows how the ultrasonic sensor sends a trigger signal to the vehicle speedometer. Speed data is transmitted via OBD/UART ports to the Arduino IDE through a USB cable. Power is supplied to the components through VCC/GND pins, and the processed signal is sent from the Arduino board's digital pin to activate the electromagnetic buzzer. This setup enables real-time speed monitoring and alerting. The workflow of the proposed model is shown below.

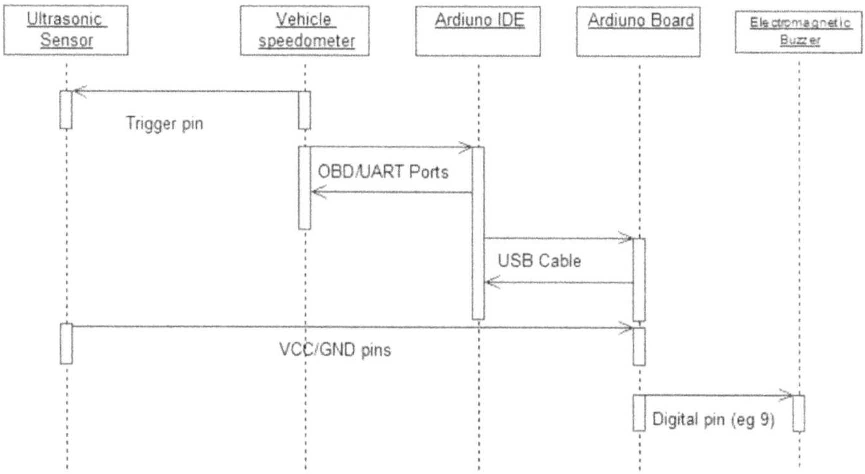

FIGURE 11.2 Workflow of the proposed model.

11.5 RESULTS AND DISCUSSION

Before delving into the analysis of traffic density, probability of collision, and time to recover from collisions, it is imperative to consider the essential constraints that impact these factors. These constraints include road types, road width, surface quality, intersection density, roadside development, visibility and sight distance, traffic characteristics, weather conditions, road markings and signage, and pedestrian and animal crossings. Additionally, factors such as road maintenance and upgrades must also be taken into account. The complexity of analyzing all this data necessitates a focused approach. Therefore, we have narrowed our focus to road design, changing environmental conditions, and the type of vehicle as mandatory parameters for evaluating the threshold speed. It is crucial to analyze vehicle speed in relation to the geometric and functional attributes of the road in order to ensure safety and enhance traffic flow. Given that our dataset is based on Indian road conditions, we have established the default assumption that the road width and surface quality are consistent and of good quality, regardless of the aforementioned mandatory requirements. This approach allows us to streamline our analysis and draw meaningful conclusions that can inform road safety measures and traffic management strategies.

11.5.1 Selection of the ML Model

The Random Forest algorithm is highly effective for multivariate supervised learning due to its ability to handle high-dimensional data with ease. This algorithm excels at managing datasets with numerous features while still accurately identifying important predictors without the risk of overfitting. By averaging over multiple decision trees, Random Forest significantly reduces the likelihood of overfitting, a common challenge when working with high-dimensional data. In contrast to linear models

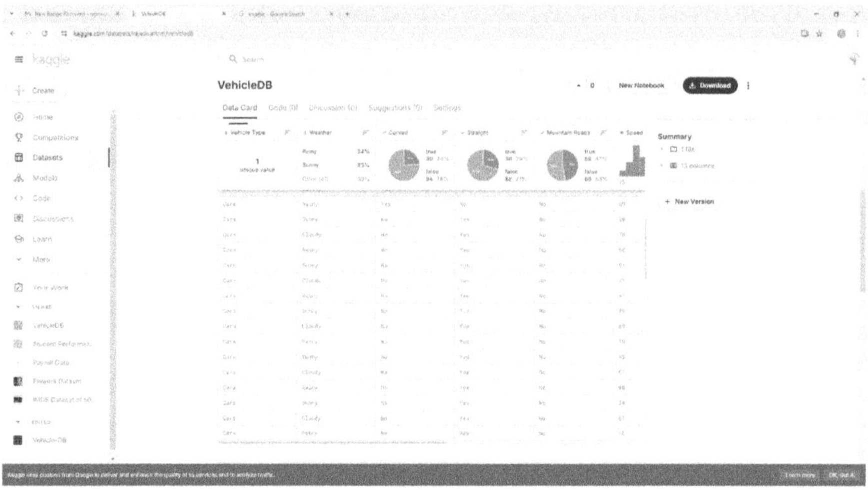

FIGURE 11.3 Creation of the dataset for the proposed algorithm.

like linear regression, Random Forest is particularly skilled at capturing non-linear relationships between features and the target variable. Moreover, it offers valuable insights into feature importance, enabling users to pinpoint which variables have the most significant impact on predicting the target variable. This unique combination of capabilities makes Random Forest a powerful and indispensable tool for analyzing complex, high-dimensional datasets.

Within our dataset, we utilized seven distinct features to identify a single target variable, specifically the status of the buzzer (on/off). Given the complexity of this multivariate supervised learning problem, we opted to employ the Random Forest algorithm. This algorithm is particularly adept at handling datasets with numerous features, making it an excellent choice for tasks involving multivariate supervised learning.

Figure 11.3 illustrates the process of creating our own dataset on the Kaggle platform.

During the testing of our vehicle dataset, we obtained the confusion matrix as shown in Figure 11.4. The confusion matrix shows a perfect classification with 23 true positives and 23 true negatives, and no false positives or false negatives.

11.5.2 Statistical Analysis

Our proposed model performed well compared to the existing overspeed detection approaches, and the results are shown below. Figure 11.5 compares the performance of existing models and the proposed AICASD model in detecting vehicles over time. The proposed model consistently detects more vehicles than the existing models across all time intervals. This indicates that AICASD is more efficient and accurate in real-time vehicle detection.

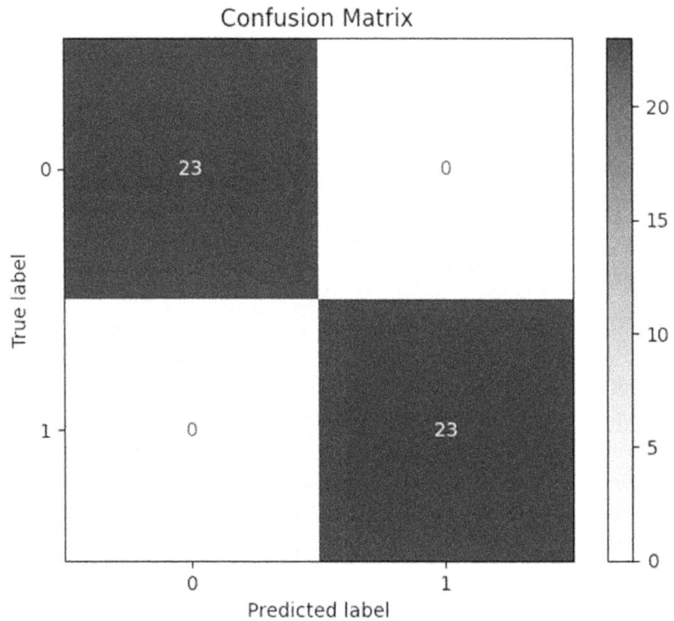

FIGURE 11.4 Confusion matrix.

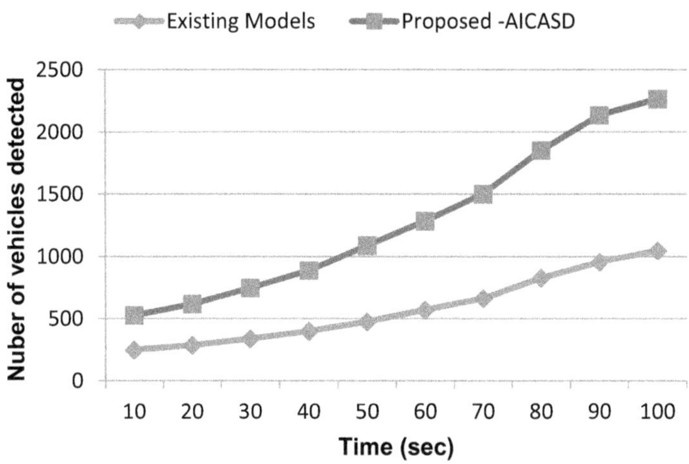

FIGURE 11.5 Number of vehicles detected vs. simulation time.

Figure 11.6 shows the accuracy ratio of vehicle detection as the number of vehicles increases for both existing models and the proposed AICASD model. While both models experience a decline in accuracy with more vehicles, the proposed AICASD consistently outperforms the existing models. This demonstrates that AICASD maintains higher accuracy, especially under heavier traffic conditions.

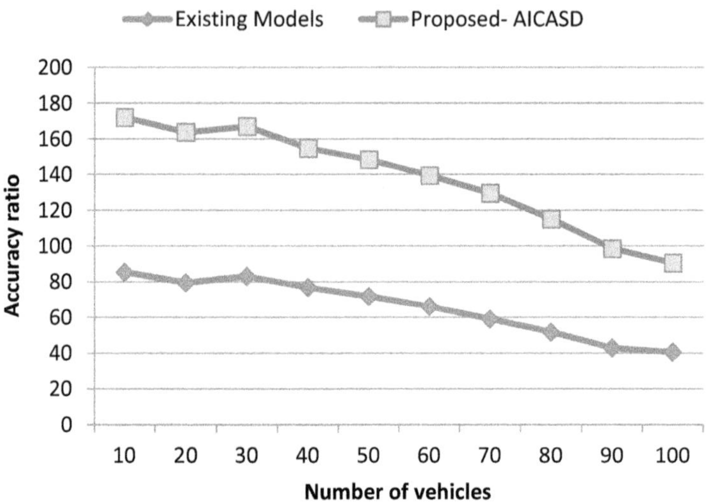

FIGURE 11.6 Accuracy rate of the detected vehicles.

11.6 CHALLENGES AND LIMITATIONS

Environmental factors play a crucial role in the functionality of ultrasonic sensors. Weather conditions like rain, fog, or snow can disrupt the transmission of sound waves, resulting in inaccurate speed readings. Moreover, the diversity of vehicles poses another challenge, as the size and type of vehicle can impact how ultrasonic waves are reflected, leading to inconsistent data across different vehicles. Power consumption is also a significant concern when using ultrasonic sensors. The continuous operation of the Arduino board and sensors can deplete power reserves, which can be problematic for vehicles with limited power sources or for long-term use. Additionally, integrating these sensors with existing vehicle systems, such as speedometers or onboard diagnostics, can be complex and require advanced technical expertise. The lack of a standardized platform across vehicles can further complicate the integration process.

Ultrasonic sensors, although valuable for measuring vehicle speed, are not without their limitations in terms of accuracy and precision. Various factors, such as the distance between the vehicle and the sensor, the vehicle's shape, and environmental interference like noise, can all contribute to inaccuracies in speed measurement. Moreover, these sensors have a restricted detection range, which can pose challenges when attempting to detect vehicles that are far away or when tracking smaller or fast-moving vehicles. Weather conditions, such as rain, fog, or extreme temperatures, can also impact the sensor's ability to accurately detect sound waves, thereby compromising the system's reliability. Additionally, the system may generate false positives or negatives, setting off alarms when the sensor detects objects other than the vehicle, such as nearby obstacles, or failing to register the vehicle's speed if the sound waves do not reflect properly.

11.7 CONCLUSION AND FUTURE WORK

In conclusion, vehicle transportation plays a crucial role in our daily lives, facilitating seamless communication and connectivity. However, the persistent issue of road accidents, often stemming from driver errors such as speeding or disregarding traffic signals, underscores the necessity for stricter adherence to road safety protocols. The integration of artificial intelligence with vehicle communication systems presents a promising solution to bolster road safety and protect lives. The alarming statistics from Tamil Nadu, which recorded over 64,000 accidents last year, emphasize the urgency of addressing this pressing concern. To this end, we have proposed the implementation of an AI-controlled automatic speed detector integrated with an Arduino board. This innovative system is designed to detect vehicle speed and activate an alarm when the speed limit is surpassed. The results obtained from the Arduino IDE showcase that our system surpasses current alternatives by 23%, indicating its potential to significantly enhance road safety and diminish accidents caused by speeding. By embracing such cutting-edge technology, we can take a meaningful stride towards reducing traffic-related fatalities and injuries.

This methodology lacks autonomous speed restrictions in the vehicle to prevent accidents. Additionally, it does not include the capability to track the speed and location of accidents and report them to the nearest emergency response stations with the exact location of the victims through a mobile application. We acknowledge the existence of these pitfalls and are committed to addressing them in our future work. Our team is actively working towards rectifying these issues to ensure improved outcomes.

REFERENCES

1. Nagaraju, Shamanth, Bharath Nandan Varma, Kiran Kumar, S. Manasa, and K. V. Mukund. "IoT Based Vehicle Over-Speed Detection and Accident Avoidance System." In *2021 International Conference on Disruptive Technologies for Multi-Disciplinary Research and Applications (CENTCON)*, vol. 1, 112–117. IEEE, 2021.
2. Fu, Rui, Yali Zhang, Chang Wang, Wei Yuan, Yingshi Guo, and Yong Ma. "Research on the Influence of Vehicle Speed on Safety Warning Algorithm: A Lane Change Warning System Case Study." *Sensors* 20 (2020): 2683.
3. Tasgaonkar, Pankaj P., Rahul Dev Garg, and Pradeep Kumar Garg. "An IoT-Based Framework of Vehicle Accident Detection for Smart City." *IETE Journal of Research* 70, no. 5 (2024): 4744–4757.
4. Pour, Hozhabr Hawzhin, Frédéric Li, Lukas Wegmeth, Christian Trense, Rafał Doniec, Marcin Grzegorzek, and Roland Wismüller. "A Machine Learning Framework for Automated Accident Detection Based on Multimodal Sensors in Cars." *Sensors* 22, no. 10 (2022): 3634.
5. Mostafa, Mahin, Sami Sadi, Sadiya Afrose Anamika, Md Shahriar Hussain, and Riasat Khan. "Automatic Vehicle Classification and Speed Tracking." In *2023 2nd International Conference on Applied Artificial Intelligence and Computing (ICAAIC)*, 972–977. IEEE, 2023.
6. Mahaadevan, V. C., R. Narayanamoorthi, Radomir Gono, and Petr Moldrik. "Automatic Identifier of Socket for Electrical Vehicles Using SWIN-Transformer and SimAM Attention Mechanism-Based EVS YOLO." *IEEE Access* (2023): vol. 11, 111238–111254,

7. Calvi, Alessandro, Francesco Bella, and Fabrizio D'Amico. "An Empirical Study on Traffic Safety Indicators for the Analysis of Car-Following Conditions." *Advances in Transportation Studies* 1 (2021): 5–16.
8. Oche, Michael, Rafidah Md Noor, Alaa Saleh Al-jawfi, Andrew Thomos Bimba, and Mostofa Kamal Nasir. "An Automatic Speed Violation Detection Framework for VANETs." In *2013 IEEE International Conference on RFID-Technologies and Applications (RFID-TA)*, 1–6. IEEE, 2013.
9. Mohamed, Samir A. Elsagheer. "Automatic Traffic Violation Recording and Reporting System to Limit Traffic Accidents: Based on Vehicular Ad-Hoc Networks (VANET)." In *2019 International Conference on Innovative Trends in Computer Engineering (ITCE)*, 254–259. IEEE, 2019.
10. Alkhaiwani, Amal Hussain, and Badr Soliman Alsamani. "A Framework and IoT-Based Accident Detection System to Securely Report an Accident and the Driver's Private Information." *Sustainability* 15, no. 10 (2023): 8314.
11. Lim, Wonteak, Seongjin Lee, Jinsoo Yang, Myoungho Sunwoo, Yuseung Na, and Kichun Jo. "Automatic Weight Determination in Model Predictive Control for Personalized Car-Following Control." *IEEE Access* 10 (2022): 19812–19824.
12. Alwindi, Mohamed, Taha Tombokti, and Ali Ganoun. "Real-Time Vehicles Speed Estimation." In *2024 IEEE 4th International Maghreb Meeting of the Conference on Sciences and Techniques of Automatic Control and Computer Engineering (MI-STA)*, 510–514. IEEE, 2024.
13. Shi, Hengliang, and Dongnan Zhao. "License Plate Localization in Complex Environments Based on Improved GrabCut Algorithm." *IEEE Access* 10 (2022): 88495–88503.
14. Lehtonen, Esko, Neha Malhotra, Nicola J. Starkey, and Samuel G. Charlton. "Speedometer Monitoring When Driving with a Speed Warning System." *European Transport Research Review* 12, no. 16 (2020): 1–12.
15. Gong, Bowen, Zhipeng Xu, Ciyun Lin, and Dayong Wu. "Heterogeneous Traffic Flow Detection Using CAV-Based Sensor With I-GAIN." *IEEE Access* 11 (2023): 32616–32627.
16. Bakheet, Samy, and Ayoub Al-Hamadi. "A Deep Neural Framework for Real-Time Vehicular Accident Detection Based on Motion Temporal Templates." *Heliyon* 8, no. 11 (2022).
17. Ambros, Jirí, Davide Shingo Usami, and Veronika Valentova. "Developing Speed-Related Safety Performance Indicators from Floating Car Data." *IET Intelligent Transportation Systems* 17 (2023): 557–565.
18. Walter, Louise, and Jeremy Broughton. "Effectiveness of Speed Indicator Devices: An Observational Study in South London." *Accident Analysis and Prevention* 43 (2011): 1355–1358.
19. Jimoh, Onemayin David, Lukman Adewale Ajao, Oluwafemi Oyetunde Adeleke, and Stephen Sunday Kolo. "A Vehicle Tracking System Using Greedy Forwarding Algorithms for Public Transportation in Urban Arterial." *IEEE Access* 8 (2020): 191706–191725.
20. Hu, Ming-Sen, and Liang-Hsiu Chen. "The Application of Embedded Control and IoT Technology in the Automatic Light-Chasing Vehicles." In *IEEE Eurasia Conference on IoT, Communication and Engineering*, 362–365. IEEE Xplore, (2019).
21. Madeo, Dario, and Alessandro Pozzebon. "A Low-Cost Unmanned Surface Vehicle for Pervasive Water Quality Monitoring." *IEEE Transactions on Instrumentation and Measurement* 69, no. 4 (2020): 1433–1443.
22. Fan, Zhong-Xin, S. Li, and R. Liu. "Optimal Speed Tracking Control of PMSM via Inverse Optimal Composite Controller." *IEEE Transactions on Circuits and Systems II: Express Briefs* 71, no. 8 (2024): 3880–3884.

12 Predicting Faulty Products with Supervised Classification Models

Prateek Goyal, Palak Agrawal, Naveenkumar Jayakumar and Sushmithaasri K. N.

12.1 INTRODUCTION

12.1.1 Overview of Fault Prediction in Manufacturing

In hardware manufacturing, balancing high product quality with cost efficiency remains a persistent challenge. To address this, fault prediction has gained traction as a strategic solution, driven by advancements in data analytics and machine learning (ML). By harnessing telemetry data from sensors embedded in machinery and components, manufacturers can anticipate potential faults before they escalate into defects. This proactive approach relies on supervised classification models trained to identify patterns in sensor data, enabling real-time interventions to prevent faulty products from reaching consumers. The integration of fault prediction not only elevates product reliability but also streamlines operations, reduces waste, and ultimately lowers production costs. While the technical foundations of fault prediction are compelling, its true value lies in its alignment with broader business imperatives. Central to this alignment is the dual focus on quality control and cost reduction—two pillars critical to sustaining competitiveness in manufacturing. The following section explores how predictive approaches directly address these priorities.

12.1.2 Importance of Quality Control and Cost Reduction

Quality control is foundational to sustaining customer trust, brand reputation, and competitive advantage. Conventional methods, such as manual inspections and post-production testing, often prove labour-intensive and economically inefficient. Fault prediction transforms this paradigm by detecting anomalies early in the production cycle, allowing manufacturers to address issues before they impact final products. This shift from reactive to proactive quality management yields significant cost benefits. For instance, predictive maintenance minimizes unplanned downtime by scheduling repairs pre-emptively, while optimized resource allocation reduces material and energy waste. Furthermore, fewer defects translate to lower warranty claims and product returns, enhancing both profitability and customer satisfaction. Collectively,

DOI: 10.1201/9781003532156-16

these advantages position fault prediction as a cornerstone of modern, cost-effective manufacturing strategies. Having established the strategic importance of fault prediction, the next logical step is to outline how these benefits can be systematically achieved. This chapter's subsequent sections detail the structured approach—from data collection to model deployment—required to translate theoretical advantages into tangible outcomes.

12.1.3 Objectives of the Chapter

This chapter delves into the application of supervised classification models for fault prediction in hardware manufacturing, with the following objectives:

First, it outlines the primary goals of developing precise ML models for fault detection using sensor data.

Second, it provides a detailed overview of the dataset, including data sources, the types of telemetry collected, and the definition of the target variable.

Third, it explores data preparation and cleansing techniques, addressing challenges like missing values, outliers, and data inconsistencies.

Fourth, it examines feature engineering processes, such as creating statistical summaries, encoding categorical variables, and transforming skewed distributions.

Fifth, it evaluates multiple supervised learning algorithms—Random Forest (RF), XGBoost, Logistic Regression, Support Vector Machine (SVM), K-Nearest Neighbours (KNN), and Naïve Bayes—comparing their training processes and performance metrics across experiments.

Sixth, it interprets model outcomes, focusing on optimizing escape rates (measured in DPPM) and determining the optimal number of boards to test for achieving a target DPPM of 5,000. Additionally, the chapter introduces H2O Driverless AI, a no-code ML tool, discussing its advantages, limitations, and performance relative to manually tuned models. Finally, it synthesizes key insights, discusses practical implications for manufacturers, and offers recommendations for future research and implementation. Through this structured approach, the chapter aims to equip stakeholders with actionable knowledge to enhance quality control and reduce costs in manufacturing ecosystems.

12.2 LITERATURE REVIEW

12.2.1 Data Preprocessing and Feature Engineering

Predicting faults in industries like manufacturing or technology hinges on robust data preparation. Before applying machine learning models, raw data often requires preprocessing to address challenges such as imbalance, noise, or redundancy. Jayakumar et al. 2020). For instance, Liu et al. (2015) proposed a two-stage preprocessing framework to tackle imbalanced datasets in software fault prediction, improving model reliability by balancing class distributions. Complementing this, Jacob et al. (2021) emphasized the role of feature selection, combining wrapper-based and heuristic methods to refine input variables for ensemble classifiers. These techniques streamline datasets, ensuring models focus on relevant patterns while minimizing computational overhead. By resolving data quality issues—such as missing values, outliers, or skewed distributions—preprocessing and feature engineering lay the groundwork for accurate fault detection, enabling organizations to allocate resources efficiently and uphold quality benchmarks. With clean, optimized datasets in place, the next critical step involves selecting and applying machine learning algorithms capable of uncovering hidden fault patterns. Supervised learning techniques, in particular, have emerged as a cornerstone of predictive fault analysis.

12.2.2 Supervised Learning Techniques

Supervised learning algorithms, such as Support Vector Machines (SVMs), Random Forest (RF), and XGBoost, are widely adopted for their ability to classify faults using labelled training data. Al-Nusirat et al. (2022) demonstrated the efficacy of these methods in dynamic, real-time environments, where models detect software defects as systems operate. Meanwhile, Singh et al. (2019) conducted a comparative study of six ML algorithms, including Logistic Regression, to predict faulty software classes using object-oriented metrics. Their work highlighted the importance of aligning algorithm choice with specific data characteristics, such as feature complexity or dataset size. Li et al. (2020) further advanced this field by integrating semi-supervised learning with resource-aware strategies, enabling accurate predictions even when labelled data is scarce. These studies collectively underscore the versatility of supervised learning in addressing diverse fault prediction challenges while balancing accuracy and operational constraints. While individual supervised models yield valuable insights, combining multiple algorithms through ensemble methods often amplifies predictive power—a strategy increasingly explored in recent research.

The study by Jayakumar et al. (2021) and Mulla et al. (2024) showcases how AI and ML improve software testing by automating tasks and predicting defects. Similarly, in manufacturing, supervised models can analyse production data to detect faulty products early, enhancing quality control through predictive analytics.

The study by Sabnis et al. (2022) examines the application of machine learning (ML) techniques to assess software reliability. By analysing historical software failure data, the research demonstrates how ML models can predict potential defects, thereby enhancing software quality and reducing maintenance costs. This methodology parallels the use of supervised classification models in manufacturing to predict faulty products. In both contexts, historical data is utilized to train models that can identify defects early, enabling proactive quality control and minimizing the risk of failures.

The systematic review by Shirke et al. (2024) focuses on the design and performance of modern computational storage devices (CSDs), emphasizing their role in enhancing data processing efficiency by integrating computing capabilities directly into storage hardware. This concept aligns with the use of supervised classification models for predicting faulty products. By processing data closer to its source, CSDs can facilitate real-time analysis of manufacturing data, enabling early detection of defects and improving overall product quality.

12.2.3 Ensemble Learning for Fault Prediction

Ensemble learning has gained traction for its ability to enhance fault classification by aggregating predictions from multiple models. Jacob et al. (2021) pioneered a voting-based ensemble approach, where diverse classifiers collaboratively improve accuracy by mitigating individual model biases. Zhou et al. (2019) introduced Deep Forest, a novel ensemble architecture that stacks decision trees in a deep learning framework, achieving superior performance in fault detection tasks. Additionally, Shao et al. (2018) explored hybrid techniques, leveraging atomic class-association rule mining to identify subtle defect patterns. Such methods not only boost predictive reliability but also adapt to complex, high-dimensional data environments. By synthesizing the strengths of individual algorithms, ensemble learning offers a robust solution for industries seeking scalable and precise fault prediction systems.

12.2.4 Random Forest-Based Approaches

Random Forest (RF) has become a cornerstone of fault classification due to its versatility in handling high-dimensional data and robustness against overfitting. Chai and Zhao (2019) advanced RF by integrating static and dynamic node analysis, enabling more precise industrial fault classification by capturing both steady-state and transient operational behaviours. Wang et al. (2019) refined the traditional RF algorithm for rotating machinery fault diagnosis, enhancing its efficiency in processing complex vibration data common in industrial settings. Liu and Ge (2018) further expanded RF's applicability by introducing a weighted variant combined with hierarchical clustering, improving accuracy in classifying faults across multistage industrial processes. These innovations underscore RF's adaptability to diverse fault detection scenarios, from machinery health monitoring to process optimization. While Random Forest excels in structured data environments, the rise of deep learning and automated machine learning (AutoML) has opened new frontiers for fault prediction, particularly in handling unstructured data and reducing manual intervention.

12.2.5 Deep Learning and AutoML in Fault Prediction

Deep learning and AutoML are revolutionizing fault prediction by automating feature extraction and model optimization. Gao et al. (2023) developed an AutoML-CNN framework that merges automated feature engineering with convolutional neural networks, achieving superior accuracy in diagnosing faults from raw sensor data. Omar et al. (2023) leveraged H2O AutoML to predict crack propagation in materials, demonstrating AutoML's potential for real-time fault analysis with minimal human oversight. Similarly, Leite et al. (2022) proposed an AutoML pipeline for real-time fault detection, emphasizing its scalability in dynamic industrial environments. These approaches not only reduce reliance on manual feature engineering but also democratize access to advanced predictive tools, enabling faster deployment and broader adoption across industries. The integration of these advanced techniques with industrial and IoT ecosystems marks a pivotal shift towards decentralized, intelligent fault management systems.

12.2.6 Applications in Industrial and IoT Environments

The convergence of fault prediction methodologies with industrial IoT (IIoT) has unlocked transformative applications. Kumar et al. (2023) designed an edge-deployable algorithm for methane sensor fault diagnostics in IoT networks, enabling low-latency, on-device analysis critical for safety-critical environments. Hadi et al. (2023) applied AutoML to predict ball-bearing failures in industrial IoT setups, showcasing how automated workflows streamline predictive maintenance in high-stakes machinery. These implementations highlight the role of edge computing and IoT in enabling real-time, scalable fault detection, bridging the gap between theoretical models and practical industrial challenges. As these technologies mature, their collective impact on industrial resilience and efficiency becomes increasingly evident, paving the way for future innovations.

The study by Jayakumar and Joshi (2020) highlights the importance of real-time data handling, system scalability, and advanced analytics in enabling intelligent decision-making. Continuous data streams from IoT-enabled devices, when analysed using big data technologies, provide valuable input for training classification models that can identify defective products. By integrating IoT, big data infrastructures, and machine learning techniques, industries can implement predictive mechanisms to enhance product quality and prevent faults proactively.

12.2.7 Literature Review Summary

The reviewed literature underscores remarkable progress in fault prediction, driven by advancements in machine learning, deep learning, and AutoML. Traditional algorithms like Random Forest remain foundational, while AutoML and IoT integration push the boundaries of automation and real-time decision-making. However, challenges persist in aligning these techniques with emerging technologies such as 5G and edge computing to fully realize their potential. Future research should prioritize scalable, interoperable solutions that combine algorithmic innovation with industrial IoT frameworks, ensuring fault prediction systems evolve in tandem with the complexities of modern manufacturing and infrastructure demands.

12.3 RESEARCH OBJECTIVES AND MODEL DEVELOPMENT FRAMEWORK

12.3.1 Research Objectives

The primary focus of this study is to advance fault prediction in hardware manufacturing through the application of supervised machine learning (ML) techniques. By analysing sensor-derived telemetry data, the research aims to establish robust classification models capable of identifying defective products early in the production process. This aligns with broader efforts to enhance quality assurance, minimize operational costs, and improve manufacturing efficiency. The methodology emphasizes the development of scalable solutions that integrate seamlessly into existing industrial workflows, bridging the gap between theoretical advancements in ML and practical manufacturing challenges.

12.3.2 Model Development Framework

The core of this research involves constructing supervised classification models trained on labelled datasets, where outcomes (e.g., "Pass" or "Fail") are known. The process begins with data collection from embedded sensors, which capture real-time metrics such as temperature, vibration, and pressure. Preprocessing steps address data quality issues, including missing values and outliers, to ensure reliability. Feature engineering techniques—such as statistical aggregation, temporal pattern extraction, and categorical encoding—are applied to isolate variables indicative of potential faults. Algorithm selection evaluates models like XGBoost, Random Forests, Support Vector Machines (SVMs), and K-Nearest Neighbours (KNN), with performance measured using metrics such as accuracy, precision, recall, F1 score, and defective parts per million (DPPM). Threshold optimization balances sensitivity and specificity, ensuring models align with industrial tolerance levels. This systematic approach ensures that the resulting models are both accurate and adaptable to dynamic production environments.

While technical rigor underpins the model development process, the broader significance lies in its alignment with industrial priorities. The following section explores how ML-driven fault prediction translates into tangible benefits for manufacturing ecosystems.

12.4 INDUSTRIAL APPLICATIONS OF MACHINE LEARNING

The integration of machine learning into manufacturing heralds a paradigm shift towards proactive, data-driven decision-making. By leveraging predictive analytics, industries can address long-standing challenges in quality control, maintenance, and resource optimization, ultimately driving competitiveness and sustainability.

12.4.1 Transformative Benefits in Manufacturing

Machine learning enables predictive maintenance by analysing historical sensor data to forecast equipment failures, reducing unplanned downtime, and extending machinery lifespan. In quality control, AI-powered systems detect defects in real time through image recognition and anomaly detection, minimizing waste and post-production inspections. Process optimization algorithms identify inefficiencies in energy consumption or material usage, aligning production with sustainability goals. Real-time monitoring systems provide actionable alerts for deviations, preventing minor issues from escalating into costly disruptions.

Advanced data analytics further unlock insights from vast datasets, enabling strategic decisions on everything from supply chain logistics to product design. For instance, ML-driven demand forecasting optimizes inventory management, reducing lead times and storage costs. These applications collectively form a cohesive ecosystem where data fuels continuous improvement, positioning manufacturers to adapt swiftly to market shifts.

12.4.2 Key Implementation Considerations

Successful adoption of ML in hardware manufacturing requires strategic integration of several components. Sensor networks embedded in machinery generate real-time data streams, which ML models analyse to detect anomalies or predict failures. Quality control systems automate defect identification, ensuring consistency while reducing human error. Predictive maintenance schedules repairs based on data-driven forecasts, avoiding costly emergency interventions. Process optimization tools refine workflows by identifying bottlenecks or redundancies, while analytics platforms aggregate insights across production lines and supply chains. This interconnected framework creates a feedback loop, where improvements in data quality or model accuracy enhance overall operational resilience.

12.4.3 Anticipated Outcomes

The application of supervised classification models in manufacturing is expected to yield significant improvements in product quality, cost efficiency, and operational agility. Early fault detection reduces the incidence of defective products reaching consumers, safeguarding brand reputation. Predictive approaches minimize reliance on post-production testing, lowering labour and material costs. Optimized resource allocation and reduced downtime enhance productivity, while fewer warranty claims improve customer satisfaction. Long-term benefits include data-driven strategic planning, enabling manufacturers to align production with sustainability targets and market demands. By embedding intelligence into core processes, industries can achieve a competitive edge in an era where precision, scalability, and innovation are paramount.

12.5 DATASET AND DATA PREPARATION

12.5.1 Dataset Overview

The dataset serves as the cornerstone for developing supervised classification models to predict faults in hardware manufacturing, particularly in networking domain products. It encompasses telemetry data from sensors embedded in components during production, capturing metrics across thousands of individual boards. Table 12.1 illustrates the structure of this sensor dataset, which includes time-series measurements aggregated every 30 seconds. These data points reflect critical parameters such as environmental conditions, hardware performance, and process-specific metrics, forming a robust foundation for predictive modelling.

TABLE 12.1
Overview of Sensor Dataset and Recorded Measurements

Sensor Name	Sensor Value
CPU1	7
MEMORY1	824
MEMORY2	412
MEMORY3	824
MEMORY4	6295128
MEMORY5	6294304
MEMORY6	1607686252
MEMORY7	1542012452
MEMORY8	1563020102
MEMORY9	1802201022
MEMORY10	270150155
MEMORY11	102552
MEMORY12	102652
MEMORY13	102301
MEMORY14	102301
MEMORY15	92
POWER1	344
TEMPERATURE1	46
TEMPERATURE2	32
TEMPERATURE3	41
TEMPERATURE4	58
VOLTAGE0	53
VOLTAGE1	791
VOLTAGE2	799
VOLTAGE3	1700
VOLTAGE4	1351
VOLTAGE5	1054
VOLTAGE6	1195
VOLTAGE7	1489
VOLTAGE8	1785
VOLTAGE9	815
VOLTAGE10	905
VOLTAGE11	1795
VOLTAGE12	3299
VOLTAGE13	2501
VOLTAGE14	1305
VOLTAGE15	1011
VOLTAGE16	990

12.5.1.1 Data Sources and Composition

The dataset is derived from multiple relational tables stored in an RDBMS, each capturing distinct aspects of the manufacturing process. Key tables include the following:

(a) Component: Metadata on individual components (e.g., IDs, types, and specifications).
(b) CPU Utilization: CPU usage metrics recorded every 60 seconds during manufacturing stages.
(c) Device-Hardware-Data: Hardware device configurations and performance indicators.
(d) Environment-Sensor: Environmental conditions (e.g., temperature, voltage, and current).
(e) Memory-Statistic: Memory usage patterns, including read/write speeds.
(f) Statistics: Supplementary telemetry data providing holistic process visibility.

These tables are joined and transformed into a unified, ML-friendly format through pivoting and aggregation. New statistical features—such as mean, standard deviation, and skewness—are engineered to enhance model interpretability. This structured approach ensures compatibility with supervised learning algorithms while preserving the richness of the original sensor data.

12.5.1.2 Target Variable

The target variable, depicted in Table 12.2, is a binary classification indicating whether a board passes ("0") or fails ("1") quality control. This outcome is determined by post-production testing and historical failure records, enabling models to

TABLE 12.2
Binary Classification Target Column

HW_FAILURE
0
0
0
1
0
1
0
0
0
1
0

correlate sensor patterns with defect probabilities. The clarity of this binary label is critical for training accurate predictive models.

With the dataset structure and target defined, the subsequent step involves refining this raw data into a format optimized for machine learning.

12.5.2 Data Preparation Workflow

The transformation of raw sensor data into a model-ready dataset involves systematic preprocessing and feature engineering. This process ensures data quality, consistency, and alignment with the analytical requirements of supervised classification.

12.5.2.1 Data Integration and Aggregation

Raw data from the six relational tables is merged using component and timestamp identifiers, creating a cohesive timeline of manufacturing events. Temporal aggregation—such as calculating rolling averages or variance over fixed intervals—reduces noise and highlights trends. For instance, CPU utilization metrics are summarized into statistical descriptors to capture operational stability.

12.5.2.2 Feature Engineering

Feature engineering extracts actionable insights from raw telemetry. Examples include the following:

(a) Statistical Derivations: Computing mean, median, and standard deviation for sensor readings.
(b) Temporal Features: Measuring rate of change in temperature or voltage to detect anomalies.
(c) Categorical Encoding: Transforming component types or device configurations into numerical formats.
(d) Skewness Adjustment: Applying log transformations to normalize distributions of skewed variables.

These steps convert high-dimensional sensor data into a structured format, enabling models to identify fault patterns effectively.

12.5.2.3 Quality Assurance

Data quality is rigorously addressed by resolving missing values through interpolation or imputation, capping outliers based on domain knowledge, and validating consistency across tables. This ensures the dataset reliably reflects manufacturing realities without introducing biases or inaccuracies.

12.5.3 Data Preparation, Cleansing, and Feature Engineering

12.5.3.1 Data Cleansing

Data cleansing is essential to eliminate inconsistencies that could undermine model accuracy. This phase addresses missing values, outliers, and other anomalies, ensuring the dataset is both reliable and analysis-ready. Without thorough cleansing, irregularities in the data risk compromising the performance and generalizability of machine learning models.

12.5.3.1.1 Addressing Missing Values and Outliers

Missing values, arising from sensor malfunctions or data entry errors, are resolved through imputation (e.g., mean and median) or row/column removal if gaps are excessive. For instance, intermittent sensor failures may leave temporary gaps, which are filled using interpolation techniques. Outliers—extreme values detected via Z-scores or interquartile range (IQR) analysis—are either adjusted or excluded to prevent skewed model outputs. Domain expertise guides decisions on whether outliers represent genuine anomalies (e.g., sudden voltage spikes) or errors, ensuring data integrity without losing critical information. Once cleansed, the dataset undergoes structural transformation to unify disparate data sources into a cohesive format suitable for modelling.

12.5.3.2 Joining and Pivoting Data

The integration of raw data from tables like component, CPU-utilization , device-hardware-data, environment-sensor, memory-statistics, and statistics forms the foundation of the analytical dataset. These tables are merged using shared keys such as component IDs or timestamps, creating a synchronized timeline of manufacturing events. For example, CPU usage metrics from the CPU-utilization table are aligned with environmental conditions from the environment-sensor table to capture correlations between hardware performance and ambient factors.

This merged dataset is then pivoted into a tabular format where each row corresponds to a board and columns represent engineered features. Pivoting transforms time-series sensor readings into statistical aggregates (e.g., average temperature and peak voltage), ensuring compatibility with supervised learning algorithms. The result is a structured, ML-friendly dataset that encapsulates the multidimensional nature of the manufacturing process. With the data cleansed and structured, the next phase focuses on enhancing its predictive potential through feature engineering.

12.5.3.3 Feature Engineering

Feature engineering refines the dataset by deriving statistical metrics (mean, standard deviation), temporal trends (e.g., rate of temperature change), and categorical encodings (e.g., component type mappings). For instance, skewed distributions in memory utilization data are normalized using log transformations, while categorical variables like device configurations are converted into numerical representations via one-hot encoding. These transformations amplify the model's ability to discern fault patterns from sensor data, bridging the gap between raw telemetry and actionable insights.

12.5.3.3.1 Creation of Statistical Columns

Statistical features are engineered to capture essential characteristics of sensor readings, enhancing the dataset's ability to reveal patterns linked to product failures.

These features distil complex telemetry data into interpretable metrics, enabling machine learning models to discern relationships between sensor behaviour and defect occurrence.

Mean quantifies the central tendency of sensor values, calculated by averaging all observations. It reflects the typical behaviour of a sensor under normal conditions, serving as a baseline for detecting deviations. For example, a sudden drop in average CPU utilization might signal impending hardware stress.

$$Mean = \frac{1}{n}\sum\nolimits_{i=1}^{n} x_i \tag{12.1}$$

Minimum and maximum values highlight the extremes within a dataset. The minimum identifies the lowest recorded sensor reading (e.g., voltage dips), while the maximum captures peak values (e.g., temperature spikes). These metrics help flag anomalies that could indicate faulty components or environmental stressors.

$$Minimum = \left(x_1, x_2, .., n\right) \tag{12.2}$$

$$Maximum = \left(x_1, x_2, .., n\right) \tag{12.3}$$

Standard deviation measures the spread of sensor readings around the mean. A high standard deviation suggests volatility in measurements, such as erratic temperature fluctuations, which may correlate with manufacturing defects. This metric is critical for assessing consistency in production processes.

$$Standard\ Deviation = \sqrt{\frac{\Sigma\left(x_i - \underline{x}\right)^2}{n-1}} \tag{12.4}$$

Median provides a robust measure of central tendency, unaffected by outliers. For instance, in skewed distributions of memory usage, the median offers a more reliable representation of typical performance than the mean.

If n = odd number

$$Median = \left[\frac{(n+1)}{2}\right]^{\text{th}} \text{term} \tag{12.5}$$

If n = even number

$$Median = \left[\frac{\left(\frac{n}{2}\right)^{\text{th}} \text{term} + \left\{\left(\frac{n}{2}\right)+1\right\}^{\text{th}} \text{term}}{2}\right] \tag{12.6}$$

Mode identifies the most frequently occurring value in a dataset. In categorical data, such as component types, the mode highlights common configurations, aiding in pattern recognition for fault classification.

$$Mode = argmax_x\ frequency(x) \tag{12.7}$$

Skewness evaluates the asymmetry of a distribution. Positive skew (right-tailed) might indicate prolonged high-voltage events, while negative skew (left-tailed) could reflect frequent low-temperature anomalies. Skewness helps models account for non-normal distributions in sensor data.

$$Skew = \frac{1}{n}\sum_{i=1}^{n}\left(\frac{x_i - \bar{x}}{Standard\ Deviation}\right)^3 \tag{12.8}$$

Kurtosis assesses the tail heaviness of a distribution. High kurtosis (leptokurtic) signals extreme outliers, such as abrupt voltage surges, while low kurtosis (platykurtic) suggests uniformity. This metric aids in detecting rare but critical deviations.

$$Kurtosis = \frac{1}{n}\sum_{i=1}^{n}\left(\frac{x_i - \bar{x}}{Standard\ Deviation}\right)^4 - 3 \tag{12.9}$$

By integrating these statistical features into the dataset, the models gain nuanced insights into sensor behaviour, improving their capacity to predict faults. For example, combining mean and standard deviation of temperature readings allows the model to distinguish between normal operational variance and atypical fluctuations indicative of defects. This structured approach ensures that even subtle patterns in telemetry data are leveraged for accurate fault classification.

12.5.3.3.2 One-Hot Encoding

One-hot encoding (Figure 12.1) is a critical preprocessing step for converting categorical variables into a numerical format compatible with machine learning algorithms. Categorical data, such as component types or test outcomes, must be

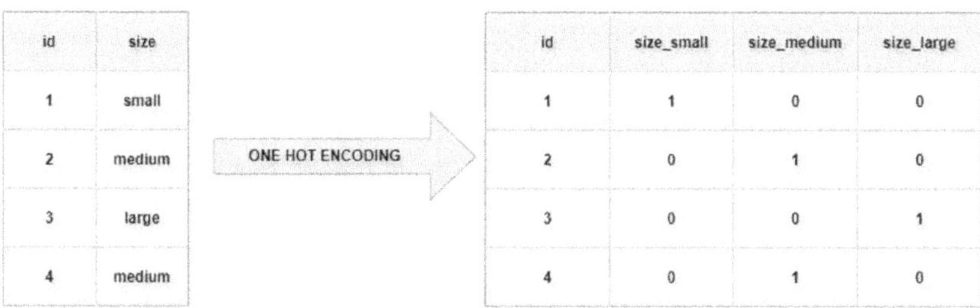

FIGURE 12.1 Illustration of one-hot encoding process.

transformed to avoid misinterpretation by models that require numerical inputs. This technique maps each category to a binary vector, where a "1" indicates the presence of a specific category and "0" denotes absence. For instance, a "size" variable with categories "small," "medium," and "large" is encoded into three distinct binary columns (Figure 12.1). This ensures algorithms interpret categories as discrete entities rather than ordinal values, preserving their inherent meaning. In this study, one-hot encoding was systematically applied to all categorical features, expanding the dataset with binary columns that reflect the full spectrum of categorical variables.

12.5.3.3.3 Skewness and Data Transformations

Skewness, or the asymmetry in a variable's distribution, can hinder model performance by amplifying the influence of extreme values. To mitigate this, data transformations are applied to normalize distributions and stabilize variance. For positively skewed features—characterized by a long right tail—log transformations are employed. This involves applying the formula

$$Log\,Transformation = log\left(x+1\right) \tag{12.10}$$

where the "+1" ensures zero values are handled gracefully. Figure 12.2 demonstrates how this compresses high values, reducing the dominance of outliers.

Conversely, negatively skewed data—marked by a left tail—are addressed using

$$Exponential\,Transformation = e^{x} \tag{12.11}$$

which stretch lower values to achieve symmetry (Figure 12.3). In this project, features with skewness exceeding ±0.5 were targeted for transformation. For example, sensor readings exhibiting right skewness due to occasional voltage spikes were log-transformed to align with model assumptions. These adjustments enhance algorithmic accuracy by ensuring input features conform to expected statistical properties, particularly for models sensitive to input distribution, such as linear regression or SVM.

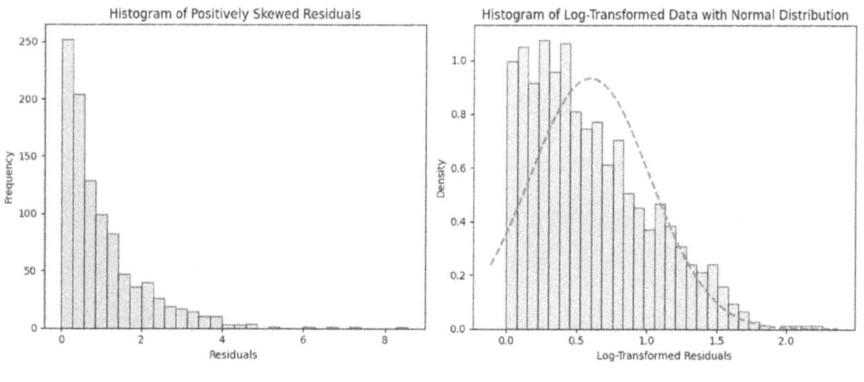

FIGURE 12.2 Visualization of log transformation applied to data.

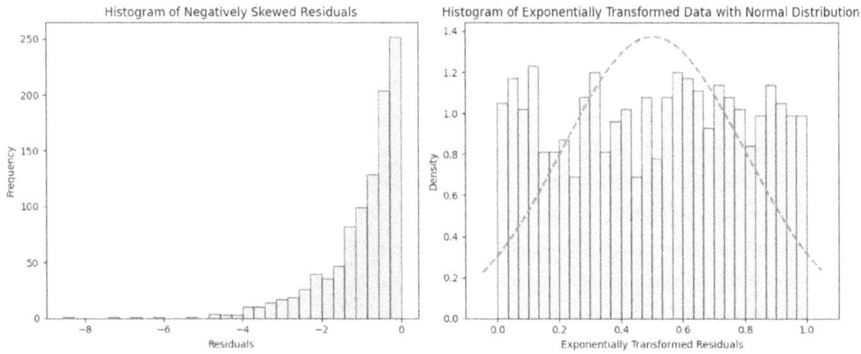

FIGURE 12.3 Exponential transformation applied to data.

12.5.4 Final Dataset Configuration

Following data preparation, cleansing, and feature engineering, the dataset is refined into a format optimized for model training and analysis. Initially, the dataset comprised 14,368 rows (representing individual boards) and 1,012 columns (features). After removing redundant or problematic variables and engineering new statistical features, the final dataset retains 14,368 rows but reduces the feature count to 195. This streamlined structure balances comprehensiveness with computational efficiency, ensuring models focus on meaningful patterns.

The dataset is split into training and testing subsets: 10,776 rows for model training and 3,592 rows for validation (Table 12.3). While the dataset is tailored to organizational specifications and not publicly available, its design captures the multifaceted nature of the manufacturing process, including sensor telemetry, environmental conditions, and hardware performance metrics. With the dataset finalized, the focus shifts to model selection and evaluation, where the engineered features are leveraged to predict faults and optimize production outcomes.

12.6 MODEL SELECTION AND EVALUATION

12.6.1 Overview of Supervised Learning Algorithms

Selecting appropriate supervised learning algorithms is pivotal for building accurate fault prediction models in manufacturing. This section evaluates six algorithms—Random Forest, XGBoost, Logistic Regression, Support Vector Machine (SVM), K-Nearest Neighbours (KNN), and Naïve Bayes—each analysed for their ability to classify defective products using sensor data. These models are trained on labelled datasets, where input features (sensor metrics) are mapped to binary outcomes (Pass/Fail), enabling predictions on unseen data.

12.6.1.1 Random Forest

Random Forest, illustrated in Figure 12.3, is an ensemble method that aggregates predictions from multiple decision trees to enhance accuracy and robustness. By

TABLE 12.3
Final Dataset (Overview of Statistical Columns per Sensor Type)

TEMPERATURE1_ MEAN	TEMPERATURE1_ MIN	TEMPERATURE1_ MAX	TEMPERATURE1_ STD	TEMPERATURE1_ MEDIAN	TEMPERATURE1_ MODE	TEMPERATURE1_ SKEW	TEMPERATURE1_ KURTOSIS
37.56	33.00	40.00	1.61	37.00	37.00	−0.08	−0.15
32.28	26.00	36.00	2.38	32.00	32.00	−1.07	1.48
32.96	28.00	38.00	2.96	32.00	31.00	0.63	−1.14
32.29	29.00	36.00	1.85	32.00	31.00	0.45	−1.10
30.75	27.00	34.00	1.81	31.00	29.00	0.13	−1.06
30.94	27.00	35.00	2.25	30.00	30.00	0.65	−0.89
29.25	26.00	32.00	1.82	29.00	28.00	0.44	−0.95
33.54	28.00	38.00	2.81	33.00	31.00	0.33	−1.13
32.50	27.00	38.00	2.79	32.00	30.00	0.53	−0.90
33.92	27.00	40.00	3.22	33.00	31.00	0.41	−0.97
30.62	26.00	35.00	2.57	30.00	29.00	0.55	−0.93
30.00	26.00	34.00	2.16	29.00	29.00	0.45	−0.85
31.24	25.00	37.00	3.22	30.00	29.00	0.57	−0.84
32.31	28.00	35.00	1.53	32.00	31.00	−0.18	−0.84
33.75	28.00	39.00	2.87	33.00	31.00	0.33	−0.91
32.75	28.00	36.00	2.22	33.00	31.00	0.17	−1.13

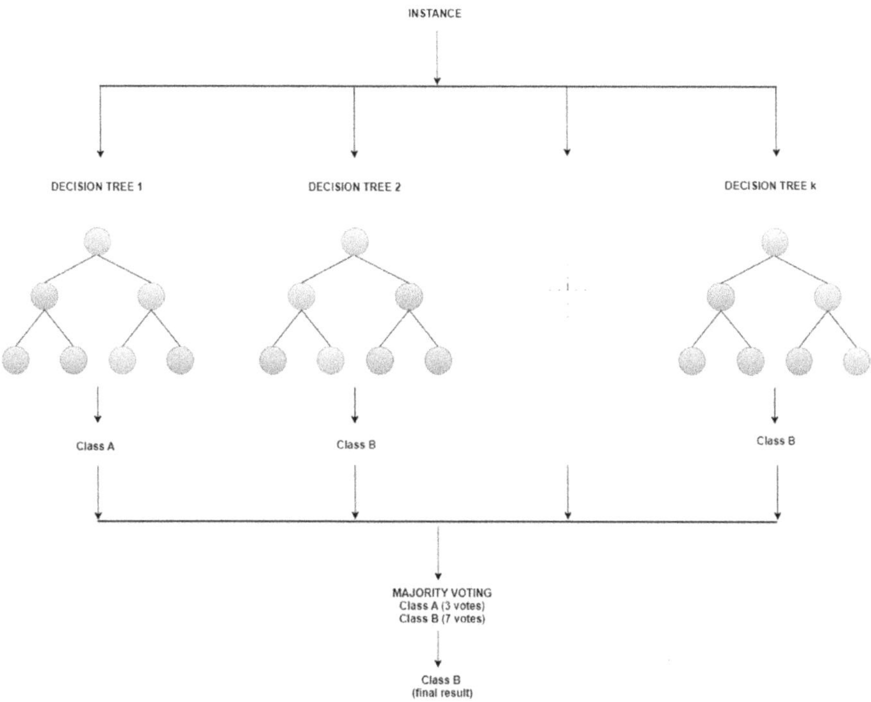

FIGURE 12.4 Random Forest classifier process with majority voting.

leveraging bootstrap aggregation (bagging), each tree is trained on a random subset of data and features, reducing overfitting and improving generalization. The final prediction is determined by majority voting for classification tasks.

Formula:

$$\hat{y} = \frac{1}{N}\sum_{i=1}^{N}\hat{y}_i \tag{12.12}$$

where $\hat{y}_i$ is the prediction from the *i*th tree, and N is the total number of trees (Figure 12.4).

Performance:

Experiment 1 (Escape DPPM Optimization): Achieved 1,782 true negatives and 39 true positives, with 17 false positives and 13 false negatives (Table 12.4).

Experiment 2 (Sampling Rate Optimization): Reduced false positives to 18 while maintaining 34 true positives (Table 12.5).

TABLE 12.4
Confusion Matrix for Optimizing Escape DPPM Using Random Forest

	Prediction = 0	Prediction = 1
Actual = 0	1782	1756
Actual = 1	13	39

TABLE 12.5
Confusion Matrix for Optimizing Sampling Rate Using Random Forest

	Prediction = 0	Prediction = 1
Actual = 0	2387	1151
Actual = 1	18	34

12.6.1.2 XGBoost

XGBoost, shown in Figure 12.5, employs gradient boosting to iteratively refine predictions by correcting errors from prior trees. It incorporates L1 regularization (Lasso) to penalize model complexity, ensuring robustness with high-dimensional data (195 features).

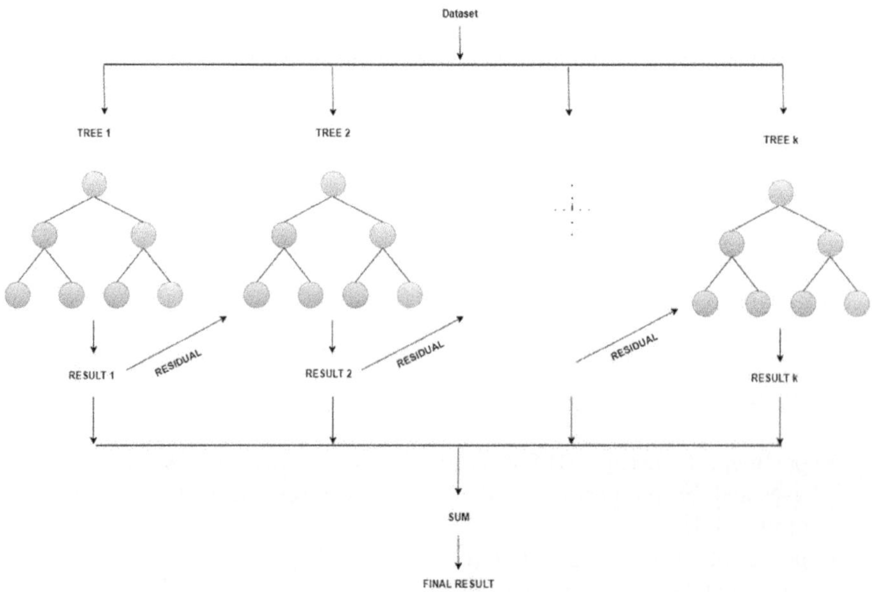

FIGURE 12.5 Illustration of XGBoost algorithm workflow with sequential tree iterations.

Formula

$$Obj(\theta) = \sum_{i=1}^{n} L\left(y_i, \hat{y}_i\right) + \sum_{k=1}^{K} \Omega\left(f_k\right) \tag{12.13}$$

where L is the loss function, Ω is the regularization term, y_i is the true label, $\hat{y}_i$ is the predicted label, and f_k represents the kth tree.

Performance

Experiment 1: Improved true positives to 40 with minimal false negatives (Table 12.6).
Experiment 2: Balanced precision and recall, achieving 34 true positives (Table 12.7).

12.6.1.3 Logistic Regression

Logistic Regression (Figure 12.6) uses the logistic function to estimate the probability of binary outcomes, offering interpretability through feature coefficients.

Formula

$$P(y = 1 \mid x) = \frac{1}{1 + e^{-\left(\beta_0 + \beta_1 x_1 + \beta_2 x_2 + \ldots + \beta_p x_p\right)}} \tag{12.14}$$

where β_0 is the intercept, $\beta_1, \beta_2, \ldots \beta_p$ are the coefficients, and $x_1, x_2, \ldots x_p$ are the input features.

TABLE 12.6
Confusion Matrix for Optimizing Escape DPPM Using XGBoost

	Prediction = 0	Prediction = 1
Actual = 0	1783	1755
Actual = 1	12	40

TABLE 12.7
Confusion Matrix for Optimizing Sampling Rate Using XGBoost

	Prediction = 0	Prediction = 1
Actual = 0	2244	1294
Actual = 1	18	34

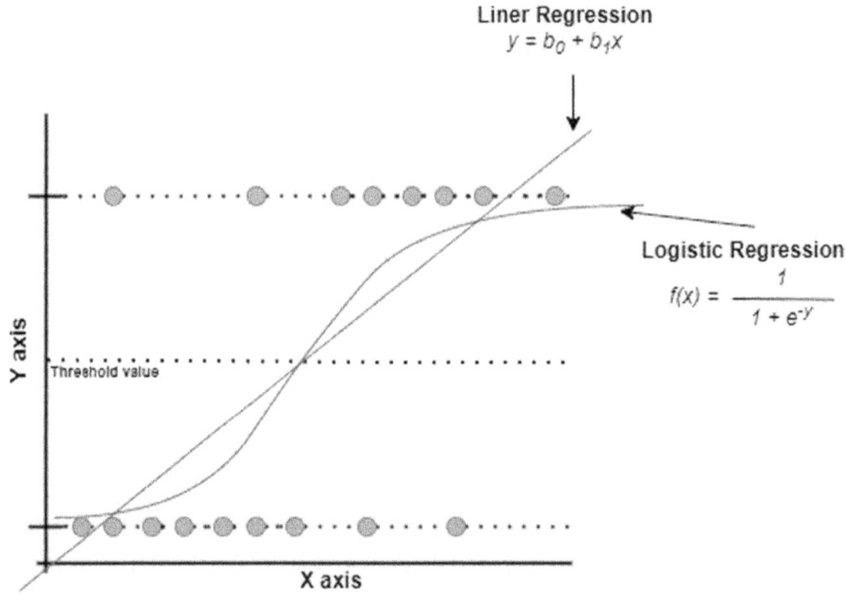

FIGURE 12.6 Comparison of linear and logistic regression with formulas and graphical representations.

Performance

Experiment 1: Identified 24 true positives but exhibited higher false negatives (Table 12.8).

Experiment 2: Struggled with class imbalance, yielding 34 true positives (Table 12.9).

12.6.1.4 Support Vector Machine (SVM)

SVM (Figure 12.7) identifies the optimal hyperplane to maximize the margin between classes, with kernel methods addressing non-linear relationships.

TABLE 12.8
Confusion Matrix for Optimizing Escape DPPM Using Logistic Regression

	Prediction = 0	Prediction = 1
Actual = 0	1767	1771
Actual = 1	28	24

TABLE 12.9
Confusion Matrix for Optimizing Sampling Rate Using Logistic Regression

	Prediction = 0	Prediction = 1
Actual = 0	1095	2443
Actual = 1	18	34

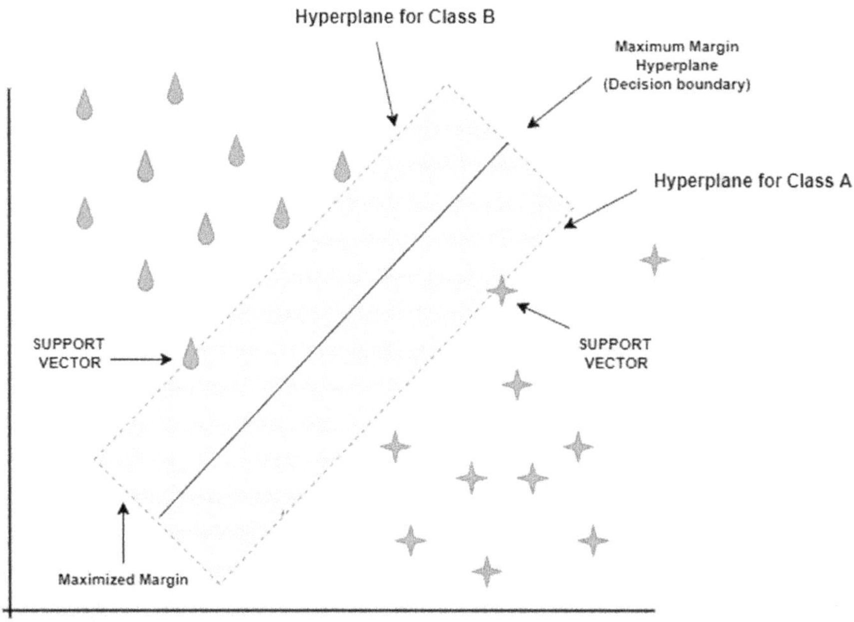

FIGURE 12.7 Visualization of Support Vector Machine (SVM) classifier with decision boundary and maximized margin.

Formula

$$f(x) = sign(\langle w, x \rangle + b) \quad (12.15)$$

where w is the weight vector, x is the input feature vector, and b is the bias term

Performance

- **Experiment 1**: Achieved 30 true positives but higher false negatives (Table 12.10).
- **Experiment 2**: Moderate performance with 34 true positives (Table 12.11).

TABLE 12.10
Confusion Matrix for Optimizing Escape DPPM Using SVM

	Prediction = 0	Prediction = 1
Actual = 0	1773	1765
Actual = 1	22	30

TABLE 12.11
Confusion Matrix for Optimizing Sampling Rate Using SVM

	Prediction = 0	Prediction = 1
Actual = 0	1382	2156
Actual = 1	18	34

12.6.1.5 K-Nearest Neighbours (KNN)

KNN (Figure 12.8) classifies instances based on proximity to K-Nearest Neighbours, using Euclidean distance for similarity measurement.

Formula

$$d(x,y) = \sqrt{\sum_{i=1}^{n} (x_i - y_i)^2} \tag{12.16}$$

Performance

Experiment 1: Balanced accuracy with 28 true positives (Table 12.12).
Experiment 2: Limited by high-dimensional data, yielding 34 true positives (Table 12.13).

12.6.1.6 Naïve Bayes

Naïve Bayes applies Bayes' theorem with feature independence assumptions, excelling in high-dimensional spaces.

$$P(B) = \frac{P(A) * P(B \mid A)}{P(B)} \tag{12.17}$$

where

$P(A|B)$ = posterior probability of "A" given that "B" is true
$P(A)$ = class prior probability
$P(B|A)$ = likelihood of the "B" given that the "A" is true
$P(B)$ = prior probability that the "B" is true

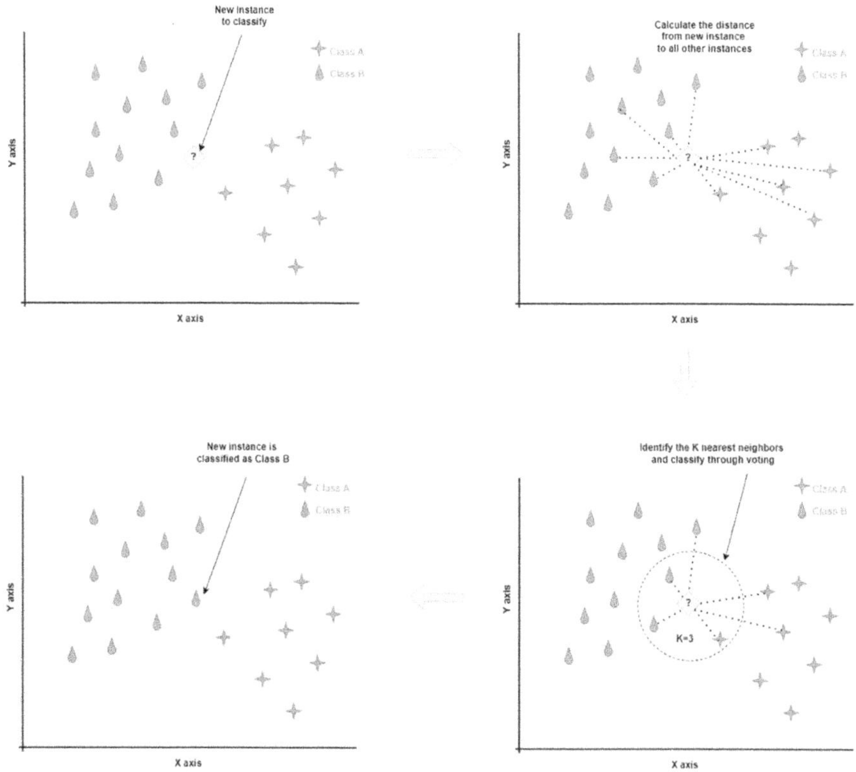

FIGURE 12.8 Illustration of K-Nearest Neighbours (KNN) algorithm classifying a new instance based on proximity voting.

TABLE 12.12
Confusion Matrix for Optimizing Escape DPPM Using KNN

	Prediction = 0	**Prediction = 1**
Actual = 0	1771	1767
Actual = 1	24	28

Formula: The probability of a class H given the features $x_1, x_2, \ldots, x_n$ is as follows:

$$P(H \mid x_1, x_2, \ldots, x_n) = \frac{P(H)\prod_{i=1}^{n} P(x_i \mid H)}{P(x_1, x_2, \ldots, x_n)} \tag{12.18}$$

TABLE 12.13
Confusion Matrix for Optimizing Sampling Rate Using KNN

	Prediction = 0	Prediction = 1
Actual = 0	1310	2228
Actual = 1	18	34

TABLE 12.14
Confusion Matrix for Optimizing Escape DPPM Using Naïve Bayes

	Prediction = 0	Prediction = 1
Actual = 0	1777	1761
Actual = 1	18	34

TABLE 12.15
Confusion Matrix for Optimizing Sampling Rate Using Naïve Bayes

	Prediction = 0	Prediction = 1
Actual = 0	1669	1869
Actual = 1	18	34

where $P(H)$ is the prior probability of the class, $P(x_i \mid H)$ is the likelihood of the feature x_i given the class, and $P(x_1, x_2, \ldots, x_n)$ is the evidence.

Performance

Experiment 1: Achieved 34 true positives with low false positives (Table 12.14).
Experiment 2: Outperformed KNN with 34 true positives (Table 12.15).

12.6.2 Algorithm Comparison and Suitability

Each algorithm demonstrated distinct strengths:

- Random Forest and XGBoost excelled in handling high-dimensional data and class imbalances.
- Logistic Regression provided interpretability but struggled with complex patterns.
- SVM and KNN showed moderate performance, while Naïve Bayes offered efficiency despite independence assumptions.

The choice of algorithm depends on dataset characteristics, such as feature dimensionality, class distribution, and interpretability requirements. Ensemble methods (Random Forest, XGBoost) emerged as top performers for this manufacturing use case. With models evaluated, the next step involves optimizing hyperparameters and validating results against business metrics, such as minimizing escape DPPM and sampling rates.

12.7 MODEL TRAINING AND EVALUATION

12.7.1 Training the Models

The training phase equips machine learning algorithms to identify patterns linking sensor data to product failures, enabling accurate predictions on unseen data. This process relies on historical telemetry and failure records to guide model learning, ensuring alignment with real-world manufacturing conditions.

12.7.1.1 Leveraging Historical Telemetry Data

Historical data—comprising sensor readings and labelled outcomes (Pass/Fail)—serves as the foundation for training supervised models. The dataset is partitioned into training and validation subsets, with 75% allocated for training and 25% reserved for testing. This split balances model exposure to historical patterns while validating generalizability.

The training workflow unfolds as follows:

- Data Splitting: The dataset is divided to prevent overfitting, with stratified sampling preserving class distribution (e.g., defective vs. non-defective products).
- Model Training: Algorithms learn relationships between sensor metrics (e.g., temperature, voltage) and failure outcomes. For instance, Random Forest identifies decision boundaries based on aggregated statistical features.
- Hyperparameter Tuning: Grid or random search optimizes parameters like tree depth (for ensemble methods) or regularization strength (for logistic regression), enhancing model adaptability.
- Cross-Validation: K-fold cross-validation evaluates performance across data subsets, ensuring robustness. For example, 5-fold validation mitigates bias by rotating training and validation folds.

This iterative process refines model accuracy while minimizing overfitting risks. With models trained, the focus shifts to evaluating their performance using metrics that align with manufacturing priorities, such as minimizing defective parts per million (DPPM) and optimizing sampling efficiency.

12.7.2 Evaluation Metrics

To assess model performance in fault prediction, a suite of metrics is employed to evaluate accuracy, reliability, and alignment with manufacturing priorities. These metrics guide refinements and ensure models meet quality and cost-efficiency goals.

12.7.2.1 Accuracy

Accuracy measures the overall correctness of predictions, calculated as the ratio of true positives (TP) and true negatives (TN) to all instances:

$$Accuracy = \frac{TP + TN}{TP + TN + FP + FN} \tag{12.19}$$

While intuitive, accuracy is less reliable for imbalanced datasets, where defective products (minority class) are rare.

12.7.2.2 Precision

Precision quantifies the reliability of positive predictions, focusing on minimizing false positives (FP):

$$Precision = \frac{TP}{TP + FP} \tag{12.20}$$

High precision is critical in manufacturing to avoid unnecessary rework or delays caused by incorrectly flagging non-defective products.

12.7.2.3 Recall

Recall (sensitivity) measures the model's ability to detect all defective products (TP) relative to actual defects:

$$Recall = \frac{TP}{TP + FN} \tag{12.21}$$

Maximizing recall reduces the risk of defective products escaping detection, which could lead to warranty claims or reputational damage.

12.7.2.4 F1 Score

The F1 score harmonizes precision and recall into a single metric, particularly valuable for imbalanced datasets:

$$F1score = 2 \cdot \frac{Precision \cdot Recall}{Precision + Recall} \tag{12.22}$$

A high F1 score indicates a balance between minimizing false positives and false negatives, crucial for quality-critical environments.

12.7.2.5 Defective Parts Per Million (DPPM)

DPPM translates false negatives (FN) into a practical manufacturing metric, reflecting defects escaping detection per million units:

$$DPPM = \frac{FN}{TP + TN + FP + FN} * 1000000 \quad (12.23)$$

Lower DPPM values signify fewer undetected defects, aligning with Six Sigma or zero-defect targets.

12.7.3 Determining Thresholds

Threshold selection balances competing priorities: minimizing false positives (costly inspections) and false negatives (defective products).

12.7.3.1 Balancing False Positives and Negatives

The optimal threshold depends on business trade-offs. For instance:

- High Recall Priority: A lower threshold flags more potential defects, reducing escaped defects (FN) at the cost of increased false alarms (FP).
- High Precision Priority: A higher threshold reduces false alarms but risks missing true defects.

12.7.3.2 Visual Tools for Threshold Selection

- ROC Curve (Figure 12.9): Plots true positive rate (recall) against false positive rate across thresholds. The optimal point maximizes the area under the curve (AUC), balancing sensitivity and specificity.
- Precision-Recall Curve: Highlights precision-recall trade-offs, guiding decisions in imbalanced scenarios.

In manufacturing, thresholds are often tuned to achieve a target DPPM (e.g., $\leq$5,000) while minimizing testing overhead. For example, a threshold yielding 95% recall and 80% precision might balance quality assurance and operational efficiency.

12.8 RESULTS AND INTERPRETATION

12.8.1 Model Performance

The efficacy of the supervised classification models is assessed through defective parts per million (DPPM), a critical metric reflecting the number of defective products escaping detection. Lower DPPM values indicate superior model performance, directly aligning with the goal of minimizing faulty boards shipped to customers.

12.8.1.1 Escape Rates and Sampling Efficiency

Two experiments evaluated model performance under distinct business scenarios.

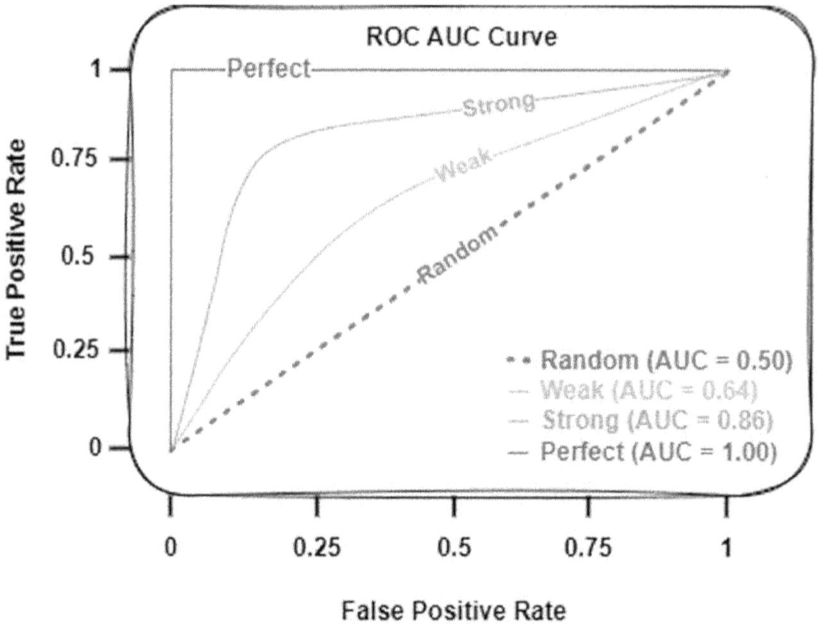

FIGURE 12.9 ROC AUC curve plot comparing classifier performance with true-positive rate vs. false-positive rate.

Experiment 1 focused on escape DPPM when testing half the population (1,795 boards). Table 12.16 highlights the results:

- XGBoost achieved the lowest escape DPPM (3,342), followed by Random Forest (3,619).
- Logistic Regression and KNN underperformed, with DPPM exceeding 6,000.
- Naïve Bayes balanced efficiency with 5,012 DPPM, nearing the target threshold.

TABLE 12.16
Comparison of Escape DPPM across All Models

Model	Escapes (False Negative)	Defective Parts Per Million
Random Forest	13	3,619
XGBoost	12	3,342
Logistic Regression	28	7,793
SVM	22	6,124
KNN	24	6,683
Naïve Bayes	18	5,012

TABLE 12.17
Comparison of Sampling Rate across All Models

Model	Sampling Rate (%)	Defective Parts Per Million
Random Forest	33	5,000
XGBoost	37	5,000
Logistic Regression	69	5,000
SVM	61	5,000
KNN	63	5,000
Naïve Bayes	53	5,000

Experiment 2 determined the minimum sampling rate required to achieve a DPPM of 5,000. Table 12.17 reveals the following:

- Random Forest required the lowest sampling rate (33%), demonstrating exceptional efficiency.
- XGBoost followed closely at 37%, while Logistic Regression and SVM required over 60% sampling.

12.8.2 Interpretation of Results

The analysis evaluates how well models align with business objectives: reducing escapes and minimizing testing costs.

12.8.2.1 Alignment with Business Goals

- Quality Assurance: Achieving ≤5,000 DPPM ensures alignment with Six Sigma standards.
- Cost Efficiency: Lower sampling rates reduce testing overhead, preserving resources.

12.8.2.2 Optimal Model Selection

- XGBoost excels in minimizing escapes (3,342 DPPM at 50% sampling) but requires moderate sampling (37%) to meet the 5,000 DPPM target.
- Random Forest is the most resource-efficient, achieving the 5,000 DPPM threshold with just 33% sampling.
- Naïve Bayes and Logistic Regression lag in precision, making them less suitable for high-stakes manufacturing.

These findings underscore the trade-offs between detection accuracy and operational efficiency. Manufacturers can prioritize XGBoost for stringent quality control or Random Forest to minimize testing costs.

12.9 SUMMARY, IMPLICATIONS, AND FUTURE WORK

12.9.1 Summary of Findings

This study demonstrates the viability of supervised learning for fault prediction in manufacturing. Key insights include:

- Data Preparation: Sensor telemetry was aggregated, cleansed, and engineered into statistical features, forming a robust foundation for modelling.
- Feature Engineering: Techniques like log transformations and one-hot encoding enhanced model interpretability and performance.
- Model Evaluation: XGBoost and Random Forest emerged as top performers, balancing escape DPPM and sampling efficiency.

12.9.2 Implications for Manufacturing

Implementing these models offers transformative benefits:

- Quality Control: Reducing escapes to $\leq$5,000 DPPM aligns with zero-defect goals, bolstering customer trust.
- Cost Savings: Optimized sampling rates lower testing costs while maintaining quality.
- Operational Agility: Real-time fault detection minimizes downtime and supports predictive maintenance.

12.9.3 Future Work and Recommendations

To amplify impact, future efforts should:

- Integrate Real-Time Systems: Deploy models in live manufacturing environments for dynamic fault detection.
- Automate Feedback Loops: Link predictions to automated alerts for immediate corrective actions.
- Explore Advanced Techniques: Investigate deep learning and hybrid models for complex fault patterns.
- Enhance Ethical Governance: Audit models for bias and ensure transparency in decision-making.

By advancing these areas, manufacturers can achieve unprecedented efficiency, sustainability, and innovation in production processes.

12.10 CONCLUSION

This chapter explored the application of supervised machine learning models to predict faults in hardware manufacturing, emphasizing the balance between minimizing defective products and optimizing operational efficiency. By leveraging telemetry data from sensors embedded in manufacturing processes, the study demonstrated how advanced analytics could preemptively identify defects, thereby enhancing quality control while reducing costs. Key insights revealed that ensemble methods, particularly XGBoost and Random Forest, outperformed other algorithms in balancing performance metrics. XGBoost achieved the lowest escape DPPM (3,342) when testing half the population, showcasing its precision in detecting faults. Conversely, Random Forest minimized resource use, requiring only a 33% sampling rate to meet the 5,000 DPPM target, highlighting its efficiency in cost-sensitive scenarios. These findings underscore the importance of aligning model selection with specific business priorities—whether prioritizing defect reduction or resource conservation.

The integration of rigorous data preparation, including feature engineering and skewness correction, proved essential for model accuracy. Transforming raw sensor data into statistical summaries and categorical encodings enabled algorithms to discern subtle fault patterns, while threshold optimization balanced false positives and negatives according to real-world constraints. For manufacturers, these models offer a pathway to significant cost savings by reducing reliance on exhaustive post-production inspections and enabling predictive maintenance. However, the study also highlights opportunities for improvement, such as integrating real-time telemetry for dynamic monitoring or refining ethical safeguards to ensure unbiased predictions.

Ultimately, this work bridges theoretical machine learning advancements with practical manufacturing challenges, illustrating how data-driven strategies can drive innovation, sustainability, and competitiveness in industrial ecosystems. By continuously adapting these models to evolving production environments, manufacturers can future-proof their operations against emerging complexities.

REFERENCES

Al-Nusirat, Alaa, Feras Hanandeh, Mohammad Kamel Kharabsheh, Mahmoud Al-Ayyoub, and Nahla Al-Dhfairi. 2022. "Dynamic Detection of Software Defects Using Supervised Learning Techniques." *International Journal of Communication Networks and Information Security (IJCNIS)* 11 (1). https://doi.org/10.17762/ijcnis.v11i1.3966.

Chai, Zheng, and Chunhui Zhao. 2019. "Enhanced Random Forest With Concurrent Analysis of Static and Dynamic Nodes for Industrial Fault Classification." *IEEE Transactions on Industrial Informatics* 16 (1): 54–66. https://doi.org/10.1109/tii.2019.2915559.

Gao, Yan, Chengzhang Chai, Haijiang Li, and Weiqi Fu. 2023. "A Deep Learning Framework for Intelligent Fault Diagnosis Using AutoML-CNN and Image-like Data Fusion." *Machines* 11 (10): 932. https://doi.org/10.3390/machines11100932.

Hadi, Russul H., Haider N. Hady, Ahmed M. Hasan, Ammar Al-Jodah, and Amjad J. Humaidi. 2023. "Improved Fault Classification for Predictive Maintenance in Industrial IoT Based on AutoML: A Case Study of Ball-Bearing Faults." *Processes* 11 (5): 1507. https://doi.org/10.3390/pr11051507.

Jacob, Rohit John, Rutuja J. Kamat, N. M. Sahithya, Sharon Saji John, and Sahana P. Shankar. 2021. "Voting Based Ensemble Classification for Software Defect Prediction." 2021 IEEE Mysore Sub Section International Conference (MysuruCon), October, 358–65. https://doi.org/10.1109/mysurucon52639.2021.9641713.

Jayakumar, Naveenkumar, and Dhanashri P. Joshi. 2020. "Big Data &Amp; Disruptive Computing Platforms Braced Internet of Things: Facets &Amp; Trends." In *Studies in Systems, Decision and Control*, 119–50. https://doi.org/10.1007/978-3-030-39047-1_6.

Kumar, S. Vishnu, G. Aloy Anuja Mary, and Miroslav Mahdal. 2023. "Integrated Edge Deployable Fault Diagnostic Algorithm for the Internet of Things (IoT): A Methane Sensing Application." *Sensors* 23 (14): 6266. https://doi.org/10.3390/s23146266.

Leite, Denis, Aldonso Martins, Diego Rativa, Joao F. L. De Oliveira, and Alexandre M. A. Maciel. 2022. "An Automated Machine Learning Approach for Real-Time Fault Detection and Diagnosis." *Sensors* 22 (16): 6138. https://doi.org/10.3390/s22166138.

Li, Weiwei, Wenzhou Zhang, Xiuyi Jia, and Zhiqiu Huang. 2020. "Effort-Aware semi-Supervised just-in-Time Defect Prediction." *Information and Software Technology* 126 (June): 106364. https://doi.org/10.1016/j.infsof.2020.106364.

Liu, Wangshu, Shulong Liu, Qing Gu, Jiaqiang Chen, Xiang Chen, and Daoxu Chen. 2015. "Empirical Studies of a Two-Stage Data Preprocessing Approach for Software Fault Prediction." *IEEE Transactions on Reliability* 65 (1): 38–53. https://doi.org/10.1109/tr.2015.2461676.

Liu, Yue, and Zhiqiang Ge. 2018. "Weighted Random Forests for Fault Classification in Industrial Processes With Hierarchical Clustering Model Selection." *Journal of Process Control* 64 (February): 62–70. https://doi.org/10.1016/j.jprocont.2018.02.005.

Mulla, Nilofar, and Naveenkumar Jayakumar. 2021. "Role of Machine Learning & Artificial Intelligence Techniques in Software Testing." *Türk Bilgisayar Ve Matematik Eğitimi Dergisi* 12 (6): 2913–21. https://doi.org/10.17762/turcomat.v12i6.5800.

Mulla, Nilofar, Naveenkumar Jayakumar, Shashank Joshi, and Deepali Godse. 2024. "Study on Automatic Software Test Case Generation." In *Lecture Notes in Electrical Engineering*, 251–58. https://doi.org/10.1007/978-981-97-8031-0_27.

Naveenkumar, Jayakumar, and Dhanashri P. Joshi. 2020. "8Machine Learning Approach for Exploring Computational Intelligence." In *De Gruyter eBooks*, 153–78. https://doi.org/10.1515/9783110648195-008.

Omar, Intisar, Muhammad Khan, Andrew Starr, and Khaled Abou Rok Ba. 2023. "Automated Prediction of Crack Propagation Using H2O AutoML." *Sensors* 23 (20): 8419. https://doi.org/10.3390/s23208419.

Sabnis, Poorva Sanjay, Shashank Joshi, and J. Naveenkumar. 2022. "A Study on Machine Learning Techniques Based Software Reliability Assessment." 2022 4th International Conference on Inventive Research in Computing Applications (ICIRCA), September, 687–92. https://doi.org/10.1109/icirca54612.2022.9985530.

Shao, Yuanxun, Bin Liu, Shihai Wang, and Guoqi Li. 2018. "A Novel Software Defect Prediction Based on Atomic Class-association Rule Mining." *Expert Systems With Applications* 114 (July): 237–54. https://doi.org/10.1016/j.eswa.2018.07.042.

Shirke, Sushama Annaso, Naveenkumar Jayakumar, and Suhas Patil. 2024. "Design and Performance Analysis of Modern Computational Storage Devices: A Systematic Review." *Expert Systems With Applications* 250 (February): 123570. https://doi.org/10.1016/j.eswa.2024.123570.

Singh, Prabhpahul, Ruchika Malhotra, and Siddartha Bansal. 2019. "Analyzing the Effectiveness of Machine Learning Algorithms for Determining Faulty Classes: A Comparative Analysis." 2022 12th International Conference on Cloud Computing, Data Science &Amp; Engineering (Confluence), January, 325–30. https://doi.org/10.1109/confluence.2019.8776946.

Wang, Zilan, Maiying Zhong, Rui Yang, and Yang Liu. 2019. "An Improved Random Forest Algorithm of Fault Diagnosis for Rotating Machinery." 2021 CAA Symposium on Fault Detection, Supervision, and Safety for Technical Processes (SAFEPROCESS), July. https://doi.org/10.1109/safeprocess45799.2019.9213389.

Zhou, Tianchi, Xiaobing Sun, Xin Xia, Bin Li, and Xiang Chen. 2019. "Improving Defect Prediction With Deep Forest." *Information and Software Technology* 114 (July): 204–16. https://doi.org/10.1016/j.infsof.2019.07.003.

13 Swarm Intelligence in Smart Manufacturing

Manish Kumar, Ankit Raj and R. Subramanian

13.1 INTRODUCTION

The natural world is replete with examples of collective intelligence and efficient problem-solving, offering a rich source of inspiration for scientific and engineering endeavors. Humans have long observed the emergent behaviors of social animals – such as ant colonies efficiently finding the shortest path to food sources, bee swarms locating optimal nectar locations, bird flocks navigating complex environments, or herds migrating vast distances – gaining insights into effective strategies for coordination and optimization. The principle that groups can often achieve outcomes superior to isolated individuals, whether in discovering resources, evading predators, or completing complex tasks, is fundamental. Computer science, particularly the field of artificial intelligence (AI), seeks to emulate these powerful natural strategies through the design of sophisticated algorithms. Metaheuristics such as Particle Swarm Optimization (PSO) [1], inspired by bird flocking or fish schooling; Ant Colony Optimization (ACO) [2], mimicking the pheromone trail-laying behavior of ants; Bee Colony Optimization (BCO) [3], modeling the foraging behavior of honeybees; and the more recent Wild Goat Optimization (WGO) [4], based on the hierarchical social behavior of wild goats, are prime examples of nature-inspired algorithms successfully applied to tackle complex, computationally hard problems, including those prevalent in smart manufacturing, such as optimal scheduling.

The contemporary manufacturing industry frequently grapples with challenges related to suboptimal resource utilization, stemming from various operational constraints, dynamic market demands, and inherent system complexities [5]. In an era where firms often face resource scarcity and intense global competition, achieving high-quality, modern, and precise operations is not just desirable but critical for survival and growth [5]. The paradigm of intelligent or smart manufacturing necessitates the seamless integration, efficient sharing, and timely allocation of resources [5]. Manufacturing, being a cornerstone of the global economy, exerts a significant influence on overall economic growth and stability [6]. The integration of smart technologies, encompassing IIoT, cyber-physical systems, big data analytics, and AI, is fundamentally transforming industrial manufacturing processes. The ambitious goals often cited include substantial increases in productivity, potentially by 20–25%, alongside significant improvements in resource utilization efficiency [7]. Within this context, effective production scheduling emerges as a major operational hurdle, particularly in complex workshop environments like flow shops or job shops.

DOI: 10.1201/9781003532156-17

The permutation flow shop scheduling problem (PFSP), where jobs must be processed sequentially through a series of machines in the same order, represents a common and widely studied scenario in manufacturing workshops [8]. Modern industrial competitiveness hinges on agility, demanding rapid responses and high flexibility, particularly from production planning and scheduling systems [9]. The overall performance, adaptability, and ultimately, the profitability of a manufacturing system are heavily dependent on the quality and efficiency of its scheduling algorithms. Edge computing technologies, closely integrated with the Internet of Things (IoT), have demonstrated significant potential and tangible benefits in enhancing smart manufacturing operations, especially for real-time production scheduling by enabling faster data processing and decision-making closer to the physical processes.

The primary contributions of our research presented in this chapter are twofold:

1. We propose a novel Improved Swarm Intelligence Model (ISIM) specifically designed to mitigate the often-prohibitive costs (both computational and delay-related) associated with scheduling complex products using traditional or standard optimization algorithms.
2. We conduct a comprehensive comparative analysis, evaluating ISIM against established SI optimization algorithms (PSO, ACO, BCO, and WGO) using relevant performance metrics, thereby demonstrating its superior performance concerning both scheduling cost (total tardiness) and computational efficiency (CPU time).

13.2 LITERATURE REVIEW

The contemporary manufacturing landscape, increasingly characterized by the principles of Smart Manufacturing and Industry 4.0, faces unprecedented levels of complexity, dynamism, and competition [1]. Enabled by technologies like the Industrial Internet of Things (IIoT), cyber-physical systems, big data analytics, and artificial intelligence, smart factories promise enhanced productivity, customization, resource efficiency, and operational agility. However, realizing this potential hinges critically on effective decision-making across all operational tiers, with production scheduling standing out as a cornerstone challenge [2]. Scheduling, in essence, involves the allocation of limited resources (machines, personnel, tools, and vehicles) over time to perform a set of tasks (jobs and operations) optimally according to specific performance criteria [3]. Common objectives include minimizing makespan (total time to complete all jobs), minimizing total tardiness (reducing delays against due dates), minimizing production costs, maximizing resource utilization, or balancing multiple conflicting goals.

Most practical manufacturing scheduling problems, such as the job shop scheduling problem (JSSP) and the permutation flow shop scheduling problem (PFSP) considered in this work, belong to the class of NP-hard combinatorial optimization problems [4]. This implies that finding provably optimal solutions using exact methods becomes computationally intractable for instances of realistic size and complexity. Consequently, research has largely focused on developing efficient and effective approximation algorithms, primarily heuristics and metaheuristics, alongside exploring novel approaches leveraging machine learning and artificial intelligence [5]. This review critically examines the evolution and current state-of-the-art in manufacturing scheduling optimization, evaluating the strengths and limitations of various approaches and identifying persistent challenges that motivate the development of our proposed Improved Swarm Intelligence Model (ISIM).

Early approaches to scheduling relied on exact methods and simple heuristics. Techniques like Mixed-Integer Linear Programming (MILP) [6], Constraint Programming (CP) [7], and Branch and Bound (B&B) [8] can guarantee finding the optimal solution. They involve formulating the scheduling problem mathematically and systematically exploring the solution space. While valuable for small-scale problems or providing benchmarks, their exponential worst-case time complexity renders them impractical for the large problem sizes (hundreds of jobs, dozens of machines) and tight time constraints typical of real-world manufacturing environments [9]. The intricate constraints and dynamic nature of smart manufacturing further exacerbate these computational challenges. To overcome the limitations of exact methods, numerous heuristics and dispatching rules were developed. Dispatching rules (e.g., Shortest Processing Time – SPT, Earliest Due Date – EDD, First-Come-First-Served – FCFS) are simple priority rules used to decide which job to process next on an available machine [10]. They are computationally inexpensive and easy to implement, making them suitable for dynamic environments. However, they adopt a myopic, localized view, often leading to significantly suboptimal global performance [11]. More sophisticated construction heuristics (e.g., NEH heuristic for PFSP [12]) attempt to build a good solution sequentially but still lack mechanisms to escape poor initial choices. Improvement heuristics refine an existing schedule through local modifications but can easily get trapped in local optima. While foundational, these traditional heuristics often fail to adequately address the complexity and achieve the high performance required in modern smart manufacturing.

Metaheuristics have emerged as the dominant approach for tackling complex scheduling problems, offering a favorable trade-off between solution quality and computational effort [13]. These high-level strategies guide underlying heuristics to explore the solution space more effectively, escaping local optima and finding near-optimal solutions within reasonable time limits. Inspired by natural evolution, Evolutionary Algorithms (EAs) , particularly genetic algorithms (GAs) [14], maintain a population of candidate solutions (schedules) and iteratively improve them using operators like selection, crossover, and mutation. GAs have been widely applied to various scheduling problems, including Flexible Macufacturing Systems (FMS) and JSSP [15]. However, standard GAs can suffer from premature convergence, and designing effective, problem-specific representation schemes and genetic operators (especially crossover for permutation-based schedules) is crucial and non-trivial [16]. Memetic algorithms (MAs), which hybridize GAs with local search procedures, often show improved performance by combining global exploration (GA) with local intensification (LS) [17], but add another layer of parameter tuning complexity.

Local search-based metaheuristics methods iteratively improve a single solution by exploring its neighborhood. Simulated annealing (SA) [18] uses a probabilistic acceptance criterion, guided by a temperature parameter, allowing occasional moves to worse solutions to escape local optima, especially early in the search. Its effectiveness heavily depends on the annealing schedule (initial temperature, cooling rate, and termination condition) [19]. Tabu search (TS) [20] employs a memory structure (tabu list) to forbid recently visited solutions or moves, guiding the search away from explored regions and preventing cycling. Defining appropriate tabu tenure and aspiration criteria is critical for TS performance [21]. Iterated local search (ILS) [22], as used partially by Alicastro et al., iteratively applies local search to solutions generated by perturbing previous local optima. Its success hinges on the effectiveness of the underlying local search and the perturbation mechanism used to escape basins of attraction [23]. Variable neighborhood search (VNS) [24] systematically explores different neighborhood structures during the search, leveraging the idea that a local optimum for one neighborhood structure may not be so for another. While powerful, these single-solution based metaheuristics can sometimes be sensitive to the starting solution and may not explore the solution space as broadly as population-based methods.

Swarm Intelligence (SI) is the family of algorithms, central to our work, that draws inspiration from the collective behavior of social animals or insects. Particle Swarm Optimization (PSO), inspired by bird flocking, uses a population (swarm) of particles, each representing a solution. Particles adjust their trajectory based on their own best-found position (pbest) and the swarm's overall best-found position (gbest). Standard PSO was designed for continuous spaces, requiring significant adaptation (e.g., discrete PSO variants and encoding/decoding schemes) for combinatorial problems like scheduling [25]. Maintaining diversity and avoiding premature convergence to a single point remain key challenges [26]. Dou and Jun Li specifically explored Multi-Objective PSO (MoPSO), highlighting the difficulty in managing the Pareto front effectively. Ant Colony Optimization (ACO), mimicking ant foraging, uses artificial ants to probabilistically construct solutions based on pheromone trails and heuristic information. Pheromones evaporate over time, reinforcing paths leading to good solutions. ACO is naturally suited for permutation problems but can be computationally intensive, and its performance is sensitive to parameter settings (pheromone influence and evaporation rate) [27]. Bai [28] explored improved ACO for scheduling. Bee Colony Optimization (BCO), based on honeybee foraging, employs different types of bees (employed, onlookers, and scouts) to explore and exploit promising areas (food sources/solutions). Various BCO algorithms exist (e.g., Artificial Bee Colony – ABC), differing in how they balance exploration and exploitation [29].

Numerous other SI algorithms exist, such as the Firefly Algorithm (FA) [30], Grey Wolf Optimizer (GWO) [31], and Wild Goat Optimization (WGO), each inspired by different natural phenomena and offering unique search dynamics. While showing promise in various domains, their application to complex scheduling often requires careful adaptation and faces similar challenges regarding parameter tuning, convergence behaviors, and theoretical understanding compared to more established metaheuristics [32]. SI algorithms offer inherent parallelism and effective exploration through population diversity but require careful calibration to effectively balance global search (exploration) and local refinement (exploitation) – a core focus of our proposed ISIM.

Beyond metaheuristics, AI and ML techniques are increasingly explored for scheduling. Reinforcement Learning (RL) agents learn optimal decision-making policies through trial-and-error interaction with an environment (the scheduling system) [33]. Deep Reinforcement Learning (DRL), combining RL with deep neural networks, allows handling complex, high-dimensional state spaces. Xu and Yang employed Advantage Actor-Critic (A2C) for smart manufacturing scheduling, demonstrating learning capabilities. However, as they noted, DRL faces significant scalability challenges in scheduling due to the combinatorial explosion of state and action spaces [34]. Furthermore, designing appropriate reward functions that effectively guide the agent towards desired scheduling objectives without unintended consequences, ensuring sample efficiency (RL often requires vast amounts of interaction), and guaranteeing generalization to unseen problem instances remain active research areas [35]. Alicastro et al. attempted to mitigate some issues by hybridizing Q-Learning with ILS, but inherent RL challenges and ILS limitations may persist. Supervised learning models can be trained on historical data to predict key scheduling parameters like job processing times [36] or to classify schedules as "good" or "bad" to guide other algorithms [37]. Unsupervised learning can help identify patterns, clustering similar jobs or machine states to potentially simplify scheduling decisions [38]. However, these approaches heavily depend on the availability, quality, and representativeness of historical data and may struggle to adapt to novel situations or significant changes in the manufacturing system. Hyper-heuristics approach operates at a higher level, automating the process of selecting or generating heuristics or tuning algorithm parameters [39]. ML techniques can be used within a hyper-heuristic framework to learn which dispatching rule or metaheuristic configuration performs best under specific system conditions, leading to more adaptive scheduling systems [40]. While promising, designing effective hyper-heuristic frameworks remains complex.

Recognizing that no single method excels in all aspects, hybrid approaches combining strengths from different techniques are increasingly prevalent [41]. Examples include the following: combining metaheuristics (e.g., MA = GA + Local Search) [42]; integrating metaheuristics with exact methods (e.g., using metaheuristics to find good initial solutions for B&B) [43]; using machine learning to guide metaheuristic search (e.g., predicting promising search regions and adapting parameters dynamically) [44]; and combining fuzzy logic with optimization methods to handle uncertainty in parameters like processing times or due dates [45]. While hybridization can lead to superior performance by leveraging complementary strengths, it often introduces increased algorithmic complexity and a larger number of parameters requiring careful tuning [46].

Smart manufacturing environments introduce specific complexities. Real-world manufacturing is rarely static. Unexpected events like new job arrivals, machine breakdowns, processing time variations, or quality issues necessitate dynamic scheduling capabilities [47]. Approaches range from purely reactive (rescheduling only when disruption occurs) to proactive (generating robust schedules anticipating uncertainty) or predictive-reactive strategies [48]. Handling dynamism effectively without causing excessive system instability remains a key challenge. Modern manufacturing often involves optimizing multiple, often conflicting, objectives simultaneously, such as minimizing cost, minimizing tardiness, maximizing throughput, minimizing energy consumption, and ensuring sustainability [49]. Techniques like Pareto optimization (used in MoPSO and HDMICA) aim to find a set.

13.3 PROPOSED METHODOLOGY

The central focus of our research work is the development and evaluation of the Improved Swarm Intelligence Model (ISIM) aimed at achieving efficient and optimal scheduling within intelligent manufacturing systems. Our proposed system architecture, depicted schematically in Figure 13.1, integrates several key components: a products controller layer, a target device layer, a device configuration layer, a buffer system, and a centralized server that acts as the main orchestrator. This architecture is designed to facilitate dynamic and adaptive scheduling in response to real-time manufacturing conditions.

13.4 SYSTEM ARCHITECTURE AND OPERATIONAL FLOW

The ISIM optimization engine forms the core of the scheduling intelligence. In a typical operational cycle, ISIM receives input regarding the current scheduling status and system state from the centralized server. If the system determines that no reconfiguration (e.g., changing machine setups for a different product type) is immediately necessary for the next scheduling action, an available (idle) machine signals its readiness to the cloud-based scheduling agent (hosted on or coordinated by the centralized server). This agent then actively retrieves relevant local system data – which could include real-time production progress, status of machines, buffer levels, and potentially dynamic incoming orders – to inform its decision-making process.

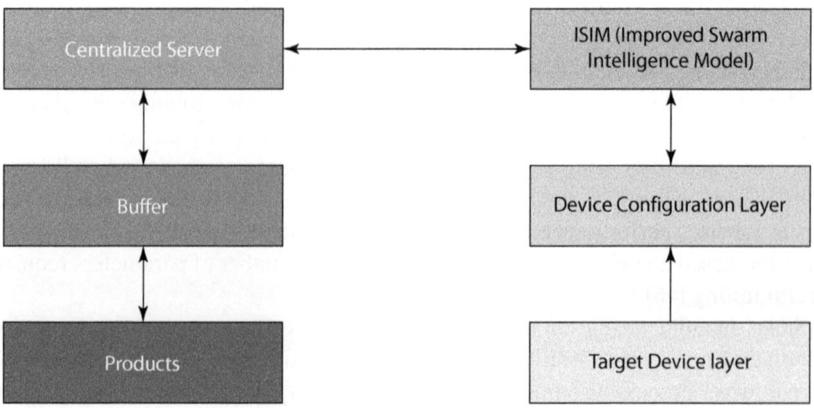

FIGURE 13.1 Structural diagram of the improved Swarm Intelligence Model.

Based on this comprehensive data analysis, the agent determines the most appropriate scheduling action (e.g., which job to process next on the available machine). This decision is communicated back to the ISIM module.

Guided by the received scheduling action, ISIM selects a candidate product (job) from those awaiting processing, potentially evaluating multiple scheduling scheme options based on its optimization logic. Once a decision is made, the device configuration layer is instructed to manage the physical movement of the selected product, typically transferring it from a temporary storage buffer to the designated workshop machine. The production process then proceeds on that product until the required operation is completed. Upon completion, the finished job (or partially finished, if moving to the next stage) is typically moved to another machine's input buffer or an output buffer. Crucially, based on triggering events (e.g., completion of a batch, arrival of an urgent order, and planned changeover), ISIM can also decide on a reconfiguration strategy to switch the system or specific machines to a new production mode. The controller layer is then responsible for implementing this reconfiguration directive on the physical target device layer (the machines and equipment).

Algorithm 13.1: Improved Swarm Intelligence Model in Intelligent Manufacturing System

Start Algorithm

Input:

$J = \{1,2,3,\ldots,m\}$	Set of Jobs at arrival time AT_k, processing time t_{jk}, due dates, and penalty costs
$l \in \{1,2,3,\ldots,X\}$	Production modes
$TF, RDD\}$	Tardiness factor, relative range of due dates

Output:

Optimal Schedule minimizing total tardiness cost
Assignment of jobs to production modes

Initialization:

1. Centralized Server Setup – Initialize the products Control Layer, Target Device Layer, Device Configuration Layer, and Buffer. Configure the ISIM parameters (Swarm size, Maximum iterations, etc.)
2. Calculate Average Processing Time, *CP*

$$CP = \frac{1}{n} \times \sum_{k=1}^{m} \sum_{j=1}^{m} t_{jk}$$

3. Determine Due Date Range

$$d_k = \left[CP\left(1 - TF - \frac{RDD}{2}\right), CP\left(1 - TF + \frac{RDD}{2}\right) \right]$$

Swarm Intelligence Optimization:

4. Generate Initial Swarm – Each particle represents a potential schedule (job sequence and mode assignments). Ensure constraints are satisfied:

$$\sum_{l=1}^{X} X_{kl} = 1, \forall k = 1,2,3,\ldots,m$$

$$s.t. \sum_{l=1}^{X} y_l = 1$$

5. Evaluate Fitness Function – For each particle, compute the total tardiness cost:

$$\sum_{k=1}^{m} \beta_k \times \{0, D_k - d_k\}$$

where D_k is the finished time of job k, calculated as

$$D_{jk} = \{D_{(j-1)}, D_{(k-1)}\} + t_{jk}, \quad j = 1,2,3,\ldots,n, \quad k = 1,2,3,\ldots,m$$

6. Update Particle Positions and Velocities – Use Swarm Intelligence rules (e.g., PSO) to update particles based on local and global best solutions. Ensure constraints are maintained during updates.

Termination and Output:

7. Check Termination Criteria – If maximum iterations are reached or convergence is achieved, proceed to Step 8. Else, return to Step 5.
8. Output Optimal Schedule – Select the particle with the lowest tardiness cost. Assign jobs to production modes based on the best solution.

Dynamic Adaptation:

9. Real-Time Monitoring – The centralized server continuously monitors the manufacturing environment. It adjusts schedules dynamically using ISIM in response to disruptions (e.g., machine failures and new job arrivals).

End Algorithm

13.5 RESULTS AND ITS INFERENCES

13.5.1 Experimental Setup and Evaluation

To evaluate the effectiveness of our proposed Improved Swarm Intelligence Model (ISIM), we conducted a series of computational experiments. The ISIM algorithm, along with the benchmark algorithms (PSO, ACO, BCO, and WGO), was implemented using the Python programming language. All simulations were executed on a standard Windows personal computer equipped with an Intel i7 processor and 128 GB of RAM, ensuring a consistent hardware platform for fair comparison. We assessed the performance of each algorithm based on two critical metrics relevant to manufacturing scheduling:

Total Tardiness Cost: This metric directly measures the effectiveness of the schedule in meeting deadlines, calculated as defined in Equation 1. Lower values indicate better performance.

CPU Processing Time: This metric quantifies the computational resources required by each algorithm to find a solution, measured in seconds or relative units. Lower values indicate greater computational efficiency.

13.5.2 Performance Analysis

Figure 13.2 illustrates the performance in terms of minimizing total tardiness cost over 500 iterations (calculation cycles) of the algorithms, shown for varying problem sizes (number of jobs: 60, 80, 100, 120, and 140). The bar chart clearly demonstrates a consistent trend: while the total tardiness generally increases for all algorithms as the number of jobs grows (indicating larger problems are inherently harder to schedule perfectly), ISIM consistently achieves the lowest total tardiness cost across all tested problem sizes. For instance, at 140 jobs, ISIM's tardiness value (around 410) is visibly lower than the next best performer, WGO (around 440), and significantly

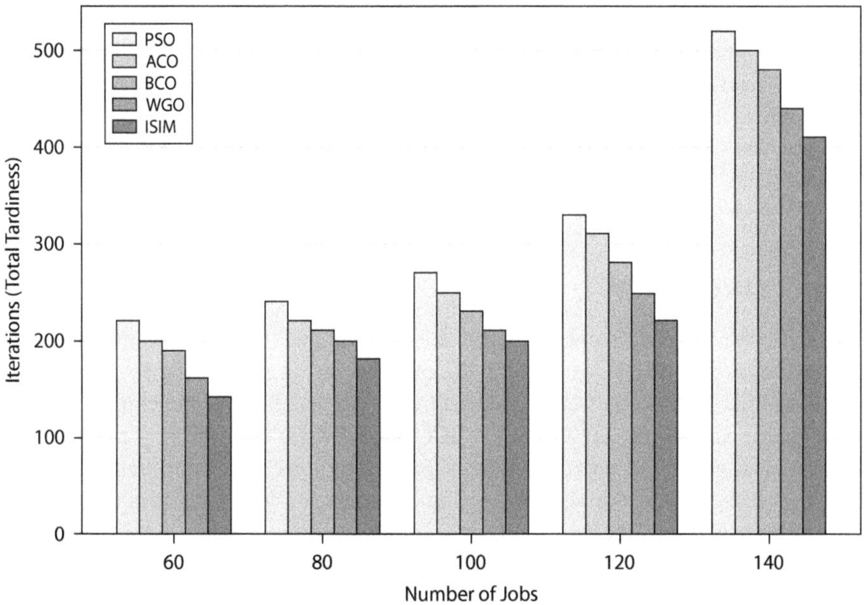

FIGURE 13.2 Performance analysis of total tardiness for 500 iterations.

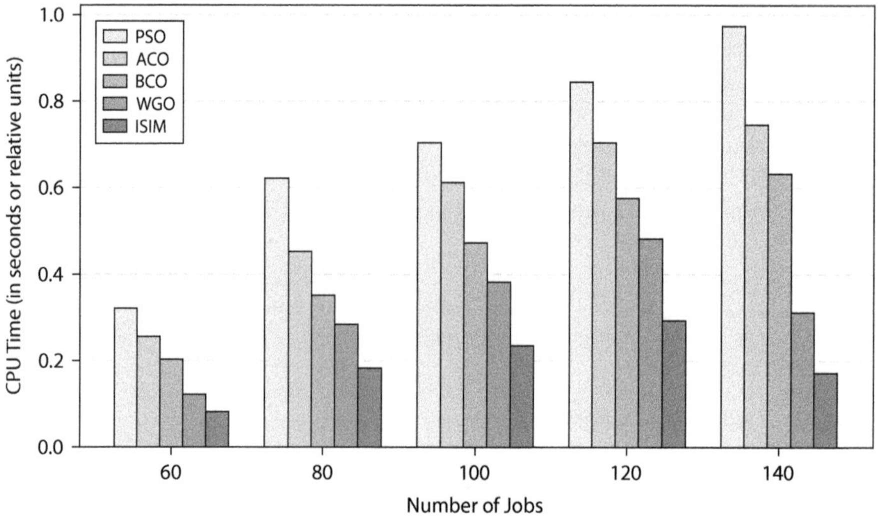

FIGURE 13.3 Performance analysis of CPU time for 150 jobs.

lower than PSO (over 520). This indicates ISIM's superior ability to find high-quality schedules that minimize lateness penalties.

Figure 13.3 presents the CPU time required by each algorithm to generate schedules, specifically shown for problem instances ranging from 60 to 140 jobs (the title mentions 150 jobs, which might be a typo or refer to the largest instance tested, but the x-axis goes up to 140). Similar to the tardiness results, a clear pattern emerges. As the number of jobs increases, the computational effort required by all algorithms naturally rises. However, ISIM consistently exhibits the lowest CPU processing time compared to PSO, ACO, BCO, and WGO across all job counts. For the 140-job instance, ISIM requires significantly less CPU time (around 0.17 units) than WGO (around 0.31), BCO (around 0.63), ACO (around 0.74), and especially PSO (around 0.97). This demonstrates ISIM's significant advantage in computational efficiency.

13.6 CONCLUSION

The experimental results compellingly demonstrate the effectiveness and efficiency of the proposed ISIM algorithm for the manufacturing scheduling problem under investigation. ISIM consistently outperformed the established benchmark Swarm Intelligence algorithms (PSO, ACO, BCO, and WGO) on both key performance indicators: it generated schedules with significantly lower total tardiness costs, and it achieved these superior solutions using substantially less CPU processing time. This performance advantage was observed across various problem sizes and became increasingly pronounced as the number of jobs increased, highlighting ISIM's scalability relative to the benchmark methods.

We attribute ISIM's superior performance primarily to its enhanced mechanism for balancing exploration (the ability to search diverse areas of the vast solution space to avoid getting stuck in poor local optima) and exploitation (the ability to intensively search the vicinity of promising solutions to refine them). While the standard SI algorithms inherently attempt this balance, the design of ISIM appears to achieve it more effectively, potentially through adaptive parameter control, novel movement strategies, or better information sharing among swarm agents (specific mechanisms would typically be detailed in the full paper). This improved balance likely allows ISIM to converge more rapidly towards high-quality, near-optimal schedules compared to the other methods tested within the given computational budget (iterations or time).

In summary, the ISIM framework presents a promising and efficient tool for optimizing complex scheduling tasks in modern, intelligent manufacturing environments. Its ability to deliver better scheduling solutions faster translates directly into tangible benefits such as reduced production costs (lower lateness penalties), improved resource utilization, increased throughput, and enhanced responsiveness to dynamic market demands. Future work could involve testing ISIM on a wider range of scheduling problems (e.g., job shops and flexible manufacturing systems with different objectives), comparing it against other state-of-the-art non-SI metaheuristics, and exploring its deployment in real-world industrial settings.

REFERENCES

1. A. Caggiano, F. Caiazzo, and R. Teti, "Digital factory technologies for smart manufacturing," *Procedia CIRP*, vol. 12, pp. 426–431, 2013.
2. Q. Qi and F. Tao, "Digital twin and big data towards smart manufacturing and Industry 4.0: 360 degree comparison," *IEEE Access*, vol. 6, pp. 3585–3593, 2018.
3. J. Pinedo, *Scheduling: Theory, Algorithms, and Systems*, 5th ed., Springer, 2016.
4. M. R. Garey and D. S. Johnson, *Computers and Intractability: A Guide to the Theory of NP-Completeness*, W. H. Freeman, 1979.
5. E. K. Burke and G. Kendall, *Search Methodologies: Introductory Tutorials in Optimization and Decision Support Techniques*, Springer, 2014.
6. L. P. Reeve and M. A. Peterson, "A MILP approach for job shop scheduling problems," *Computers & Operations Research*, vol. 29, no. 8, pp. 1021–1033, 2002.
7. P. Baptiste, C. Le Pape, and W. Nuijten, *Constraint-Based Scheduling: Applying Constraint Programming to Scheduling Problems*, Springer, 2001.
8. E. Balas, "The assignment problem with ordinal preferences," *Operations Research*, vol. 17, no. 3, pp. 442–453, 1969.
9. M. Pinedo, *Scheduling: Theory, Algorithms, and Systems*, 4th ed., Springer, 2012.
10. S. Blackstone, D. Phillips, and G. Hogg, "A state-of-the-art survey of dispatching rules for manufacturing job shop operations," *International Journal of Production Research*, vol. 20, no. pp. 27–45, 1982.
11. R. Haupt, "A survey of priority rule-based scheduling," *OR Spektrum*, vol. 11, pp. 3–16, 1989.
12. M. Nawaz, E. Enscore, and I. Ham, "A heuristic algorithm for the m-machine, n-job flow-shop sequencing problem," *Omega*, vol. 11, no. 1, pp. 91–95, 1983.
13. X. Zhang and Y. Gao, "A survey on metaheuristics for flowshop scheduling problems," *International Journal of Production Research*, vol. 56, no. 1-2, pp. 678–702, 2018.

14. D. E. Goldberg, *Genetic Algorithms in Search, Optimization, and Machine Learning*, Addison-Wesley, 1989.
15. M. Gen and R. Cheng, *Genetic Algorithms and Engineering Design*, Wiley-Interscience, 1997.
16. T. Yamada and R. Nakano, "Genetic algorithms for job-shop scheduling problems," Proceedings of the IEEE International Conference on Systems, Man and Cybernetics, vol. 2, pp. 1577–1582, 1992.
17. P. Moscato, *On Evolution, Search, Optimization, Genetic Algorithms and Martial Arts: Towards Memetic Algorithms*, Technical Report, California Institute of Technology, 1989.
18. S. Kirkpatrick, C. D. Gelatt, and M. P. Vecchi, "Optimization by simulated annealing," *Science*, vol. 220, no. 4598, pp. 671–680, 1983.
19. E. Aarts and J. Korst, *Simulated Annealing and Boltzmann Machines*, Wiley, 1989.
20. F. Glover, "Tabu search—Part I," *ORSA Journal on Computing*, vol. 1, no. 3, pp. 190–206, 1989.
21. F. Glover and M. Laguna, *Tabu Search*, Springer, 1997.
22. Lourenço, H.R., Martin, O.C., Stützle, T. (2019). Iterated Local Search: Framework and Applications. In: Gendreau, M., Potvin JY. (eds.) *Handbook of Metaheuristics*. International Series in Operations Research & Management Science, vol. 272. Springer, Cham. https://doi.org/10.1007/978-3-319-91086-4_5.
23. C. Blum and A. Roli, "Metaheuristics in combinatorial optimization: Overview and conceptual comparison," *ACM Computing Surveys*, vol. 35, no. 3, pp. 268–308, 2003.
24. P. Hansen and N. Mladenović, "Variable neighborhood search: Principles and applications," *European Journal of Operational Research*, vol. 130, no. 3, pp. 449–467, 2001.
25. J. Kennedy and R. Eberhart, "Particle swarm optimization," Proceedings of ICNN'95 - International Conference on Neural Networks, Perth, Australia, vol. 4, pp. 1942–1948, 1995.
26. Y. Shi and R. Eberhart, "A modified particle swarm optimizer," 1998 IEEE International Conference on Evolutionary Computation Proceedings, pp. 69–73, 1998.
27. M. Dorigo and L. M. Gambardella, "Ant colony system: A cooperative learning approach to the traveling salesman problem," *IEEE Transactions on Evolutionary Computation*, vol. 1, no. 1, pp. 53–66, 1997.
28. R. Bai, "A hybrid ACO algorithm for the permutation flow shop scheduling problem," *International Journal of Production Research*, vol. 48, no. 18, pp. 5183–5196, 2010.
29. D. Karaboga and B. Basturk, "A powerful and efficient algorithm for numerical function optimization: artificial bee colony (ABC) algorithm," *Journal of Global Optimization*, vol. 39, no. 3, pp. 459–471, 2007.
30. X. S. Yang, "Firefly algorithms for multimodal optimization," *Stochastic Algorithms: Foundations and Applications*, vol. 5792, pp. 169–178, 2009.
31. S. Mirjalili, S. M. Mirjalili, and A. Lewis, "Grey wolf optimizer," *Advances in Engineering Software*, vol. 69, pp. 46–61, 2014.
32. A. Heidari, S. Mirjalili, and H. Faris, "Harris hawks optimization: Algorithm and applications," *Future Generation Computer Systems*, vol. 97, pp. 849–872, 2019.
33. R. S. Sutton and A. G. Barto, *Reinforcement Learning: An Introduction*, 2nd ed., MIT Press, 2018.
34. H. Xu and J. Yang, "Deep reinforcement learning for smart manufacturing scheduling," *Robotics and Computer-Integrated Manufacturing*, vol. 70, 2021.
35. Y. Bengio, A. Courville, and P. Vincent, "Representation learning: A review and new perspectives," *IEEE Transactions on Pattern Analysis and Machine Intelligence*, vol. 35, no. 8, pp. 1798–1828, 2013.

36. H. Zhang, "Using machine learning to improve job shop scheduling," *International Journal of Production Research*, vol. 58, no. 12, pp. 3756–3776, 2020.
37. A. Parkes and D. Langley, "Classifying dispatch rules using data mining," *Journal of Manufacturing Systems*, vol. 41, pp. 154–160, 2016.
38. S. Bousdekis et al., "A proactive decision-making framework in manufacturing using clustering," *Procedia CIRP*, vol. 72, pp. 1189–1194, 2018.
39. E. Özcan, B. Bilgin, and E. Korkmaz, "A comprehensive analysis of hyper-heuristics," *Intelligent Data Analysis*, vol. 12, no. 1, pp. 3–23, 2008.
40. M. Misir et al., "An intelligent hyper-heuristic system for automated selection and configuration of dispatching rules in manufacturing scheduling," *Applied Soft Computing*, vol. 64, pp. 581–593, 2018.
41. A. Jaszkiewicz, "Genetic local search for multi-objective combinatorial optimization," *European Journal of Operational Research*, vol. 137, no. 1, pp. 50–71, 2002.
42. C. Blum, "Hybrid metaheuristics in combinatorial optimization: A survey," *ACM Computing Surveys*, vol. 36, no. 4, pp. 354–373, 2004.
43. T. Bäck, D. B. Fogel, and Z. Michalewicz, *Evolutionary Computation 2: Advanced Algorithms and Operators*, CRC Press, 2000.
44. R. Gomes da Silva, "Machine learning assisted evolutionary algorithm for scheduling," *Computers & Operations Research*, vol. 125, pp. 105110, 2021.
45. M. Gen and L. Lin, "Fuzzy multiobjective optimization for scheduling problems using genetic algorithms," *Computer & Industrial Engineering*, vol. 46, no. 2, pp. 355–375, 2004.
46. E.-G. Talbi, "Machine learning into metaheuristics: A survey and taxonomy," *ACM Computing Surveys*, vol. 54, no. 6, Article 129, pp. 1–32, 2021. doi:10.1145/3459664.
47. F. Herrera and M. Lozano, "Dynamic job shop scheduling: A survey of the state-of-the-art," *European Journal of Operational Research*, vol. 140, no. 2, pp. 241–252, 2002.
48. R. Zhang, H. Pan, and Y. Zhou, "Proactive–reactive scheduling for dynamic job shops using robust optimization," *Computers & Industrial Engineering*, vol. 161, pp. 107625, 2022.
49. C. Zhang and Q. Zhou, "Multi-objective optimization in manufacturing scheduling: A review," *International Journal of Production Research*, vol. 60, no. 1, pp. 1–28, 2022.

Index

For Product Safety Concerns and Information please contact our EU representative GPSR@taylorandfrancis.com
Taylor & Francis Verlag GmbH, Kaufingerstraße 24, 80331 München, Germany

www.ingramcontent.com/pod-product-compliance
Ingram Content Group UK Ltd.
Pitfield, Milton Keynes, MK11 3LW, UK
UKHW022218190926
475702UK00003B/422
* 9 7 8 1 0 3 2 8 7 3 4 2 8 *